THE TRANSLATOR'S GUIDE TO CHINGLISH

中式英语之鉴

by Joan Pinkham
with the collaboration of Jiang Guihua

琼·平卡姆[美]　编著
姜 桂 华　　　协助

外语教学与研究出版社
FOREIGN LANGUAGE TEACHING AND RESEARCH PRESS

D1343081

（京）新登字 155 号

图书在版编目(CIP)数据

中式英语之鉴/[美]平卡姆(Pinkham, J.)编著. -北京:外语教学与研究出版社,1998.12
ISBN 7-5600-1559-X
Ⅰ.中… Ⅱ.平… Ⅲ.英语-翻译 Ⅳ.H315.9
中国版本图书馆 CIP 数据核字(1999)第 03296 号

中式英语之鉴

编著: 琼·平卡姆[美]

协助: 姜桂华

* * *

责任编辑: 吴文子
出版发行: 外语教学与研究出版社
社 址: 北京市西三环北路 19 号 (100089)
网 址: http://www.fltrp.com.cn
印 刷: 北京市鑫鑫印刷厂
开 本: 850×1168 1/32
印 张: 18
字 数: 455 千字
版 次: 2000 年 5 月第 1 版 2000 年 5 月第 1 次印刷
印 数: 1—11000 册
书 号: ISBN 7-5600-1559-X/H·874
定 价: 22.90 元

* * *

如有印刷、装订质量问题出版社负责调换

序

英语学了多年,虽说高不成低不就,纯正的英语总还是一直在听、在读。可是,"纯正"的中式英语(Chinglish),却是第一次有机会如此集中地赏析。琼·平卡姆女士的这部作品搜取了大量中式英语的实例,分别部居,详剖细解,将中国人写英语易犯的文体修辞毛病揭出了大半。

中式英语,因其半英半汉、不英不汉,被作者戏称为"具有汉语特色的英语"。这样的英语每天都在我们中间出现,见于街头的广告词,见于我们的英语报刊,见于政府报告的英译文本。而我们早已看惯,并不觉得怪异,如今由作者一一指出,才知道这种中式英语的可笑。比如"农业获得丰收",表达为"there have been good harvests"蛮好,在后面添上"in agriculture"便成蛇足,因为"harvest"本来就指农业。再如"生活水平不断提高",有人译为"living standards for the people continued to rise",其中的"for the people"也属多余。"红"就是"red","很少"就是"few",既简单又清楚,何必赘言"red in color","few in number"?(均见正文3-4页)诸如此类的现象,作者在本书的第一部分**多余的词**里作了分析,所述分为"多余的名词和动词"、"多余的修饰语"、"同义堆叠"、"重复指称"等类。

第二部分题为**句子结构**,从"名词肿胀症"、"代词与先行词"、"短语和子句的位置"、"垂悬成分"、"平行结构"、"逻辑连词"六个方面,分析了中式英语的构句特点。这里仅就第一个方面举一个例子。

所谓"名词肿胀症",指的是句子里名词过多,且要位都被抽象名词占尽。例如下面一句(172页):

A. The prolongation of the existence of this temple is due to the solidity of its construction.

书中没有提供汉语原文，想来是"这座寺庙的能够持久，是因为其建筑的牢固"之类。经作者改译，成为：

B. This temple *has endured* because *it was solidly built*.

再转译入汉语，可作"这座寺庙建造得十分牢固，因此能历久不败"。句 A 的四个抽象名词在句 B 中由两个动词和一个副词取代，名词当家一变而为动词主宰，句子顿时有了生气。作者主张多用动词，少用名词，多用意义具体的词，少用抽象含混的词。其实，一般的英语修辞书或写作教科书上也都是这么教的，只是写作者为使文体显得"威严"、"科学"，不知不觉便用起了抽象名词。英美人写英语，中国人写汉语，又何尝不是如此。所以作者补充说，这样的弊病并不能算中式英语的特色。

关于本书的用途，平卡姆女士在书前的"致读者"中已经说明。它可以作教材，供高年级学生练习汉英翻译；又可以作读本，供翻译工作者自行修习。为此，每一小节的后面都附有 20 个正误句例和 20 个待改的病句。在作者看来，"翻译不是一门科学，而是一种手艺。"研究翻译理论、构建翻译学的人，听了会作何想？或许我们应该这样来理解她的话：翻译要想被尊为一门"学"，先得成为一种"艺"，就像"烹饪学"那样，写一本烹调书，终不及做一手好菜更能证明"学"的价值。

除了提高汉英翻译的技艺，本书还有一个更广的用途，那就是帮助各行各业的中国人写好英语。两个用途其实有点相通，因为许多中国人写英语，大概是心里先有了汉语的句子，再把它译过去。我自己写英语总不能自如，怕也是落了这个毛病，但读了这本书，虽然谈不上彻底摆脱汉语思维，竟也有一种豁然明亮的感觉，因此愿把它推荐给那些想在英语写作上进一大步、却苦于找不到帮手的朋友。

姚小平
2000 年 2 月
于外研社研究发展中心

TABLE OF CONTENTS

TABLE OF CONTENTS

To the Reader

This book can be used either in the classroom or for independent study. It is addressed primarily to Chinese translators and to advanced students of English who are practicing translation. I hope, however, that it will prove equally useful to other Chinese who are called upon to write English and who wish to improve their mastery of it — people working in journalism, foreign affairs, business, tourism, advertising, and many other fields.

Naturally, readers who open this book will have reached varying levels of skill in their second language. But to one degree or another, the work of all but the most highly trained and experienced among them will inevitably contain elements of Chinglish. Chinglish, of course, is that misshapen, hybrid language that is neither English nor Chinese but that might be described as "English with Chinese characteristics."

In writing this Guide, I have assumed that my Chinese readers have a basic knowledge of English grammar and that if they want a review of the subject, they can find it in other books. My purpose is rather to show translators — and, by extension, others who are writing directly in English — how to recognize elements of Chinglish in a first draft and how to revise it so as to eliminate those elements. In other words, this book is intended to help them turn their work into real English such as might have been written by an educated native speaker of the language.

At institutions like Xinhua News Agency, *China Daily*, Foreign Languages Press, and the Central Translation Bureau, this task is commonly entrusted to senior translators or editors or to foreign "polishers" (who may be more or less competent to perform it). But in principle, much of the work could be done by the original translators — or writers — themselves. That is why throughout these pages I have sometimes referred to the "translator," sometimes to the "polisher" or "reviser." The terms are not mutually exclusive: every translator rereading a first draft can and should be his or her own polisher.

The examples of Chinglish presented here (the "A-version" in each case) are authentic. That is, although some of them have been simplified for instructional purposes, none are invented. Most were found in draft translations that were corrected before the text appeared in print. Some were found in published materials — official documents, *China Daily*, the several English-language magazines, and so on. The source of an example is indicated only when it appeared in a foreign publication, such as the *Far Eastern Economic Review* or a U.S. newspaper.

When an example of Chinglish is taken from a draft translation, the revision offered here (the "B-version") is, with few exceptions, the one decided upon by the polishers who revised it. If, however, the A-version appeared in print, the revision is one that I think should have been made and that I am suggesting now. In either case, the proposed B-version is not necessarily the only "correct" one. Translation is not a science but a craft, and craftsmen in any field may have different opinions as to the best solution to a given technical problem.

It may seem presumptuous for a person who knows little of the Chinese language to proffer a work of this kind. My qualifications are that I am a lifelong student of English and a professional translator (from French to English) who has given much thought to problems of translation. In addition, during the 1980s and 1990s I spent eight years working as a polisher in Beijing, first at Foreign Languages Press and later at the Central Translation Bureau (Bureau for the Compilation and Translation of Works of Marx, Engels, Lenin and Stalin). During those years I had the opportunity to work closely with a wide range of Chinese translators, from beginners fresh out of school to the most capable senior professors. I learned much from them all.

Even with this background, however, I could not have produced this Guide without the help of two invaluable consultants who have kindly read and reread my manuscript. The first is my good friend Jiang Guihua, the retired chief of the English section at the Central Translation Bureau, who has examined every example with the critical eye of a skilled reviser. The second is my husband Larry, who has given me the benefit of his expertise as a writer and as a professor of journalism who has had long experience both teaching and polishing in China. The criticism and advice of these two knowledgeable editors, one native speaker of each language, have been, quite simply, indispensable.

Joan Pinkham
Amherst, Massachusetts
1 April 1999

致 读 者

本书可用于课堂教学,也可用于自学。其主要对象是中国的翻译工作者以及做翻译练习的高年级英语学生。但是,我希望这本书对需要用英语写作的其他中国人(包括新闻工作者、外事工作者、从事商业、旅游业、广告业以及许多其他行业需要使用英语的工作者)同样有帮助,而他们又都希望解够更好地掌握英语。

自然,当读者翻阅这本书时,他们使用第二语言的技能所达到的水平是不同的。但是,除了那些造诣很深的,一般人的翻译中都会不同程度地含有中式英语的成分。当然,所谓中式英语就是那种畸形的、混合的、既非英语又非汉语的语言文字,也可称其为"具有汉语特色的英语"。

在写这本书的过程中,我心目中的中国读者已经掌握了基本的英语语法;如果有人想复习一下他们的语法,可以去求助于有关这方面的书籍。而我的目的则在于帮助翻译工作者以及其他直接用英语写作的人懂得如何在初稿中找出中式英语的成分并将其修改掉。也就是说,这本书是为了帮助他们将自己的写作修改成为地道的英语,就像一个受过教育的以英语为母语的人写的一样。

在一些像新华社、《中国日报》社、外文出版社、中央编译局的单位里,这项工作一般是由高级翻译、审校或外国专家做的(他们或多或少能够胜任这项任务)。但是,原则上,大部分工作可由译者(或作者)自己来完成。为此,在整部书中,我有时用"译者",有时用"润色者"或"改稿人"。这些词并不相互排斥：每位译者在审阅其初稿时都可以而且应当是他自己的润色者。

书中所提供的中式英语的例句(每一条初译文：A-version)都是有根据的。虽然其中有的例句为了便于说明而简化了，但都不是编造出来的。绝大部分例句是从初译稿中搜集的，出书之前都作了修正。有些是从出版物中找到的，如：正式文件、《中国日报》、几种英语杂志等等。给出处的例句都是引自外国出版物，如：《远东经济评论》或某份美国报纸。

书中凡是为从初译稿里引用的例句提供的修改译文(B-version)，除个别例外，都是由改稿人定的。但是，如果 A-version 是从已出版的书中引用的，那么所提供的修改译文则是我认为当初应该改而未改、现在建议这样改的。无论是哪一种情况，这里所提供的修改译文不一定是惟一"正确"的。翻译不是一门科学，而是一种需要特殊技能的专业。每个行业的技术工人对于解决某个技术问题的最佳办法都会有不同的见解。

对于一个不懂汉语的人来说，向读者提供这样一部作品似乎有些不自量力。而我所具备的条件是：我一生都在学习英语而且是一名职业翻译(法译英)，因此，对翻译问题考虑甚多。在80年代到90年代期间，我在北京做了八年的修改译文工作。先是在外文出版社，后来在中央编译局(马恩列斯著作编译局)。在这些年里，我有机会同许多中国的翻译工作者密切合作，他们中间有刚走出校门的新手，也有水平很高的教授。我从他们那里都学到不少东西。

尽管如此，如果没有两位不可多得的人一遍又一遍地帮我审阅我的手稿，这本书是不可能写出来的。首先是我的好朋友姜桂华，她退休前任中央编译局英文处处长，她以一名有水平的改稿者身份严格地检查了每一个例句。其次是我先生拉里，他是一名作家和新闻学教授，曾多年在中国任教并从事修改译文工作，他的专长使我受益非浅。这两位有知识的审校人，一位的母语是英语，一位的母语是汉语,他们提出的批评和建议很简单,但却是不可或缺的。

琼·平卡姆
马萨诸塞州,阿默斯特
1999 年 4 月 1 日

Part One: Unnecessary Words

All authorities on the style of English prose agree that good writing is concise. Careful writers say what they mean in as few words as possible.

A classic statement of this precept appears in the famous little book of William Strunk, Jr., and E. B. White, *The Elements of Style* [p. 23]* :

> Vigorous writing is concise. A sentence should contain no unnecessary words, a paragraph no unnecessary sentences, for the same reason that a drawing should have no unnecessary lines and a machine no unnecessary parts.

It follows that any words which perform no useful function in the sentence — that is, which add nothing to the meaning — should be edited out.

Almost every text that has been translated into English from Chinese, (or that has been written directly in English by a native speaker of Chinese) contains unnecessary words. Draft translations are commonly full of them, and even polished final versions are seldom free of them.

Read anything that has been published in English for foreign readers — a magazine article, a news story, an advertisement, a government report — and you are likely to find superfluous words. Read even the shortest of English texts — the label on a food product, a

---

* For identification of all works quoted in this Guide, see the Selected Bibliography beginning on page 560.

billboard on Chang'an, the company name on the front of a building — and, if you are on the alert to recognize them, chances are that you will find words that could and should have been omitted. Unnecessary words are the hallmark of Chinglish.

The late Sol Adler was the most distinguished practitioner of the English language who ever turned his attention to "polishing" in China. One of his most frequent marginal comments on translations of the works of Mao Zedong, Zhou Enlai, Deng Xiaoping, and other leaders was a laconic "Unnec."

"Unnec." words can be any part of speech — nouns, verbs, adjectives, adverbs, prepositions, articles, and so on. In the following chapters we shall consider the most important types, starting with unnecessary nouns and verbs, which often go hand in hand.

I. Unnecessary Nouns and Verbs

Nouns

Most unnecessary nouns in Chinglish appear not alone but in short phrases, combined with articles and prepositions. When you eliminate the nouns, you eliminate the articles and prepositions as well.

Many of these nouns are easy to recognize. They are plainly redundant because their sense is already included or implied in some other element of the sentence. Here are a few examples ("A") with suggested revisions ("B") and comments in brackets.

A: to accelerate the pace of economic reform
B: to accelerate economic reform
   ["To accelerate" = "to increase the pace of."]

A: there have been good harvests in agriculture
B: there have been good harvests
   ["Harvests" implies agriculture: there are no harvests in industry.]

A: living standards for the people in both urban and rural areas continued to rise
B: living standards in both urban and rural areas continued to rise
   [The notion of living standards applies only to people.]

A: these hardships are temporary in nature
B: these hardships are temporary
   [Any adjective describes the "nature" or "character" of the

3

noun it modifies. To say that hardships are "temporary in nature" is like saying that the Chinese flag is "red in color" or that pandas are "few in number."]

A: the development of our economy in the future will, to a large extent, depend on . . .

B: the development of our economy will depend to a large extent on . . .

[The future tense of the verb ("will depend") is sufficient to express futurity.]

A: we should adopt a series of measures to ensure that . . .

B: we should adopt measures to ensure that . . .

[Here the plural form of "measures" covers the sense of a "series."]

Other unnecessary nouns (or gerunds) may be less easy to identify. Nevertheless, a little thought will reveal that they add nothing to the meaning of the sentence. When they are deleted the sense is not diminished, only clarified. Some examples:

A: following the realization of mechanization and electrification of agriculture

B: following the mechanization and electrification of agriculture

A: it is essential to strengthen the building of national defense

B: it is essential to strengthen national defense

A: these constitute important conditions in striving for the fulfillment of the general task in the transitional period

B: these are important conditions for fulfilling the general task in the transition period

A: at that time the situation in northeast China was still one where the enemy was stronger than the people's forces

B: at that time the enemy was still stronger than the people's forces in northeast China

["Situation" is a particularly dangerous noun. Not only is it generally unnecessary, but it drags other unnecessary elements after it (in this instance, "one where").]

A: the key to the solution lies in the curtailment of expenditure

B: the solution is to curtail (*or*: cut back on) expenditure

["Key" is sometimes useful, but usually it too can be dispensed with. And like "situation," it often leads to further unnecessary complications (here, "lies in").]

A: inner-Party democracy is a subject that has been discussed in detail

B: inner-Party democracy has been discussed in detail

Category nouns

There is one type of noun that deserves special mention, because it is the commonest unnecessary word in Chinglish. This is the general noun that serves only to introduce a specific noun (or gerund) to follow: "a serious mistake in the work of planning."

In such constructions, the first noun announces the category of the second; in this case, it tells readers that "planning" falls into the category of "work." That is something they already know. Accordingly, the first noun should be deleted: "a serious mistake in planning."

Other examples:

A: promoting the cause of peaceful reunification

B: promoting peaceful reunification

A: reforms in <u>the sphere of</u> the economy

B: reforms in the economy (*or*: economic reforms)

A: to ensure <u>a relationship of</u> close cooperation between...

B: to ensure close cooperation between...

A: we must oppose <u>the practice of</u> extravagance

B: we must oppose extravagance

A: these principles apply to all <u>cases of</u> relations between China
   and other countries

B: these principles apply to relations between China and all other countries

A: this, coupled with <u>the factor of</u> price instability, caused...

B: this, coupled with price instability, caused...

Whatever function the category noun serves in Chinese, in English it is generally useless. All it adds to the sentence is weight without substance.

Verbs

Like unnecessary nouns, most unnecessary verbs in Chinglish
occur in phrases. Usually, they are combined with nouns (plus the
inevitable articles and prepositions that nouns bring with them).
These phrases are of two principal types:

1. unnecessary verb plus noun
2. unnecessary verb plus unnecessary noun plus third word

We shall look at first one and then the other.

1. *Unnec. verb + noun*

The commonest type is a phrase like "we must <u>make an</u>

6

improvement in our work." Here the verb ("make") is a weak, colorless, all-purpose word having no very specific meaning of its own, while the real action is expressed in the noun ("improvement"). Since the verb is not contributing anything to the sense, it can be edited out: "we must *improve* our work."

The basic pattern is unnec. verb + noun. Both translators and polishers tend to overlook constructions of this sort, because they are grammatically correct and because — precisely — everyone is so accustomed to them. Once you become alert to the pattern, however, it is easy enough to eliminate the unnecessary words by substituting plain verbs:

A: it is impossible for us to accomplish the transformation of the whole society overnight

B: it is impossible for us to *transform* the whole society overnight

A: they should conduct a careful examination of...

B: they should carefully *examine*...

A: trying to entice the Korean army to launch an attack against them

B: trying to entice the Korean army to *attack* them

A: to bring about a change in this state of affairs

B: to *change* this state of affairs

A: they must make up their minds to implement the reform of the current system

B: they must make up their minds to *reform* the current system

A: until China realizes industrial modernization

B: until China *modernizes* its industry

The construction may also appear in passive voice. That is, instead of "we must make an improvement in our work," we find "an improvement must be made in our work." But this is only a variation of the same pattern, and the solution is the same too: substitute a plain verb. The result is "our work *must be improved*" (because "to make an improvement in" = "to improve").

More examples in passive voice:

A: approval should be given to all these projects
B: all these projects *should be approved*
  [Because "to give approval to" = "to approve."]

A: solutions to these problems can be found only through...
B: these problems *can be solved* only through...
  [Because "to find solutions to" = "to solve."]

A: grain rationing was implemented
B: grain *was rationed*
  [Because "to implement rationing" = "to ration."]

The verb most frequently found in these combinations with nouns is to make:

to make an investigation of = to investigate
to make a careful study of = to study carefully
to make a decision to = to decide to
to make a proposal that = to propose that
to make efforts to = to try (*or*: attempt) to
to make an analysis of = to analyze

The runner-up is doubtless to have:

8

to have a dislike for = to dislike

to have trust in = to trust

to have an influence on = to influence

to have adequate knowledge of = to know enough about

to have the need for = to need

to have respect for = to respect

But many others can be seen on every page as well:

to give guidance to = to guide

to provide assistance to = to assist

to carry out the struggle against = to struggle against

to conduct reform of = to reform

to engage in free discussion of = to discuss (it) freely

to achieve success in = to succeed in

to accomplish the modernization of = to modernize

to realize the transformation of = to transform

to bring about an improvement in = to improve

to place stress on = to stress

to exercise control over = to control

to register an increase = to increase

You should be on the watch for all of them.

2. *Unnec. verb + unnec. noun + third word*

As we have seen, in the first type of phrase a vague and general verb, incapable of expressing specific action, shifts the responsibility for that task onto a noun. In the second type, however, the noun cannot perform the task either.

Consider "our efforts to reach the goal of modernization." Here

9

the noun ("goal") is no more precise than the verb ("reach"). (Indeed, "the goal of" is only another example of the superfluous category noun.) This means that the work of the verb has to be done by still another word, a second noun ("modernization"). Since now the first noun is not doing anything useful in the sentence, it too can be eliminated, along with the all-purpose verb. The result is, "our efforts to *modernize*."

In phrases of this type, the basic pattern unnec. verb + noun has been expanded to unnec. verb + unnec. noun + third word. As in the example above, the third word is usually another noun (or gerund). Since this new noun is performing the function of a verb, it should be given the form of a verb.

A: our troops used the method of slow advance
B: our troops *advanced* slowly

A: three garrison divisions were necessary to perform the task of guarding warehouses
B: three garrison divisions were necessary to *guard* warehouses

A: we adopted the policy of withdrawal
B: we *withdrew* (*or*: decided to withdraw)
  [This was a particular tactical retreat, not a general military policy.]

A: in all matters we must assume the attitude of admitting what we do and do not know
B: we should always (be ready to) *admit* what we do and do not know

A: we should adopt the principle of combining solutions to

> people's immediate difficulties with long-term develop-
> ment
>
> B: we should *combine* solving people's immediate problems
> with promoting long-term development
>
> [A further simplification would be: we should try to solve
> people's immediate problems and at the same time to pro-
> mote long-term development.]

> A: we need to achieve the objective of clarity in ideology
> B: we need to *be clear* in our ideology

But sometimes the third word called upon to do the verb-work is
an adjective. Then it is the adjective that should be promoted to the
rank of verb, while the idle words are dismissed from service:

> A: this measure will have a restrictive effect on the activities of
> speculators
> B: this measure will *restrict* the activities of speculators

And sometimes the third word is another verb. Again, only the
functioning word need be retained:

> A: we failed to take care to ensure that there must be an all-
> round balance between the various planned targets
> B: we failed to *ensure* an all-round balance between the planned
> targets
>
> ["There must be" merely duplicates the sense of "ensure."
> "Various" adds nothing to the plural "targets."]

Like the category-noun phrases on which they are often based
("to reach the goal of modernization"), these unnec. verb + unnec.
noun combinations are only empty preliminaries to other words that

11

carry real content. They add no more to the meaning of the sentence than a cough. The writer is merely clearing his throat before he comes to the point.

Overworked introductory verb phrases

Chinglish texts typically contain many of these throat-clearing verb phrases, but there is one group of them which recurs so constantly, especially in official statements, that it merits special attention. As noted below, these particular verb + noun combinations have a few plain-verb equivalents that are sometimes found as well. However, no matter whether the verbs appear combined with nouns or standing independently, they do nothing but delay the advent of the main action:

A: it is especially necessary to <u>make great efforts to</u> assimilate the achievements of other cultures

B: it is especially necessary to *assimilate* the achievements of other cultures

[What is especially necessary is to assimilate. It is obvious that this process is going to take effort, so we don't have to say so.]

Variants: <u>make every effort to</u>, <u>try our best to</u>, <u>do our utmost to</u>, <u>do everything possible to</u> (also, plain verbs: <u>strive to</u>, <u>endeavor to</u>, <u>work hard to</u>), etc.

A: all enterprises must <u>pay attention to</u> promoting excellent workers

B: all enterprises must *see to it that* excellent workers *are promoted*

[The point is not that the enterprises must "pay attention"

12

to doing something but that they must <u>do</u> it. If they promote workers, they are clearly paying attention to promoting them.]

Variants: <u>pay heed to</u>, <u>lay stress on</u>, <u>attach importance to</u> (also, plain verbs: <u>stress</u>, <u>emphasize</u>), etc.

A: the principal task at present is to <u>do a good job in</u> disseminating and applying the results of scientific and technological research

B: the principal task at present is to *disseminate* and *apply* the results of scientific and technological research

[Logically, the task is not to do a good job but to disseminate and apply. It can be taken for granted that people should try to do it well.]

Variants: <u>make a success of</u>, <u>achieve success in</u>, <u>do successful work in</u> (also, verb + adjective: <u>be good at</u>), etc.

In these examples the phrases "make great efforts to", "pay attention to," "do a good job in" are used indiscriminately, without logical necessity. And because they are not needed, they only clutter up the sentence and obscure its point. For that reason alone they should be eliminated.

But there is another reason as well. The expressions in this group have been so weakened by constant repetition that they have lost their power of exhortation. Thus when they <u>are</u> needed — that is, when their sense is really intended — they carry no force. They have degenerated into tedious formulas to which the reader no longer pays any attention.

While overworked introductory verb phrases are characteristic of

13

Chinglish, they can also appear in the speech or writing of any native speaker of English who is not careful about language. For example, my American grandfather-in-law, a carpenter from rural New England, used to say, "I'm going to go to work and build a set of steps" or "I'm going to go to work and shell those peas."

At first I took the phrase to be an expression of the old man's admirable energy and determination. He used it so often, however, that it gradually ceased to impress me in that way. Then one afternoon when he was preparing to lie down to rest, he declared, "I'm going to go to work and take a nap." With the exception of myself, a newcomer to the family, none of his listeners noticed anything contradictory in the remark. It was clear that for them, as for Grandpa himself, the oft-repeated phrase had long since lost any literal meaning: it was only his habitual way of announcing an intended action.

A warning about revision

It is natural enough for unnecessary nouns and verbs to slip into a draft translation. Most often they have been dutifully carried over from the Chinese original, where they are apparently useful or, at least, tolerable. But in accordance with Professor Strunk's principle, in English they are unacceptable: "A sentence should contain no unnecessary words...." When you reread your work with a critical eye, you should confidently edit them out.

A word of warning, however. First, you have to make sure that the words are indeed "unnec." With a few exceptions, all of the phrases discussed so far sometimes have real content. While three times out of four they are mere cotton padding, the fourth time they may convey an element of meaning that would otherwise be lacking.

In that case, of course, they should be allowed to stand.

For example, the noun phrase expressing time is not always redundant with the verb tense: "at present it is necessary to..." may mean that the necessity is only temporary. The usually worthless category noun can occasionally perform a valid function: "in accordance with the principle of self-reliance, all army units should...."

Phrases such as "make great efforts to," "pay attention to," and "do a good job in" are sometimes perfectly legitimate: "we must make great efforts in education" conveys meaning. And even when such a phrase serves to introduce another verb, it is not necessarily superfluous: "we must make great efforts to overcome this difficulty" may indicate that the task will be particularly arduous.

This means that whenever you come across one of these suspect phrases in a draft translation, you are called upon to make a judgment. In context, is it justified? Is it necessary for the sense of the passage? Or has it been put into the English version simply because it was present in the Chinese?

Consider "the bourgeoisie followed a policy of vacillating." The statement is absurd in English, because to vacillate — that is, to be undecided, to alternate between different positions, to lean now this way and now that — is, precisely, to have no policy. Not only do the words add nothing to the meaning but, as in Grandpa's "I'm going to go to work and take a nap," they actually contradict it. Plainly, they should be deleted ("the bourgeoisie vacillated"). But how about "China has always followed a policy of peaceful coexistence"? That statement makes sense, and here the words are essential to express the meaning. Plainly, they should be retained.

Sometimes, however, the choice is not so clear. What should be done, for example, with "we must <u>follow the policy of</u> putting quality first"? Was the phrase used in Chinese only from force of habit? Is this just Chinglish for "we must always put quality first"? Or did the writer really mean to stress the notion of a policy? Perhaps we should keep the "policy" and even recast the sentence to emphasize it: "we must make it our policy to put quality first." The translator must decide.

Machines have been devised to perform certain types of translation, but they cannot distinguish between meaningful and meaningless uses of the same phrase. That is the difference between you and a machine.

Twenty more examples of revision

Here are twenty more examples of superfluous nouns and verbs, together with suggested revisions.

In the A-versions the unnecessary nouns and verbs are underlined. In the revisions some of them were simply deleted; others were replaced by different words, and the new versions are italicized. The comments in brackets at the end of each example explain the reasons the changes were made. (The explanations in parentheses refer to other faults that were corrected in addition to those discussed in this chapter.)

Note that in every case the edited version is not only shorter but also simpler and easier to understand.

1) A: when making revolution in Guangzhou <u>in the past</u>, we were young and arrogant

   B: when we were making revolution in Guangzhou, we were

16

young and arrogant

[The past tenses of the verbs ("were making" and "were") suffice to place the action "in the past."]

2) A: this accounts for the inadequate efficiency <u>in the performance of their duties</u>

B: this accounts for their inefficiency

[People's "efficiency" normally refers to the way they do their work (perform their duties), so there is no need to spell it out.]

3) A: these nine years <u>constitute a period in which</u> the national economic strength has increased

B: in these nine years the economy has grown stronger

[- "Constitute a period in which" is mere filler, adding nothing to the sense of "nine years."

- ("National" was omitted in the revised version because it is assumed that "the economy" means the national economy.)]

4) A: it is also necessary to <u>put an end to the situation in which</u> the leading organizations accompany the guerrilla units here and there

B: also, leading organizations *should stop* accompanying the guerrilla units wherever they go

["Situation" adds nothing but a more complicated sentence structure. "We must put an end to the situation in which students are late for class" is only a roundabout way of saying "students must stop being late for class."]

5) A: the reason why the contracts are so lifeless and out of gear with actual conditions <u>lies in the fact that</u> the trade union

leadership didn't understand that . . .

B: the reason the contracts are so lifeless and unrelated to actual conditions *is that* the trade union leadership didn't understand that . . .

[Professor Strunk is particularly stern in his condemnation of the expression "the fact that." He says unequivocally [p. 24], "It should be revised out of every sentence in which it occurs."]

6) A: the Civil Aviation Administration of China has decided to start the business of advance booking and ticketing on connecting and return flights

B: the Civil Aviation Administration of China has decided to start advance booking and ticketing for connecting and return flights

["The business of" is an unnec. category noun.]

7) A: The efforts . . . are all focused on the objective of effectively strengthening the vitality of large and medium-sized state-owned enterprises.

B: The efforts . . . are all focused on *revitalizing* (*or*: designed to revitalize) large and medium-sized state-owned enterprises.

[- "The objective of" is another unnec. category noun.

- "To strengthen vitality" = "to revitalize" (pattern: unnec. verb + noun).

- ("Effectively" was edited out because to "revitalize" means to revitalize "effectively.")]

8) A: the main forces of the East China Field Army marched down south into the Henan-Anhui-Jiangsu plains in order to

18

carry out the task of fighting on exterior lines

B: the main forces of the East China Field Army marched south into the Henan-Anhui-Jiangsu plains to *fight* on exterior lines

[- "To carry out the task of fighting" = "to fight" (pattern: unnec. verb + unnec. noun + third word).

- (Note that "in order" is often superfluous with a following infinitive.)]

9) A: instead of <u>introducing the method</u> of confiscation, we have adopted a policy of redemption to change the capitalist ownership

B: instead of *confiscating* property to change capitalist ownership, we have adopted a policy of redeeming it

[- "Introducing the method of confiscation" = "confiscating" (pattern: unnec. verb + unnec. noun + third word).

- "Adopt a policy of" was retained because in this context it is an important element of the meaning, not just a thoughtless cliché.

- Note how changing the nouns "confiscation" and "redemption" to gerunds ("confiscating" and "redeeming") enables us — indeed, requires us — to clarify the sense by adding direct objects ("property" and "it").]

10) A: it is therefore imperative, both politically and economically, to <u>attach importance to</u> promoting the work in the old base areas

B: it is therefore imperative, both politically and economically, to *promote* the work in the old base areas

[What is imperative is not to "attach importance to promoting

19

the work" (i.e., to recognize its importance in principle)
but to promote it (i.e., to take practical action).]

11) A: we must attach great importance to <u>the role of</u> scientific re-
    search institutes

    B: we must attach great importance to (*or*: recognize the great
    importance of) scientific research institutes

    [- If "the role of" is dropped, the sentence means exactly the
    same thing.

    - But here "attach great importance to" expresses the cen-
    tral idea; it can be modified but not edited out. Compare
    the use of the same phrase in the preceding example,
    where it is merely a superfluous introduction to the main
    action.]

12) A: <u>the target</u> of capturing Changsha failed <u>to be achieved</u>
    B: they failed to *capture* Changsha

    ["To achieve the target of capturing" = "to capture" (pat-
    tern: unnec. verb + unnec. noun + third word).]

13) A: the Japanese army concluded that in suppressing the Commu-
    nist Party the dependence on the armed forces alone could
    not <u>achieve success</u>

    B: the Japanese army concluded that it could not depend on the
    armed forces alone to *suppress* the Communist Party

    ["To achieve success in suppressing" = "to suppress" (pat-
    tern: unnec. verb + unnec. noun + third word).]

14) A: in order to accomplish this, <u>an approach</u> of gradual transition
    <u>will be adopted</u>

    B: we *shall accomplish this by* a gradual transition

    [- The structure "adopt an approach of" can be dropped

20

without any loss of meaning.

- (The sentence was changed from passive voice — "this will be accomplished" — to active voice — "we shall accomplish this" — in accordance with the English preference. Active voice is more natural, more direct, more forceful, and more readily understood.)

- (Here again, as in example 8, "in order" can be eliminated.)]

15) A: departments of scientific research should take steps to make a proper readjustment of ...

B: departments of scientific research should *readjust* ...

[- "Take steps to" is another empty introductory phrase.

- "Make a readjustment" = "readjust" (pattern: unnec. verb + noun).

- (It goes without saying that the readjustment should be "proper.")]

16) A: the national economic strength experienced the most rapid increase during this period

B: the economy *grew* most rapidly during this period

[- "To experience increase" = "to increase" = "to grow" (pattern: unnec. verb + noun).

- (As in example 3 above, "economic strength" was changed because it is only a further abstraction for "the economy," and "national" was omitted because it can be taken for granted.)]

17) A: the work of clearly stipulating their functions, organization and personnel should be done well

B: their functions, organization and number of personnel *should be clearly stipulated*

[- "The work of" = unnec. category noun.

- "Should be done well" is a variant of "do a good job." The point here is not that the work should be done well but that it should be done. In any case, the sense of "well" is expressed in "clearly."]

18) A: <u>a</u> good <u>job must be done in</u> medical-care <u>work</u> for the urban residents too

   B: good *medical care must be provided* for city people too

   [- Here, on the contrary, the point is indeed that the work must be done well, so the standard phrase is not just a mindless addition. It can be tightened by eliminating "job", but "good" has to be retained.

   - Note, incidentally, how the revision turns a vague, abstract statement into one that is precise and concrete.]

19) A: plunging yourselves into practical work is very important for you to <u>find solutions to</u> <u>all sorts of</u> problems

   B: if you want to *solve* problems, it is important for you to plunge into practical work

   [- To "find solutions to" = "to solve" (pattern: unnec. verb + noun).

   - Like "a series of," mentioned at the beginning of this chapter, "all sorts of," "various kinds of," etc. are often redundant with a plural noun.

   - ("Very" was removed because it only weakens the force of "important.")]

20) A: it is essential to <u>make vigorous efforts to</u> reform the system for determining the purchasing and selling prices of grain

and take further steps to <u>establish the institution</u> of regulating the reserves of grain, cotton, and other such major products

B: it is essential to *reform* the system for determining the prices at which the state purchases and sells grain and to take further steps to *regulate* the stockpiling of grain, cotton, and other major (*or*: basic) products

[- "Make vigorous efforts to" is a variant of "make great efforts to."

- "To establish the institution of regulating" = "to regulate" (pattern: unnec. verb + unnec. noun + third word).

- (The phrase "the purchasing and selling prices of grain" was slightly expanded to make the system of distribution clearer to foreign readers. "Such" was omitted because in this sentence it means the same thing as "major.")]

Twenty exercises

Here are twenty more examples for you to practice on. Appropriate revisions will be found in the Key to Exercises beginning on page 526. As mentioned in the opening note to the reader, your own versions do not have to be exactly the same as the ones proposed.

1) the new state we have just inaugurated is unusual in character, entirely different from the empire of the Qing dynasty

2) throughout this period there was a severe shortage in the supply of a great variety of goods

3) Comrade Chen Yun paid constant attention to analyzing his experience

4) it is only by employing the method of discussion, criticism, and reasoning that we can really foster correct ideas

5) At first they adopted the method of slow advance to achieve perfect results in the agrarian reform.

6) the one and only policy to be adopted by us is to try our best to mobilize the people

7) we must get rid of the practice of supplying materials in an unplanned way

8) This state of affairs concerning the waste of the most precious resource of the state must be eliminated.

9) the Army must solve the problem of raising work efficiency

10) Chiang Kai-shek, for his part, ceaselessly expanded the scope of the war

11) to date, some 1,900 enterprises in 27 provinces and municipalities have carried out the practice of separating taxes from profits

12) the government departments concerned should do a good job in drawing up development plans for the special economic zones

13) we should regulate patterns of consumption in such a way as to adapt them to the characteristics of China's agricultural resources

14) we should strengthen the work in all facets of public security

15) we shall further reform the banking system by following a policy of controlling total supply and demand for currency and credit

16) it is a question of paramount importance to have a sober understanding of our basic conditions

17) our policy is to work hard and ensure that not a single person shall perish from starvation

18) Sun Yat-sen's firm support for cooperation between the two parties thwarted the efforts of the KMT Right-wingers to undertake activities to split the KMT

19) enterprises should be granted decision-making power in the area of foreign trade

20) we should take effective measures to implement the strategy of invigorating agriculture by applying scientific and technological advances

II. Unnecessary Modifiers

For our purposes, these can be divided into five categories:

1. redundant modifiers
2. self-evident modifiers
3. intensifiers
4. qualifiers
5. clichés

Let us examine them in turn.

1. Redundant modifiers

Many adjectives and adverbs that are carried over into translations from the Chinese originals are simply redundant in English. That is, their sense is already contained or implied in the word they modify or in some other element of the sentence. Including them in the English version adds nothing but a useless duplication.

a) *Obvious redundancies*

Following are some obvious examples — all of which, incidentally, have appeared in print in Chinese publications:

advance forecasts   female businesswoman Liu Zhihua

new innovations   a serious natural disaster

mutual cooperation   an unfortunate tragedy

residential housing   financial revenue and expenditure

positive guidance   a family relative

Here are some more. As in Chapter I, in each example A-version is the original translation, B-version is the suggested revision, and any comments are given in brackets.

A: that theory too is a <u>valuable</u> ideological treasure of the Party

B: that theory too is an ideological treasure of the Party

[A treasure is valuable by definition.]

A: quadrupling GNP will provide a new starting point from which, in another 30 to 50 years, we shall approach the level of the <u>economically</u> developed countries

B: quadrupling GNP will provide a new starting point from which, in another 30 to 50 years, we shall approach the level of the developed countries

[The term "developed countries" means those that are developed economically (not necessarily in other ways).]

A: Singapore will bar America's <u>popular</u> <u>female</u> pop star Madonna from staging a show in its territory

B: Singapore will bar America's pop star Madonna from staging a show in its territory

[She wouldn't be a star if she were not popular, so "popular" is unnecessary. (Another objection is that it repeats "pop," which here means "popular music.") And to Western readers, even those who might never have heard of the performer, "female" is redundant with the universally recognizable feminine name "Madonna" (Italian for "my lady" and commonly used in Christian religion and art to refer to the Virgin Mary).]

A: the Chinese government took all <u>possible</u> eventualities into account when it made this policy decision

B: the Chinese government took all eventualities into account when it made this policy decision

[An "eventuality" is a possible occurrence. "All
eventualities" therefore means "all possible occurrences."]

A: Chiang was able to complete the <u>all-round</u> encirclement of
the Central Soviet Area after having defeated the Fujian
People's Government

B: having defeated the Fujian People's Government, Chiang was
able to complete the encirclement of the Central Soviet
Area

[A completed circle is necessarily "all-round." (The change
in structure clarifies the logical connection between the
two events: <u>because</u> Chiang had defeated ... he was now
able to complete ....)]

b) *Adverbs of time*

One kind of redundant modifier that often appears in Chinglish
is the adverb indicating the time of an action. We noted in Chapter I
that the noun phrases expressing time ("at present," "in the
future," and "in the past") are usually superfluous in English, where
their function is served by the tense of the verb. The same is true of
adverbs expressing time:

A: <u>now</u> the government is working hard to improve taxation
B: the government is working hard to improve taxation

A: <u>previously</u> we used to overemphasize the need for class struggle

B: we used to overemphasize the need for class struggle

c) "*Various*"

Another redundant modifier typical of Chinglish is the adjective
"various." Again, we saw in Chapter I that the noun phrases "a

28

series of," "all sorts of," and "various kinds of" do not generally need to be carried over in translation. While in Chinese they are often necessary to indicate a plural, in English the plural is shown by the form of the noun ending in -s. "Various" is usually superfluous for the same reason:

A: more and more of our <u>various</u> construction projects require the efforts of the intellectuals

B: more and more of our construction projects require the efforts (*or*: assistance, *or*: collaboration) of intellectuals

A: hundreds of transnational firms have started <u>various</u> businesses in China

B: hundreds of transnational firms have started businesses in China

d) *Other examples*

It is not hard to find plenty of other redundant modifiers. Here is a sampling:

A: with the <u>final</u> completion of construction, the plant will reach an annual capacity of 100,000 medium-size trucks

B: with the completion of construction (*or*, *better*: when construction is completed), the plant will have an annual capacity of 100,000 medium-size trucks
[Completion is final by definition.]

A: imports of <u>foreign</u> automobiles have declined sharply this year

B: imports of automobiles have declined sharply this year
[You cannot import a domestic product.]

A: the long-term stability and prosperity of Hong Kong will be assured as long as China <u>widely</u> unites the Hong Kong people from all walks of life

B: the long-term stability and prosperity of Hong Kong will be assured as long as China unites the Hong Kong people from all walks of life

[The phrase "from all walks of life" by itself indicates that the unity is to be "wide."]

A: they must also have some <u>necessary</u> knowledge about history and geography

B: they must also know something about history and geography

[- "Must have" means that it is necessary.

- (<u>Review</u>: "Have knowledge" is one of those "unnec. verb + noun" phrases discussed in Chapter I. In the revision, it was changed to a plain verb, "know.")]

A: We should continue to take measures to <u>further</u> improve regular education, adult education, and on-the-job training programs.

B: We should continue to improve regular education, adult education, and on-the-job training programs.

[- "Continue" to improve = "further" improve.

- (<u>Review</u>: "Take measures to improve" = unnec. verb + unnec. noun + third word, which is the true verb, "improve." In the revision, the unnecessary introductory phrase "take measures to" was dropped.)]

2. Self-evident modifiers

These, while not strictly redundant with another word, are still superfluous because the information they provide can be taken for granted. We have already met the first two of the following examples in Chapter I.

A: these nine years constitute a period in which the <u>national</u> economic strength has increased

B: in these nine years the economy has grown stronger
   [- Unless otherwise stated, "the economy" means the national economy.
   - (Review: "Constitute a period" adds nothing to the sense of "nine years" and is therefore unnecessary.)]

A: departments of scientific research should take steps to make a <u>proper</u> readjustment of . . .

B: departments of scientific research should readjust . . .
   [- We can take it for granted that the readjustment should be "proper."
   - (Review: "Make a readjustment" is another unnec. verb + noun combination that can be replaced by a plain verb, "readjust." "Take steps to," like "take measures to" above, is an unnec. introductory phrase that can be omitted entirely.)]

A: we should <u>appropriately</u> raise the purchasing prices of grain and cotton, so as to increase the income of the peasants considerably

B: we should raise the purchasing prices of grain and cotton, so as to increase the income of the peasants considerably
   [We should always do everything "appropriately," just as we should always "do a good job."]

A: the Congress elected a new leading body, ensuring <u>adequate</u> continuity for our policies of reform and opening to the outside world

B: the Congress elected a new leading body, ensuring the continuity of our policies of reform and opening to the outside world

[Clearly, "continuity" here means "adequate" continuity.]

A: the editorial notes that in 1992, China will open wider to the outside world and do an even better job in running the five special economic zones, as well as the new Pudong development zone in <u>China's</u> leading industrial city of Shanghai

B: the editorial notes that in 1992, China will open wider to the outside world and do an even better job of running the five special economic zones, as well as the new Pudong development zone in the leading industrial city of Shanghai

[It can safely be assumed that even foreign readers know what country Shanghai is in.]

3. Intensifiers

Intensifiers are adjectives (like "serious" and "great") or adverbs (like "extremely" and "certainly") that are intended to heighten the effect of the words they modify. They should be looked upon with suspicion: more often than not, an English text is better off without them.

a) *Intensifiers with weak words*

Sometimes an intensifier is used to modify a weak or inadequate word in the hope of increasing its power. In English, this is a mark of the inexperienced writer.

A skilled writer will try to find, in the rich vocabulary the language has to offer, a strong, precise word that by itself will convey the meaning of both the intensifier and the weak word. Thus, instead of "extremely important," he or she might say "essential," "imperative," "vital," "indispensable," or "crucial"; instead of "they absolutely wanted to," the translator might choose "they were determined to," "had resolved to," "were bent on," or "insisted upon."

More examples:

A: the people have a strong aversion to graft, bribery, embezzlement, and other dirty practices

B: the people *detest* graft, bribery, embezzlement, and other dirty practices

A: I think there will definitely be genuine stability and unity

B: I *am certain* that there will be genuine stability and unity

A: I firmly believe that our army will be able to steadfastly maintain its own character

B: I *am convinced* that our army will be able to (steadfastly) maintain its own character

A: I can surely tell you that nobody is able to stop the reform and opening up in China from continuing

B: I can *assure you* that no one can stop China's reform and opening to the outside world

A: the KMT government overestimated its own strength and was thoroughly optimistic as to the outcome of the war

B: the KMT government overestimated its own strength and was *confident* of the outcome of the war

b) *Intensifiers with strong words*

It is bad enough to use an intensifier to shore up a weak word,

33

as in the examples just given. It is worse to use one to support a word that can stand perfectly well alone. Such a word gives full expression to the writer's thought, and the intensifier adds nothing to its meaning. That is, the modifier is redundant, like those in the first category.

The classic example of this is the combination "great historic," as in "great, historic contributions," "an event of great, historic significance," and so on. Both Professor Cheng Zhenqiu and Sol Adler — two distinguished scholars and longtime students of translation — have criticized this usage. Professor Cheng [p. 44] gives "a great, historic victory" as an example of a phrase in which the Chinese modifier ("great"), if retained in the English translation, "would be redundant and would weaken the effect." Sol Adler [p. 17] put it like this: "The word 'historic' is so strong in English that if you say 'This is a historic change,' there's no need to say it's 'great.' By definition it's great. 'Historic' already contains implicitly in it the idea of greatness."

The same logic condemns many other combinations in which the idea expressed by the intensifier is "implicitly contained" in another word. Consider the following:

From the Far Eastern Economic Review, *quoting Deng Xiaoping*:

A: if there is <u>serious</u> chaos in Hongkong, the Chinese government would be forced to reconsider . . .

B: if serious *disturbances* occurred in Hong Kong, the Chinese government would then be compelled to reconsider . . .

["Chaos" is very strong in English: it means a state of utter confusion in which nothing is organized or predictable. In politics, such a condition is necessarily "serious."]

A: "all this conduct has severely damaged the reputation of the medical profession and must be <u>firmly</u> banned," the minister said

B: "all this conduct has severely damaged the reputation of the medical profession and must be banned," the minister said

[To ban something is to prohibit it, to make it illegal in the English sense of "against the law." It is by definition a "firm" action.]

A: the Civil Aviation Administration of China <u>strongly</u> demanded that the Taiwan authorities take all measures possible to secure the safety of the plane and its passengers

B: the Civil Aviation Administration of China demanded that the Taiwan authorities take all measures possible to secure the safety of the plane and its passengers

[A demand is a firm, even imperative request: it is strong by definition.]

A: these practices should be <u>totally</u> abolished

B: these practices should be abolished

["Abolish" already contains the idea of "totally"; you can't abolish something partially. The same is true of such expressions as "<u>thoroughly</u> eliminated," "<u>completely</u> smashed," and "<u>totally</u> destroyed."]

A: during the entire process of reform and opening, we must <u>persistently</u> oppose corruption

B: throughout the process of reform and opening, we must combat corruption

["Persistently" is redundant with "during the entire"

(which can be neatly replaced by "throughout").]

And although they have been consecrated by long usage, we should place in the same category:

A: the <u>broad</u> masses of the people
B: the masses
 [The masses are necessarily " broad "— there are no "narrow" masses. (And since " the masses" = " the people," we can eliminate one or the other as well.)]

A: a <u>tiny</u> handful of troublemakers
B: a handful of troublemakers
 ["A handful" is a metaphor for a very small number. As with "broad masses," "serious chaos" etc. , the opposite formulation, "a large handful of troublemakers," would be a contradiction in terms.]

c) *Common redundant intensifiers*

In any translation that has not been well edited, either by the original translator or by a polisher, a practiced eye will light upon a great number of redundant intensifiers. An informal count suggests that the following are the most common:

 * active/actively

A: <u>active</u> efforts should be made to develop small-scale mining
B: efforts should be made to develop small-scale mining
 [Efforts are active by definition: you can't make an inactive effort.]

A: I think we should <u>actively</u> promote the establishment of a new international political and economic order
B: I think we should promote the establishment of a new

36

international political and economic order

[- "Actively" is redundant because you can't promote anything passively.

- If emphasis is wanted, it should be provided by other means: "we should vigorously promote," "make every effort to promote," "use all means to promote," "do everything possible to promote," or the like.]

* effective/effectively

A: to benefit the people by means of an effective control of the Yellow River

B: to benefit the people by controlling the Yellow River
   [Control is not control unless it is effective.]

A: we should effectively protect the legitimate rights and interests of foreign investors

B: we should protect the legitimate rights and interests of foreign investors
   [To protect something means to protect it effectively.]

* actual (true, real)/actually (truly, really)

A: the people's procuratorates must always pay attention to actual facts

B: the people's procuratorates must always pay attention to facts
   [A fact is "actual" ("true," "real") by definition. If not, it is not a fact.]

A: he devised tactics for battle according to the actual situation

B: he devised tactics for battle according to the *particular* situation
   [- The point here is that each situation is different and that

37

he devised tactics to match the "particular" one he was facing. A situation, like a fact, is always "actual" ("true," "real"), so there is no need to say so.

- Note that the same goes for "circumstances" and "conditions," which are also objective realities needing no certification by an adjective.]

* successful/successfully

A: to successfully accomplish the arduous and complicated tasks defined at this congress . . .

B: to accomplish the arduous, complicated tasks defined at this congress . . .

[To successfully accomplish = to succeed in accomplishing = to accomplish.]

A: we should keep in mind the days when scientists of the older generation successfully developed the atomic and hydrogen bombs

B: we should keep in mind the days when scientists of the older generation developed the atomic and hydrogen bombs

[If they developed the bombs, they were successful.]

d) *Effect of intensifiers*

Another problem with intensifiers is that, redundant or not, their effect is not always the one intended. Sometimes they produce an overemphasis that is unacceptable in English. For example, it is overdoing it to say that "all social circles are tremendously enthusiastic about providing education." "Enthusiastic" is emphatic enough: the adverb is simply excessive.

At other times, instead of making a statement too strong, an intensifier only weakens it. If we say, for example, "historical experience has proved that . . . ," the reader tends to accept the statement as fact. But if we say, "historical experience has <u>convincingly</u> proved that . . . ," the reader's suspicions are aroused. "Evidence" may or may not be convincing, but "proof" is convincing by definition. The unadorned verb is stronger.

A notable example of this principle of English appears in the First Amendment to the Constitution of the United States: "Congress shall make no law respecting an establishment of religion, or prohibiting the free exercise thereof . . . ."

The men who drafted that amendment more than two hundred years ago did not say "Congress shall <u>absolutely</u> make no law," or "Congress shall <u>definitely</u> make no law," or Congress shall <u>resolutely</u> refrain from making any law . . . . " They understood that the unmodified statement was absolute and that, for future generations, its power would lie precisely in its simplicity.

Here are some examples from Chinglish sources:

A: we are confident that we shall <u>assuredly</u> surpass imperialism through peaceful competition

B: we are confident that we shall surpass imperialism through peaceful competition

A: I am deeply convinced that the normalization of Sino-Japanese relations can <u>certainly</u> be realized

B: I am deeply convinced that Sino-Japanese relations can be normalized

[<u>Review</u>: To realize the normalization of = to normalize (unnec. verb + noun replaced by a plain verb).]

39

A: we cannot endure turmoil and whenever we encounter it later we will <u>definitely</u> enforce martial law

B: we cannot tolerate turmoil, and whenever it arises we will enforce martial law

[- If more emphasis is needed to match the effect of the Chinese, it could be provided, for example, by saying: "we are determined to enforce martial law."

- (Note that the adverb "later" is unnec. with a verb in the future tense, "will enforce.")]

A: their speech is <u>very</u> dull and meaningless

B: their speech is dull and meaningless

A: the people's living standards are <u>truly</u> rising, the country is thriving, and China's international prestige is <u>genuinely</u> growing

B: the people's standard of living is rising, the country is thriving, and its international prestige is growing

[If "rising" has to be supported by "truly," and "growing" has to be confirmed by "genuinely," how can we be sure that "thriving" by itself really means "thriving"? Each of the verbs is more convincing when it stands alone.]

e) *Advice from the experts*

It is safe to assume that the British and American authors of current handbooks for writers have never heard of Chinglish. Nevertheless, their advice on unnecessary intensifiers is so relevant to the work of translators and polishers in China that it might have been addressed specifically to them. Here is a sampling:

- William Zinsser [pp. 109 – 110]: Most adverbs are unnecessary.

You will clutter your sentence and annoy the reader if you choose a verb that has a precise meaning and then add an adverb that carries the same meaning.... Again and again in careless writing, strong verbs are weakened by redundant adverbs.

- Claire Cook [pp. 15 – 16]: You probably should delete all intensive adverbs — *very*, *really*, *truly*, *actually*, and the like. If you've chosen the right word, adding a *very* defeats your purpose. If you haven't got the right word, the *very* offers poor compensation. Readers pay no attention to this overused word. If you want to put a *very* in front of a *large*, you should consider substituting *enormous*, *huge*, *gigantic*, or *massive*.... [The intensive adverbs] attenuate rather than strengthen. Consider *really terrific*, *absolutely stunning*, *truly sensational*, *extremely vital*, and *very devastating*. The adverbs reduce powerful adjectives to conversational gush, depriving them of their stark force. Almost all writers succumb to these trivializing intensives. Be on guard.

- Lauren Kessler and Duncan McDonald [pp. 117 – 118]: When you intensify an already intense word, be it adjective or verb, you do more than add clutter. You sap the word of its strength. Once you have chosen a powerful word, you must trust it to stand on its own ....

- H. W. Fowler [p. 10]: Constant association with an intensifying adjective deprives a noun of the power of standing on its own legs. Thus *danger* must always have its *real*, *part* its *integral*, and *crisis* its *grave* or *acute*, and *understatements* must be *masterly*. The only hope for a noun thus debilitated is for the combination to be recognized as a cliché and killed by ridicule ....

- Ernest Gowers [pp. 50, 52]: Cultivate the habit of reserving

41

adjectives and adverbs to make your meaning more precise, and suspect those that you find yourself using to make it more emphatic. Use adjectives to denote kind rather than degree. By all means say an *economic crisis* or a *military disaster*, but think well before saying an *acute crisis* or *a terrible disaster*. Say if you like 'The proposal met with noisy opposition and is in obvious danger of defeat'. But do not say 'The proposal met with considerable opposition and is in real danger of defeat'. If that is all you want to say it is better to leave out the adjectives and say 'The proposal met with opposition and is in danger of defeat'.... Strong words like *urgent*, *danger*, *crisis*, *disaster*, *fatal*, *grave*, *overriding*, *prime*, *paramount*, and *essential* lose their force if used too often. Reserve them for strong occasions, and then let them stand on their own legs, without adjectival or adverbial support.

- Jacques Barzun [p. 100]: An important subclass of clichés consists of what an English rhetorician [Gowers] has called "adverbial dressing gowns": *seriously consider*, *utterly reject*, *thoroughly examine*, *be absolutely right*, *make perfectly clear*, *sound definitely interested*. All these are clichés and the adverb is the dressing gown: the writer thinks the verb or adjective would not seem decent if left bare. The truth is that the meaning is strengthened by the removal of the automatically remembered adverb. Nothing is easier than to strike it out when it crops up unbidden in your prose. Reread yourself and you will feel how much more firm the tone and final the thought of "I reject the accusation" than the spluttering: "I utterly reject the accusation."

4. Qualifiers

Qualifiers are adverbs designed not to intensify the force of a statement but to lessen it. They are words like "quite," "rather," and "relatively."

There is nothing wrong with using such words on occasion, when the bald statement would be too absolute without some qualification. However, when qualifiers are used indiscriminately, as they often are in Chinglish, they give the reader an impression of hesitancy, timidity, and indecisiveness, as if the writer were unable or unwilling to commit himself to anything definite.

The leading Party cadre who described a forthcoming history of the CPC as "a reasonably substantial book giving a comparatively complete history of the Party" meant to praise it. His Chinese readers doubtless understood that. But to anyone who reads his comment in English translation, he appears so reluctant to express wholehearted approval of the work that his words are only a lukewarm recommendation at best. In Alexander Pope's famous phrase, he seems to "damn with faint praise."

a) *Examples*

Here are more examples of qualifiers that weaken the writer's statement when there is no logical reason for doing so:

A: we have dozens of thousands of students studying abroad, and it is quite important to create suitable conditions for their work after they come back

B: we have tens of thousands of students studying abroad, and it is important to create suitable conditions for their work after they return

[-There is no need to hang back from saying straight out that this is important; that is clearly what the speaker means.

- ("Dozens of thousands" was changed simply because it is

43

not idiomatic in English.)]

From a Reuters dispatch printed in the Boston Globe:

A: Chinese officials voiced shock yesterday at a decision by the
US Export-Import Bank to delay loans for a subway project for the southern city of Guangzhou.... "The impact
of this will be quite huge," an official said by telephone.

B: ... "The impact of this will be huge," an official said by
telephone.

[If the officials "voiced shock," they plainly thought the decision would have an enormous impact. "Quite" saps the
meaning of "huge."]

A: "[artist] Zhao's images are somewhat primitively aggressive,
forcing themselves on the viewer as if they, together with
the strong feelings they convey, must never be ignored
and overlooked," critic Geng Jian comments on his art

B: "Zhao's images are primitively aggressive," says critic Geng
Jian, "forcing themselves on the viewer as if they, and the
strong feelings they convey, were not to be ignored"

[- Here the qualifier is at war with the meaning: if the images were only "somewhat" aggressive, they could not
"force themselves" upon us.

- (Note that in this context, "overlooked" simply dupli-
cates the sense of "ignored.")]

A: under the most difficult circumstances, Zhou Enlai resolutely
and carefully set to work, basically guaranteeing the
peaceful resolution of the Xi'an incident

B: under the most difficult circumstances, Zhou Enlai carefully
set to work, guaranteeing (*or*: ensuring, *or*: bringing

44

about) the peaceful resolution of the Xi'an incident

[- Premier Zhou's diplomatic efforts did indeed bring about the peaceful resolution of the Xi'an incident, so "guaranteeing" needs no qualification.

- "Resolutely" is an unnecessary intensifier and a cliché; it is particularly undesirable in the same sentence with "resolution," which repeats the sound.]

A: I do not think that that part of history [the Cultural Revolution], a <u>fairly</u> significant part of our lives for my generation, has gone with the wind

B: I do not think that that part of history, which for my generation was a significant part of our lives, has gone with the wind

[The writer, born in 1952, is speaking of a "part of history" that transformed the lives of young people of her generation and marked many of them profoundly. To refer to it as "fairly significant" is a needless understatement that only undercuts her following remarks about its importance.]

b) *"Perhaps," "maybe," "possibly"*

In this same category of qualifiers, there are three — "perhaps," "maybe," and "possibly" (or "possible") — which, even when they are perfectly legitimate, are often unnecessary. They can be neatly replaced by "may" or "might." In other words, the doubt expressed in Chinglish by one of these modifiers is commonly expressed in English by a special form of the verb.

A: <u>perhaps</u> it will take a decade to accomplish this

B: it *may* take a decade to accomplish this

45

A: twelve to thirteen percent of China's people, or more than
100 million of the total, live in cities, and <u>maybe</u> the figure will go up in coming years

B: twelve to thirteen percent of our people, or more than 100
million, live in cities, and that figure *may* go up in years
to come

A: experts predict that the reduction of interest rates will lead to
a <u>possible</u> loosening of credit this year

B: experts predict that the reduction of interest rates *may* lead
to a loosening of credit this year

c) <u>*Comments by the experts*</u>

Unnecessary qualifiers, like unnecessary intensifiers, are unanimously condemned by the writers, editors, and scholars who have a
professional concern for the English language.

- Gowers [p. 51] cites <u>unduly</u>, <u>relatively</u>, and <u>comparatively</u> as
the most fashionable "adverbial dressing-gowns," pointing out that
those words "can only properly be used when something has been
mentioned or implied which gives a standard of comparison." When
there is no standard of comparison, "their use is merely a shrinking
from the nakedness of an unqualified statement."

- Strunk and White [p. 73] call qualifiers like <u>rather</u> and <u>a little</u>
"leeches that infest the pond of prose, sucking the blood of words."

- And the Fowler brothers, writing in 1906 [p. 363], refer to
the indulgence in qualifying adverbs (<u>perhaps</u>, <u>possibly</u>, <u>probably</u>,
<u>rather</u>, <u>a little</u>, <u>somewhat</u>, and so on) as a disease of British journal-
ists. They deplore the "intemperate orgy of moderation" that they
find renewed every morning in the daily newspapers.

46

Here again, although the remarks are addressed to writers who are native speakers of English, they apply with equal force to Chinese translators who are working into English as a second language.

5. Clichés

Clichés are the most troublesome category of unnecessary modifiers in Chinglish. This category overlaps all the others: it consists of adjectives and adverbs which, while they may or may not be objectionable for one of the reasons discussed above, are so overworked that they have become nearly meaningless. They are used with such regularity to accompany certain words that those words are seldom found standing alone.

a) *Examples*

Translators and polishers at units that deal with official reports and speeches are only too familiar with the following formulas, lifted straight out of the Chinese:

arduous tasks	overwhelming majority
painstaking efforts	scientific analysis
correct understanding	appropriate readjustment
bold experiments	clearly defined
firm and effective measures	basically accomplished
vigorously promote	gradually improve
energetically develop	further reform
carry out unswervingly	properly combine
study conscientiously	fully mobilize
resolutely enforce	firmly forbid

Staff members at other units could no doubt compile similar lists of clichés found in the particular texts with which they work.

b) *Effect of repetition*

Professor Cheng Zhenqiu [p. 47] suggests that the Chinese language tolerates more adjectives and adverbs than the English. Referring to a government report thick with relentlessly repeated modifiers, he warns that "if all [of them] are translated literally into English, the effect would be deadening. Too much emphasis means very little emphasis."

This problem of the "deadening effect" often arises in English versions of political documents. When all tasks are "arduous," when it is "imperative" to perform them all, and when we are constantly exhorted to execute them "conscientiously," "diligently," "resolutely," "energetically," "vigorously," "unswervingly," "persistently," and "unremittingly," the reader, exhausted at the end of the first page, mentally throws up his or her hands and stops listening.

For the native reader of English, the meaning of such ubiquitous adjectives and adverbs grows fainter with each repetition. At last they degenerate into familiar background noises, like the Beijing street sounds that accompany a cyclist's stream of thought without intruding upon it.

In other words, these overworked modifiers have met the same fate as the overworked verb phrases discussed in Chapter I: "make great efforts to," "pay attention to," and "do a good job in." They have been used so often that they have lost all power of persuasion. Thus, when they are needed for a legitimate purpose, the translator finds them too enfeebled to serve.

c) *Avoiding repetition*

The easiest way to deal with a cliché modifier is simply to omit it from the English version. That is often a perfectly acceptable solution. Sometimes, however, when the word cannot be deleted without diminishing the meaning of the original, a fresh variation is enough to relieve the monotony. For a change, an "arduous" task might be described as "demanding." "Vigorous" development might be called "intensive." "Further" efforts could be changed to "renewed." And "resolute" measures could be made "determined." (In the search for alternative renderings of this sort, *Roget's International Thesaurus* or another dictionary of synonyms is often helpful.)

Plainly, you should try to steer clear of weak and colorless modifiers like "very" and "fully," which have been overused in innumerable pieces of writing. They have long since succumbed to the process of deterioration and have become empty clichés. But it should be remembered that even a forceful and unusual word, if it appears too often in any one text, can quickly be reduced to the same impotence.

For example, in the draft translation of the first volume of the *Selected Works of Zhou Enlai*, the pieces dating from the 1920s and 1930s were full of references to "rampant" reaction and "frenzied" enemy attacks. Concerned about the constant repetition of such striking adjectives, the two English-language polishers did their best to delete or change them where possible. They also made it a rule that the strong adverb "resolutely" was to be allowed no oftener than twice a page, lest it lose its force (a rule that they were not always able to abide by).

49

The importance of judgment

We have now examined the five main types of unnecessary modifiers in Chinglish: redundant modifiers, self-evident modifiers, intensifiers, qualifiers, and clichés. From this discussion, it is clear that no adjective or adverb should be automatically included in the English version of a text simply because its equivalent appears in the Chinese. But, let us hasten to add, neither should it be automatically eliminated.

In Chapter I we saw that a noun or verb that is usually superfluous can nevertheless be useful at times. The same is true of adjectives and adverbs. In each instance, a judgment must be made. Is the modifier necessary? Should it be carried over into English? Should it be replaced, along with the noun or verb it modifies, by a single, more expressive word? Or should it simply be edited out?

Confronted with a modifier of the first category, you need not hesitate:

1. *Redundant* : new innovations = innovations.

But modifiers in the other categories often require more consideration. Here are examples from each in which, for one reason or another, it was decided that a word that is generally dispensable should nevertheless be retained:

2. *Self-evident* : he called for ... further reform efforts to push State cultural organizations and performing art troupes into the marketplace

   [- The Minister of Culture is calling for additional efforts, so here the "further" seems justified.

   - When, however, in the next few sentences he also calls

for "more cultural events to <u>further</u> boost the market" and vows to "<u>further</u> improve the management of the cultural market," the word adds only an idea that can be taken for granted, and it should therefore be cut.]

3. *Intensifiers*: the <u>complete</u> prohibition and <u>thorough</u> destruction of nuclear weapons

[Here political considerations intervene. It is probably better to tolerate the redundancy than to correct it at this late date, when, as Professor Cheng Zhenqiu has warned, a change in wording might be interpreted abroad as a change in China's long-standing policy.]

4. *Qualifiers*: looking back to the war years, I should say that our Second Field Army accomplished its tasks <u>fairly</u> well at every stage of the war

[Although "fairly," like "quite," "rather," and "somewhat," usually expresses only unnecessary hesitation, here it is a deliberate understatement. The speaker is Deng Xiaoping, and he is referring in particular to the heroic Dabie Mountains campaign, which he himself had commanded together with Liu Bocheng. The intentional modesty of the remark would be lost if the qualifier were eliminated.]

5. *Clichés*: Jiang said that the central idea running through Deng Xiaoping's remarks was the need to carry out <u>unswervingly</u> the Party's basic line of "making economic construction the central task and adhering to the four cardinal principles ..."

[This is a public pronouncement by Jiang Zemin speaking in

his capacity as General Secretary of the Party. Better to keep his emphasis, even if it means retaining an overworked adverb.]

In sum, given the markedly different habits of the Chinese and English languages with regard to modifiers, it behooves you to examine each one critically before deciding how to deal with it.

Twenty more examples of revision

Here are twenty more examples of sentences containing unnecessary words, together with proposed revisions. This time it is the superfluous modifiers that are underlined in the A-versions. Again, explanations of the revisions are given in brackets. Remarks on unnecessary nouns and verbs that were also removed appear in parentheses and are marked "Review."

1) A: however, these troops, which were what remained after severe tempering, were the valuable cream of the Communist Party of China and the Red Army

   B: however, these troops, which were what remained after severe tempering, were the cream of the Communist Party and of the Red Army

   [- The metaphor "cream" means the best or most valuable part, so "valuable" is redundant.

   - "Of China" is understood.]

2) A: some people are worried whether China will abide by the agreement consistently

   B: some people are worried whether China will abide by the agreement

   ["To abide by" means to remain faithful to. That is, it

implies the idea of always or consistently.]

3) A: the decision also <u>clearly</u> set forth the basic principles, policies, and measures for the rectification

   B: the decision also set forth the basic principles, policies, and measures for the rectification

   [We assume a statement (explanation, definition etc.) is clear unless there is some reason to doubt it.]

4) A: the <u>current</u> great peril facing the <u>whole</u> country and the entire nation was brought on by the erroneous policy pursued by the KMT, which must be <u>thoroughly</u> revised

   B: the great peril facing the entire nation was brought on by the erroneous policy pursued by the KMT, a policy that must be *reversed*

   [- The sense of "current" is clear from "facing."

   - The "entire" nation was retained, because in this context it was important, but "the whole country" seemed redundant.

   - "Thoroughly revised" was replaced by a single strong word, "reversed." The word was justified because it was clear from the context that the KMT must do the opposite of what it had been doing.]

5) A: the editorial calls on the Chinese people to <u>fully</u> implement the CPC's basic line, deepen reform and further opening to the outside, so as to <u>further</u> push forward the political, economic, and social development of the country in a steady way

   B: the editorial calls on the Chinese people to implement the basic line of the CPC, deepen the reform, and promote the opening to the outside, so as to steadily push forward the political, economic, and social development of the country

[- "Fully" is unnec. because its sense can be taken for granted: policies should always be fully carried out.

- If the word conveys something more specific in Chinese, that must be spelled out for the reader of English. We might say, for example, "to implement the CPC's basic line in all its aspects," or "in every respect."

- As for "further," it is obvious that at this point in history, any push given to development will be a "further" push (not the initial push).

- The repetition of "further" in A-version is particularly undesirable because the word is used in two different senses. It appears first as a verb ("to further opening"), then immediately after as an adverb ("to further push ahead"), so that the reader is obliged to go back and read the sentence again in order to make sense of it.]

6) A: we shall continue to <u>effectively</u> prevent and treat plant diseases and insect pests and spread the use of improved strains and advanced, <u>suitable</u> techniques

B: we shall continue to prevent and treat plant diseases and insect pests and to spread the use of improved strains and advanced techniques

[- Unless you prevent diseases "effectively," you do not prevent them.

- We can take it for granted that techniques used should be "suitable" (which means no more than "appropriate," "proper," etc.). If the sense of the Chinese is that the techniques should be "suited to local conditions," we

54

should say that.]

7) A: the land reform conducted across this vast area represented a
tremendous social transformation unparalleled in Chinese
history

B: the land reform conducted across this vast area represented a
social transformation unparalleled in Chinese history

["Unparalleled" is so strong that there is no need for the intensifier "tremendous." Cf. "great historic."]

8) A: according to the record, the population of the city of Nanjing
had dropped drastically by 80 per cent after the Japanese
occupation

B: according to the record, the population of the city of Nanjing
had dropped by 80 percent after the Japanese occupation

[In this context, 80 per cent is in itself a "drastic" figure, so
the adverb is redundant.]

9) A: The efforts to further deepen reforms, accelerate readjustment
of the economic structure, and constantly promote scientific and technological progress and improve economic performance are all focused on the objective of effectively
strengthening the vitality of large and medium-sized state-
owned enterprises.

B: The efforts to deepen reforms, accelerate readjustment of the
economic structure, promote scientific and technological
progress, and improve economic performance are all designed to revitalize large and medium-sized state-owned
enterprises.

[- This was written in 1992. By then, any efforts to deepen
the reforms initiated in 1979 were clearly "further"

efforts.

- It can be taken for granted that the efforts to do all these things are "constant."
- "Effectively" is a redundant intensifier.
- (<u>Review</u>: "The objective of" = unnec. category noun. "Strengthen the vitality of" = unnec. verb + noun, here replaced by the plain verb "revitalize.")]

10) A: the situation was <u>fairly</u> <u>grim</u> and perilous for us, but on the whole, I should say we accomplished our task of strategic counteroffensive <u>quite</u> smoothly

B: the situation was perilous, but on the whole, I should say we accomplished the strategic counteroffensive smoothly

[- This is again Deng Xiaoping speaking about the Dabie Mountains campaign in which he himself played a leading role. The translator will therefore want to retain the modesty of the statement, but "on the whole" is a sufficient qualifier, obviating the need for "quite."

- "Fairly," on the other hand, is plainly an unnecessary understatement.

- "Grim" was deleted as a mere duplication of "perilous."

- (<u>Review</u>: "Our task of" was omitted as an unnec. category noun.)]

11) A: [Liu] Bocheng firmly supported the Party's policy of marching north to resist the Japanese invaders and <u>resolutely</u> opposed Zhang Guotao's activities to split the Party and the Red Army

B: Bocheng firmly supported the Central Committee's policy of marching north to resist the Japanese invaders and opposed

Zhang Guotao's attempts to split the Party and the Red Army

[- "Resolutely" was omitted on the principle that one should eliminate an overworked modifier whenever it serves only decorative purposes.

- Another consideration was that "firmly" and "resolutely" mean virtually the same thing and, used together in the same sentence, produce overemphasis.]

12) A: we must <u>resolutely</u> shift the emphasis of construction to technological transformation

B: we must shift the emphasis of construction to technological transformation

[- The adverb seemed to have been included only because there was one in the Chinese. Emphasizing technological transformation is not a task that calls for special resolve.

- Again, better to save the word for a place where it is necessary and more appropriate.]

13) A: <u>effective</u> measures must be taken to bring the number of <u>various</u> mentally ill persons under control

B: measures must be taken to bring the number of mentally ill persons under control

[- If the measures bring the number under control, they are necessarily effective.

- "Various persons" is meaningless here, and the adjective seems to have been automatically carried over from the Chinese where, presumably, it was needed to indicate a plural.]

14) A: first, seize the <u>favorable</u> opportunity and <u>actively</u> create

conditions to seek a faster and better development speed

B: first, seize the opportunity to create conditions for faster and better development

[- An opportunity is by definition an opportune or "favorable" occasion.

- The notion of "actively" is implicit in "create."

- (Presumably, the revised version reflects the intended meaning. "Better" must apply to "development" rather than "speed"; it is hard to think what a "better" speed could be if not a "faster" one.)]

15) A: the people as a whole are strongly dissatisfied with the phenomena of serious bureaucratism and corruption

B: the people are *indignant* over (*or*: outraged by) bureaucratism and corruption

[- "The people" means all or most of the people, so "as a whole" was dropped.

- A single strong word, "indignant," was used to replace the combination of intensifier + weak "dissatisfied".

- The people would not be indignant unless the problems were serious, so the adjective was omitted as self-evident.

- (Review: "The phenomena of" = unnec. category noun.)]

16) A: all members of the Party should conscientiously, actively, and gladly plunge into the reform

B: all members of the Party should plunge *eagerly* into the reform

[- "Actively" was deleted as being redundant with "plunge."

- It was felt that the sense of both "conscientiously" and "gladly" could best be expressed in the single word "eagerly." (It might also be argued that in this context "plunge" alone implies eager, voluntary action.)]

17) A: <u>successful</u> handling of the two above-noted problems [relating to the minority nationalities] is a responsibility that rests largely with the State organs and government departments <u>concerned</u>

B: the responsibility for handling these two problems rests largely with State organs and government departments

[- Their responsibility is to handle the problems; it is understood that they are to try to handle them successfully — that is, to "do a good job."

- "Concerned" was deleted as redundant with "responsibility." In A-version all we have said is that the responsibility rests with those who are responsible for it.

- It is possible that a different sense was intended, one in which "concerned" was not merely redundant. In that case, we would have to spell out its meaning: "the responsibility for handling these two problems rests largely with those State organs and government departments that are concerned with the minority nationalities."]

18) A: after completing their preparations for war, the KMT authorities <u>immediately</u> revealed their true nature and tore up the truce agreement by <u>flagrantly</u> launching an all-out attack on the Liberated Areas

B: *as soon as they had completed* their preparations for war, the KMT authorities revealed their true nature and their *contempt* for the truce agreement by launching a full-scale attack on the Liberated Areas

[- We can dispense with "immediately" by combining it with "after" in the phrase "as soon as."

- "Flagrantly" is a wrong collocation with "launching" (although we might have said "in flagrant violation of the truce agreement"). It can be neatly replaced by "contempt," which includes both the meaning of the metaphor "tore up" and the writer's indignation as expressed in the adverb.]

19) A: in the letter [to the KMT] the CPC <u>earnestly</u> stated, "We want to form a solid, revolutionary, united front with you . . ."

B: in the letter the CPC stated (*or*: declared), "We want to form a solid, revolutionary, united front with you . . ."

["Earnestly," like "sincerely," can be taken for granted. If the point needs to be emphasized here, a solution would be "the CPC declared in good faith."]

20) A: through three years of hard effort, Jiang noted, the tasks of rectifying the economy have <u>basically</u> been completed

B: through three years of hard effort, Jiang noted, the rectification of the economy has *basically* been completed

[- In this instance, the qualifier seems necessary. It would scarcely be correct to say that so enormous and open-ended a task as "rectifying the economy" had been completed in so short a time.

- (<u>Review</u>: "The tasks of" = unnec. category noun.)]

Twenty exercises

Here are twenty examples for you to edit. It may help to under-line all the modifiers in each sentence and then decide which ones to retain and which to delete. Again, suggested revisions are given in the key at the back of the book.

1) we discovered this long ago but were never able to successfully solve the problem

2) the General Secretary pointed out that to speed up the construction of the new economic system it is imperative to resolve several key problems currently

3) Beijing plans to make greater efforts to further improve sanitation conditions

4) the unchecked spread of bourgeois liberalization may have grave consequences

5) I believe that these policies will definitely not be changed

6) the reform and opening up must be carried out in light of the actual conditions in each country, because countries differ from one another in many respects

7) first, every year we must truly solve some of the intellectuals' problems, producing real results

8) we should have a sober view that there are still many defects yet to be wiped out

9) we shall continue to severely crack down on smuggling

10) we shall unswervingly follow a policy of opening to the outside world and actively increase exchanges with foreign countries

on the basis of equality and mutual benefit

11) I believe that the unhealthy practices which can now be found in society will certainly decrease gradually and disappear eventually

12) the decree says the country firmly forbids import and export of rhinoceros horn and tiger bone and ready-made traditional Chinese medicines which include them

13) you can make suggestions to the responsible departments concerned for an extension of time

14) China will work to soundly implement the Uruguay Round of trade accords, a Beijing representative said on Wednesday

15) I hope you will sit down together to carefully study and discuss this question

16) however, it will be hard to avoid completely an occasional delay of ten to fifteen days

17) the Third Plenary Session of the Eleventh Central Committee defined the central task for the whole Party and the entire country as development of the productive forces

18) while there has been a significant and phenomenal increase in output, it has not solved the problem of fragmentation of production

19) in this way, we can seize the favorable opportunity to raise the national economy to a new level

20) agricultural growth remains the important foundation for the development of China's national economy as a whole

III. Redundant Twins

One of the distinguishing characteristics of Chinglish is the constant use of two words so close in meaning that one would do. The pairs can be nouns, verbs, adjectives, or adverbs:

help and assistance　　　　stir up and incite
views and opinions　　　　prudent and cautious
sentiments and feelings　　fair and equitable
encourage and promote　　firmly and resolutely
discuss and debate　　　　ceaselessly and unremittingly

This sort of duplication is apparently acceptable in Chinese. It may even be necessary — to avoid ambiguity, to reinforce meaning, to provide balance and symmetry, or just to satisfy the ear. But as we saw in the preceding chapter, the presence of two words in Chinese is never in itself a sufficient justification for using two words in an English translation.

Recognizing redundancies

Confronted with a pair of English words in a draft translation, whether your own or someone else's, you must decide whether both are needed to convey the meaning of the Chinese. The temptation is to retain both words, on the grounds that they do not mean exactly the same thing. But no two words in English ever do mean exactly the same thing.

For historical reasons, and because of its innumerable borrowings from other languages, English has an exceedingly rich vocabulary. That is, it contains many words that are nearly synonymous.

63

Some pairs in which the two words are drawn from separate language streams (the first having Germanic roots, the second Latin) may appear to be exact equivalents. Consider, for example:

friendship/amity   wonderful/marvelous

handbook/manual   motherly/maternal

undertaking/enterprise   underwater/submarine

foretell/predict   wrong/erroneous

oversee/supervise   before/prior to

Yet even in these pairs whose dictionary definitions are for practical purposes identical, subtle distinctions can be made. The words have acquired different connotations and associations and have come to be used in different contexts. "Foretell" has an aura of mystery and prophecy that is lacking in the scientific "predict." "Erroneous" carries none of the moral condemnation that can be expressed by "wrong."

So the question for the translator is not: Is there a difference between these two words? There is always a difference. The right question is: In this particular context, is the difference important? In other words: Does the second word add anything significant to the first? Is a second word necessary to express some element in the Chinese that one alone does not convey? If the answer is no, you have identified an example of what may be called "redundant twins."

Eliminating redundancies

In most instances, the best way to deal with redundant twins is simply to <u>delete one of them</u>. (And, as we have seen in preceding chapters, whenever unnecessary words are removed, the statement gains in clarity and force.) For example, "geographical surveys and

64

explorations" can be reduced to "geographical surveys" without loss of meaning. Cadres who are urged to be "attentive and meticulous in their work" will not grow careless if they are asked only to be "meticulous in their work."

At other times, it is preferable to replace both members of the pair with a new word that expresses the thought better than either of the original two. For example, "faraway, distant areas" could be described as "remote." And instead of calling upon people to "be alert and wake up," you could call upon them to "rouse themselves."

Occasionally, it turns out that neither of these operations — deleting one twin or replacing both — produces an adequate version, one that covers all the sense of the original Chinese. This suggests that two or more words really *are* needed in English, but the translator has selected the wrong ones. He or she has tried to condense too much meaning into two words that cannot convey it and has unwittingly produced redundant twins instead.

The best solution in such a case may be to add a word or two that will clarify the intended meaning of one or both terms. Depending on context, of course, "conditions and environment" might be changed to "working conditions and social environment." "Reconnaissance and investigation" might be expanded to "military reconnaissance and investigation among the people."

When the attempt at clarification is successful, the new version matches the full sense of the original and incidentally, by differentiating between the two words used in English, eliminates the redundancy as well. When you "spell out" the meaning in this way, however, you are making explicit in English something that may be only implicit in Chinese. For this reason, there is always the danger of

65

mistranslation — that is, of misunderstanding the original and of introducing into the English version a meaning that is not present or intended in the Chinese. You should think hard before adding the explanatory words.

Categories of redundant twins

It is useful to distinguish three types of redundant twins, the first of which is by far the most common:

1. a pair of words in which the meaning of one is virtually the same as that of the other
2. a pair in which the meaning of one is contained in or implied by the other
3. a pair in which the meaning of one is so vague and general that it cannot be differentiated from the other

Following are examples of each type, with appropriate revisions.

1. *Meaning of one is virtually the same as that of the other*

A: this is the only road leading to <u>affluence and prosperity</u>

B: this is the only road to *prosperity*

A: although the road before us is <u>rough and bumpy</u>, we believe that the favorable situation will continue

B: although the road before us is *rough*, we believe that the favorable situation will continue

A: a country that wants to develop needs to pay close attention to maintaining extensive international <u>contacts and dealings</u> with all kinds of people

B: a country that wants to develop needs to maintain extensive international *contacts* with all kinds of people

[Review: "Pay close attention to" is one of the unnec. introductory verb + noun phrases.]

A: even if problems do emerge, they can be easily corrected or
    solved

B: even if problems do emerge, they can be easily *solved*

From the leaflet of a silk store in Beijing:

A: our store also accepts orders for blouses, shirts, pajamas …
    etc., the sewing work being fine and excellent

B: our store also accepts orders for blouses, shirts, pajamas …
    etc., all of which are *finely* sewn

2. *Meaning of one is contained in or implied by the other*

A: representatives in the Sino-British talks failed to reach an
    agreement, despite the Chinese side's best and thorough
    efforts toward that end

B: representatives in the Sino-British talks failed to reach an
    agreement, despite the *best* efforts of the Chinese side
    ["Best" contains the sense of "thorough." ("Toward that
    end" is self-evident.)]

A: biographical background data on cadres should be correctly
    evaluated and comprehended

B: biographical background data on cadres should be correctly
    evaluated
    [You can't evaluate something correctly if you haven't un-
    derstood it; "evaluated" implies "comprehended."]

A: the present boom of foreign investment in China has prompt-
    ed the country to consider and eventually work out ways to
    use such investment more efficiently

B: the present boom of foreign investment in China has prompt-
ed the country to *work out* ways to use such investment
more efficiently

[Again, you can't determine what measures to take without
studying possible alternatives; "considered" is implicitly
contained in "work out."]

A: the Chinese Foreign Ministry spokesman called the decision
"yet another attempt by British Hong Kong authorities to
<u>interfere with and undermine</u> the Sino-British talks"

B: the Chinese Foreign Ministry spokesman called the decision
"yet another attempt by British Hong Kong authorities to
undermine the Sino-British talks"

[To "undermine talks" is to "interfere with" them in a particularly damaging way.]

A: the KMT government arbitrarily arrested, imprisoned, and
executed workers, students, and other patriotic democrats
and <u>promulgated and implemented</u> a series of reactionary
laws and decrees

B: the KMT government arbitrarily arrested, imprisoned, and
executed workers, students, and other patriotic democrats
and *promulgated* a series of reactionary laws and decrees

["Promulgated" implies "implemented." Unless there is a
statement to the contrary, it can be assumed that once a
law has been publicized it is put into effect.]

3. *Meaning of one is so vague and general that it cannot be differ-*
entiated from the other

A: So long as the two sides work together, bilateral relations
will continue to <u>grow and develop</u> further.

68

B: So long as the two sides work together, bilateral relations will continue to *grow* (*or*: expand).

  [- "Develop" is too imprecise to add anything to the meaning of "grow."

  - (<u>Review</u>: The sense of "further" is already expressed in "continue to.")]

A: the editorial said that the working class should help to <u>further and develop</u> production and concentrate their efforts on economic development

B: the editorial said that the working class should help *expand* production and concentrate (its efforts) on economic development

  ["Develop" production is passable, but the more concrete "expand" is preferable, especially in the same sentence with "development." "Further" is so broad in meaning that it cannot be distinguished from either "develop" or "expand."]

A: the editorial also calls for <u>strengthening and building</u> the Party

B: the editorial also calls for *strengthening and expanding* the Party

  [Here both words are vague and general, so it is hard to see a difference in meaning. If, however, "building" is used in the sense of expanding the membership, it is better to use the more precise word.]

A: we should <u>strengthen and improve</u> the system under which governments at all levels are responsible for attaining given objectives for birth control

B: we should *strengthen* the system under which governments at all levels are responsible for attaining given objectives for birth control

　　[Again, since neither word conveys a particular action, they seem to mean the same thing: to "strengthen" a system is to "improve" it. If the original Chinese suggests two different meanings, the translator has to find more specific words in English to convey them.]

A: effective guidance by the government is especially important for a <u>healthy and rational</u> development of this industry in a socialist market economy

B: governmental guidance is especially important for the *rational* development of this industry in a socialist market economy

　　[- "Healthy" is so vague a metaphor that it can add nothing to "rational," which itself is open to broad interpretation.
　　- (<u>Review</u>: "Effective" is an unnec. intensifier.)]

Proliferation of redundancies

That redundant twins do proliferate in Chinglish is evident to anyone who reads attentively even a single page of unedited copy. The following are examples that have appeared, some of them many times, either in print or in draft translations from which they were later eliminated.

Category 1 (meaning the same)

<u>Nouns</u>:
discussions and deliberations
skills and abilities

70

setbacks and defeats

errors and mistakes

practices and customs

troubles and problems

trials and tests

paths and routes

divisions and splits

functions and responsibilities

shortcomings and weaknesses

consciousness and awareness

forecasts and predictions

shrinkage or decrease

steps and measures

instructions and commands

plots and intrigues

complaints and dissatisfactions

disputes and dissension

restrictions and shackles

Verbs:

consider and study

endorse and support

introduce and put into effect (measures)

(dikes) give way and collapse

triumph and overcome

defeat and overthrow

flee and retreat

unmasked and revealed

absorbing and incorporating

following and putting into effect (advice)

71

Adjectives:

strong and solid

weak and faint

firm and staunch

upright and honest

experienced and seasoned

irresolute and hesitant

major and important

trivial and insignificant

accurate or precise (statistics)

short and brief

Adverbs:

correctly and properly

wholly and completely

conscientiously and painstakingly

vividly and dramatically

earnestly and sincerely

Category 2 (*meaning contained or implied*)

accusations and attacks

corruption and degeneration

wise and sensible

appropriate and advisable

firm and unshakable

precious and useful

necessary and imperative

unprecedented and unique

forward-looking and far-sighted

mentally and ideologically (confused)

the situation and circumstances
the conditions and situation
advances and developments
enhance and improve
healthy and sound

Hundreds more could be added to the list.

Again, the need for judgment

Despite the abundance of examples in which a pair of words represents an unnecessary duplication, it cannot be assumed that every two-word combination is objectionable.

It would be understandable if, confronted with a seemingly endless parade of redundant twins marching hand in hand down page after page, an exasperated polisher were to begin automatically striking out one word of every pair encountered. But that would be no more justifiable than letting every pair stand. Each case must be considered on its merits.

As stated at the outset, the question is: Is there a significant difference between the two words, and are both needed to express the sense of the Chinese? Unfortunately, the answer is not always obvious. The same two words may be needed in one context and not in another, the Chinese text may be open to different interpretations, and often there is room for disagreement.

When, on reflection, you cannot make a sure judgment about a given pair of words (or find a better version), it is probably advisable to retain both. Especially if you are dealing with a government document or an official statement that will be closely examined by foreign readers, it is generally better to risk including a redundancy than to risk losing an element of the intended sense. As Sol Adler [p. 27] rightly said with regard to the English translation of Volume V of the *Selected Works of Mao Zedong*, "meaning must have priority over elegance."

Here are a few instances in which, after some debate, the polishers decided that both words were justified and should be retained (or replaced by two preferable ones):

A: "Trade unions should voice their <u>opinions and demands</u> in time and truly protect their legitimate <u>rights and interests</u>," the President said.

B: "Trade unions should voice their *opinions and demands* in time and protect their legitimate *rights and interests*," the President said.

[- Significant distinctions can be made between the members of each pair.

- (<u>Review</u>: "Truly" is an unnec. intensifier.)]

A: Party leader Jiang Zemin has urged the nation to <u>grasp and implement</u> Deng Xiaoping's recent remarks on reform

B: Party leader Jiang Zemin has urged the nation to *understand and apply* Deng Xiaoping's recent remarks on reform

[The two words clearly represent different ideas. The problem is that they are ill chosen. The "collocations" are wrong: one can grasp an idea and implement a policy, but one can neither grasp nor implement a remark.]

A: China is of special importance to the world and is related to the <u>stability and security</u> of the international situation

B: China is of special importance: what happens in China can affect world *stability and security*

[- It was felt here that neither "stability" nor "security"
alone would suffice to convey the sense of the Chinese.

- ("To the world" was judged unnec. and eliminated,
along with "the international situation," both expressions
being reduced to the single adjective "world.")

- (The vague "China is related to" was changed to the precise "what happens in China can affect," which the polishers understood to be the intended meaning.)]

A: The session <u>examined and adopted</u> the "Decision of the CPC
on ... " It also <u>discussed and approved</u> the report on ...

B: At this session the Central Committee *examined and adopted* the "Decision of the CPC on ..." It also *discussed and
approved* the report on ...

[- It might be argued that a committee always examines a
decision before adopting it and discusses a report before
approving it, so that in each pair of words the second implies the first. But the polishers (one native speaker of
each language) decided that neither in China nor in western countries could this be taken for granted, so in each
expression both words were retained.

- (The sentence was, however, revised to make the Central
Committee the subject. It is the committee, not the session — which is literally a "sitting" of the committee —
that makes decisions. Cf. Chapter II, page 62, exercise
17, and Key, page 529.)]

A: the cause of our Party has enjoyed the <u>support and assistance</u>
of progressive people and friendly countries throughout the

75

world

B: the cause of our Party has enjoyed the *support and assistance* of progressive people and friendly countries throughout the world

[- Here the polishers were reluctant to suppress either element. They speculated that there was an intended distinction in the Chinese between moral support and tangible assistance. They felt, however, that if they made that meaning explicit they would be adding too much of their own interpretation to the original. They were being particularly conservative because the phrase appeared in a speech delivered by a senior Party leader at a national Party congress.

- Working on another text, the same two polishers might have been less cautious. For example, had they been asked to review the *China Daily* editorial that stated, "with the assistance and support of the central government, Tibet has made great strides," they would no doubt have treated the words as simple redundant twins and eliminated one or the other.]

Redundant twins in native English

It should be noted that the impulse to employ redundant twins is by no means limited to Chinese translators. Native speakers of English, if they do not pay attention to what they are saying — or if they affect a pretentious style — readily succumb to it.

Thus, a U. S. trade representative is quoted as saying that a plan announced by the Japanese government is both "significant and historic." The trustees of a great hospital write that they will "promote the vigorous scrutiny and speedy resolution of any <u>issues or problems</u> identified in the realm of patient care" and that they will "<u>strengthen and enhance</u> emotional support for patients and their families." A large real estate agency offers to its "<u>clients and customers</u>," for their "<u>benefit and knowledge</u>," documents designed to "<u>inform and explain the process</u> of purchasing property in Hawaii."

Indeed, some redundant twins have been seen together in public so often that they have gained a kind of respectability. They include such expressions as:

rules and regulations	bits and pieces
trials and tribulations	by leaps and bounds
betwixt and between	lo and behold
by hook or by crook	right and proper
vim, vigor and vitality	various and sundry
first and foremost	pure and unadulterated
hale and hearty	the strait and narrow (path)
winking and blinking	the one and only
ranting and raving	above and beyond (the call of duty)
huffing and puffing	really and truly

And so on and so forth. Some of these pairs, like those in the left-hand column, have a jaunty alliteration or rhyme that may make them tolerable in a humorous context. Others, like "null and void," "each and every," "without let or hindrance," "aid and abet," and many others, were originally legal terms and are still deemed useful by lawyers. But with these exceptions, the professional guardians of the English language — teachers, writers, and editors — reject them as pointless duplications.

Meanwhile, however, the vast majority of the population — the casual speakers and writers who neither notice nor care that there is no significant difference between the two elements in these tired formulas — cheerfully continue to use them.

The result is that such common redundancies inevitably come to sound familiar and hence acceptable. They exert an influence not only on native speakers of English (including foreign polishers) but on Chinese translators as well, reinforcing the habits of their own language. No doubt this influence contributes to the abundance of twins in Chinglish.

Twenty more examples of revision

As in the previous chapters, the words under particular consideration — here, redundant twins — are underlined, the revised versions are italicized, and the changes are explained in brackets. Also as before, comments about material already covered or about incidental points appear in parentheses.

1) A: While deepening reform and quickening the pace of economic development, we should strengthen efforts to build a clean and honest government.

   B: While deepening reform and accelerating economic development, we should strengthen efforts to build a *clean* government.

   [- "Clean" is a familiar metaphor for "honest." It needs no second word to make its meaning plain.

   - (Review: The sense of "pace" is included in "quickening." Both were replaced by "accelerating.")]

2) A: Not everything that can be done in one country can be done in another. We must define our system and management

methods in light of China's actual <u>conditions and charac-</u>
<u>teristics</u>.

B: Not everything that can be done in one country can be done in
another. We must determine our system and management
methods in light of our own *conditions*.

[- The "characteristics" of China (its huge population, shortage of arable land, etc.) cannot be distinguished from its
"conditions."

- (<u>Review</u>: "Actual" is an unnec. intensifier. As for
"China's," it is clear from context that what the speaker
means is the particular conditions in China, hence "our
own" conditions.)]

3) A: Once the new leading group is established, you must be responsible for everything — that is, for your mistakes,
<u>merits and contributions</u>.

B: Once the new leading group is established, you must be responsible for everything— that is, for your mistakes and
for your *achievements*.

[- The polisher felt that "merits" and "contributions" were
too close in meaning for both to be needed here.

- Moreover, the three terms "mistakes," "merits," and
"contributions" were not of the same order. One could
make mistakes or contributions, but "merits" were qualities; they would not be opposed to "mistakes" but rather
to "defects" or "failings." Of the two twins, she therefore
dropped "merits."

- Then, thinking that "mistakes" and "contributions" were
not entirely parallel either, she substituted
"achievements."]

4) A: With the <u>support and promotion</u> of Deng Xiaoping, the Central Committee of the Party and the State Council ratified the program in November of the same year.

B: With the *support* of Deng Xiaoping, the Central Committee of the Party and the State Council ratified the program in November of the same year.

[- In this context, there is no significant difference between "support" and "promotion."

- Moreover, the phrase "with the support and promotion of Deng Xiaoping" is ambiguous at best. On first reading, the reader might well understand not that Deng was urging ratification but that he enjoyed wide support and had therefore been promoted to a higher post.]

5) A: we should eliminate all factors that <u>hinder or oppose</u> our socialist cause or which might lead to unrest and turmoil

B: we should eliminate all factors that *impede our progress toward* socialism or that might lead to unrest and turmoil

[- "Hinder" a cause is dubious. In careful English, what is "hindered" (= delayed, hampered, obstructed, etc.) is not the cause itself but the progress or success or advancement of the cause. Also, it is people — not abstract "factors," which can take no action — who "oppose" (= resist, combat) a cause.

- Thus, in the revised version both words were abandoned for a clearer and less questionable expression, "impede our progress toward."

- This version, however, may have been faulty. It is possible that in the Chinese phrase that the translator rendered by the redundant twins "hinder and oppose," the second term was meant to be stronger than the first, just as "turmoil" is stronger than "unrest." If so, a better solution would have been "all factors that impede or block our progress toward socialism."]

6) A: as victory [in the war with Japan] drew near, the Chinese people were presented with the choice of two possible <u>destinies or prospects</u>

B: as victory drew near, the Chinese people were presented with a choice between two different *visions of the future*

[Another instance where a different and more idiomatic expression can be substituted for redundant twins.]

7) A: Once this point is made clear, it will help us understand the nature of problems and learn <u>experience and lessons</u>.

B: Once this point is made clear, it will help us understand the nature of problems and learn from *experience*.

[- If the distinction suggested in the Chinese is between successes and failures, we might say, "and learn from both positive and negative experience."

- (Incidentally, you cannot "learn" experience in English. You can gain it, acquire it, or learn something from it.)]

8) A: The comrades concerned should look at the <u>influence and effect</u> that their wrong words and actions, pernicious writings, and cheap performances have on young people and others.

B: The comrades concerned should look at the *influence* that their wrong words and actions, pernicious writings, and cheap performances have on young people and others.

[- Presumably, the influence is the effect.

- If "effect" is intended to convey a separate meaning, that

81

would have to be spelled out: "... should look at the influence that their wrong words and actions, pernicious
writings, and cheap performances have on young people
and others and at the consequences of that influence."]

9) A: we also adopted the Seventh Five-Year Plan, which is designed to create the necessary conditions for China's <u>pro-
longed, stable, and sustained</u> development in this century
and the next

B: we also adopted the Seventh Five-Year Plan, which is designed to create the necessary conditions for *prolonged*,
stable development in this century and the next

[- The Plan was adopted in 1986, fourteen years before the
end of the century. Clearly, development that was to continue "in this century and the next" would be "prolonged"
as well as "sustained." It could therefore be argued that
these are redundant triplets and that "stable" alone would
suffice.

- (<u>Review</u>: In this context, "China's" is obvious.)]

10) A: further efforts should be made to <u>choose and promote</u> young
people to leadership

B: more young people should be *promoted* to positions of leadership

[- Choosing people to be promoted is part of the promotion
process.

- (<u>Review</u>: "Efforts should be made to" is only a variation
of "make great efforts to," one of the superfluous introductory formulas discussed in Chapter I.)]

11) A: the Communists in any country should <u>consider and settle</u> the

question of the revolutionary road by themselves

B: the Communists in any country should *settle* the question of the revolutionary road by themselves

[If they settle the question, they have necessarily considered it.]

12) A: we must carefully <u>study and ascertain</u> better ways to implement the policy of combining education with productive labor

B: we must *ascertain* (*or*: find) better ways to implement the policy of combining education with productive labor

[- Plainly, if we are to find better ways we have to study possible ones and choose among them: "ascertain" implies "study."

- (<u>Review</u>: "Carefully" can be taken for granted: anything that has to be studied should be studied carefully.)]

13) A: we must give full attention to the <u>study and adoption</u> of policies that will ...

B: we must *formulate* policies that will ...

[- Adopting a policy usually implies that you have studied it first. But the pair of words can be neatly replaced here by "formulate," which suggests the meaning of both.

- (<u>Review</u>: "Give full attention to," a variation on "pay attention to," is another of the classic empty introductions.)]

14) A: administrative departments for industry and commerce and courts at all levels are authorized to <u>investigate, handle, and hear</u> cases of trademark <u>counterfeiting and infringement</u>

83

B: administrative departments for industry and commerce and courts at all levels are authorized to *investigate and hear* cases of trademark *counterfeiting*

[- "Handling" a case includes investigating the facts and hearing testimony and argument. Better to use the more specific words and simply omit the general one.

- "Counterfeiting" a trademark is an "infringement" of the trademark laws. If "infringement" here is meant to refer to other possible violations, we would have to say: "cases of counterfeiting and other infringements of trademark laws."]

15) A: Official statistics show that by the end of 1991 individual <u>savings and deposits</u> amounted to 911 billion yuan ($ 167. 16 billion).

B: Official statistics show that by the end of 1991 individual *savings* amounted to ￥911 billion ($ 167. 16 billion).

[- From the point of view of the bank, "savings" = "deposits."

- If a distinction was intended between the two words, we would have to study the Chinese, in context, to determine what was meant and then clarify the meaning in English. Possibly: "personal savings and institutional deposits."

- (Since we don't spell out "dollars," it is better to be consistent and use the symbol for "yuan" as well.)]

16) A: To bring about sustained, rapid, and sound development of the national economy, all localities and departments should, proceeding from the overall interests, make rational arrangements in order of <u>importance and urgency</u> to

use financial and material resources first in ....

B: To bring about sustained, rapid, and sound development of the economy, all local authorities and all departments should make rational arrangements for the use of financial and material resources. Projects to be supported should be selected in the order of *priority*, based on the overall national interest. First should come ....

  [- A project would scarcely be considered urgent if it were not important: "urgency" includes the sense of "importance." But here we can substitute for both twins a single word, "priority," that perfectly expresses the intended meaning.

  - (The long sentence was broken into three parts so that the reader would not have too many ideas to absorb all at once.)

  - (The order of ideas was changed in the interest of logic and clarity.)]

17) A: Wen also called for work to <u>introduce and improve</u> a system under which the State will be able to <u>back, guarantee</u>, control, and serve agricultural production

B: Wen also called for the *introduction* of a system under which the State would *support*, control, and serve agricultural production

  [- Although "introduce" does not always imply "improve," we can take it for granted that once the system is in place, its defects should be corrected.

  - In a socialist society, any new measure should be first proposed, then studied, then introduced, then improved, then gradually perfected (or abandoned, if it ceases to be

85

useful) — we don't have to rehearse the entire process every time a new idea is put forward.

- As for "back" and "guarantee," they seem to be true redundant twins. If not, the ideas they represent need to be stated more explicitly. It is hard to know how the state can "guarantee" agricultural production other than by supporting it.

- (Review: In the first clause "work" was eliminated as an unnec. noun. "Called for work to introduce" means no more than "called for the introduction of.")]

18) A: There are three important criteria for judging the soundness of a country's political <u>system and structure</u> and the policies it has adopted.

B: There are three important criteria for judging the soundness of a country's political *system* and the policies it has adopted.

[Two all-embracing words that in this context can hardly be differentiated. Using both only invites the reader to puzzle over the distinction between "system" and "structure," instead of quickly grasping the real distinction, which is between "system" and "policies."]

19) *Subtitle in a government report*:

A: Further rationalizing price relations and <u>fostering and developing</u> a market system.

B: Further rationalizing price relations and *developing* a market system.

[The meaning of both words is so general that neither adds anything perceptible to the other.]

20) A: we should draw up correct <u>development and construction</u>
plans for all these zones

B: we should draw up correct (*or*, *better*: sound) *development*
plans for all these zones

[- Two more large abstractions that are plainly used here to
mean the same thing.

- (To avoid using the noun "development" as an adjective,
we could say: "we should draw up correct plans for the
development of all these zones." That would be the simplest, most natural word order in English.)]

Twenty exercises

1) Since the publication of China's Automotive Industrial Policy last
July, the "family car" has been one of the hottest topics of
discussion and debate in the Chinese press.

2) the drafting of important documents or reports [for the National
People's Congress] has been finalized or completed ahead of
schedule

3) we should strengthen and improve the overall balance of the national economy

4) this will convince the people that you are sincerely and wholeheartedly carrying out the policies of reform and opening to
the outside world

5) in the final analysis, the growth and expansion of the CPC,
China's achievement of national independence, and her advance toward strength and prosperity were closely linked to
the drive to liberate and develop the forces of production

6) The last decade of this century will be the key to laying a foundation and creating good conditions and environment for economic development in the first half of the next century.

7) as long as the ranks of the Party forge the closest unity and are vigorous and vital, the cause of socialism will grow and flourish

8) if the reform is successful, it will lay a solid foundation for sustained and stable development in China over the next few decades

9) political reform aims at improving and revitalizing China's socialist system

10) actually, as means or methods adopted in developing the social productive forces, different managerial forms can serve both capitalism and socialism

11) when we have dealt with those problems, our established principles and policies will only be carried out more smoothly, steadily, and perseveringly

12) What problems or obstacles are we going to run into? As I see it, there are two or three problems that might hold up the growth of our economy . . . .

13) Mou Xinsheng, Vice-Minister of Public Security, urged public security organs to support and closely cooperate with banks in cracking down on white-collar crime.

14) Leading comrades of Party committees and governments at all levels should often visit schools, listen to the opinions and voice of the teachers and students, and help them overcome their anxieties and difficulties.

15) We are not rich and cannot offer you much financial help, but we can tell our friends our experiences and lessons, which is also a kind of help.

16) It was then that Mao Zedong showed his distinguished ability to draw experience and lessons from practice.

17) So China must not allow itself to get out of control; we have that responsibility to ourselves and also to the whole world and mankind.

18) We must therefore continue to uphold Mao Zedong Thought and enrich and develop it with new principles and new conclusions corresponding to reality.

19) Of course, the report reflects my views and opinions, but chiefly collective opinions.

20) After years of consideration and study, the State Bureau of Cultural Relics has agreed to unearth the much-talked-about No. 2 vault of terra-cotta soldiers, Yuan Zhongyi, President of the Terra-cotta Museum, said recently at Lintong, where the museum is located.

IV. Saying the Same Thing Twice

As we have seen, there is a governing principle of English usage that rejects unnecessary duplication. We have examined many individual words and short phrases, typical of Chinglish, that are condemned by this principle — "temporary in nature," "new innovation," "help and assistance," etc. Now we shall look at some larger groups of words, including whole clauses, to which it also applies.

This principle, which the American authority on usage Wilson Follett [p. 377] calls "the maxim against redundancy," insists that no idea should be expressed twice in the same passage. In English, sentences that present as new information something that has just been said, or that is plainly implied in what has just been said, are considered a waste of the reader's time. The more frequently such sentences occur, the more they clog the flow of ideas and the more annoying they become.

Perhaps the most forceful condemnation of needless repetition is expressed by the British writers Robert Graves and Alan Hodge [p. 103]: "Unless for rhetorical emphasis, or necessary recapitulation, no idea should be presented more than once in the same prose passage.... [R]epetitiveness is nowadays considered a sign of pauperdom in oratory, and of feeble-mindedness in narrative."

Other advisers on English likewise make a point of warning writers not to repeat themselves. That is because even educated native speakers are often tempted to say the same thing twice, and because the effect is generally deplorable.

For example:

- An American banker (cited by Claire Cook [p. 15]) can hardly say anything without at once restating it in other words. Thus, he refers to "unprecedented interest rates that set an all-time record." He thanks stockholders for having "assisted us with their help." And he reports that his institution has "continued to maintain success since the outset of our entry into the computer field."

- A U.S. politician, Vice-President J. Danforth Quayle, gained a reputation in the early 1990s as a master of mindless repetition. Indeed, he is still remembered for many solemn redundancies that provided much amusement to newspaper readers. These included profundities like "A low voter turnout [in an election] is an indication of fewer people going to the polls," and "If we don't succeed, we run the risk of failure."

- Even journalists, who, as professional writers, should know better, sometimes produce twin statements that convey what is perfectly self-evident. A user of the Internet has drawn attention to such newspaper headlines as "If Strike Isn't Settled Quickly, It May Last a While" and "Enfields Couple Slain; Police Suspect Homicide."

There are times, of course — as Graves and Hodge concede — when it is entirely legitimate to state an idea twice over. Repetition for emphasis, for example, is an ancient and honorable device. But to be effective it must be used deliberately and, above all, sparingly. In draft translations from Chinese, the times when it is superfluous far outnumber the times when it is useful.

91

Accordingly, when you are revising a translation you should be constantly on the watch for unnecessary repetitions. Any word or group of words that states the same thing expressed elsewhere in a sentence is quite probably redundant.

Forms of repetition in Chinglish

A study of many draft translations reveals that the repetition of ideas in Chinglish appears in one of the three following forms:

1. simple restatement (same idea presented twice in different words)
2. self-evident statement (one idea implicit in another)
3. mirror-image statement (same idea presented first in positive form, then in negative)

Let us consider each of these.

1. *Simple restatement*

This sort of repetition is already familiar: it is only an expanded version of a pair of redundant twins. Instead of two words that mean virtually the same thing, we have two parts of a sentence that mean virtually the same thing. Usually, the pattern is: "we must arrive at the station on time and be punctual." Here are some examples:

- we must practice economy and reduce unnecessary expenditures

- We must be clear whether a mistake has really been made and if it has, we must be able to tell whether it is a major or a minor one and whether it is serious or not.

- in industrial production we should maintain a policy of safety first, with prevention of accidents as our main concern

Sometimes the conjunction joining the two parts of the sentence is not "and" but "in order to." This produces a statement that is essentially circular, on the pattern "we must <u>arrive at the station on time</u> in order to <u>be punctual</u>":

- we must further <u>strengthen the building of national defense</u> in order to <u>enhance our defense strength</u>

- it is essential to <u>control environmental pollution</u> so as to <u>protect the environment</u>

No doubt the reason these "circular" sentences turn up in draft translations is that often there is nothing in the Chinese to indicate the logical relation between the two parts of the sentence. With no clear guidance from the original, the translator is obliged to insert a conjunction on his or her own — "and" or "in order to" (sometimes even " or "). Unfortunately, none of these can solve the basic problem, which is the double statement itself.

2. *Self-evident statement*

In this type of repetition, one part of the sentence, while it is not just another version of the other, is nevertheless implicit in it. The result is a statement in which one element is so obvious that it can be taken for granted. The patterns vary, but the most common one is: "we must <u>arrive at the station on time</u> in order to <u>catch the train</u>":

- By renovating and expanding a number of chemical fertilizer plants, we shall increase the output of standard fertilizer by 15 million tons in the five-year period. . . . Meanwhile, to <u>increase soil fertility</u>, we should <u>promote widespread scientific application of fertilizer and greater use of farm manure</u>.

["To increase soil fertility" (like "to catch the train") goes without saying. The reader does not need to be told that the purpose of applying fertilizer and manure is to make soil more fertile.]

- we should reduce taxes on enterprises so as to <u>allow them to retain more of their profits</u> and thus <u>increase their financial capacity</u>

[Plainly, if enterprises are allowed to keep more of their profits, they will be stronger financially. It is not necessary to spell this out.]

- China's socialist <u>system of law has now been basically established,</u> so that the <u>situation in which there were no laws has changed</u>

[It is obvious that a situation in which there are laws is different from a situation in which there were none.]

3. *Mirror-image statement*

In this construction, the same idea is stated first in positive form, then in negative (or vice versa). The second part of the sentence is only a mirror image of the first — the identical picture presented from the opposite point of view. Here, the pattern is: "we must <u>arrive at the station on time</u> and <u>not be late</u>":

- We should <u>pay close attention to</u> the formulation of annual plans and <u>not neglect it</u>.

- we must <u>maintain our vigilance</u> and <u>never be off guard</u>

- financial expenditures should be <u>arranged in order of priority,</u> rather than <u>be given equal status</u>

Dealing with repetition in translations

Confronted with a repetition of ideas in an English translation, you should begin by asking some questions. Was the repetition intentional in the original, or did the Chinese writer merely slip unconsciously into a cliché pattern? If the repetition was used deliberately to provide emphasis, is there a better way to achieve that effect in English? How many times has the same construction already appeared in this piece? If I use it here, will it serve to make a point, or will it just sound . . . well, "feeble-minded"?

The answers to such questions will help determine whether the repetition is useful in English. If you decide that it is not, you have four options:

1. find further (or different) meaning in the original
2. delete the redundant words
3. change the wording
4. let the repetition stand

1. *Finding further (or different) meaning*

First, you should re-examine the original Chinese. Perhaps it will yield another element of meaning, one which the translator has misunderstood or overlooked and which, if introduced into the English version, will eliminate the redundancy. For example:

A: this shows that all advanced <u>means of communication</u> and <u>communications equipment</u> are controlled by the people, so the difficulties of the past no longer exist

B: this shows that all advanced *means of transportation* and *communication* are controlled by the people, so the difficulties of the past no longer exist

95

[- Simple restatement: "communications equipment" = "means of communication." A closer study of the original suggested that "communication" should be understood as "transportation," in the sense that roads are means of "communication." Also, that "equipment" had been introduced only in an attempt to make a distinction from "communication."

- In short, the repetition of ideas was due only to a misunderstanding of the Chinese. A more thoughtful reading produced a perfectly acceptable sentence in English.]

A: We must continue to strengthen basic research and increase scientific and technological strength and staying power for future development.

B: *To enhance our ability to make further advances* in science and technology, we must continue to *expand basic research* .

[- Again, simple restatement: "increase scientific strength" = "strengthen basic research." Reviewing the Chinese, the polishers decided that (1) "strength and staying power" were merely redundant twins; (2) "strength for future development" meant the ability to continue making progress; and, most important, (3) the logical connection (unexpressed in Chinese) between "strengthen basic research" and "increase scientific strength" was not and but in order to.

- This reinterpretation of the original made it possible to eliminate the repetition of ideas and, by so doing, to clarify an exceedingly vague statement.]

Revisions of this sort, in which the redundancy in English is removed thanks to the discovery of further (or different) meaning in the Chinese, are the most successful. Unfortunately, they are not always possible.

2. *Deleting the redundant words*

If you cannot find more sense in the original, the next best solution is to delete one of the repetitive elements or replace them both with another expression:

A: He stressed that all State Council departments <u>have an important responsibility</u> in the struggle [against corruption] and said they <u>are in a very important position</u>.

B: He stressed that all State Council departments *have an important responsibility* in the struggle.

[Since the second clause ("they are in a very important position") is only a simple restatement of the first ("departments have an important responsibility"), it can be omitted without sacrificing any element of substance. This kind of judicious pruning is no more radical than deleting one of two redundant twins.]

A: Has the political status of the Shanghai workers undergone any change since Liberation? Yes, it has, and <u>the change is an essential</u>, <u>not an insignificant one</u>, for they have changed from members of an exploited class into members of a ruling class.

B: Has the political status of the Shanghai workers undergone any change since Liberation? Yes, it has, and *the change is absolutely fundamental*, because they are no longer members of an exploited class but members of a ruling (*or*: leading) class.

[Both elements of this mirror-image statement can be replaced by a single strong expression ("the change is absolutely fundamental") that more neatly conveys not only the meaning of the Chinese but also the intended emphasis.]

3. *Changing the wording*

In principle, the decision to cut or not to cut should be made on purely technical considerations — how best to convey the sense of the Chinese in English. In practice, however, you may feel obliged to take into account the nature of the text and its intended audience.

Is this an article addressed to the casual readers of a general-interest magazine, or is it an official pronouncement that will be closely studied abroad in foreign ministries or in corporate headquarters? Is this just a spontaneous remark, or is it a quotation from a prepared speech? And so on.

When dealing with an important text — a legal document, say, or a formal statement by a government spokesman — you may feel you lack the authority to "correct" even an obviously useless repetition. In that case, you may still try to make the repetition less obtrusive by a change of wording:

A: people of all the different nationalities have made enormous contributions to safeguarding the unity of the motherland and promoting stability and unity and prosperity

B: people of all the different nationalities have contributed enormously to *safeguarding the unity* of the motherland and *promoting* stability, *solidarity*, and prosperity

A: to maintain steady growth of the economy, we must implement a long-term policy of steady economic growth

B: to *keep the economy growing* we must implement a long-
term *policy favorable to steady economic development*

Both of these examples are, basically, simple restatements. Despite the changed language in the B-versions, a careful reader may
recognize that the author is only saying the same thing twice. In the
first example, "safeguarding unity" and "promoting solidarity" are
barely distinguishable notions. And in the second, the revision still
boils down to "to maintain steady growth, we must have a policy of
steady growth."

Nevertheless, versions like these are more acceptable because
they are less obviously redundant.

4. *Letting the repetition stand*

Sometimes, especially with statements of the mirror-image
type, a case can be made for retaining the repetition on the ground
that it provides needed emphasis:

- Speaking of the diverse cultures around the world, Jiang said,
  "It is a good thing, not a bad thing, that the world is a
  diverse and colorful place."

- there is no question that we will win and the enemy will be defeated

And even where the necessity for the positive/negative construction is debatable, you may wish to give a writer the benefit of the
doubt, so as to reflect his or her characteristic style and way of thinking. Translators of the works of Chairman Mao, for example, have
generally respected his mode of expression:

- The Chinese people, now at the high tide of revolution, need friends, and they should remember their friends and not forget them.

- In agriculture, those labour-exchange teams and organizations, which were in the grip of bureaucrats and which harmed the people instead of benefiting them, have all collapsed.

Sometimes, however, a repetition may be allowed to stand not because it serves a useful purpose in English, but simply because, for the reasons suggested above, the translator is reluctant to cut, and no other solution is available. The result is seldom satisfactory:

- we must work hard to gain professional proficiency and become skilled in our work

- we must strengthen public health services in rural areas in order to improve our people's health

In these examples (both taken from published documents), one half of the statement tells readers something they already know, either because they have just been told it (simple restatement in the first case), or because it is perfectly obvious (self-evident statement in the second).

Constructions of this sort, although they are grammatically correct and "faithful" renderings of the Chinese, are nevertheless to be avoided wherever possible. Not only are they full of unnecessary words but, worse, they cast doubt on the value of the text as a whole. When readers find that a considerable part of what the writer is saying is not worth listening to, they are unlikely to pay much attention to the rest.

Twenty more examples of revision

This section follows the same format that has been used in corresponding sections in chapters I through III.

1) A: We should <u>exercise centralized control</u> over the management of foreign exchange and foreign debts and <u>centralize such power</u> <u>in the hands of central authorities</u>.

   B: We should *place the power to manage* foreign exchange and foreign debt *in the hands of the central authorities*.

   [Three statements of the same idea can be easily reduced to one.]

2) A: In areas that are suitable for grain growing, <u>a good job must be done in grain production</u> and <u>efforts be made to raise per-unit yield, increase variety, and improve quality</u>.

   B: In areas that are suitable for the production of grain, *we must try to raise per-unit yield, increase variety, and improve quality*.

   [- It is hard to see what "doing a good job in grain production" could mean other than achieving the three goals mentioned.

   - (<u>Review</u>: To "make efforts" is only the unnec. verb + noun form of "to try.")]

3) A: Naturally, the Chinese side resolutely <u>opposed the propositions</u> and <u>did not accept them</u>.

   B: *Since* the Chinese side firmly *opposed the propositions*, *naturally it refused to accept them*.

   [- In A-version the two statements are virtually identical in meaning. To remedy this, the polisher reinterpreted the

original: because the Chinese side was against the propositions, it rejected them.

- This new understanding, expressed in the conjunction
"since," produced an acceptable revision that differentiated between "opposed" and "did not accept."]

4) A: After the decision made at the August 7th [1927] Meeting to
wage armed resistance against the butchery policy of the
Kuomintang reactionaries, the fundamental question of
how to achieve the victory in armed struggle and what
road the revolution should take lay before the Party.

B: After the decision made at the August 7th Meeting to resist
the murderous policies of the Kuomintang reactionaries
with armed struggle, the fundamental question before the
Party was *how to achieve victory* in that struggle.

[- At this stage of history the question "what road should the
revolution take?" could only mean "what must we do to
achieve a military victory over the KMT?" In A-version
the second expression is only a metaphor for the first and
can therefore be edited out.

- (Note that since "armed resistance" = "armed struggle,"
one of them can also be dispensed with.)]

5) A: Party organizations must set up a centralized leadership in each
guerrilla area and remedy the lack of centralized leadership
where the working group, the county Party committee,
and the guerrilla forces are operating separately.

B: In each guerrilla area the Party organization must *set up a
centralized leadership to remedy the lack of coordination*
between the working group, the county Party committee,

102

and the guerrilla units.

[- Plainly, to establish an institution = to remedy the lack of it.

- By introducing a "to," indicating purpose, and the key word "coordination," the polisher not only eliminated a pointless repetition but clarified the central idea.]

6) A: <u>The large numbers</u> [of Hui people] <u>are due to</u> their assimilation of other ethnic groups, <u>which contributes to their population growth</u>.

B: *Their large numbers are due to* their assimilation of other ethnic groups.

[- A-version says that the population is large because of a factor (assimilation) that contributes to a large population. The logic is as circular as in Dan Quayle's remark that "a low voter turnout is an indication of fewer people going to the polls."

- Since the entire subordinate ("which") clause merely repeats the sense of the main clause in different words, it was edited out.]

7) A: it is essential to <u>delegate powers of</u> operation and <u>management</u> to enterprises and institutions so as to <u>let them manage their own affairs</u> in accordance with the principle of <u>having full authority for management</u> and administration

B: it is essential to *delegate powers of* operation, *management*, and administration to enterprises and institutions, so as to *let them manage their own affairs with full authority*

[- In A-version, the same idea is presented not twice but three times.

103

- B-version, while it is an improvement, still contains a repetition (to "delegate powers of management" to enterprises = to "let them manage their own affairs"). However, the sentence appeared in a government report, and the polishers did not feel authorized to cut it further.]

8) A: Our policy is <u>unswerving</u> and <u>will not be shaken</u>, and <u>we shall always follow it</u>.

B: Our policy *will not change*, and *we shall always follow it*.

[- Again A-version says the same thing three times over, and again B-version still says it twice.

- But here the polishers were satisfied with the revision, because the repetition seemed justified to match the speaker's intended emphasis.]

9) A: The Party member <u>must put the interests of the revolution and the Party first</u>, dealing with all his personal problems in accordance with the principle that <u>the interests of the revolution and the Party are paramount</u>, instead of <u>placing his own interests above those of the revolution and the Party</u>.

B: The Party member *must put the interests of the revolution and the Party first*, dealing with all his personal problems in accordance with the principle that *those interests are paramount*.

[- Another instance in which the same idea was expressed in three different ways, of which the polishers eliminated only one (the mirror-image "instead of" clause).

- Here they thought the idea that the general interests must come first was usefully reinforced by being restated as a principle.

- ("Those interests" was used in the B-version to avoid repetition of the long phrase "of the revolution and the Party.")]

10) A: We should <u>speed up housing construction</u> in cities and towns, especially the building of medium and low-grade housing estates, <u>so as to improve the housing conditions</u> of the inhabitants there.

B: We should *speed up construction of* urban *housing* , especially medium- and low-income (*or* : low-cost) units.

[- The construction of housing clearly implies the desire to improve housing conditions, so there is no need to state its purpose.

- ("Low-grade" was changed because the term means low quality — shoddy workmanship, poor materials, etc.)]

11) A: We should improve techniques of raising animals and reward the development of better breeds. In order to <u>prevent</u> and cure <u>animal diseases</u> and <u>improve animal breeds</u>, we should set up <u>disease-prevention organizations</u> and <u>breeding stations</u> in a planned way.

B: We should improve techniques of raising livestock and reward the development of better breeds. We should draw up plans for *establishing breeding stations* and *centers for the prevention* and treatment *of animal diseases* .

[- The only possible purpose of a disease-prevention organization is to prevent disease. Breeding stations are obviously designed to improve breeds, and in any event, this has been made clear in the preceding sentence.

- Again, the entire content of the subordinate ("in order

105

to") clause is self-evident.]

12) A: All this means that the advances in science and technology will decide fundamentally the progress of China's modernization and <u>are an important matter</u> <u>on which hinges the future and destiny of our nation.</u>

B: All this means that advances in science and technology will basically determine the progress of China's modernization and that the *revitalization of our nation hinges upon them*.

[- Any factor on which the future of the nation depends is obviously important, and there is no need to say so.

- (<u>Review</u>: "Future and destiny" = redundant twins. While "revitalization" is not an obvious equivalent, the context made it clear that that was the intended meaning.)]

13) A: Within the people's governments, the standard for judging whether a person who performs official duties is competent to handle financial and economic affairs is not merely that of <u>embezzlement or honesty. The former is a crime, and</u> <u>the latter is essential.</u> The principal standard is whether one is wasteful or not.

B: In the people's governments, the criterion for judging if a cadre is competent to handle financial and economic affairs is not merely whether he is honest or commits embezzlement. *Of course*, *embezzlement is a crime and honesty is indispensable*, but the principal criterion is whether he is wasteful.

[- In A-version the second statement — that embezzlement

106

is a crime and honesty is essential — seems entirely self-evident.

- Rather then omit it, however, the polishers decided simply to reduce its importance.
- In B-version the statement is merely a preliminary to the following sentence, which makes the speaker's new and important point. By starting with "Of course," he recognizes that he is saying something that everyone knows.
- ("But" was added to provide the logical connection between the two ideas, which was not stated in the Chinese.)
- (Note that a "person who performs official duties" in a local government can be designated by many shorter names, depending on the historical period: a cadre, an official, a functionary, a staff member, a government employee, a civil servant, etc.)]

14) A: Private capital has to meet two conditions to make profits: First, <u>illegal profits are not allowed</u>, <u>only legal ones are allowed</u>. Second, <u>excessive profits are not acceptable</u>, <u>only reasonable profits are allowed</u>.

B: To be allowed to make profits, private capital has to meet two conditions: 1) *the profits must be legal*, and 2) *they must not be excessive*.

[In each case, the second or mirror-image statement adds nothing to the sense of the first. It was therefore edited out.
- (Note, incidentally, that "illegal" in English has a very strong and precise meaning: something that is "illegal" is literally "unlawful," or against the law, and is therefore

107

forbidden by definition. Consequently, to say "illegal profits are not allowed" is to say no more than "profits that are not allowed are not allowed." This sort of statement, technically known as a truism, tells readers nothing they do not already know.)]

15) A: Meanwhile, China began to export technology, which means that we are no longer restricted to importing technology.

B: Meanwhile, *China's technology began to enter the international market*, which means that *we are no longer restricted to importing technology*.

[Again the second statement says exactly the same thing as the first and could in principle be omitted. But here the polishers, dealing with a carefully prepared government document, contented themselves with changing the wording to make the repetition less obtrusive.]

16) A: During the period of the Seventh Five-Year Plan we must in no way neglect, even in the slightest degree, the production of grain, but should keep it growing steadily.

B: During the period of the Seventh Five-Year Plan *we must never neglect* grain production. *On the contrary, we must steadily increase it*.

[- In this example, the mirror-image statement serves the legitimate function of providing emphasis. The revised version ("on the contrary") heightens the effect by underlining the contradiction.

- "In the slightest degree" = "in no way," and "never" is strong enough to reflect the sense of both.)]

17) A: After public grain and taxes are placed under the administration of

108

the Central People's Government, local comrades should not only <u>refrain from adopting a passive and irresponsible attitude</u> toward financial and economic work, but also <u>show a more active and responsible attitude</u> toward it.

B: After public grain and taxes are placed under the administration of the Central People's Government, comrades in local governments, *far from losing interest in* financial and economic work, *should take even greater responsibility* for it.

[- Here the contradiction between the two "attitudes" (passive/irresponsible vs. active/responsible) is an important element.

- The revised version ("far from") retains that element but eliminates the tiresome mirror images and, at the same time, clarifies the meaning.

- (Note that both "attitudes" have disappeared and been replaced by more precise, concrete expressions.)

- (Review: To "show a responsible attitude" is one of the constructions discussed in Chapter I: unnec. verb + unnec. noun + third word. Here the "third word" is the adjective "responsible," which expresses the real action, to "take responsibility.")]

18) A: Compared with the more than a hundred million workers and staff members in state-owned enterprises and institutions of the whole country, <u>the number of hired workers is very small</u>. Judging from the situation as a whole, <u>their number is only a very small one</u>.

B: Compared with the more than a hundred million workers and administrative personnel in public enterprises and institutions throughout the country, *the number of privately hired workers is very small. In terms of the overall situation, there are only very few of them.*

[- Here the polishers were able to solve the problem of repetition by means of a better interpretation of the original.

- In A-version the second sentence appears to add nothing to the sense of the first. A closer reading of the Chinese, however, suggested that "judging from the situation as a whole" (which the reader slides over as almost meaningless) should rather be "in terms of the overall situation."

- With this change, the second sentence could be understood as a legitimate repetition, reinforcing the idea expressed in the first. Still, to avoid repeating the identical words, the polishers changed "their number is only a very small one" to "there are only very few of them."

- (For greater clarity, "privately" was inserted before "hired workers" and, to underline the difference, "state-owned" was changed to "public.")

- ("Staff members" was changed to "administrative personnel" because in English all employees of an organization, both white-collar and blue-collar, are usually considered to be on the "staff" of the organization.)]

19) A: Things <u>are getting better</u> with us every passing day and <u>can't be getting worse</u>.

   B: Things *are getting better* for us with every passing day, and *the tide of progress cannot be turned back*.

   [- Plainly, if things are getting better, they can't be getting worse. The mirror-image construction simply doesn't work.

- When a translator has unwittingly produced a sentence as pointless as this one, it suggests that he or she has either misunderstood the Chinese or made a mistake in English.

- In this instance, it proved to be the latter. What the translator had meant to say was "things <u>are getting</u> better (now) and they can't <u>get</u> worse (in future)." This new understanding quickly led to a sensible B-version.]

20) A: China's strategy for scientific and technological development must be both forward-looking and far-sighted, and <u>it must serve the development of the present and future</u>, <u>not the past</u>, Zhou said.

B: China's strategy for scientific and technological development must be both forward-looking and far-sighted, and *it must be adapted to the present and the future*, *not the past*.

[- Here the mirror-image construction itself was reasonable enough (present and future vs. past), but by choosing the wrong verb the translator had inadvertently turned it into nonsense: how can a strategy for (future) development "serve" the past?

- Again, once the problem had been identified, it was not hard to find a solution.]

Twenty exercises

1) Enterprises with exclusively foreign investment should abide by China's laws and regulations and operate according to law.

2) we should try our best to slow price rises and prevent them from

rocketing

3) The initiative has been moved from the enemy side to our side, and we have grasped the initiative of the war.

4) there will be a great many economic imbalances, which will take much time, instead of a short while, to remedy

5) people who have made mistakes should be allowed to compensate by performing good deeds, provided they quickly come to realize their mistakes and make up their minds to mend their ways and turn over a new leaf

6) industrial enterprises should combine military with civilian production and manufacture products for both peacetime and wartime use

7) We must develop the production of import substitutes and speed up the process of substituting China-made goods for ones manufactured abroad.

8) although the campaign is necessary, it should be limited to these three months and should not go beyond them

9) We should expand the patriotic health campaign and improve the system of primary health care and the training of health workers at the grass roots to protect people's health.

10) We veterans should take advantage of this opportunity to read and increase our knowledge, instead of letting it slip; otherwise we may regret it when it's too late.

11) The work of family planning should be combined with efforts to help poor areas cast off poverty and become prosperous.

12) cadres should adopt an active attitude toward this work and not

take a passive attitude

13) *Subtitle in a government report*:
Attending to ideological and cultural work and promoting socialist cultural and ideological progress.

14) All people will be employed, and there will be no job-waiting laborers.

15) We are firm with our policy; we shall not change it but will persist in it.

16) friendly contacts and trade relations between the Chinese and Japanese peoples have continuously developed, instead of being interrupted

17) To promote democracy at the village level and to advance rural development, governments at different levels must implement the Organic Law of Villagers' Committees of the People's Republic of China, ensuring that villages govern themselves and that the masses manage their own affairs, as provided by law.

18) This does not mean, however, that we can neglect agriculture, concentrating our efforts on industrial development to the total disregard of agriculture, which now accounts for nearly 90 per cent of the economy.

19) We must, in particular, put a stop to the unauthorized use of arable land and the destruction of forests, and promote the planting of trees and grass in both town and country, which will benefit the people.

20) This year we hope to take great strides and achieve noteworthy successes in this regard.

V. Repeated References
to the Same Thing

There is one more group of unnecessary words in Chinglish that we need to examine. These words occur when, in a given sentence or brief passage, there are two or more references to the same thing.

Sometimes, after the first mention of an idea, the subsequent references to it can be dispensed with entirely; more often, they need to be retained but can be shortened. We shall consider examples of both types.

Repeated references that can be dispensed with

In some sentences where the same idea is mentioned two or more times, there is no logical necessity for it. In the following examples, the repetition adds nothing to the meaning of the passage. Accordingly, it is only another form of redundancy, and the superfluous words should simply be edited out.

A: Statistics show that from 1990 to 1994, imported <u>vehicles</u> totalled 960,000 <u>units</u>, compared with the four million <u>vehicles</u> produced in the country.

B: Statistics show that from 1990 to 1994, 960,000 *vehicles* were imported, while four million were produced domestically.

[Vehicles = units. The sentence can easily be revised so that the idea is mentioned only once.]

A: A minimum of 50,000 kilometers of road test is <u>required</u> for the prototype of a regular truck, as <u>mandated</u> by the central government, before it can be approved for quantity production.

B: The prototype of a regular truck is *required* to go through 50,000 kilometers of road test before the central government will approve it for mass production.

[- Required = mandated.

- ("A minimum" can be dispensed with because the notion is implicit in "required.")]

A: Now let me discuss how we can overcome our <u>financial and economic</u> difficulties this autumn and how we should strive for a turn for the better regarding our <u>financial and economic</u> situation next year.

B: Now let me discuss how we can overcome our *financial and economic* difficulties this autumn and how we can improve the situation next year.

[- The meaning of "situation" is clear from the context, even without the second "financial and economic."

- ("Strive for a turn for the better regarding" is only a wordy expression for "improve.")]

Repeated references that need to be retained

Repetition, however, is not always redundancy. Indeed, certain types of repetition are indispensable to normal, consecutive discourse.

Consider the following outline of a paragraph:

<u>The National Conference on Iron and Steel Production</u> was held in Beijing from this date to that, by such-and-such a ministry under the auspices of so-and-so. <u>The National Conference on Iron and Steel Production</u> drew up a national plan for this and

laid down the principle of doing that. <u>The National Conference on Iron and Steel Production</u> also discussed the problem of such-and-such. <u>The National Conference on Iron and Steel Production</u> decided to take the following measures. All in all, <u>the National Conference on Iron and Steel Production</u> was a great success.

Plainly, if we were forbidden ever to refer to the same thing twice in succession, there could be no logical progression of ideas as there is here. Every sentence would have to have a different subject, and the result would be incoherent nonsense.

This does not mean, however, that every time an idea is repeated it must be spelled out in full. In the sample paragraph above, the constant repetition of the entire title is an enormous waste of words (and, to the ear of a native speaker, decidedly irritating). Since in Chinese this is not so, or so only to a lesser extent, draft translations tend to contain many more exact repetitions than are tolerable in English.

Ways of shortening repeated references

In English, once an idea has been expressed, subsequent references to it can almost always be shortened. The means vary, depending on whether the idea in question is based on a verb or a noun.

If <u>the idea is based on a verb</u>, the second reference might be replaced with an expression like "do so," "do the same," "do likewise," or "do this":

A: It took three years for rural reform to <u>show results</u>, and it will take longer, three to five years, for urban reform to <u>show results</u>.

B: It took three years for rural reform to *show results*, and it

116

will take longer, three to five years, for urban reform to *do so*.

A: The United States needs to extend trade privileges to China permanently. Chen says that only by making those privileges permanent can the U.S. government ensure the long-term stability of American investments in China.

B: The United States needs to *extend trade privileges* to China *permanently*. Chen says that only by *doing so* can the U.S. government ensure the long-term stability of American investments in China.

A: We must strengthen our leadership and quickly correct our deficiencies as a means of mobilizing and developing the potential of our intellectuals. To mobilize and develop the potential of our intellectuals, we must first of all . . . .

B: We must strengthen our leadership and quickly correct our deficiencies so as to *mobilize our intellectuals and develop their potential*. To *do this*, we must first of all . . . .

[The word order of the second sentence has been changed to give " mobilizing " its proper object, which is "intellectuals," not "potential" as in A-version.]

If, as is more usual, the idea is based on a noun accompanied by modifiers, there are a number of means of abbreviating repeated references. Here we shall deal only with the three principal ones, plus a fourth that is available in special cases:

1. eliminating the modifiers
2. replacing the expression with a summary noun
3. replacing the expression with a pronoun
4. (in special cases) replacing the expression with initials

117

Following are examples of each.

1. *Eliminating the modifiers*

The second reference to a noun accompanied by modifiers can often be made more concise simply by using the noun alone. As can be seen from the following examples, the meaning remains perfectly clear, confirming that the words omitted are indeed "unnec."

A: The National Conference on Iron and Steel Production was held in Beijing from this date to that, by such-and-such a ministry under the auspices of so-and-so. The National Conference on Iron and Steel Production drew up a national plan for this and laid down the principle of doing that.

B: *The National Conference on Iron and Steel Production* was held in Beijing from this date to that, by such-and-such a ministry under the auspices of so-and-so. *The Conference* drew up a national plan for this and laid down the principle of doing that.

A: This year we have issued one hundred million *fen* of government bonds, which has done much to withdraw currency from circulation and stabilize prices. However, we issued more government bonds than necessary.

B: This year we have issued one hundred million *fen* of *government bonds*, which has done much to withdraw currency from circulation and stabilize prices. However, we issued more *bonds* than necessary.

A: As far as the work of the Central Advisory Commission is concerned, its general functions are set forth in the new Constitution of the Communist Party of China. According to the Party Constitution, the members of the Central

118

Advisory Commission are to act as political assistants and consultants to the Central Committee.

B: As far as the work of *the Central Advisory Commission* is concerned, its general functions are set forth in the new Constitution of the Communist Party of China. According to the Party Constitution, the members of *the Commission* are to act as political assistants and consultants to the Central Committee.

[Note than in A-version, the "Constitution of the Communist Party of China" has already been shortened, in the second reference, to "the Party Constitution," the modifiers "Communist" and "of China" being understood.]

Another way of eliminating modifiers in a second reference is to substitute a single word that represents them. The words most often used for this purpose are the demonstrative adjectives (this, that; these, those) and the possessive pronouns (my, your, his/her/its; our, your, their), which function as adjectives:

A: For our part, we have already made a concession by putting forward the principle of "one country, two systems." We believe that eventually our motherland will be reunified based on the principle of "one country, two systems."

B: For our part, we have already made a concession by putting forward *the principle of "one country, two systems."* We believe that eventually our motherland will be reunified on the basis of *that principle*.

A: The first question is whether the line, principles, and policies formulated at the Third Plenary Session of the Party's Eleventh Central Committee, and our "three-

119

stage" development strategy, are correct or not. Has the correctness of the line, principles, and policies we have formulated become a problem because of the turmoil?

B: The first question is whether *the line*, *principles*, *and policies formulated* at the Third Plenary Session of the Party's Eleventh Central Committee, including our "three-stage" development strategy, are correct. Has *their* correctness been placed in doubt because of the turmoil?

[The conjunction "and," which was probably lacking in the Chinese, was replaced with "including" for reasons of logic.]

A: Government sources reveal that Japanese manufacturers are stepping up their efforts to establish auto-parts joint ventures in China. Up to now 18 Japanese companies have set up 25 auto-parts joint ventures in a dozen provinces in China.

B: Government sources reveal that Japanese manufacturers are stepping up their efforts to establish *auto-parts joint ventures* in China. Eighteen Japanese companies have already set up 25 *such ventures* in a dozen provinces.

[Review: "In China" was omitted because it is understood.]

2. *Replacing the expression with a summary noun*

In each of the three examples just given, a noun is present in A-version ("principle," "correctness," "ventures"), and all that is needed is to replace its accompanying modifiers with an all-purpose adjective. Sometimes, however, it is necessary to supply a general noun that, with or without an adjective, will neatly sum up the entire phrase being replaced:

120

A: it [the problem of bureaucracy and commandism] means failure to make clear the <u>policy limits and the proper style of
work</u> when giving assignments, in other words, failure to
give the cadres at the middle and lower levels receiving assignments thorough instructions on <u>policy limits and proper style of work</u>

B: it means failure to make clear the *policy limits and the proper style of work* when giving assignments, in other words,
failure to give cadres at the middle and lower levels receiving assignments thorough instructions on *these matters*

A: We must adhere to the principle that <u>economic development</u>
relies on <u>science and technology</u>, while development of <u>sci-
ence and technology</u> is geared to the needs of <u>economic de-
velopment</u>, and promote the organic combination of <u>sci-
ence and technology</u> with the <u>economy</u>.

B: We must adhere to the principle that the *development of the
economy* should be based on *science and technology* and
that the *development of science and technology* should be
geared to the needs of *the economy*. *The two* must be or-
ganically combined (*or* : must be integrated).

[- The first two mentions of economic development and science and technology are necessary to make the writer's
point. The third mention, however, becomes tedious repetition and can be replaced simply by "the two."

- ("Economic development" was changed to " the
development of the economy" to make it parallel in form
to "the development of science and technology.")]

A: The practice of the past decade has proved that the lines,

121

principles, and policies adopted by the Party since the Third Plenary Session of the Eleventh Central Committee are correct and that it is correct to carry out <u>the reform and opening up</u>.... <u>The reform and opening up</u> will not be accomplished in a short period of time.

B: The practice of the past decade has proved that the lines, principles, and policies adopted by the Party since the Third Plenary Session of the Eleventh Central Committee are correct and that we are right to carry out *the reform and opening up*.... *These two tasks* will not be completed in a short time.

[- (The second use of "correct" was changed to "right" simply to avoid repeating the same sound.)

- (<u>Review</u>: "A short period of time" is no more than "a short time," so "period" is an unnec. noun.)]

3. *Replacing the expression with a pronoun*

The commonest means of condensing repeated references to an idea is to replace the spelled-out version with a pronoun. While pronouns appear relatively seldom in Chinese, their use is deeply rooted in English.

A: Why cannot <u>these lines and policies</u> be changed? Because the practice of the past ten years has proved that <u>these lines and policies</u> are completely correct.

B: Why cannot *these lines and policies* be changed? Because the practice of the last ten years has proved that *they* are correct.

[<u>Review</u>: "Correct" is sufficient (and stronger) without the adverb "completely."]

A: So the difficulties of the past no longer exist, and it is there-fore possible to introduce <u>centralized management</u> sooner than we expected. We should not be afraid of minor diffi-culties from <u>centralized management</u>; otherwise . . . .

B: So the difficulties of the past no longer exist, and it is there-fore possible to introduce *centralized management* sooner than we expected. We should not be dissuaded by the mi-nor difficulties *this* will cause; otherwise . . . .

[Here "this" stands for the introduction of centralized man-agement.]

A: The ongoing <u>movement to eliminate counterrevolution</u> in the society at large is different from the previous <u>movements to suppress counterrevolution</u>.

B: The ongoing *movement to eliminate counterrevolution* in the society at large is different from the previous *ones*.

4. *Replacing the expression with initials*

When the thing referred to is an organization, institution, offi-cial body, or the like, a special means is available for abbreviating subsequent references to it: the entire name can frequently be reduced to initials. For example, the former Union of Soviet Socialist Re-publics, generally so called only at first mention in a formal context and usually shortened to "the Soviet Union," can, and very often is, further shortened to "the USSR." The Communist Party of China, spelled out, perhaps, at the beginning of a passage, becomes in later references "the Party" or just "the CPC."

Since in Chinese there are no initials — and since even the longest title can be expressed in just a few characters — translators often tend to overlook this means of avoiding wordiness. In English,

123

however, its use is standard practice. Indeed, certain organizations become so well known by their initials that they are seldom referred to by their full names.

Thus, in defiance of logic, the Strategic Arms Limitation Talks are often spoken of as "the SALT talks." The United Nations International Children's Emergency Fund remains "UNICEF" decades after its official name was changed to the United Nations Children's Fund, to which the initials no longer correspond.

And sometimes the full name disappears entirely. Who now remembers that the "Care" package we send to a friend, containing food, clothing, or other useful gifts, was originally one sent to needy people abroad, after World War II, by the private U.S. charity, Cooperative for American Remittances to Europe (later, the Cooperative for Assistance and Relief Everywhere)?

Occasionally, initials can be used to replace the full name of an entity even when it is not a capitalized title. For example, in an article in the magazine *Asiaweek*, the authors use initials not only for China's "gross domestic product" but also for phrases that are less familiar but equally awkward to spell out repeatedly: "special economic zones," "state-owned enterprises," and "township and village enterprises."

Readers of the newsweekly need no explanation of "GDP," which is never spelled out in the article. It should be noted, however, that before the other initials are used alone, they are carefully introduced in such a way as to make their meaning unmistakable:

- The nation's first four special economic zones — Zhuhai,

Shenzhen, Xiamen and Shantou *SEZs* — were created in 1979 as labs for industrial reform.

- [Deng Xiaoping] brought Zhu to the capital permanently in 1991 to help revive the economy and tackle one of its most pressing and perplexing problems: the dismal performance of state-owned enterprises (*SOEs*).

- Township and village enterprises expanded their share of industrial output from 22.4% in 1978 to 34% in 1994. That year nearly 25 million *TVEs* employed about 120 million people, many of them former farmers put out of work by earlier reforms.

Once the meaning of these abbreviations has been established, they can be used lightly and flexibly, as in this later sentence:

- TVEs have an average of about five workers each, a size nimble enough to respond to market changes the way their SOE cousins can't.

The proliferation of initials in current English has no doubt been encouraged by journalistic practice, which sets a premium on economies of space and time. Their use, like any other device in writing, can be carried to excess. Still, you should bear in mind the possibility of replacing repeated references to the National People's Congress with "the NPC," the Chinese Academy of Social Sciences with "CASS," the Special Administrative Region of Hong Kong with "the SAR," the US-China Peoples Friendship Association with "the USCPFA," and so on. The longer the full title, and the more frequently it appears, the greater the saving in words.

Another reason for avoiding exact repetition

These means of effecting economies — the omissions and substitutions that can be used to shorten repeated references to the same thing — serve another function as well. They are useful, indeed required, not only because, as the early nineteenth century British grammarian William Cobbett says of pronouns [p. 13], they "make speaking and writing more rapid and less encumbered with words," but also because they prevent the repetition of the same sounds.

Most readers "hear" what they are reading (just as, on some level, they "hear" what they are thinking), and the ears of native speakers of English are highly sensitive to repetition. Where it is not used deliberately — as in poetry, for example, or for clarity, emphasis, or humorous effect — it is perceived as an annoyance and a distraction from the content.

The principle here is the simple one enunciated by Graves and Hodge [p. 164]: "The same word should not be so often used in the same sentence or paragraph that it becomes tedious." And it should be remembered that the point of tedium is reached very quickly.

Thus, even when, as in some of the B-versions offered above, there is only a small net saving of words or none at all, the revision, which avoids the immediate repetition of the same word or words, is still more natural and more acceptable in English than the draft version.

Following are two more examples in which the change of wording — here, the substitution of a pronoun — does little or nothing to make the statement more succinct but does much to make it more satisfying to the ear.

126

A: We have not met with too many difficulties in the course of the reform, and in general the reform is proceeding smoothly.

B: We have not met with too many difficulties in the course of *the reform* , and in general *it* is proceeding smoothly.

A: I think this suggestion can be adopted; it is a good suggestion.

B: I think this *suggestion* can be adopted; it is a good *one* .

Twenty more examples of revision

The format here is the same as in preceding chapters.

1) A: We must oppose corruption and promote clean government. We should not do this for only a couple of days or months but should oppose corruption in the whole process of reform and opening to the outside world.

B: We must *oppose corruption* and promote clean government. We should *do this* not just for a few days or months but throughout the process of reform and opening to the outside world.

[- In A-version the translator has already substituted "do this" for a second reference to opposing corruption. He or she failed to notice, however, that the third reference could simply be omitted without in any way affecting the meaning.

- (Review: It could be argued that the first sentence says the same thing twice, in the mirror-image construction.)]

2) A: Those who wrongly or too repeatedly criticized people and those who correctly criticized people but overdid it should

127

apologize to them for <u>doing that</u>.

B: Those who have *criticized people* wrongly, excessively or too often should apologize to the persons concerned.

［- "Excessively" expresses "overdid it" and makes it possible to eliminate the second "criticized people."

- "Doing that" is a good alternative to a third "criticizing," but the sense is implied in "apologize," so it too can be dispensed with.］

3) A: Many comrades, having been expelled from the Party, have come to <u>the Organization Department</u> of the Central Committee to <u>appeal</u>, or have sent letters of <u>appeal</u> to <u>the Department</u>.

B: Many comrades, having been expelled from the Party, have *appealed* to *the Organization Department* of the Central Committee, either in person or by letter.

［Here a simple change of structure suffices to eliminate the repetition.］

4) A: In order to satisfy the needs of <u>industrial enterprises</u> for various kinds of <u>materials</u>, and to spare <u>these enterprises</u> the trouble of sending out many people simply for the purchase of some necessary types of <u>materials</u>, the State Council has decided that . . . .

B: To meet the needs of *industrial enterprises* for *materials* and to spare *them* the trouble of sending out many purchasing agents, the State Council has decided that . . . .

［- The second reference to "industrial enterprises" can be replaced by the pronoun "them."

- Once "people for the purchase of" is reduced to "purchasing

128

agents," the second "materials" can be eliminated: the meaning remains clear.

- (Review: "Various kinds of" and "types of" are both unnec. with the plural "materials." The adjective "necessary" is redundant because we have already spoken of "needs.")]

5) *From the quarterly* U.S.-China Review:

A: The word "socialism" is explained [in a dictionary] by quoting Deng Xiaoping's words that the essence of socialism is to free productive forces, develop productive forces, abolish exploitation, abolish polarization and achieve common wealth finally.

B: The word "*socialism*" is explained by quoting Deng Xiaoping's statement that the essence of *socialism* is to free and develop the *productive forces*, *abolish* exploitation, *eliminate* polarization, and eventually achieve common prosperity.

[- The repetition of "socialism" is plainly necessary and, in this context, unobjectionable.

- There is no need, however, for two references to the "productive forces" or for two uses of the word "abolish."]

6) A: Another achievement [of the Congress] is that it elected a new leading body that will ensure continued and accelerated implementation of our policies of reform and opening to the outside world. Before the Thirteenth National Congress, the world's people and the Chinese people were somewhat concerned that our policies of reform and opening to the outside world might not be continued. But

129

the Thirteenth National Congress has addressed this question, reassuring the Chinese people and our international friends.

B: Another achievement is that it elected a new leading body that will ensure continued and accelerated implementation of *our policies of reform and opening to the outside world*. Before *the Thirteenth National Congress*, *people at home and abroad* were concerned that *those policies* might not be continued. But *the Congress* has addressed this question, reassuring *the Chinese people* and our international friends.

[- At second reference, the modifiers of "Congress" were dropped, and the modifiers of "policies" were replaced by the demonstrative adjective "those."

- To avoid having "the world's people," "the Chinese people" and "the Chinese people" all in one sentence, the polisher combined the first two into "people at home and abroad."

- (Review: "Somewhat" is superfluous because "concerned" is mild enough without a qualifier.)]

7) A: After the local authorities have turned over their public grain and tax receipts, the central authorities must ensure the funds needed to cover the expenses of local governments.

B: After *local governments* have turned over their public grain and tax receipts, the central *authorities* must provide them with funds to cover *their* expenses.

[- Local governments = local authorities, so the second reference to them can be reduced to the possessive pronoun "their." The pronoun "them" was added for clarity.

- "Local authorities" was changed to "local governments" to avoid repeating "authorities."]

8) A: While fighting corruption, we must demonstrate our will not to change the policies of <u>reform and opening to the outside world</u> and our resolve to <u>deepen the reform and open even wider to the outside world</u>.

B: While fighting corruption, we must demonstrate our resolve not to change *the current policies* but, on the contrary, to *deepen the reform and open even wider to the outside world*.

[- "Current" can be used to replace one of the two long formulas.
- ("Will" and "resolve" are so close in meaning that we don't need both.)
- (Adding "but, on the contrary," provides the logical connection between the ideas that is understood in Chinese but needs to be made explicit in English.)]

9) A: Our biggest experiment is the economic restructuring. <u>Reform</u> started first in the rural areas. It was after the <u>reform</u> there had produced results that we had the courage to carry out the urban <u>reform</u>. In fact, the urban <u>reform</u> is a <u>reform</u> of the economic structure as a whole and is very risky. The <u>reform</u> has just begun and some problems have already appeared.

B: Our biggest experiment is the restructuring of the economy. We started the *reform* first in the rural areas. It was only after *it* had produced results there that we had the courage to launch *it* in the cities. In fact, the urban *reform* is a *reform* of the economic structure as a whole and is very risky. *It* has only just begun, and some problems have already appeared.

[- Three of the six "reforms" can be readily replaced by "it."

- (The two "only"s were introduced to clarify the logic, which, again, is implicit in the Chinese but should be spelled out in English. In the third sentence, "only" underlines the meaning "we didn't dare begin in the cities until it had proved successful in the countryside," and in the last sentence, it prepares for and supports the "already.")]

10) A: Naturally, there are disagreements about <u>the reform</u>; however, the difference is not about whether we should carry out <u>the reform</u> but about how deep <u>the reform</u> should go, and <u>how to reform</u> and open to the outside world.

B: Naturally, there are disagreements about *the reform*; but the disagreements are not over whether we should carry *it* out but over how deep *it* should go, *how it should be conducted* and how we should go about opening to the outside world.

[- Four "reform"s in one sentence are unacceptable, especially when the unsuspecting reader is required to recognize that although the first three are nouns, the fourth is suddenly a verb.

- The problem is easily solved by a change of structure. The fourth "reform" was converted to a noun also (not "how to reform" but "how the reform should be conducted"). The pronoun "it" could then be substituted for the last three.]

11) A: The cost of moving grain is high: on average, it is equal to the price of the grain transported, and in some places transportation charges exceed the price of the grain.

B: *The cost of shipping grain* is high: on average, it is equal to *the price of the grain* transported, and in some places *it* exceeds *that price*.

[- Transportation charges = the cost of moving grain, so the second term was replaced by "it."
- The second reference to the price of grain was replaced with "that price."]

12) A: For this reason, we have decided to increase our cotton purchases both at home and abroad and to commission private cotton mills in Shanghai to produce more cotton fabric for us by using the cotton we offer them.

B: For this reason, we have decided to buy more *cotton* both at home and abroad and to commission privately owned mills in Shanghai to process *it* into cloth for us.

[- A little critical attention reveals that only the first of the four mentions of cotton is necessary.
- Mills that produce cotton fabric are obviously "cotton" mills; only "cotton" fabric can be produced from cotton; and "the cotton we offer them" is plainly the same as the cotton we are buying, which can now become "it."]

13) A: The target of the revolution is to change the old system, which hindered the development of the productive forces, and prepare new means for the development of the productive forces.

B: The goal of the revolution is to change the old system, which hindered *the development of the productive forces*, and to prepare new means for *their development*.

[- In principle, the entire second mention of "the development of the productive forces" could be replaced by the pronoun "it."

- That much tightening, however, would have left the meaning unclear, so the phrase was simply shortened with the help of the possessive pronoun "their."]

14) A: Asked whether he wanted to <u>own</u> a car, Xia said, "I've never even thought of <u>owning</u> a car. It's too expensive. No one in my factory is rich enough to <u>own</u> a car. Most of the people in the city who now <u>own</u> automobiles are <u>owners</u> of private businesses.

B: Asked whether he wanted to *own* a car, Xia said, "I've never even thought about *that*. It's too expensive. No one in my factory can afford to *own* a car. Most of the people in the city who *have* automobiles are *owners* of private businesses."

[- A short, commonplace word like "own" doesn't draw so much attention to itself as a longer, more unusual phrase like "development of the productive forces," so it can be repeated more often without intruding on the reader's consciousness.

- Even so, five appearances of any word in four short sentences must be considered excessive, and replacements ("that" and "have") were not hard to find.]

15) A: When the Ministry of Finance of the Central People's Government, after careful consideration, issues an order

to transfer public grain from one province to another, no province should refuse to transfer its public grain to meet the needs of other areas.

B: When the Ministry of Finance, after careful consideration, issues an order to *transfer public grain* from one *province* to another where it is needed, no *local authorities* may refuse to *do so*.

  [- The useful "do so" served to replace the second reference to transferring public grain.

  - "Local authorities" was substituted for the second "province" partly to avoid repetition and partly to avoid personifying "province" — that is, to introduce some people to do the refusing.

  - (Note that "to meet the needs of other areas" was tightened to "where it is needed.")

  - (Review: "Of the Central People's Government" is a superfluous modifier because, in any state, a ministry is always an organ of the central government.)]

16) *Footnote referring to the Ministry of Trade*:

A: Established in October 1949, the Ministry of Trade under the Central People's Government was in charge of domestic and foreign trade. It was abolished in August 1952, when the Ministry of Commerce and the Ministry of Foreign Trade were established to handle domestic trade and trade with other countries, respectively.

B: The Ministry of Trade was established in October 1949 to be in charge of *domestic and foreign trade*. It was abolished in August 1952, when *its functions* were divided between two new ministries, the Ministry of Commerce and the

Ministry of Foreign Trade.

[- It is self-evident that the Ministry of Foreign Trade will handle trade with other countries, and clear in context that the Ministry of Commerce will handle domestic trade.

- The sentence was recast to express the notion more succinctly and without the repetition.

- (<u>Review</u>: Again, "under the Central People's Government" is understood.)]

17) A: In order to familiarize <u>the central Financial and Economic Commission</u> with <u>preparations</u> in the <u>various regions</u> and to ensure coordination in this effort, the <u>local authorities</u> should report to <u>the former</u> on their <u>preparatory work</u>.

B: To keep *the central Financial and Economic Commission* informed and to ensure coordination, *local authorities* should report to *the Commission* on the *preparations* they are making.

[- These repetitions too are unnec. "Preparatory work" = "preparations," "local authorities" represent the "various regions," and there is no need to refer to either notion twice.

- The Financial and Economic Commission was repeated, however, in shortened form, because in this sentence·"the former" doesn't work.

- "The former" can be used only to refer to one of two preceding items — here, there would have to have been a mention of two different government bodies. In other words, we cannot speak of the "former" (= the first) unless there is also a "latter" (= the second).

- ("In this effort" was deleted as self-evident.)]

18) A: One thing that has to be done is to establish a new international political order. The other is to establish <u>a new international economic order</u>. With regard to <u>a new international economic order</u>, I spent a long time on it when I spoke at the United Nations General Assembly in 1974.

B: One thing that has to be done is to establish a new international political order; the other is to establish *a new international economic order*. With regard to *the latter*, I spent a long time on the subject when I spoke at the United Nations General Assembly in 1974.

[Unlike in the preceding example, here there are two comparable items (the two "new international orders"). It is therefore possible to refer to the second of them as "the latter."]

19) A: Xuzhou's strategy, says Xia, has been to build reliable and affordable <u>specialized vehicles</u>. Xia sees an expanding market in China for <u>specialized vehicles</u>. "Large automakers cannot possibly manufacture all kinds of <u>specialized vehicles</u>," he says, "and those of us in <u>specialized vehicle</u> production have a niche in meeting the market demands."

B: Xuzhou's strategy, says Xia, has been to build reliable and affordable *specialized vehicles*. Xia sees an expanding market in China for *such vehicles*. "Large automakers cannot possibly manufacture all kinds of *specialized vehicles*," he says, "and those of us who produce *them* have a niche in the market."

[- Four "specialized vehicles" in three successive sentences is

137

distressing to the ear of a native speaker. It is easy
enough, however, to reduce them to an acceptable two.

- At the second reference, the adjective "specialized" was
  replaced by "such." At the fourth, both adjective and
  noun were replaced by the pronoun "them."

- (Note that the primary meaning of "niche" — derived
  from the Latin word for "nest" — is a small recess in a
  wall. Metaphorically, it is a special place or position in
  some larger structure. Accordingly, one can speak of a
  "niche in the market" but not of a "niche in meeting demands.")]

20) *From a footnote referring to the "Joint Declaration of the Gov-
    ernment of the United Kingdom of Great Britain and
    Northern Ireland and the Government of the People's Re-
    public of China on the Question of Hong Kong":*

   A: The Joint Declaration states: "The Government of the
      People's Republic of China will resume exercise of
      sovereignty over Hong Kong with effect from 1 July
      1997, and the Government of the United Kingdom will
      restore Hong Kong to the People's Republic of China with
      effect from 1 July 1997." The Government of the People's
      Republic of China expounds in the Joint Declaration the
      basic policies of the People's Republic of China regarding
      Hong Kong.

   B: *The Joint Declaration states: "The Government of the
      People's Republic of China will resume exercise of
      sovereignty over Hong Kong with effect from 1 July
      1997, and the Government of the United Kingdom will
      restore Hong Kong to the People's Republic of China with*

effect from 1 July 1997." In *this document the Chinese government sets forth its* basic policies regarding Hong Kong.

[- Although "the People's Republic of China" occurs twice in the first sentence, there can be no question of abbreviating the title or replacing it with a pronoun because this is a direct quotation from the Joint Declaration and cannot be altered.

- In the second sentence, however, it is the editor of the book speaking, and there is no reason to continue in the same formal tone.

- Accordingly, "the Government of the People's Republic of China" can be reduced to "the Chinese government," and thereafter to a simple "its."

- And to avoid repetition, we can now use a general noun to refer to the Joint Declaration: "this document."]

Twenty exercises

1) Our present standard of living is still very low, and we have a long way to go to attain a relatively high standard of living.

2) We have just held the Twelfth National Congress of the Party. Since the Twelfth National Congress, the political situation of our country has been more stable than ever before.

3) For two consecutive years, production of passenger cars has failed to reach the target, says Lu Fuyuan, Vice Minister of Machinery Industry, who is in charge of day-to-day administration of the automotive sector. Last year production of passenger cars was 80,000 short of the expected total.

4) If you want to find out whether the present policy is here to stay, you should first examine whether the policy is correct, whether the policy is right for the country and the people, and whether the life of the people is gradually improving under the policy. I believe that the people's eyes are discerning. If the present policy is altered, the standard of living of the people will definitely come down.

5) Wang Ming was criticized at the Sixth Plenary Session of the Sixth Central Committee, and as many cadres raised their political consciousness Wang Ming gradually became isolated. Even Chiang Kai-shek rejected Wang Ming, refusing to appoint him a minister.

6) Party branches should regularly transfer good cadres to higher-level Party committees, so long as the work of the branches does not suffer as a consequence.

7) Local governments are bound to encounter difficulties in the early days of centralized management. But those difficulties and their consequences will be far less serious than the difficulties that would result from the serious fluctuations in monetary value and prices that would occur under a system of decentralized management.

8) The central task of the congress was to accelerate and deepen reform. The congress expounded the theory of the primary stage of socialism in China and defined the basic line of our Party in building socialism with Chinese characteristics during the primary stage of socialism.

9) We failed to attach equal importance to both types of work, and

there was no proper coordination between the two types of work.

10) The principles our Party has laid down since the Third Plenary Session of the Party's Eleventh Central Committee can be summed up in two points.

11) China must have a leading collective with the image of people who favor reform and opening to the outside world. I hope you will pay special attention to this point. We cannot abandon the policies of reform and opening to the outside world.

12) Lin believes that it is important for a foreign company to keep its [joint-venture] negotiating team intact from beginning to end and that it would be a good idea for the Chinese partner to keep its team intact too.

13) At the beginning of this year, the Central Committee of the Communist Party of China and the State Council called a meeting on nationality work. At the meeting, general experience on nationality work was analyzed and major tasks and policies for nationality work in the 1990s were put forward.

14) In 1995, 42 percent of the automotive manufacturers operated at a loss, a 42 percent increase over the previous year. The total amount of loss for automotive producers in 1995 increased by 41 percent, and their inventory increased by 14.2 percent over a year ago, amounting to 200,000 units.

15) Despite the fact that officials from the automotive industry and central government took stern measures in fighting smuggling of vehicles, foreign motor vehicles, especially sedans, have kept pouring into the country.

16) In the letter, they outlined the state of affairs in the study of high-energy physics and made suggestions on developing research on high-energy physics.

17) After that he became Chairman of the Central Committee of the Communist Party of China, Chairman of the Central Military Commission and Premier of the State Council. In September 1980 he resigned from the post of Premier of the State Council.

18) the purpose of making advances in technology is to improve the economic performance of enterprises by greatly disseminating applicable new scientific and technological findings

19) In 1995 total medium trucks produced were 249,800 units, 21 per cent fewer than in 1994, and the number of heavy trucks produced was 29,800 units, a 17.5 per cent drop from the previous year. Sales of medium trucks and heavy trucks were down 21.4 and 16.2 per cent respectively.

20) Contrary to some people's misconceptions, Americans have a deep love for their families and spend as much time as they can with their families.

VI. Summing it All Up

Throughout the preceding chapters, Chinese polishers who are reviewing a draft translation in English, whether it is their own work or that of another translator, have been encouraged to tighten loose sentences. That is, they have been urged to edit out superfluous words that waste the reader's time, obscure the writer's meaning and make any text seem heavy and longwinded.

This advice flows from the widely agreed-upon rule that writers of English should be concise. The rule is summed up in the classic injunction of Professor Strunk quoted on the first page of this book: "A sentence should contain no unnecessary words ... for the same reason that a drawing should have no unnecessary lines and a machine no unnecessary parts."

At the same time, you have been cautioned to exercise care in eliminating a word or phrase that seems unnecessary. Often, you will need to refer back to the original text to check the translation: it may be that in a more accurate version the apparent redundancy will disappear. But even if you confirm your initial judgment that the expression in question serves no purpose, there may be special reasons for retaining it. The degree to which you feel free to depart from a literal version of the Chinese will inevitably depend to some extent on the kind of text you are dealing with and on the kind of readers to whom it is addressed.

The decision to allow an unnecessary word to stand, however, must remain an exception. The "golden rule" for translators writing English is the same as that proposed by the respected authority

143

Ernest Gowers [p. 3] for British civil servants: "to pick those words that convey to the reader the meaning of the writer and to use them and them only."

The professional responsibility of the translator is not to trade English words for Chinese equivalents but to select those English words that "convey to the reader the meaning of the writer." It is to give Chinese authors fair exchange for their characters, not in equal measure but in equal value.

Twenty more examples of revision

We have now studied the five major categories of unnecessary words in Chinglish: superfluous nouns and verbs, superfluous adjectives and adverbs, redundant twins, repeated ideas and repeated references to the same thing. By way of review, here are twenty final examples representing all five.

Since most of these examples present more than one problem, it should be noted that not all problems need be solved simultaneously. Revision is typically accomplished not all at once but in stages. Polishers may do something to tighten a wordy passage, but if they then, or later, reread the revised version, they will often think of further improvements. (The hope, of course, is to think of all of them before, rather than after, the work appears in print.)

This means that the "A-version, B-version" format used in this book is only a convenience. In practice — especially if more than one person is involved in the revision — there is likely to be not just a B-version but a C and perhaps even a D.

In the following examples the changes that appear in the revisions are explained in the order in which they were made. This will show the successive steps by which the polisher arrived at a final version. As will be seen, redundant twins and superfluous modifiers, being the easiest to recognize and eliminate, were often dealt with first, before the more difficult problems were addressed.

Only the unnecessary or repetitive words are underlined in the A-versions, with revisions italicized in the B-versions. Some A-versions present other faults which have not been discussed but which the polisher has also corrected in B. These are not highlighted in the same way, but most of them are mentioned in parentheses at the end of the explanation of revision.

1) A: We should enthusiastically explore both the international and domestic markets, opening up new international markets and further exploring the rural market.

   B: We should try to *open up* new *international* and domestic *markets*, especially *exploring* (*or*, *better*: expanding) the rural market.

   [- As soon as the polisher read A-version she deleted "enthusiastically" as an overemphatic and superfluous modifier.

   - She then noted the two references to international markets. As there seemed to be no difference between "exploring" markets and "opening up" new ones, she decided to eliminate one mention. Accordingly, she dropped "explore," which was the vaguer of the two and was repeated a few words later.]

2) A: On the whole, however, financial and economic work was still decentralized, because we had not adopted measures to bring financial revenue under unified management; only expenditure was unified, not revenue.

B: On the whole, however, financial and economic work was still decentralized, because we had *brought expenditure under unified management, but not revenue*.

[- First the polisher eliminated "financial" revenue as redundant. Except when there is some reference to taxes in kind (grain, for example), all revenue is "financial."

- Next she replaced "adopted measures to bring" (an unnec. verb + unnec. noun + third word construction) with the plain verb "brought."

- Then she noticed that the idea that revenue had not been "unified" was expressed in two ways ("we had not brought revenue under unified management" and "not revenue"). She recast the sentence to eliminate one of them.]

3) A: Foreign <u>experience</u> has shown that some countries have <u>experienced development periods</u> or <u>undergone a number of high-growth stages</u>, as demonstrated in Japan, South Korea and parts of Southeast Asia.

B: The *experience* of other countries shows that some of them — Japan, South Korea and parts of Southeast Asia, for example — *have gone through one or more periods of rapid development*.

[- To avoid an annoying repetition of the same word, the polisher immediately changed "have experienced" to "have gone through."

- Then she considered the "development periods" and "high-growth stages," which looked suspiciously like the same thing. The difference between them was not explained, and she could see none.

- But before deciding that the sentence merely said the same thing twice, she checked the Chinese. The repetition, she discovered, was only in the English version. It had apparently come about because the translator had not clearly understood the original.

- The distinction the speaker was making was not between "development periods" and "high-growth stages" but rather between countries that had experienced one period or stage of rapid development and others that had experienced several.

- That understanding made it possible to eliminate the redundancy and also to combine the two expressions into one: "some of them . . . have gone through one or more periods of rapid development."]

4) A: The offices of the Military Control Commission were located in an area where board and lodging, and public transport and <u>communication facilities were easily available</u> and where <u>telephone contacts could be made with much convenience</u>.

B: The offices of the Military Control Commission were located in an area where board and lodging, public transportation, and *communication facilities, including telephones, were readily available*.

[- Rereading the end of A-version, the polisher wondered why "telephone contacts" should be mentioned separately, as if they were something apart from "communication facilities." The entire last clause ("where telephone contacts could be made . . . .") was redundant, she thought, and should be eliminated.

- Checking against the original, however, she decided that

147

telephones were specifically mentioned because they were of special importance.

- Accordingly, she retained the telephones, but only as a component of "communication facilities."]

5) A: Moreover, they are in the habit of <u>taking more than their due</u> and do not make compensation for or return the <u>things which they are not entitled to</u> but which they <u>have taken into their own possession</u>.

B: Moreover, they *take things to which they are not entitled* and never return *them* or make compensation.

[- When she first read A-version the polisher had an impression of constant repetition. She read it again to see why that was so.

- "Things which they are not entitled to" was plainly the same as "more than their due." Of the two, she chose "which they are not entitled to," using the preferred order, "to which they are not entitled."

- This produced: "Moreover, they are in the habit of taking things to which they are not entitled and do not make compensation for or return the things which they have taken into their own possession."

- Now it was clear that the end of the sentence merely repeated the beginning. The things "which they have taken into their own possession" were the same as the things "they are in the habit of taking." She dispensed with the repetition, replacing the second "things" with "them."

- The revision now stood as follows: " Moreover, they are in the habit of taking things to which they are not entitled and do not make compensation for or return them." A more logical order seemed to be, "and do not return them or make compensation," so the polisher made that adjustment.

- Finally, for further tightening, she changed "in the habit of taking" to "take." That version eliminated the noun "habit" and conveyed more concisely the notion of habitual action. To reinforce the idea she changed "not" to "never."]

6) A: Therefore, we should approach, study and solve the problem of development from the high plane of all mankind. Only in this way can we understand that the problem of development is the responsibility of the developing and the developed countries as well.

B: We should therefore *consider and solve the problem of development* from the perspective of a broad concern for all mankind. Only then can we understand that *this problem* is the responsibility of both the developing and the developed countries.

[- The polisher first took a critical look at "approach, study and solve." "Approach," she thought, was so vague that it could not be distinguished from "study." She decided they were redundant twins and replaced both with "consider."

- Seeing that "the problem of development" was repeated, she shortened the second reference by means of a demonstrative adjective: "this problem."

- But now she saw that the "this" she had introduced repeated the one used just before in "Only in this way." To remedy that she changed "only in this way" to "only

149

then."

- (Lastly, she tackled the most difficult problem, rewriting "from the high plane of all mankind" to make a clearer and more idiomatic version. After discussing the meaning of the Chinese with another polisher, she came up with "from the perspective of a broad concern for all mankind.")]

7) A: Of course, we must have <u>a certain number</u> of <u>professional revolutionaries</u> who may not get involved in the <u>specific production activities</u> and <u>a proper number</u> of physicians as well as <u>a certain number</u> of <u>personnel specializing in literary, artistic and other related activities</u>.

B: Of course, we must have *a certain number of revolutionary professionals* — doctors, *writers*, *artists*, *and other specialists* — who are not involved in *production*.

[- On first reading, the polisher could make no sense of A-version. She was only aware that it was wordy and repetitive and needed to be edited down.

- As a start, she reduced "specific production activities" to "production."

- Next she saw that "personnel specializing in literary, artistic and other related activities" was only a circumlocution for "writers, artists, and other specialists," which she accordingly substituted.

- Then she added "physicians" to the list of specialists, using the simpler term "doctors." This change eliminated one of the three references to "a certain (or proper) number."

- The revision now stood as follows: "Of course, we must have a certain number of professional revolutionaries who may not get involved in production and a certain number of doctors, writers, artists and other specialists." That version was not so wordy, but the meaning was no clearer than before.

- It was only when the polisher consulted the Chinese that she understood what the difficulty was: the key words had been mistranslated.

- The speaker was not talking about "professional revolutionaries" (i.e., persons whose profession in life was to make revolution) but rather about "revolutionary professionals" (i.e., persons who had a profession — medicine, writing, etc. — and who were revolutionary in their thinking).

- Once the doctors and other specialists had been identified as the revolutionary professionals, the misleading "and a certain number of doctors" and so on could be eliminated: "we must have a certain number of revolutionary professionals who are not involved in production — doctors, writers, artists and other specialists."

- That was both clear and concise. All that remained was to improve the word order: "we must have a certain number of revolutionary professionals — doctors, writers, artists and other specialists — who are not involved in production."]

8) A: Various departments should quickly establish and strengthen necessary research organs to carry out work in coordination with the Chinese Academy of Sciences in a joint effort for expanding the scientific force.

B: Various departments should quickly *establish* research organs

151

to *work jointly with* the Chinese Academy of Sciences to expand the scientific force.

[- A-version, the polisher saw, was clear enough and needed only some tightening that would not be difficult.

- She first spotted the redundant twins "establish and strengthen." Although the words did not mean the same thing, she thought that in this context they were never-theless redundant because one implied the other. Any in-stitution, once established, should be strengthened, im-proved, perfected, etc. She deleted "strengthen."

- That the research organs were "necessary" was implicit in the statement that they should be established, so she deleted that word too.

- Next she replaced "carry out work," an unnec. verb + noun construction, with the plain verb "work."

- Finally, since "in coordination with" merely duplicated the sense of "in a joint effort" — a double reference to the same idea — she replaced both with the adverb "jointly."]

9) A: We shall step up medical <u>research</u>, <u>focusing on</u> the causes for <u>incidence of</u> common illnesses and their prevention and treatment, and <u>concentrating on tackling</u> the key <u>research</u> projects.

B: We shall step up medical *research*, *concentrating on* key pro-jects *for the study of* the cause, prevention, and treat-ment of common illnesses.

[- The cause of the incidence of a disease = the cause of the disease, so the polisher deleted "incidence."

- Concentrating on tackling projects = concentrating on the

152

projects, so she deleted "tackling" as well.

- "Focusing on" = "concentrating on," so she changed the structure of the sentence to condense them into one.

- At the same time, she eliminated the repetition of "research" by changing "research projects" to "projects for the study of." That was plainly the intended meaning, and it tied the two parts of the sentence together.]

10) A: In this decision [of the Central Committee] the <u>necessity and urgency</u> of <u>rectification</u> was <u>explicitly</u> expounded and the basic tasks for the <u>rectification</u> were <u>clearly</u> defined as follows: to unify thinking, <u>rectify</u> the style of work, tighten discipline and purify the organizations.

B: In this decision the Central Committee explained the *urgency* of *rectification* and defined *its* basic tasks as follows: to unify the members' thinking, *improve* their style of work, tighten discipline and weed out those who were unqualified.

[- The polisher paused as soon as she came to the twins "necessity and urgency." If a task was "urgent," it was not only "necessary" but pressing; in short, the second idea included the first. (She noted in passing that the translator also evidently thought of the two words as one, since he or she had used the singular verb "was" instead of the correct plural "were.")

- Of the two words, she retained the one that was more inclusive, "urgency."

- Reading on, she quickly deleted the two adverbs "explicitly" and "clearly." Explanations and definitions are assumed to be explicit and clear unless there is some indication to the contrary.

- Then she considered how to eliminate the repetition "rectification"/"rectification"/"rectify." She replaced the second "rectification" with the possessive pronoun "its" and changed "rectify" to "improve."

- (To make the sentence more vigorous and direct, she put it in active voice by introducing "The Central Committee" as the subject. Then, to give a concrete anchor to the unattached "thinking" and "style of work," she brought in "the members.")

- (She had left until last the more difficult question of "purify the organizations." This was a political metaphor that might not be readily understood by foreign readers. After reflecting on the meaning of the phrase, she substituted a different expression that was more familiar in English: "weed out those who were unqualified.")]

11) A: With regard to the <u>existing practices</u> of <u>vying for gaining</u> investments <u>and for undertaking</u> construction projects <u>in an unchecked way</u>, we must stop <u>them</u> by strictly implementing the state's industrial policies, improving the scientific feasibility appraisal and management of projects and tightening control over <u>the amount of</u> bank credit.

B: *We must put a stop to the blind competition for investments and construction projects* by strictly implementing the state's industrial policies, improving the (scientific) feasibility studies and the management of projects, and tightening control over bank credit.

[- On reading A-version the polisher realized it would need considerable revision, so she looked first for easy changes with which she could make a start.

- "The amount of" added nothing to the sense of "bank credit." She deleted the phrase.

- Since only "existing" practices need to be stopped, "existing" could be taken for granted. She eliminated that word also.

- And now that she thought about it, "practices" itself was only a superfluous category noun, so it too could come out. But that left "With regard to vying for . . . , we must stop them." Since the pronoun "them" no longer had an antecedent, it had to be replaced by the noun it stood for: "we must stop these practices."

- At this point, the polisher backed up. The source of these complications, she now realized, was the opening phrase "With regard to." Why not abandon that construction and just say, "We must put a stop to vying etc."? That took care of "practices"/"them" and was in any event simpler and more direct. Done.

- So far, the revision of the first part of the sentence read as follows: "We must put a stop to vying for gaining investments and for undertaking construction projects in an unchecked way by strictly implementing etc."

- On rereading, the polisher saw that the two gerunds, "gaining" and "undertaking," were superfluous. The idea could be expressed perfectly well without them: "We must put a stop to vying for investments and construction projects."

- Next she addressed the awkward expression "vying for . . . in an unchecked way." The whole thing, she

155

thought, could be neatly replaced by "blind competition
for."

- These changes produced: "We must put a stop to the
blind competition for investments and construction projects by strictly implementing . . . ."

- (Turning to the end of the sentence, the polisher paused
over "feasibility appraisal." There was nothing wrong
with that term, but she substituted the more usual one,
"feasibility studies.")

- As for "scientific," she was tempted to eliminate the adjective on the grounds that it was merely decorative (such
studies are always supposed to be "scientific"). Still,
since it was there in the Chinese . . .]

12) A: In combating international <u>terrorism</u>, we emphasize the prevention of <u>terrorists</u> from inciting <u>terrorist</u> incidents in
China or taking China as a base for <u>terrorist</u> activities.

  B: In combating international *terrorism* , our chief concern is to
prevent *terrorists* from inciting incidents in China or using
China as a base for *their* activities.

  [- The polisher thought that in one sentence four references
to the same idea in virtually the same terms were both intolerable and unnecessary.

  - She judged the first two references ("terrorism," "terrorists") to be unavoidable. The third, however ("terrorist"
incidents) was self-evident in context: the reader assumes
that incidents incited by terrorists are "terrorist"
incidents. Accordingly, she deleted it.

  - The fourth use of the term was equally superfluous: the
activities of terrorists are, by definition, "terrorist"

156

activities. She therefore replaced the adjective with a possessive pronoun, "their."]

13) A: The <u>orientation and aim</u> of political reform are . . . to improve the socialist legal system and to <u>effectively</u> guarantee the rights of the <u>masses of</u> people as masters of the country.

   B: The *aim* (*or*: goal) of political reform is . . . to improve the socialist legal system and guarantee the rights of the people as masters of the country.

    [- The polisher first eliminated the redundant intensifier "effectively": a "guarantee" is "effective" by definition (otherwise, it does not guarantee anything).

    - Next she deleted "masses of," since "the masses" = "the people."

    - Then she considered "orientation and aim." What, she wondered, was the "orientation" of a program of reform? The word seemed to have no meaning here, or so vague and abstract a meaning that it added nothing to the plain sense of "aim." She edited "orientation" out too.]

14) A: During the three-year period of <u>improvement of the economic environment and rectification of the economic order</u>, the State Council, the various ministries and commissions and local governments at different levels issued a series of documents. Generally speaking, these documents have <u>played a positive role in promoting</u> the program of <u>economic improvement and rectification</u>.

   B: During the three-year period of *improvement of the economic environment and rectification of the economic order*, the State Council, the various ministries and commissions and local governments at different levels issued a series of documents. Generally speaking, these documents *helped achieve the objectives of that period*.

[- First, to avoid repeating a long phrase heavy with nouns, the polisher replaced the second reference to "economic improvement and rectification" with a summary expression: "the objectives of that period." This made it possible to eliminate "the program of" as well.

- Next, seeing that "played a positive role in promoting" was only an elaborate way of saying "helped promote," she substituted the simpler version. On reflection, she then changed "helped promote" to the stronger "helped achieve."]

15) *The next sentence after the preceding example*:

A: Now that this program has ended, the State Council, various ministries and commissions and all local governments should earnestly check up these documents, continuing to implement those that still play a positive role at present and revising or abolishing by formal decree those that do not suit the current real conditions and the needs of economic development.

B: Now that *it* has ended, however, *the State Council and the other issuing authorities* should review these documents, continuing to implement those that *are still useful* and revising or *formally* withdrawing those that are no longer appropriate to current conditions or the needs of economic development.

[- On first reading A-version, the polisher had the impression that it needed a good deal of cutting but that none of the necessary changes would require much thought. She therefore went back to the beginning and dealt with the superfluous words in the order in which they appeared.

- Since the "program" had been edited out of the preceding sentence, she substituted "it," referring to the three-year "period" just mentioned.

- "The State Council, various ministries and commissions and all local governments" had just been spelled out above (see example 14). To avoid repeating so much material, she used a summary expression, "the State Council and the other issuing authorities."

- She unhesitatingly cut "earnestly" on the grounds that it was merely a cliché modifier (everything should always be done earnestly, carefully, conscientiously, etc.).

- Next she replaced the wordy and abstract "play a positive role at present" with the short, concrete "are still useful."

- She reduced "by formal decree" to "formally." (At the same time, she changed "abolish" to "withdraw," because one cannot "abolish" a document.)

- Since "current conditions" are "real" by definition, "real" was then eliminated as an unnec. intensifier.

- (Finally, having gotten rid of the unnecessary words, she added a necessary one. She introduced a "however" near the beginning of the sentence to express the logical progress of the argument that was implied in Chinese but needed to be stated outright in English: the documents were useful then; however, they may no longer be useful now.)]

16) A: In the rural areas we should pay attention to economical use
       of land and try our utmost to use less or no arable land in
       rural housing construction.

    B: As for housing construction *in rural areas*, we should *try* to
       be economical in our use of land and *especially* to use little
       or no arable land.

    [- The polisher saw at once that there was no need for both
       "In the rural areas" and "in rural housing construction."
       She combined them into a single opening phrase, "As for
       housing construction in rural areas."

     - Next she condensed the two verb phrases — the meaning-
       less "pay attention to" and the overworked "try our ut-
       most" — into a single plain verb, "try."

     - Then, to replace the emphasis that had been lost when
       she eliminated "utmost," she added "especially."]

17) A: Waste does not simply mean extravagance and squandering
       but handling affairs or spending money without consider-
       ing importance and urgency and the need to subordinate
       the part to the whole. That is to say, revenue is not ap-
       propriately used on the most important undertakings, but
       rather unwisely on the unimportant ones.

    B: Waste does not simply mean *squandering* money. Also and
       particularly it means *spending money* without considering
       priorities and the need to subordinate the part to the
       whole — that is, *spending it unwisely on unimportant
       projects*.

    [- The dictionary definition of "squandering" money is
       spending it "extravagantly or wastefully." "Extravagance"
       and "squandering" were therefore redundant twins, and

160

the polisher began by eliminating one.

- She chose to retain "squandering," partly because it was the more unusual word and partly because with the obligatory direct object "money" it made a clearer statement than "extravagance" alone would have done.

- Next she paused over "without considering importance and urgency": importance and urgency of what? Various projects, presumably, but that was not stated. She substituted "priorities," which was neater and did not raise the same question.

- The first sentence now read: "Waste does not simply mean squandering money, but handling affairs or spending money without considering priorities and the need to subordinate the part to the whole."

- That was better, but "handling affairs" was exceedingly vague. Since the topic was wasting money, the "affairs" in question could only be affairs involving decisions about expenditure. And if that was so, the phrase was redundant with "spending money" and could therefore be omitted.

- Proceeding to the next sentence, the polisher recognized it as a mirror-image construction in which the same idea was expressed twice. Once it was stated that revenue was not used on important undertakings, there was no need to say it was used on unimportant ones. Or vice versa — either the first statement of the idea or the second could be dispensed with.

- Considering which to eliminate, the polisher saw that if she retained the second statement (that revenue was used unwisely on unimportant projects), she could attach it neatly to the preceding sentence: "... spending money without considering priorities and the need to subordinate the part to the whole — that is, spending it unwisely on unimportant projects."

- (But now the sentence was too long. She decided to break it after the first clause: "Waste does not simply mean squandering money. It also means spending money without considering priorities etc.")

- (The first polisher, a foreigner who did not read Chinese, left the passage in that form. It was a second polisher who, reviewing the work of the first and comparing it with the Chinese, found that the original translator had omitted an element of meaning. To correct this, she changed "It also means" to "Also and particularly it means.")]

18) A: <u>Great efforts are required</u> to achieve the goal that by the year 1990 the <u>freight</u> volume of <u>various kinds of cargo</u> will <u>register an increase</u> of <u>about</u> 30 per cent over 1985.

B: *We must try to increase* the volume of *freight* handled annually, so that by 1990 it is 30 per cent greater than in 1985.

[- Judging that in this case "Great efforts are required" was only a variation on the empty introductory phrase "make great efforts," the polisher changed it to "We must try." That revision had the further advantage of putting the statement in active voice.

- Analyzing the remainder of the sentence, she saw that what "we must try to do" was in skeleton form "achieve

162

the goal that x will register an increase." Most of that, she decided, was "empty words."

- "Achieve the goal that" was merely a superfluous preliminary. "Register an increase" was just the familiar combination of unnec. verb + noun. The only real action was expressed in the noun "increase."

- Since the essential "verb work" was being performed by "increase," she promoted that word to the status of verb, made "we" the subject and dispensed with all the rest: "We must try·to increase x ...."

- "Various kinds of," she thought, could be taken for granted. For the matter of that, "cargo" was only an unnecessary repetition of "freight." After a moment's reflection, she deleted the entire phrase.

- The "30%" was clearly only an approximate target figure, so "about" could come out too.

- (After cutting all these words, the polisher inserted two that she thought were needed for clarity: "handled annually.")]

19) A: <u>Earnest efforts will also be made</u> in the <u>exploitation and utilization</u> of solar, wind and geothermal energy.

   B: Solar, wind and geothermal energy *will also be exploited*.

   [- The polisher first deleted one of the redundant twins "exploitation and utilization."

   - She recognized "Earnest efforts will be made in the exploitation" as a passive-voice version of "we shall make earnest efforts to exploit" — that is, another variation on "make great efforts."

   - She was about to remove the expression, but this sentence

163

appeared in an important document (the Seventh Five-Year Plan), and the team of translators were being particularly careful with it. She therefore consulted the senior reviser first.

- Talking it over, the two polishers decided that the government expected to make "earnest efforts" to fulfill all of the many tasks set forth in the Plan, and that there was no particular reason for underlining its determination to accomplish this one.

- They thought, in short, that in this case the emphasis in the Chinese was merely habitual and did not have to be carried over into English — better to save it for a passage where it was needed. Accordingly, they used a simple statement of intent: " ... will also be exploited."]

20) A: To enrich the people's lives, <u>conscientious efforts should be made</u> to <u>bring about a thriving situation</u> in <u>literary and artistic spheres</u> such as <u>literary creations</u>, drama, operas, music, dance ....

   B: To enrich people's lives, *we must ensure that literature and art flourish*. This includes *novels*, *poems*, plays, operas, music, dance ....

   [- This sentence also appeared in the Seventh Five-Year Plan.

   - As soon as the polisher finished reading A-version, she reduced "literary and artistic spheres" to "literature and art" and changed "such as" to "including."

   - Returning then to the beginning of the sentence, she edited out "conscientious efforts should be made," for the same reason that "earnest efforts will be made" had been eliminated in the preceding example. At the same time, she changed the verb to active voice.

- These revisions produced: "To enrich people's lives, we should bring about a thriving situation in literature and art, including etc."

- But that was not quite right: what had to be "thriving" was not the situation but the arts. Indeed, the polisher now saw that, as usual, "situation" added nothing but a needless complication. She revised it out: "we must ensure that literature and art thrive." Then, because she felt a longer word was wanted for better rhythm, she substituted "flourish."

- To avoid the repetition "literature"/"literary creations" (and also because this latter expression would include "drama"), she substituted for "literary creations" "novels and poems," which she understood to be the intended meaning.

- (Finally, because the sentence was very long, she dropped "including" and started fresh with "This includes.")]

Twenty more exercises

These exercises also include examples representing all the categories of unnecessary words discussed in this book.

1) during this period an increase was registered in the state's reserves of foreign currency

2) The Peugeot model 505SX has been ranked the third best passenger car in terms of quality produced in the country.

3) we shall continue to make further efforts to do a good job of family planning

4) certain comrades even adopt an attitude of maintaining a certain respectable distance between themselves and non-Party members

5) We should actively expand the scale of using foreign funds and introducing advanced technology.

6) it is essential to introduce these measures so that the aim of rational utilization of grain may be achieved

7) We must take determined measures to correct this practice of bureaucratism, factionalism, and sectarianism in handling personnel, so that specially trained talents are assigned to the units that deserve them most.

8) Seeing that we had scored remarkable achievements in the transformation of the old society, some people began to show a varying degree of negligence toward problems of class struggle.

9) Yi pointed out that some automakers, facing rising inventories, have encouraged their salesmen to sell cars for a much lower price than the price set in their contracts with trading companies.

10) The practice of hegemonism and use of power politics are the root cause of the turbulent international situation, and China is opposed to hegemonism and power politics.

11) In waging our struggle against the counterrevolutionary elements, we must not involve those whose relationship with the counterrevolutionary elements is merely social. This is a

166

very important point, for there are many among the intellectuals who have such relationships.

12) In view of the unique importance of the Northeast in the development of China's iron and steel industry and of the serious shortage of technical personnel in the region, the conference decided on the transfer to the Northeast of large numbers of technical personnel from North, East and Central-South China.

13) Analysts expect that the demand for Jeeps in China will reach 240,000 units by 2000 and the number will further increase to 560,000 by the end of the first decade of the 21st century.

14) The cotton mills must make sure that their products, instead of lower quality, are up to the standards required by the State Cotton Textile Company.

15) He added that to reform the old economic system means removing the obstacles to the development of the productive forces and further liberating the productive forces.

16) Even among the champions and advocates of reform it is good for them to be a bit skeptical.

17) we must pay close attention to the prevention and treatment of various diseases seriously harming people's health

18) In accordance with the principles of separating the functions of the government from those of the enterprise and appropriately separating ownership from management authority, government departments should continue to change their functions and strengthen and improve macro-economic regulation and control.

19) we shall ... improve the performance and quality of investments

using foreign funds and make efficient use of foreign funds

20) industrial and agricultural production has been raised greatly, with the total output value of industry and agriculture in 1957 estimated to increase by more than 60 per cent compared with 1952

Part Two: Sentence Structure

In Part One we dealt with various types of unnecessary words. All the chapters in that part related to one central concern: the need to make an English sentence concise.

In Part Two we shall deal with various aspects of sentence structure. All the chapters in this part will relate to another central concern: the need to make an English sentence clear and logical.

The faults we shall consider in Part Two are, in general, harder to identify and harder to remedy than those we studied in Part One. But by the same token, they are more interesting. And once we have named and analyzed these mistakes, you will be able to recognize and correct them, just as you have learned to recognize and correct unnecessary words.

VII. The Noun Plague

Plain English is a language based on verbs. It is simple, concise, vigorous and, above all, clear. Chinglish is a language based on nouns — vague, general, abstract nouns. It is complicated, long-winded, ponderous, and obscure.

As we saw in Chapter I, Chinglish contains many nouns that are unnecessary. We examined three types that contribute nothing to the meaning of a sentence and can simply be eliminated:

- redundant nouns ("to accelerate the <u>pace</u> of economic reform" = "to accelerate economic reform"; "there have been good harvests in <u>agriculture</u>" = "there have been good harvests")

- empty nouns ("following the <u>realization</u> of mechanization" = "following the mechanization"; "we must pay <u>attention</u> to promoting" = "we must promote")

- category nouns ("opposing the <u>practice</u> of extravagance" = "opposing extravagance"; "to achieve the <u>objective</u> of clarity" = "to be clear")

At the same time, we looked at two groups of nouns that do carry necessary meaning but that drag unnecessary words along with them. To express their meaning more concisely, we changed them to verbs:

- nouns in the construction unnec. verb + noun ("to make an <u>improvement</u> in" = "to improve")

- "third word" nouns in the construction unnec. verb + unnec.

noun + third word ("to reach the goal of <u>modernization</u>" = "to modernize")

There are also many constructions involving nouns like "improvement" and "modernization" that we did not discuss in Chapter I because they do not include unnecessary words. Yet those too should be edited out wherever possible, simply because the nouns are abstract.

In this chapter we shall consider abstract nouns as a class and see both why and how to avoid them.

Perils of using abstract nouns

Authorities on English consistently condemn the use of abstract language. The consensus is perhaps best summed up by the American scholar Jacques Barzun, a master of the crafts of writing and translation. In his guide for writers, significantly entitled *Simple and Direct*, he makes this recommendation [pp. 16 – 17]:

> Prefer the concrete word to the abstract. Follow that advice and
> you will see your prose gain in lucidity and force. Unneces-
> sary abstraction is one of the worst faults of modern writing
> — the string of nouns held together by prepositions and re-
> lying on the passive voice to convey the enfeebled sense.

In the same way, Ernest Gowers [pp. 78 – 79], addressing British civil servants, singles out the preference for the abstract word as "the greatest vice of present-day writing." He warns in particular that "an excessive reliance on the noun at the expense of the verb will ... insensibly induce a habit of abstraction, generalisation and vagueness."

The authors of books on writing often use metaphors comparing the use of abstract nouns to an infection. Fowler [p. 5] calls it the "disease" of "abstractitis." William Zinsser [pp. 116 – 117] speaks of "dead" sentences and the blight of "creeping nounism." And Wilson Follett, whose *Modern American Usage* is as much a classic as Fowler's *Dictionary of Modern English Usage*, urges writers [p. 230] to "avoid abstract nouns like the plague."

Sentences based on abstract nouns

To see how abstract nouns undermine straightforward communication we have only to look at the following example, in which the same idea is expressed in two different ways:

A: The <u>prolongation</u> of the <u>existence</u> of this temple is due to the <u>solidity</u> of its <u>construction</u>.

B: This temple *has endured* because *it was solidly built*.

The first version contains four abstract nouns, while the second has none. Not only do the nouns make the statement nearly twice as long, but they also make it pretentious, wooden, and hard to understand.

Chinglish abounds in sentences that rely chiefly on nouns to express their meaning. Here are three examples taken from draft translations:

- A curtailment of both city and town population as well as streamlining of administrative personnel for an enhancement of work efficiency constitutes an important aspect in our tasks of adjustment.

- With stability of currency and prices achieved, there had to be readjustment of industry and commerce as well as improved communications throughout the country, in accordance with the new conditions and demands, so that they could serve the restoration of production.

- The basic requirements of the struggle against Right-leaning conservatism are the further development and consolidation of the people's dictatorship in our country, the early accomplishment of socialist transformation, the overfulfillment of the state plan for industrial development, and the rapid progress of the technical transformation of the national economy.

The preference for abstract language is not, of course, unique to Chinglish. If the advice-givers make such a point of condemning it, that is precisely because it pervades so much of the writing of native speakers of English.

Abstract nouns are the common coin of academic institutions, government bureaucracies, the military establishment, large corporations, and so on (groups for which obscurity is often an advantage). Abstract nouns are also favored by many ordinary citizens, when they wish to sound authoritative or scientific.

Following are three more examples, this time from the English produced by native speakers, of what has been termed "the noun style." Like the Chinglish sentences cited above, they illustrate what Gowers [p. 79] calls "the habit of using abstract words to say in a complicated way something that might be said simply and directly."

Note that the proposed revisions are based on strong verbs in the active voice and on concrete nouns that one might use in everyday speech.

173

- From an article in a U.S. journal of higher education :

A: The age distribution of higher education faculty necessitates immediate implementation of innovative early retirement programs.

B: Because *there are so many older teachers in colleges and universities, we should* immediately *introduce* innovative programs for early retirement.

- From the instructions by a manufacturer of cookware, explaining what to do if the screw attaching the handle to a pot works loose :

A: In such a case, simple application of a screwdriver should be used to tighten screw. Failure to tighten the screw can eventually lead to disengagement of the handle.

B: *If this happens,* simply *tighten* the screw with a screwdriver; *otherwise,* the handle *may come off*.

[Apparently, in the attempt to imitate scientific jargon, the writer of these instructions failed to notice that one cannot use "application" to tighten a screw.]

- From a clothing manufacturer's advertisement for a seminar entitled "Dressing for Objectives":

A: It's a highly informative presentation on image packaging and impression management for business professionals.

B: It's a highly informative presentation that *shows how* business executives *can dress to create a favorable impression*.

As can be seen from these examples, even a few abstract nouns in a short sentence make it difficult to grasp what the writer is trying to say. In a longer sentence, if nouns begin to multiply, they impede understanding even more.

And if nouns proliferate to the point where they spread first throughout the paragraph, then down the entire page, the reader, tired of having to go over every sentence twice in order to make sense of it, may simply abandon the struggle. When that happens, the nouns have indeed become a deadly plague, and it is the reader who has succumbed.

Combating the plague

As we saw in Chapter I, if a noun is empty or redundant, it can simply be deleted. If, however, it carries a necessary element of meaning, the translator must find some other way of dealing with it.

The usual solution is to transform the noun into a different part of speech. We shall look at three ways of doing this and then at an alternative solution that may be useful if these do not work.

1. *Replacing the noun with a verb*

This is the commonest device and the first to consider. It is the one we have used repeatedly, starting in Chapter I, to deal with the unnec. verb + noun constructions ("make an improvement" = "improve").

It can be used in many other situations as well. For example:

A: Adherence to Marxism is vital to China, and so is adherence to socialism.

B: It is vital for us to *adhere* to Marxism and socialism.

A: otherwise, there can be no achievements in our work

B: otherwise, we can *achieve* nothing

A: such behavior on the part of leading cadres will encourage extravagance

175

B: if leading cadres *behave* that way, they will encourage extravagance

A: <u>reading</u> of newly published materials is also important

B: it is also important to *read* newly published materials

2. *Replacing the noun with a gerund*

As you will recall from your study of English grammar, a gerund is the "-ing" form of a verb that functions as a noun. In the example just above, "reading" is a gerund; "replacing" in the subtitles is another.

Gerunds, which are part verb, part noun, partake of the nature of both. Like nouns, they can be heavy and awkward — that is why we changed "reading" to "to read." But they also inherit some of the virtues of their parent verbs. Like verbs, gerunds can impart motion to a sentence that is stiff and lifeless. And because, like verbs, they usually require the writer to express a subject or a direct object — that is, to say plainly who is doing what — they can clarify meaning.

For these reasons, it is often useful to substitute gerunds for nouns, as in the following examples:

A: economic <u>revitalization</u> will be an arduous task

B: *revitalizing* the economy will be an arduous task

A: the company began its <u>issuance</u> of 100 million foreign currency B shares yesterday

B: the company began *issuing* 100 million foreign currency B shares yesterday

A: we shall transform the national bourgeoisie through <u>cooperation</u> with it

B: we shall transform the national bourgeoisie by *cooperating*

176

with it

A: we have to concentrate our efforts on agricultural <u>reinforce-ment</u>

B: we have to concentrate on *strengthening* agriculture

[Review: "Efforts" was eliminated because it is understood in "concentrate."]

3. *Replacing the noun with an adjective or adverb*

Sometimes good results can be achieved by substituting an adjective (or a verb + adjective) or, more rarely, an adverb:

A: this accounts for the <u>unsoundness</u> in organization of these enterprises

B: this accounts for the *poor* organization of these enterprises

A: silk undershirts are rich in <u>elasticity</u>

B: silk undershirts are (highly) *elastic*

A: facts will prove the <u>correctness</u> of these policies

B: facts will prove that these policies are *correct*

A: we must guard against <u>blindness</u> in action

B: we must guard against acting *blindly*

[Note that the second noun, "action," has been replaced by the gerund "acting."]

An alternative solution : "spelling it out"

Sometimes the noun construction is so condensed, or so vague, that it takes more than a change of form to produce an understandable sentence in English. In that case, the translator may have to introduce a few new words to "spell out" the meaning:

A: The practice of indiscriminate <u>abolition</u> tallies with neither

177

Mao Zedong Thought nor the scientific method.

B: *Abolishing all rules* indiscriminately is not consistent either with Mao Zedong Thought or with the scientific method.

[Review: "The practice of" is only a useless category noun.]

A: A Beijing computer newspaper even makes the point that China is entering a PC era that is going to be characterized by the <u>dominance</u> of national brands.

B: A Beijing computer newspaper even makes the point that China is entering a PC era in which national brands *will dominate the market*.

A: Can anyone imagine that Hong Kong is free from <u>obstacles</u> or sabotaging <u>forces</u>?

B: Can anyone imagine that there are no forces in Hong Kong *that might engage in* obstruction or sabotage?

A: it is important to give full scope to the <u>role</u> of experts

B: it is important to take full advantage of the *knowledge and abilities* of experts

Here, of course, as at any time when you add to the English version an element that is not explicit in the Chinese, you must be particularly careful that your interpretation of the original is correct.

A special form of the plague

There is one particular form of the over-use of nouns that deserves special consideration. It is the tendency to employ them as adjectives modifying other nouns.

Using a single noun as an adjective

First, it should be acknowledged that using a single noun as an

178

adjective is entirely legitimate in English. Nothing could be more natural than to refer to "an <u>army</u> officer," "the <u>street</u> corner," "<u>drug</u> addiction," or "an <u>income</u> tax." The meaning of such neat phrases is clear at once. No one would suggest that it is necessary to revise them using prepositions: "an officer in the army," "the corner of the street," "addiction to drugs," or "a tax on income."

Longer nouns can be used in this way just as easily, when no equivalent adjectives are available. "<u>Government</u> department," "<u>application</u> form," "<u>university</u> education," "<u>television</u> set," and countless other such phrases are no more awkward and no more difficult to understand than the ones just cited.

This does not mean, however, that you should feel free to use any given noun to modify any other. Outside the circle of familiar combinations like the ones above, it is well to exercise caution. Most often the sentence will be clearer and flow more naturally if the noun is not made to serve as an adjective.

Take this sentence for example:

- The method of <u>work</u> evaluation and <u>workpoints</u> allotment should be changed.

Here the use of "work" to modify "evaluation" and of "workpoints" to modify "allotment" gives readers pause. These are not combinations that they are used to encountering. And their understanding is slowed by the unnatural word order, which in each pair conceals the true relation between adjective and noun.

In ordinary, straightforward discourse, the idea would be expressed like this:

- The method of evaluating work and allotting workpoints should

179

be changed.

In this version, "work" and "workpoints" are plainly the direct objects of "evaluating" and "allotting," and the clarification speeds readers on their way.

Using two nouns as adjectives

The use of two nouns to make a compound adjective is also acceptable when its sense is easy to grasp. There is no need, for instance, to spell out the meaning of "a hospital maternity ward" as "a ward set aside for the care of maternity cases in a hospital." There are a great many familiar combinations like this: "water conservancy project," "malaria eradication campaign," "minority nationality areas," "Peking opera company," and so on.

Using three or more nouns as adjectives

In special circumstances, even compounds made of three nouns can be understood. Probably no reader would stumble over "a State Planning Commission document." The capital letters tie the elements of the compound together as the title of an organization, preventing confusion.

Instances of this sort, however, are exceptional. The general rule is that no more than two nouns should be combined into an adjective modifying another noun.

The phrases "lung cancer," "cancer research," "research project" and "project design" are all perfectly intelligible and commonly used. In an article in which such terms came up frequently, we might even be able to speak of "lung cancer research" without slowing the reader down. But that does not give us license to write "the lung cancer research project design," in the pleasant belief that

180

we have come up with a more concise substitute for "the design of the research project on lung cancer."

Compound modifiers as long as this one are not uncommon in Chinglish. Typically, they consist of several nouns (or nouns plus adjectives) strung together without prepositions or other connecting words. Diligent readers who take the trouble to study a sequence like "the lung cancer research project design" may eventually perceive what the writer has in mind. But what are they to make of a sequence like "State key protection relic sites"? Can anyone tell which word modifies which, or what these sites might be?

The following strings of nouns have all appeared in Chinese publications for foreigners:

- power supply business regions
- China's conformity assessment system
- 1998 China Daily Newspaper Group Subscription Consultancy Day
- China's first National Urban Construction Archive Sector Achievements Expo

In the last example, the series includes not only nouns but also some true adjectives ("first," "National," "Urban"). But even when that is the case, phrases like these are so highly compressed that one can only guess at their meaning.

The reason that strings of nouns appear so often in draft translations is, of course, that they are literal renderings of the original. Chinese characters are commonly juxtaposed without written links, and Chinese readers readily understand the invisible connections between them. But carried over into English, the pattern is both awkward and ambiguous, when it is not simply incomprehensible.

181

When a noun-as-adjective construction is difficult to understand, the translator should revise the sentence to clarify the relations between the words. Following are three principal ways to do this — plus a fourth, if all else fails.

1. The construction can be treated like any other manifestation of the noun plague. That is, when there are two or three nouns together, one of them can be converted into another part of speech. Here are some examples, starting with the one cited above:

A: The method of work evaluation and workpoints allotment should be changed.

B: The method of *evaluating* work and *allotting* workpoints should be changed.

[In this instance, the second noun of each pair — the one being modified — was changed to a gerund. "Work" and "workpoints" then automatically found their normal places as direct objects.]

A: measures adopted by local governments in soil erosion control include the following

B: measures adopted by local governments to *control* soil erosion include the following

[Here again, the noun being modified was changed, this time to a verb. As a result, "soil erosion" followed naturally as the direct object of "control."]

A: the Party's expanded leadership capacity in struggles

B: the Party's expanded capacity to *lead* struggles

[In this instance, it was the noun being used as an adjective that was changed to a verb. This put the three ideas "leadership," "capacity" and "struggles" in their normal English order, making the relations between them instantly understandable.]

A: "Most of the technology transformation should be placed under the control of the market," Lu said.

B: "Most of the *technological* transformation should be placed under the control of the market," Lu said.

[Here again, it was the noun being used as an adjective that was changed, this time to the corresponding true adjective.]

In certain circumstances, changing a noun to another part of speech will also serve to break up a longer sequence of nouns (or of nouns plus adjectives):

A: China's meteorological system modernization drive

B: China's drive to *modernize* its meteorological system

A: the reform of the science and technology management system

B: the reform of the system for *managing* science and technology

A: the State assets management institutions

B: the institutions responsible for *managing* State assets

In the first example, one of the nouns was changed to a verb. In the second and third, a noun was changed to a gerund. In each case the other nouns in the phrase became direct objects. Thus, an undifferentiated series of words was sorted into grammatically related parts.

2. In some constructions made of two or three nouns it is possible to retain all of them as nouns, providing a preposition is

183

<u>introduced</u> to show the connection between them:

A: during the economic <u>recovery period</u> in the early 1950s

B: during the period *of* economic recovery in the early 1950s

A: scientific and technological experts now take part in economic and social <u>policy decisions</u>

B: scientists and technicians now take part in decisions *on* economic and social policy

A: <u>research topic selection</u> should also be guided by the market

B: the selection *of* research topics should also be guided by the market

~This method too can sometimes be used to break up a string of nouns. Even a very long sequence will become intelligible when appropriate prepositions are inserted:

A: Golmud is an important <u>personnel and materials transfer center</u>

B: Golmud is an important center *for* the transfer *of* personnel and materials

A: Wan Wenpeng, leader of the provincial <u>drug abuse control consultancy expert group</u>

B: Wan Wenpeng, leader of the province's group *of* expert consultants *on* the control *of* drug abuse

[Note that the abstract "consultancy" was changed to concrete "consultants."]

A: the <u>China Foreign Experts Employment Contract Disputes Arbitration Commission</u>

B: China's Commission *for* Arbitration *of* Contract Disputes *with* Foreign Experts

184

[Review: "Employment" can be omitted as a self-evident modifier.]

3. Sometimes the same clarifying effect can be achieved by <u>using a hyphen</u>. Take a phrase like "two noun combinations that form compound adjectives." This expression leaves the reader in doubt about its meaning.

A revision that supplies the preposition "of" dispels the doubt at once. "Combinations of two nouns that form compound adjectives" makes it clear that we are not talking about "two combinations of nouns."

But a revision that supplies a hyphen will serve as well. If we write "two-noun combinations that form compound adjectives," the "two" plainly modifies "noun," and both together modify "combinations."

In the same way, to make sure the reader does not have even a brief moment of misunderstanding, "mobile phone users" could be changed either to "users of mobile phones" or to "mobile-phone users." "An increase in grain and cotton production" could become either "an increase in production of grain and cotton" or "an increase in grain- and cotton-production."

There are many such hyphenated adjectives so common that the reader slides over them as easily as if they were single words: "twentieth-century writers," "Right-wing attacks," "a fur-bearing animal," "a low-salt diet," etc. Apart from such familiar compounds, however, the structure using the preposition is generally preferable, being simpler and more readily understood.

If you do decide to employ a hyphen, you should give some

185

thought to its placement and to the placement of the compound created. The everyday English written by native speakers of the language shows often enough that carelessness in these matters can create confusion.

For example, the American nursery school that advertised for a "3-year-old teacher," adding "experience preferred," would have been better advised to seek a "teacher of 3-year-olds." If the cancer clinic in the U.S. that urged women to "perform monthly self-breast exams" had advised them instead to "examine their breasts every month," it would not have raised the question of what a "self-breast" might be. (It would also have avoided a Chinglish construction that only contributes to the gross national product of nouns: to perform exams = to examine.)

4. Sometimes the translator has tried to cram so much information into a noun-as-adjective phrase that it is not enough to change the noun into another part of speech or to insert a preposition or hyphen. Here again, as for other forms of the noun plague, when the usual methods are insufficient, the alternative solution is <u>adding a few words to spell out the meaning</u>.

A: In addition, we should encourage workers to make technological innovation, and put forward <u>rationalization suggestions</u>.

B: In addition, we should encourage workers to make technological innovations and to *suggest ways of rationalizing production*.

A: The establishment of a <u>local specialties company</u> will enable us to use our foreign exchange effectively.

B: If we establish a *company for the export of local specialties*, we shall be able to use our foreign exchange effectively.

A: Shareholding restructuring of State enterprises was encouraged during the landmark 15th Party Congress held last month.

B: During the landmark 15th Party Congress held last month, State enterprises were encouraged to *restructure by introducing a system of shareholding*.

Twenty more examples of revision

The same basic format that was used for the twenty examples of revision in each chapter of Part One is used here and in corresponding sections throughout Part Two.

1) A: Analysis is also necessary even for the imperialist camp.

B: It is also necessary to *analyze* even the imperialist camp.

[- A classic example of the ambiguity of abstract nouns. "Analysis" is a vague, floating notion, without either subject or object (whose analysis? of what?). The reader of A-version might just as well understand it to mean that even the imperialist camp has to analyze the opposing forces.

- The noun ("analysis") was changed to a verb ("analyze"). This anchored "analysis" to a direct object ("the imperialist camp") and thus made the meaning unmistakable.]

2) A: On the contrary, refusal to make an effort to examine the mistake and draw lessons from it is bound to lead to loss of face.

B: If, on the contrary, he [the Party member] *refuses* to examine the mistake and to learn from it, he is bound to *lose*

187

face.

[- "Refusal" was changed to a verb with a subject ("he").

- The introduction of a subject then made it possible to replace "lead to loss" with a simple verb ("lose").

- (Review: "Make an effort to" was eliminated as a pointless introductory phrase. "Draw lessons" = unnec. verb + noun, replaced by plain verb "learn.")]

3) A: A man's <u>ascent</u> to the position of a high official meant the <u>advent</u> of a comfortable and wealthy life for his whole family and his <u>attainment</u> to the top of the social ladder signified the <u>rise</u> of all his relatives as well.

B: When a man *ascended* (*or*: climbed) to high position, his whole family *was assured* of an affluent life, and when he *reached* the top of the ladder, all his relatives *rose* as well.

[- "Ascent" was changed to a verb ("ascended").

- "Advent" became a verb + adjective ("was assured of").

- "Attainment" and "rise" were also changed to verbs ("reached" and "rose").

- (Review: "Comfortable and wealthy" = redundant twins, replaced by a single word better than either: "affluent.")]

4) A: <u>Keeping</u> our employees honest and industrious and <u>combating</u> corruption of all kinds are an essential <u>guarantee</u> for the smooth advance in the reform and economic development.

B: If we want to *guarantee* the smooth advance of the reform and economic development, it is essential to *keep* our employees honest and industrious and to *combat* corruption of

188

all kinds.

[- Both gerunds ("keeping" and "combating") and the noun ("guarantee") were changed to verbs.

- (The word order was changed to put the important point — what we must do — at the end of the sentence.)]

5) A: A <u>readjustment</u> of the production targets will facilitate the <u>planning</u> of a more realistic program.

B: *Readjusting* the production targets will make it easier to *plan* a more realistic program.

[- The noun "readjustment" was changed to a gerund, "Readjusting."

- The gerund "planning" was upgraded to a verb, "to plan."]

6) A: Paishanlou gold mine, which formally started operation in June, is a gold mine with the largest <u>production scale</u> and the highest <u>degree</u> of <u>modernization</u> in China.

B: Paishanlou gold mine, which formally started operation in June, is the *largest* and *most modern* in China.

[- First the reviser changed the noun-as-adjective construction in the usual way, using a preposition and returning "production" to its original function as a noun ("the largest scale of production").

- It then became clear that both "scale" and "production" were redundant: a mine "with the largest scale of production" is simply the "largest" mine. Similarly, the mine "with the highest degree of modernization" is the "most modern." Thus, the revision reduced four abstract nouns to two everyday adjectives.

189

- (Review: The second reference to a "gold mine" was simply omitted as an unnec. repetition.)]

7) A: Government departments, schools, factories, and enterprises should fix the number of their employees and set work loads for all of them in accordance with the units' needs. Furthermore, every possible <u>reduction</u> and <u>postponement</u> should be made.

B: Government departments, schools, factories, and enterprises should fix the number of their employees and set work loads for all of them in accordance with the units' needs. Furthermore, whenever it is possible to *reduce* or *postpone an expenditure*, they should do so.

[- Confronted with A-version, the reader wonders "reduction and postponement of <u>what</u>?" This sentence, coming immediately after the one about the number of employees, seems to call for reductions in staff and postponement of any new appointments.

- When the reviser studied the passage as a whole, however, she concluded that the intended sense was reduction and postponement of expenditure.

- By changing the abstract nouns to verbs ("reduce," "postpone"), she made it both possible and necessary to specify a direct object ("an expenditure") that made the meaning clear.]

8) A: Only when the masses feel that the Party and socialism are good in deed can our ideological and disciplinary <u>education</u> or <u>education</u> of socialism and patriotism be effective.

B: Only when the masses see concrete evidence that the Party and

190

socialism are good can we *teach* them to cherish ideals and observe discipline and *imbue* them with socialism and patriotism.

[- Here the noun structure was so compressed that the sense was hard to grasp. The polishers therefore used verbs ("teach," "cherish," "observe" and "imbue") to spell out their understanding of the meaning.

- (The phrase "are good in deed" was changed because the natural expression in English is not "to be good in deed" but "to do good deeds." The sense was apparently that the masses would see "good deeds" as a demonstration of the worth of the Party and socialism. This led to the more idiomatic version "see concrete evidence.")]

9) A: a state firm in Shaoguan, Guangdong Province, was auctioned off to the public last Sunday as a result of its <u>loss-making operation</u>, the China News Service reported

B: a state firm in Shaoguan, Guangdong Province, was auctioned off to the public last Sunday because it *was operating at a loss* (*or*: losing money), the China News Service reported

[- By replacing "as a result of" with "because," the polisher was able to turn the second noun ("operation") into a verb ("was operating").

- Thus the awkward and unusual compound adjective "loss-making" could be transformed into an idiomatic expression familiar to the reader: "operating at a loss."]

10) A: A <u>gift registration system</u> and an <u>income declaration system</u> for government officials have already been established in

some regions of China.

B: Systems under which government officials must *register* gifts and *declare* their income have already been established in some regions.

[- In the first noun-as-adjective phrase, the second noun ("registration") was again converted to a verb ("must register"), with the first noun ("gift") as its direct object.

- The second phrase was revised in the same way ("must declare their income").

- (Review: The use of a plural eliminated the need to repeat "system." "Of China" was dropped as a self-evident modifier.)]

11) A: To participate in social labor is an important <u>prerequisite</u> for the <u>emancipation</u> of women.

B: If women *are to be emancipated*, it *is essential* for them to participate in social labor.

[- "Prerequisite" was recast as a verb + adjective ("it is essential").

- "Emancipation" was changed to a verb.

- (The revision is not only simpler and more direct, but has the further advantage of placing the important point — women must participate — in the place of emphasis, at the end of the sentence. Cf. example 4.)]

12) A: This resulted from our <u>lack</u> of <u>vigilance</u> against attack and also from <u>lack</u> of cadres and battle-seasoned troops.

B: This was partly because we *were not sufficiently vigilant* (*or*: on guard) against attack, and partly because we *did not have enough* cadres and battle-seasoned troops.

[- Replacing "this resulted from" with "because" made it possible to turn the first "lack" into a verb + adjective ("were not vigilant").

- By the same token, the second "lack" became a simple verb ("did not have").]

13) A: There was a <u>lack</u> of a sense of urgency in solving these problems [serious accidents caused by criminal negligence] and the <u>fear</u> of some <u>procuratorate officials</u> of offending important people by probing into such cases.

B: There was *no* sense of urgency about solving these problems, and some officials *of* the procuratorates *were afraid* of offending important people by probing such cases.

[- It would have been preferable to convert this "lack" — like the second "lack" in the example above — into a verb with a subject.

- But since it was impossible to tell from the context just who it was that "lacked a sense of urgency" (procuratorates in general? certain officials? local governments?), the polishers had to leave the subject vague.

- Still, they were able to dispose of the noun "lack" by substituting the adjective "no."

- "Fear," for which a subject was provided (the "officials"), could be changed to a verb + adjective ("were afraid").

- The noun-as-adjective construction ("procuratorate officials") was simplified by restoring "procuratorate" to its function as a noun and introducing the preposition "of."]

193

14) A: This unhealthy tendency has emerged partly due to cadres' shortage of the spirit to serve the people and partly due to their lack of understanding of the current situation in the Northeast.

B: This unhealthy tendency has emerged partly because cadres *are not sufficiently dedicated* to serving the people and partly because they *do not understand* the current situation in the Northeast.

[- "Due to" is another phrase that ends in a preposition and therefore leads inevitably to a noun, a pronoun or, at best, a gerund. Cf. "as a result of" in example 9 and "resulted from" in example 12.

- As in both of those examples, the solution here was to substitute "because," which leads to a verb.

- This made it possible to replace both nouns in "shortage of the spirit to serve" with the more idiomatic verb + adjective construction "are not sufficiently dedicated to serving."

- It also made it possible to change the two nouns in "lack of understanding" to a simple verb, "do not understand."]

15) A: This would not only be a hindrance to the people of different nationalities in exchanging experience with and learning from each other but also a great disadvantage to the development of culture.

B: This would not only *make it difficult* for people of different nationalities to *exchange* experience and *learn* from each other, but would also *impede* the development of culture.

[- "Be a hindrance" (an unnec. verb + noun) was changed

194

to "make it difficult" (a verb + adjective).

- This made it possible to convert the gerunds "exchanging" and "learning" to verbs ("exchange," "learn").
- "Be a disadvantage" was then turned into a verb as well: "would impede."]

16) A: there is the <u>likelihood</u> that you will easily commit errors of national <u>discrimination</u>

   B: you *are likely* to make the mistake of *discriminating* against the minority nationalities

   [- The noun "likelihood" was changed to a verb + adjective ("you are likely").

   - The ambiguous phrase "national discrimination" was spelled out with a gerund ("discriminating against"). (Note that "national discrimination"— if it means anything — would be "discrimination on a national scale" or "nationwide discrimination," which is not the intent here.)]

17) A: it is also imperative for <u>success</u> to improve the <u>leadership structure</u> of the enterprises and give fuller <u>scope</u> to the <u>role</u> of the Party organization as the political core

   B: to *be successful*, an enterprise must improve the structure *of* its leadership and *ensure* that the Party organization *functions* as the political core

   [- The noun "success" was changed to a verb + adjective ("to be successful").

   - The noun-as-adjective phrase "leadership structure" was broken up with the preposition "of" ("the structure of its leadership").

- "Scope" and "role" — two of the vaguest abstract nouns in Chinglish — were both dispensed with, in favor of a simple structure using two precise verbs ("ensure" and "functions").]

And now let us see what the revisers did to lighten up the three examples of the noun plague in Chinglish that were cited in the beginning.

18) A: A <u>curtailment</u> of both <u>city and town population</u> as well as <u>streamlining</u> of administrative personnel for an <u>enhancement</u> of <u>work efficiency</u> constitutes an important aspect in our <u>tasks</u> of <u>adjustment</u>.

B: An important aspect of *adjusting* the economy is to *reduce* the population *of* cities and towns and to *streamline* administrative personnel so as to *increase* efficiency.

[- "Adjustment" was replaced with the gerund "adjusting." This made it possible to introduce a direct object ("the economy"), which clarified the meaning.

- "Curtailment," "streamlining," and "enhancement" were all changed to simple verbs, ("reduce," "streamline," and "increase").

- The noun-as-adjective construction "city and town population" was simplified with the preposition "of."

- (As in examples 4 and 11, the order of ideas was changed to place the main point — the need for "curtailment" and "streamlining" — at the end of the sentence rather than the beginning.)

- (<u>Review</u>: "Work" and "tasks" add nothing to the sense and were therefore deleted.)]

196

19) A: With <u>stability</u> of currency and prices achieved, there had to
be <u>readjustment</u> of industry and commerce as well as improved communications throughout the country, in accordance with the new conditions and demands, so that they
could serve the <u>restoration</u> of production.

B: Once the currency and prices *were stabilized*, to *help restore*
production we had to *readjust* industry and commerce and
improve communications throughout the country, in accordance with the new conditions and new demands.

[- "Stability" was replaced by a verb. (<u>Review</u>: "To achieve
stability" = "to stabilize").

- "Readjustment" was changed to a verb in the active voice,
which meant introducing the subject "we." It followed
that "improved" would also become a verb, with the same
subject.

- "Serve" was replaced with "help." This made it possible
to change "restoration" to a verb ("restore"), with "production" as its direct object.

- (Again the order of ideas was changed. "To help restore
production" was moved up toward the beginning of the
sentence. This left the more important position to the
more important idea, "we had to readjust ... and
improve ....")]

20) A: The basic requirements of the struggle against Right-leaning
conservatism are the further <u>development</u> and <u>consolida-
tion</u> of the people's dictatorship in our country, the early
<u>accomplishment</u> of socialist transformation, the
<u>overfulfillment</u> of the state plan for industrial
development, and the rapid <u>progress</u> of the technical

transformation of the national economy.

B: The basic requirements of the struggle against Right-leaning conservatism are that we must *consolidate* the people's dictatorship, *complete* the socialist transformation as quickly as possible, *overfulfill* the state plan for industrial development, and *speed up* the technical transformation of the economy.

[- "That we must" was brought in. This simple addition made it possible to change most of the nouns that followed to active verbs with a subject and direct objects ("consolidate," "complete," "overfulfill," and "speed up").

- (Review: The first "development" was deleted because the polishers thought that its sense was included in "consolidation" — that is, that in this context the two were redundant twins. "In our country" was eliminated as a self-evident modifier. "National" was dropped because it too could be taken for granted.)]

Twenty exercises

Before working on an exercise, you may find it useful to underline the abstract noun or nouns you wish to eliminate, as was done in the examples above.

Remember that, as in Part One, the versions suggested in the Key to Exercises at the back of the book (starting on page 538) are not necessarily the only acceptable ones.

1) we do not have the facilities necessary for the production of alloy steel

2) Without the mastery of essential skills, you will prove unequal to

this kind of job.

3) we must make them understand the protracted nature of the struggle in the Northeast

4) One reason is our lack of understanding about certain theories and principles, which explains why there is a need to study more theory.

5) At the same time, the U. S. government announced the severance of its diplomatic relations with the Taiwan authorities, termination of the U. S.-Taiwan Joint Defense Treaty, and withdrawal of American troops from Taiwan.

6) The principal criteria for judging the reform and the open policy are whether they serve the development of the productive forces of our socialist society, the increase in the overall national strength of our country, and the improvement of the people's living standards.

7) the transformation of these different sectors of the economy calls for the adoption of different forms and speeds

8) The training of cadres for the land reform and people's tribunals and the expansion and reorganization of peasants' associations are now in progress.

9) "Zhang is always ready to offer help to the farmers, who usually lack knowledge of planting and caring for fruit trees," says Cai Lihong, a doctoral student under Zhang's tutorship.

10) The implementation of general policies in the transition period and the building of socialism call for improving the people's health.

11) In order to stabilize currency and prices, there had to be a balancing of national expenditure and revenue and a guarantee of sufficient supplies of goods.

12) We shall abolish this class through utilization, restriction, and transformation of the capitalist economy.

13) The practice in the nine months since the Third Plenary Session of the Twelfth Central Committee has proved the correctness of the price reform.

14) It is our estimate that once the money supply in the various localities has been reduced there will be nationwide price stability prior to November 25.

15) unless these problems are handled satisfactorily, there will be no successes in the implementation of various policies

16) The Asian Development Bank on Wednesday approved two loans, totaling $ 256 million, to finance water shortage alleviation and air pollution reduction projects.

17) "An efficient residential property development and management system is to our advantage," said Tan Kian Siew, executive deputy general manager of BJ Minghua Properties.

18) He made these remarks during a talk with Sakurauchi Yoshio and other leading members of the Japanese International Trade Promotion Association delegation.

19) This practice has helped ensure that no needy student will drop out because of the self-pay tuition.

20) "The State assets administrative authorities should contribute toward the promotion of the process," said Zhang at a seminar

organized by the Chinese Institute for State Property Management.

VIII. Pronouns and Antecedents

As you will recall from your studies, there are many different types of pronouns in English. Grammar books distinguish seven or eight, but here we need concern ourselves with only three — the ones that are generally used to replace nouns.

These three are as follows:

- <u>personal pronouns</u>: I, you, he, she, it, we, they (plus their objective and possessive forms — me/my/mine, him/his, etc.)
- <u>relative pronouns</u>: which, that, who/whom/whose, etc.
- <u>demonstrative pronouns</u>: this, that, these, those

Many examples of the use of such pronouns have already been given in Chapter V, Repeated References to the Same Thing. It will be useful to recall two of them (from pages 127 and 140 − 141/535):

A: We have not met with too many difficulties in the course of <u>the reform</u>, and in general <u>the reform</u> is proceeding smoothly.

B: We have not met with too many difficulties in the course of *the reform*, and in general *it* is proceeding smoothly.

A: We failed to attach equal importance to both <u>types of work</u>, and there was no proper coordination between the two <u>types of work</u>.

B: We failed to attach equal importance to both *types of work*, and there was no proper coordination between *them*.

These are simple examples. Presented with a second reference to "the reform" or to "types of work," any advanced student of English would recognize the need for a pronoun to avoid repetition and would have no trouble selecting the right one.

Unfortunately, pronouns are not always so easy to handle; even for native speakers of English, their use presents numerous pitfalls. Jacques Barzun, whose book *Simple and Direct* is primarily addressed to educated American adults, begins his remarks on the subject [p. 75] with an ominous subtitle, "Pronouns: The slightest slip is fatal," and a warning that the reader is about to enter "the dangerous wilderness of Pronouns."

For native speakers of Chinese, the difficulties with English pronouns are compounded by the differences between the two languages. As you know, pronouns are used in many places in English where they are not required in Chinese. Indeed, some English pronouns — the relatives, for instance ("which," "that," "who," etc.) — do not even have Chinese equivalents. Also, most pronouns in English have more forms to choose from than do the corresponding pronouns in Chinese.

It is only to be expected, then, that Chinese who have not yet gained a complete mastery of English might make mistakes in using pronouns. In fact, they often do. In this chapter we shall examine the most common types of errors and discuss how to correct them.

Correct use of pronouns

Early on in your study of English you learned that certain pronouns (the personal pronouns and "who") had different "cases" — that is, that their form varied according to their grammatical function. For native speakers of Chinese, which seldom makes such

203

distinctions, case is no doubt a difficult notion at first. But by now, it can be assumed, you automatically use the right forms: "he," "they," "who," etc. for the subject of a verb; "him," "them," "whom," etc. for its direct or indirect object; "his," "their," "whose," etc. for the possessive.

Using the correct case is a great help to readers, because it shows them what role the pronoun plays in the grammatical structure of the sentence. But that is not all they need to know. If readers are to understand what you have written, they also need to be certain what noun the pronoun is replacing.

Every pronoun — whether or not its form varies with case — must have a clear, logical antecedent. And that antecedent must be a stated word that readers can immediately recognize as the one to which the pronoun refers. Otherwise, they will be either confused or, worse, misled.

Rules governing the use of antecedents

Barzun [p. 75] describes the problem of providing clear antecedents for pronouns as "the greatest difficulty in the writing of English prose." This difficulty will be much reduced, however, if you bear in mind four common-sense rules.

To be clear, the antecedent of a pronoun must be:

1. explicitly stated (not merely implied)
2. unambiguous (not possibly one word, possibly another)
3. close to the pronoun (not so far away that the connection between the two words is hard to perceive)
4. in grammatical agreement with the pronoun (i.e., in the same "person," number and gender)

Returning to the examples cited above, we find that in both revisions all four of these rules have been respected:

B: We have not met with too many difficulties in the course of the <u>reform</u>, and in general <u>it</u> is proceeding smoothly.

   [- 1. *Explicit* : The antecedent of the pronoun "it" is stated earlier: "reform."

   - 2. *Unambiguous* : There is no other word in the sentence that the pronoun could refer to.

   - 3. *Nearby* : The antecedent "reform" comes only a few words before the pronoun "it."

   - 4. *In agreement* : The pronoun "it" agrees with its antecedent, "reform," in person (both are third person), in number (both are singular), and in gender (both are neuter). This grammatical agreement cements the bond between the two words.]

B: We failed to attach equal importance to both <u>types</u> of work, and there was no proper coordination between <u>them</u>.

   [- 1. *Explicit* : The antecedent of the pronoun "them" is plainly stated: "types."

   - 2. *Unambiguous* : No other noun is competing for the role of antecedent (there are no other plural nouns).

   - 3. *Nearby* : The antecedent "types" is close to the pronoun "them."

   - 4. *In agreement* : The pronoun "them" agrees with its antecedent, "types," in person (both are third person), in number (both are plural), and in gender (both are neuter). Again, the grammatical agreement confirms the close relation between the two words, indicating that they mean the same thing.]

We shall now consider examples of the problems that arise for readers when the antecedent of a pronoun is *not* clear — that is, when one or another of these four rules has been neglected.

1. When antecedents are not explicitly stated

If the antecedent of a pronoun is not clear, most often it is simply because the antecedent is missing. It may be implied, but it is not present on the page.

When a pronoun has no stated antecedent, it will either a) remain unattached, or b) attach itself to some word that it was not intended to refer to. Consequently, the reader trying to understand the sentence in question will either a) be left in doubt, or b) mistake the sense.

Following are examples of both kinds of errors.

a) *Unattached pronouns: reader is left in doubt*

Here is a simple example of a pronoun which, having no expressed antecedent, remains afloat:

- The second question concerns close planting. It should neither be spread out too thinly nor planted too closely.

Since the subject of the second sentence was only implied in the Chinese, the translator supplied one, the pronoun "it." But he or she neglected to provide an antecedent.

The polisher, a more experienced translator, discarded the pronoun and introduced a specific noun to serve as the subject, even though the equivalent character did not appear in the original:

- The second question concerns close planting. *Crops* should be neither spread out too thinly nor planted too closely.

In this instance, a reader of the draft version could probably have guessed what the first translator meant. Often, however, a pronoun without an expressed antecedent can be genuinely baffling. Here is another "it" left unattached:

- The shareholding system and joint stock partnership which have been introduced in China over the past few years have also raised doubts among some people. They can get an answer from Jiang Zemin's report to the recently completed 15th National Congress of the Communist Party of China held last week — it is because China is in the primary stage of socialism.

Could any reader of this paragraph tell what "it" represents — in other words, what is to be explained by the fact that China is in the primary stage of socialism? Since the nature of the "doubts" is never specified, the reader does not know what question is answered by the statement, "it is because China is in the primary stage of socialism."

There are several possible meanings. One is that the shareholding system and joint stock partnership are necessary because China is in the primary stage of socialism. Another is that those institutions are legitimate because China is in this stage. Another is that they are only temporary or experimental for that reason. It is impossible to tell.

This passage, which appeared in a Chinese publication, was probably not translated from Chinese but written directly in English. Since we cannot refer to an original Chinese text to establish the

207

meaning, it is not possible to suggest a revision. The example is cited here only to show how a pronoun for which no antecedent is provided can make a sentence unintelligible.

b) *Wrongly attached pronouns*: *reader mistakes the sense*

In both of the examples just given ("It should neither be spread out too thinly etc." and "it is because China is in the primary stage etc."), the pronoun, having no stated antecedent for an anchor, simply remains adrift. More often, however, a pronoun with a missing antecedent will fasten onto some other word that *is* available.

A pronoun that is separated from its true partner has a tendency to form an attachment to any potential mate at hand. (In this respect, it resembles the fellow in the song who candidly confesses, "When I'm not near the girl I love, I love the girl I'm near.") And when that happens, the reader is inevitably given the wrong impression.

Following is an example with a personal pronoun, "his." It is the draft version of a footnote identifying a text that appeared in Volume I of the *Selected Works of Zhou Enlai*:

- Minutes of an interim telephone report to <u>Mao Zedong</u> during <u>his</u> investigation in Handan Prefecture, Hebei Province.

The true antecedent of "his" — the person making the investigation — is Zhou Enlai. But Zhou is nowhere to be seen, and the pronoun attaches itself instead to the person who is visible on the page, Mao Zedong. The reader's inevitable interpretation is that Mao is the one doing the investigating.

Since all the pieces in this book were the works of Premier Zhou, the polishers thought it was unnecessary to specify who had

208

written this one. Accordingly, in the published version the misleading pronoun was simply omitted:

> - Minutes of an interim report telephoned to Mao Zedong during an investigation in Handan Prefecture, Hebei Province.

Here is another example of a pronoun which, given no true antecedent, tries to tie itself to a false one. This time, it is the demonstrative pronoun "this":

> - The Shanghai chapter of the Democratic National Construction Association, the Shanghai Association of Industrialists and Merchants for Progress, and the Chongqing Chamber of Commerce, among others, issued statements in support of the students' patriotic actions and demanded the <u>withdrawal</u> of U.S. troops. <u>This</u> became a broad-based people's movement, a united front against the U.S. and Chiang Kai-shek.

Although "this" can sometimes be used to refer not just to a single word but to the whole idea expressed in a preceding clause or sentence, in this instance it is not clear what that idea might be. Is it the fact that these organizations issued statements? That they demanded withdrawal of the foreign troops? No — because neither of those elements could become a "movement." Since the translator has provided no antecedent for "this," it attaches itself to the nearest preceding singular noun: "withdrawal."

Thus, the readers' first impression is that the <u>withdrawal</u> of the foreign troops became a broad-based people's movement. Since that reading makes no sense, their next thought is that it was the <u>demand</u> for withdrawal of the troops that became a broad-based people's movement. But there is no "demand" on the page — only

209

"demanded," which cannot serve as the antecedent of "this" because it is not a noun but a verb. So that interpretation cannot be right either. At this point, even an interested reader is likely to give up on the sentence and move on.

When the polisher came upon this problem, he studied the original Chinese passage in context. It was clear to him that the translation was misleading. "This" was indeed intended to refer to the whole preceding sentence. It was supposed to mean "All this" — that is, all the actions taken by other sectors of society. Only, those actions themselves did not "become" a broad-based movement; the sense was rather that they helped to form one.

On the basis of that understanding, he was able to revise the sentence, dispensing with the ambiguous "This":

- The Shanghai chapter of the Democratic National Construction Association, the Shanghai Association of Industrialists and Merchants for Progress, and the Chongqing Chamber of Commerce, among others, issued statements in support of the students' patriotic actions and demanded the withdrawal of U. S. troops. *All this* helped form a broad-based people's movement, a united front against the U.S. and Chiang Kai-shek.

The missing subject

No doubt the frequent appearance in Chinglish of pronouns without antecedents is due to the elliptical nature of the Chinese language. As you know, compared to English, Chinese relies much more on readers to grasp ideas that are not actually spelled out.

For example, Professor Cheng Zhenqiu points out [p. 68] that

210

in Chinese "the grammatical subject is often left out if it can be inferred from the context." He goes on to say that because such an omission is generally unacceptable in English, the translator often has to supply a missing subject. Providing instructive examples — including some in which pronouns were wrongly introduced and others where it was judged better to leave the subject vague — Professor Cheng concludes with the warning [p. 72]: "supplying logical subjects is a very delicate matter and requires a good deal of caution."

That does not mean, however, that you should be discouraged from introducing into an English sentence a subject (or any other element) that is absent from the original but can be "inferred from the context" by Chinese readers. On the contrary, it is precisely the translator's duty to identify those ideas that a native speaker of Chinese understands by implication and to give them overt expression in English.

Admittedly, that is harder (and riskier) than to evade the difficulty by simply supplying a vague "it" or "this," in the hope that readers will somehow "get the idea." But if you make the effort, you will be rewarded with the knowledge that you have met the challenge and successfully communicated the Chinese author's meaning — in other words, that you have produced a professional piece of work.

2. When antecedents are ambiguous

If there is more than one word in a sentence to which a pronoun might refer, readers may not be sure which is the intended antecedent. Here is an example:

- Since the purchase of grain is mostly entrusted to state companies, and grain traders are allowed to carry no more than

50 *jin* with them, <u>their</u> regulating role is restricted.

In this sentence it is not clear whose regulating role is restricted. Does "their" refer to "companies," to "traders," or to both? The simplest way to dispel the doubt is to abandon the pronoun and, referring again to the original to determine the sense, use the noun it was supposed to replace. Better a repetition than an ambiguity:

- Since the purchase of grain is mostly entrusted to state companies, and grain traders are allowed to carry no more than 50 *jin* with them, the *traders'* regulating role is restricted.

[<u>Review</u>: In the final version, in order to replace the abstract noun "role" with a verb and, at the same time, to clarify the meaning, the reviser changed the end of the sentence to: "the traders can do little to regulate the market."]

Antecedents can be even more ambiguous when the same pronoun appears twice in one passage but refers to two different things. Readers are then left on their own to match up the pairs correctly. Consider the following sentence:

- The <u>price</u> of one <u>ton</u> of crude oil is 1,300 yuan ($ 175) on the market, while <u>it</u> is only 800 yuan ($ 96) if <u>it</u> is sold to the government.

There is nothing to indicate that the first "it" refers to the "price" of oil, while the second refers to the "ton" being sold. Readers will no doubt understand what the writer means, but only because they either slide over the shift in antecedents or backtrack and make the mental correction.

A careful reviser would have recast the sentence in such a way

212

that both pronouns had the same antecedent:

- The price of one *ton* of crude oil is 1,300 yuan ($ 175) if *it* is sold on the market but only 800 yuan ($ 96) if *it* is sold to the government.

It is hard to recognize ambiguous antecedents in one of your own sentences, because you know what you meant when you wrote it. Remember, though, that your readers do not, and that you should try to leave them no opportunity to mistake your meaning.

3. When antecedents are too remote

When a pronoun stands too far away from its antecedent, readers may fail to connect the two words. And when the antecedent is too remote, just as when it is missing, the fickle pronoun will very probably cling to another, closer word, distorting the meaning.

Personal pronouns

Here is an example with a personal pronoun, "they":

- In the meantime, the U.S. government increased its aid to the KMT government. In March 1946 the United States successively organized army and navy advisory teams. On June 17 they signed the Sino-American Lend-Lease Agreement, which transferred 51.7 million U.S. dollars' worth of military equipment to the KMT government.

There is only one possible way to understand the "they" in the third sentence: it represents the immediately preceding "teams." But that understanding is quite wrong — it was not the military advisory teams that signed this high-level agreement.

In the revision, the pronoun "they" was dropped and replaced

213

by the true subject of the sentence:

- In the meantime, the U.S. government increased its aid to the KMT. In March 1946 the United States successively organized army and navy advisory teams. On June 17 *the two governments* signed the Sino-American Lend-Lease Agreement, which transferred 51.7 million U.S. dollars' worth of military equipment to the KMT.

Here is another example of a personal pronoun ("their") so far removed from the word it is meant to refer to that the reader mistakes its meaning:

- Li Yili points out that these northern <u>tribes</u> were still in the early stage of feudalism or slavery when they conquered the Han-Chinese populated areas where feudalism had enjoyed its zenith. The refined literature and the wanton lifestyle of the noble <u>Han Chinese</u> were too powerful to resist, while maintaining <u>their</u> own military might became a burden.

It is virtually impossible to read this passage without getting the impression that the Han Chinese were finding it a burden to maintain their military might. It takes at least a second reading to realize that the "their" in the last clause is meant to refer to the northern "tribes" that appeared at the beginning of the preceding sentence. By the time the reader reaches "their own," he or she has already forgotten the "tribes," and the recent mention of "Han Chinese" (also plural) makes them a plausible candidate for the role of antecedent.

It would not have been hard to clarify the meaning of this passage. A polisher would only have had to repeat the noun "tribes," placing it nearer to the pronoun than the competing "Han Chinese"

214

and thus making it the obvious antecedent of "their":

- Li Yili points out that these northern tribes were still in the early stage of feudalism or slavery when they conquered the areas populated by Han-Chinese, where feudalism was at its zenith. The refined literature and luxurious lifestyle of the noble Han Chinese were too powerful for *the tribes* to resist, while *they* found it an increasing burden to maintain *their* own military might.

Relative pronouns

The examples just discussed show that to prevent misunderstanding, personal pronouns ("they," "their," etc.) must stand close to their antecedents. The same principle applies with even greater force to relative pronouns ("which," "that," "who," etc.).

Readers encountering a relative pronoun assume not just that it will be somewhere near the element it refers to, but that it will come immediately after that element. The following examples show the expected arrangement of words:

- Jiang has instructed legal departments to severely punish <u>lawbreakers</u> <u>who</u> have been involved in making and dealing in illegal alcoholic drinks.

- The main peak of this range, <u>Mount Qogir,</u> <u>which</u> stands outside the Qinghai-Tibet Plateau to the northwest, is second in elevation only to Qomolangma.

This unconscious expectation on the reader's part — that the relative pronoun will refer to the immediately preceding noun — is very strong. So strong that if any other noun intervenes between the true antecedent and the relative pronoun, the pronoun will — again

215

— affix itself to that one, whether the connection is logical or not. As may be seen from the following three examples, the result can completely subvert the writer's meaning.

1) First, a simple example taken from a native source (a U.S. newspaper):

- Wanted: Man to take care of <u>cow that</u> does not smoke or drink.

The intended antecedent of "that" is the "man" whose services are being sought in the advertisement. Unfortunately, the pronoun attaches itself to the intervening noun, thus describing the blameless habits of the cow.

To connect the pronoun "that" to the right antecedent, one would only have to move the relative clause — which is merely a misplaced modifier — next to the noun it logically modifies:

- Wanted: *Man that* (*or*, *better*: who) does not smoke or drink to take care of cow.

2) Now, a more complex example taken from Chinglish:

- In October of the same year [1976], the Political Bureau of the CPC Central Committee took decisive measures to shatter <u>the Gang of Four</u>, in <u>which</u> he [Hua Guofeng], Ye Jianying, Li Xiannian, and others played an important role.

In this sentence the translator is trying to use "which" not to represent a single word but to sum up a whole preceding idea. Like the similar use of "this" mentioned on page 209 above, the practice can be useful, and it is generally considered acceptable.

216

But such a construction works only when the antecedent is unmistakable. It may be grammatically defensible, but if it suggests that a specific word (as opposed to a whole clause) is the antecedent of the relative pronoun, it will mislead the reader nonetheless.

It must therefore be used with great care. Barzun [pp. 77 – 78] warns that when "which" and "this" are used to refer "to antecedent ideas — sentences or statements taken as a whole — only the closest attention will prevent ambiguity or blunders."

In the example under consideration, the "which" is intended to refer to the entire preceding clause: "the Political Bureau ... took decisive measures etc." But after the manner of relative pronouns, it fastens upon the nearest preceding noun instead, the "Gang of Four." Consequently, the only possible interpretation of the sentence is that Hua Guofeng and the other leaders played an important role in the Gang of Four. There is no "ambiguity" here, just an outright "blunder" of major proportions.

Unlike the sentence about the virtuous cow, this one cannot be fixed simply by moving the relative clause to another position. To break the unintended link between the pronoun "which" and the false antecedent, "the Gang of Four," we have to provide the pronoun with an appropriate and nearby antecedent:

> - In October of the same year, the Political Bureau of the CPC
>   Central Committee took decisive measures to break up the
>   Gang of Four, *an operation* in *which* he, Ye Jianying,
>   Li Xiannian, and others played an important role.

In this revision the idea to which the pronoun was meant to refer — "the Political Bureau ... took decisive measures etc." — has been summed up in a single word, "operation." And it is now that word,

217

positioned directly before the "which" (the spot formerly occupied by "the Gang of Four"), that stands in the place where readers expect to find the antecedent.

3) Lastly, another example from Chinglish. Here again, the relative pronoun, intended to refer to an entire preceding statement, rejects that antecedent in favor of a closer word, with a result that sabotages the meaning.

> - To enforce the people's democratic dictatorship, we must launch an unremitting struggle against <u>bureaucracy</u>, <u>which</u> is of great importance.

The "which" is meant to represent "we must launch an unremitting struggle etc." But it is attracted instead to the immediately preceding noun "bureaucracy." Thus, the sentence appears to be saying that bureaucracy is very important — the opposite of what the translator intended to convey. No doubt readers who are misled will quickly realize their mistake, but why should they be subjected to even momentary confusion?

As before, to rewrite the sentence so that it says without the slightest ambiguity what it is supposed to mean, we must break the link between the "which" and the false antecedent. In the "Gang of Four" example above, this was accomplished by supplying a proper antecedent and placing it close at hand.

That can be done here too, if we consider that what is important is not "to launch" the struggle but the "struggle" itself — a slightly different interpretation that means virtually the same thing:

> - To enforce the people's democratic dictatorship, we must launch an unremitting struggle against bureaucracy, *a*

struggle which is of great importance.

Another solution would be to discard the "which" and start over with a different construction. Here is one possibility:

- To enforce the people's democratic dictatorship, we must launch an unremitting struggle against bureaucracy. *It is very important to conduct such a struggle.*

The last two examples confirm Professor Barzun's warning about the risks of using "which" to refer to an entire preceding idea. Whenever you come across such a construction in a text you are revising, you should ask yourself if the pronoun clearly refers to the idea in question.

If you find that the antecedent is vague, or that it is not immediately obvious, the possible solutions are the two demonstrated above. You can either (1) sum up the idea in a word or phrase that can serve as a specific and unmistakable antecedent for the "which," or (2) change the relative clause to another construction.

4. When pronouns do not agree with their antecedents

To repeat: a pronoun "agrees" with its antecedent when it is in the same person, number, and gender as the word it represents. As we have seen, this agreement helps the reader recognize that pronoun and antecedent are simply two ways of referring to the same thing. Indeed, the agreement is essential. If the pronoun disagrees with its antecedent, readers have no way of identifying one with the other.

Chinese translators (or journalists writing directly in English) rarely make mistakes in the first and third categories, person and gender. For example, when the antecedent is "recent events" (third person), they are not likely to refer to them with the pronoun "you"

219

(second person). And if the antecedent is "the report" (neuter), they will not refer to it as "he" (masculine).

When Chinese make a mistake in the agreement between pronoun and antecedent, it is almost always a question of number.

Examples of disagreement in number

In the following sentences one of the two words is singular, the other plural:

- If each enterprise goes it alone, they will never be able to improve the quality of their products.

"Each enterprise" is singular, as shown by the singular verb "goes." The pronouns "they" and "their," however, are plural. Correction: "... *it* will never be able to improve the quality of *its* products."

- In the past decade we scored great achievements. These should be attributed to the efforts of the collective and not to me, though I played a part in it.

The antecedent "These" is plural, but the pronoun "it" is singular. Correction: "... though I played a part in *them* ."

In these examples, readers may overlook the errors and correctly guess the intended meaning. But sometimes disagreement between pronoun and antecedent can be quite misleading, as in the following sentence:

- The Carter administration committed itself to the withdrawal of American troops from Taiwan, but in the meantime they adopted the Taiwan Relations Act, which constituted interference in China's internal affairs.

The "Carter administration" is thought of as singular, as

220

evidenced by the singular "itself," but the pronoun that represents the administration is the plural "they." This discrepancy prevents readers from recognizing at once that "administration" is the antecedent of "they" and, worse, leads them to assume for a moment that the antecedent is the American "troops," which are plural like the pronoun. Correction: "... but in the meantime, *it* adopted the Taiwan Relations Act."

Mistakes made by native speakers of English

As Barzun suggests, pronouns cause almost as much trouble to native speakers of English as they do to persons who have learned it as a second language. It is not surprising, then, that native speakers make all the same mistakes that are found in Chinglish. They too use pronouns whose antecedents are missing, ambiguous, too far away, or in grammatical disagreement.

This last error is probably the most common. The following examples betray the writers' confusion as to whether a given antecedent is singular or plural:

- *From a letter from a U.S. health insurance company to a*
   client :

At this time <u>Medicare</u> is updating <u>their</u> files and is requesting a
   copy of your Medicare Card.

[Medicare starts out singular ("<u>is</u> updating"), immediately afterward becomes plural ("<u>their</u> files") and then reverts to singular ("<u>is</u> requesting").]

- *From the description on the cover of a tape recording of the*
   Bible in English :

Alexander Scourby's dramatic and moving <u>narration</u> of the Bible has touched and inspired millions — as they will you!

[Again the switch from singular ("has touched") to plural ("they will"). Perhaps the writer was distracted by the intervening plural "millions."]

- *From the U.S. newsweekly* The Nation:

By muffling its own voice, the media limit their own usefulness.

[One group of writers holds that "media" is singular ("its"), while another insists that it is plural ("their"). Here it has been made first one, then the other — a compromise that surely neither party to the dispute would find acceptable.]

- *From an advertisement for tennis rackets, quoted by William Safire in the* New York Times:

Anyone who thinks a Yonex racquet has improved their game, please raise your hand.

[Here, the inconsistency as to number is compounded by inconsistency as to person. "Anyone" (third person, singular, as shown by "thinks") is referred to first by "their" (third person, plural), and then by "your" (second person, singular). Since the writer was no doubt a well educated professional, this spectacular disregard for agreement should probably be attributed not to an ignorance of English grammar but to an ill-advised attempt at "folksy" informality.]

Twenty more examples of revision

Missing antecedent

1) A: I can give you some records made by Cheng Yanqiu. I enjoy

his records very much. When I can't sleep well, I listen to them a while. In the old society they were looked down upon. Now we call them performing artists, and we are all on an equal footing.

B: I can give you some records made by Cheng Yanqiu. I enjoy his records very much. When I can't sleep, I listen to them for a while. In the old society *Peking opera performers* were looked down upon. Now we call them performing artists, and we are all on an equal footing.

[- In A-version the inescapable assumption is that "they," like the preceding "them," refers to "records."

- In B-version the logical subject is substituted for the pronoun: "Peking opera performers."]

2) A: When you [Chancellor Helmut Kohl of the then Federal Republic of Germany] visited China in 1974, you and I talked about the danger of war. Now we have slightly different views. We feel that although the danger of war still exists and we still have to remain vigilant, the factors that can prevent a new world war are growing.

B: When you visited China in 1974, you and I talked about the danger of war. Now *we Chinese* have slightly different views. We feel that although the danger of war still exists and we still have to remain vigilant, the factors that can prevent a new world war are growing.

[- The "we" in the second sentence of A-version is meant to represent the Chinese leaders, but they are never mentioned.

- Accordingly, the only possible way of understanding the "we" is that it refers to "you and I" — that is, to

223

Chancellor Kohl and the speaker. This applies to the following "we"s as well.

- To prevent this blunder, the reviser specified "we Chinese."]

3) A: They [the people's governments at all levels] must direct the departments of justice, civil affairs, public security, and culture and education ... to implement the [Marriage] law and combine it as much as possible with the central tasks of agrarian reform and the democratic consolidation of local governments.

B: They must direct the departments of justice, civil affairs, public security, and culture and education ... to ensure that the law is enforced, combining *that task* as much as possible with the central tasks of agrarian reform and the democratic consolidation of local governments.

[- In A-version "it," having no true antecedent, attaches itself to the "law," which is immediately preceding and with which it agrees grammatically. As all but the least attentive readers will recognize by the end of the sentence, the difficulty is that one cannot combine a "law" with "tasks."

- In B-version "it" has been replaced with a sensible noun, "that task" (i.e., the task of implementing the law).

- ("To implement the law" was changed to "to ensure that the law is enforced" for reasons of logic. The government departments named cannot themselves carry out the provisions of the Marriage Law; they can only ensure that the citizens do so.)]

224

4) A: In Africa too, the strong and common voice of the Organization of African Unity is to ask other countries not to interfere in their internal affairs.

B: The African *countries* too, through the Organization of African Unity, demand with one voice that no other country interfere in *their* internal affairs.

[- The "their" in A-version refers to the closely preceding "other countries," which is in any event the only plural antecedent available. Thus "other countries" are being asked not to interfere in their own affairs, which is nonsense.

- In the revision "their" internal affairs is given its missing antecedent, the "African countries."

- "Other countries" (plural) was changed to "no other country" (singular) so that there would be no competing plural antecedent for "their."

- (Review: The sense of "strong" in A-version was incorporated into the verb in B-version: "ask" became "demand," making it possible to eliminate the adjective.)]

5) A: The several million people we have provided for [demobilized KMT troops and former government personnel, shortly after Liberation] will play some useful role. It is our determination to make them productive. We are quite certain of this because this principle was implemented during the War of Resistance Against Japan.

B: The several million people we have provided for will play some useful role. We should be determined to turn them into a productive force. We are quite certain that *this can be done*, because the principle was applied successfully during

225

the War of Resistance Against Japan.

[- In A-version "this" is afloat without a specific antecedent.
There is no way for the reader to tell just what "we are
certain" of. Strictly speaking, the pronoun refers to the
preceding sentence and means "we are quite certain that
we have this determination." Clearly, that is not the intended sense.

- The reviser judged from the Chinese passage as a whole
that the meaning was: "We are quite certain that this can
be done." That is what he put in the revision.]

6) A: Is it possible that a country like this will be brought down so
easily? No, it is not. Neither people in China nor those in
other countries, such as the superpowers and the rich
countries, will be able to do that.

   B: Is it possible that a country like this will be brought down so
easily? No, it is not. Neither people in China nor those in
other countries, such as the superpowers and the rich
countries, have the ability to *bring China down*.

   [- A-version seems logical enough at first, but in fact its
structure will not bear examination.

   - The final pronoun ("will be able to do that") has nothing
to refer to. If the reader, looking back to find an antecedent, asks: "none of these people will be able to do
what?" the only available answer is "be brought down,"
which makes no sense.

   - The problem is that the intended antecedent is in passive
voice — the wrong grammatical form. To serve as an antecedent for "do that" (or "do this" or "do so"), a verb
has to be in active voice.

- Rather than rewrite the first sentence to provide a usable antecedent, the reviser discarded the pronoun. In B-version "to do that" was replaced with the phrase it was meant to represent, "to bring China down."]

Ambiguous antecedent

7) A: Government departments, schools, factories and enterprises should fix the number of <u>their</u> workers and other employees and according to <u>their</u> specific work and production requirements set work loads for all of them.

B: Government departments, schools, factories and enterprises should fix the number of *their* employees and set work loads for all of them in accordance with *the units'* needs.

[- In A-version the first "their" plainly refers to the "government departments etc." The second "their" is meant to do the same, but because of the intervening "workers and other employees" it attaches itself to them instead. Since both antecedents seem to make sense, the reader does not know which is the correct one.

- In B-version the second "their" has been replaced by the noun it represents, "the units'," so that no misunderstanding is possible.

- (In this context there was no need to distinguish between "workers" and "other employees," so both were included in the general term "employees.")

- (Review: There also seemed no need to distinguish between the "work" requirements of some units and the "production" requirements of others; indeed, in context, both words were unnecessary modifiers. "Specific" was

227

likewise judged superfluous. Thus the A-version phrase "specific work and production requirements" was reduced to the single word "requirements," which was then changed to "needs.")]

8) A: Under such circumstances, the comrade presiding over the meeting should explain to <u>them</u> [members of Party branches] how to go about the work, pointing out that <u>they</u> should first talk to those workers and peasants who are usually enthusiastic about <u>their</u> work or who are willing to join the Red Army.

B: Under such circumstances, the comrade presiding over the meeting should explain to *them* how to go about the work. He should advise *them* to talk first to those workers and peasants who are usually enthusiastic about *the Party's* work or who are willing to join the Red Army.

[- In A-version all three pronouns are intended to have the same antecedent: the members of Party branches. "Their," however, attaches itself to "workers and peasants" instead.

- Readers inevitably understand that the workers and peasants are enthusiastic about their own work, and since that is not an unreasonable interpretation, they may never realize that they have been led astray.

- In the revision the pronoun has been replaced by an unambiguous noun: "the Party's work."

- (The sentence was broken into two so that readers would not have too many ideas to absorb all at once.)]

9) A: Here I must make it clear that new intellectual cadres have

228

quite a few shortcomings. It is the duty of veteran cadres to help <u>them</u> overcome <u>their</u> weaknesses and lead <u>them</u> onto the correct path. Veterans should not be jealous of <u>their</u> knowledge and ability nor should <u>they</u> put on airs. <u>They</u> should learn from <u>them</u>.

B: Here I must make it clear that new intellectual cadres have quite a few shortcomings. It is the duty of veteran cadres to help *them* overcome *their* weaknesses and lead *them* onto the correct path. Veterans should not be jealous of *the new cadres'* knowledge and ability, and *they* should not put on airs because of *their* seniority. Rather, *they* should learn from *their new comrades*.

[- In the A-version of these four sentences, there are no less than seven pronouns, all third person plural, sharing two different antecedents.

- The first three pronouns ("help them," "their weaknesses," "lead them") all plainly refer to the "new intellectual cadres." But after that, the reader enters upon the "dangerous wilderness" to which Professor Barzun refers.

- "Their" (in "their knowledge and ability") is powerfully drawn to the nearby "Veterans," which is the subject of the sentence, but actually it refers again to the new cadres.

- The next "they" ("they should not put on airs") now does mean the veterans, but could just as logically mean the new cadres.

- In the last sentence ("They should learn from them"), "they" again represents the veterans, while "them" represents the new cadres, although the reverse reading would be equally plausible.

- To straighten out this tangle, the polisher first replaced "their knowledge and ability" with "the new cadres' knowledge and ability."

- This left "they should not put on airs" plainly referring to the subject "Veterans," as did also "They should learn."

- Then she made the final "them" explicit by replacing the pronoun with "their new comrades."

- The net result of these changes was that starting with the third sentence, all the pronouns now had the same antecedent, "Veterans."

- The polisher could even introduce two more pronouns — "because of their seniority" (added to clarify the sense), and "their new comrades" — without causing readers to lose their way: the new pronouns had the same antecedent as the others.]

10) A: At this time, "Left" adventurism represented by Wang Ming was already dominant in the Provisional Central Committee. It failed to understand and deal with these questions correctly.

B: At this time, "Left" adventurism represented by Wang Ming was already dominant in the Provisional Central Committee. The Committee failed to understand and deal with these questions correctly.

[- In A-version the "It" at the head of the second sentence is meant to refer to the immediately preceding "Provisional Central Committee." But a noun that is the subject of a sentence exercises a strong attraction on a following pronoun.

- Thus, despite the proximity of the true antecedent, the reader thinks at first that "It" refers to the subject of the preceding sentence, "adventurism."

- To dispel this ambiguity, the polisher discarded the pronoun and substituted the noun it stood for, "the Committee."]

11) A: At last they [the Chinese people] have chosen their present political system and government. <u>It</u> was by their efforts that the Chinese revolution triumphed. <u>It</u> was certainly not imported from outside.

B: At last they have chosen their present political system and government. *It* was thanks to their efforts that the Chinese revolution triumphed. *The revolution* was certainly not imported from outside.

[- In A-version the first "it" is merely an idiomatic device for anticipating the subject of the sentence ("that the Chinese revolution triumphed"). Readers do not perceive it as a pronoun with an antecedent, any more than they would in the construction "<u>It</u> is true that the Chinese revolution triumphed."

- When readers come to the second "it" — standing, like the first, as subject at the head of the sentence — they automatically assume that it is performing the same function as the first. If only unconsciously, they expect parallel structure: "<u>It</u> was by their efforts that the revolution triumphed. <u>It</u> was certainly not (by the efforts of anyone else)."

- Only when they come to the end of the sentence do

readers realize that the two "it"s are being used in two different senses.

- To prevent this momentary misunderstanding, the reviser simply replaced the second "it" by its antecedent, "the revolution."]

12) A: Currently the proportion of private industry and commerce in the economy is quite large. In industry the private sector accounts for 42 per cent and in retail trade for 68 per cent. Workers and shop assistants employed in private industry and commerce (excluding handicrafts and family-run shops) total roughly 3.8 million, as against the 4.2 million employed in state-owned factories and state commerce. This is a great asset to the state and still plays a large part in the national economy and the people's livelihood.

B: Currently the proportion of private industry and commerce in the economy is quite large. In industry the private sector accounts for 42 per cent and in retail trade for 68 per cent. Workers and shop assistants employed in private industry and commerce (excluding handicrafts and family-run shops) total roughly 3.8 million, as against the 4.2 million employed in state-owned factories and state commerce. *Private industry and commerce* are a great asset to the state and still play a large part in the national economy and the people's livelihood.

[- In A-version the translator has tried to make "This" sum up the entire content of three fact-laden sentences. That is too heavy a task for a demonstrative pronoun. At best, it can refer only to the immediately preceding sentence, suggesting that the high proportion of workers in private employ is a great asset to the state.

- Studying the passage, the polisher noted that the second and third sentences merely gave statistics to support the first. It was this opening statement that was the important one and, remote though it was, the true antecedent of "This."

- This understanding of the meaning made it possible for the polisher to provide the logical subject for the fourth sentence. Abandoning the "This" as unusable, he substituted "Private industry and commerce."]

13) A: If anyone sets out to make revolution but insists on demonstrating his talent in ways that harm the revolution, then we will say to him: Sorry, but we have to impose restraints on you. If this is not the case, no one would feel restrained in any way. We all acknowledge the talent of Marx, Engels, Lenin, Stalin, and comrade Mao Zedong, and all of them are models of discipline. Therefore comrades need not have any worry about that.

B: If anyone sets out to make revolution but insists on demonstrating his abilities in ways that harm the revolution, then we have to say to him: Sorry, but we must impose restraints on you. If we didn't, no one would feel restrained in any way. We all acknowledge the abilities of Marx, Engels, Lenin, Stalin, and comrade Mao Zedong, and all of them are models of discipline. So comrades need not worry *that discipline will inhibit their abilities*.

[- The antecedent of "that" is vague at best. It appears to mean that comrades need not worry about how disciplined

233

Marx and the others are... surely not what the speaker intended.

- Again the polisher studied the original in context to determine the true meaning of the passage. His conclusion was spelled out in B-version: "comrades need not worry that discipline will inhibit their abilities."

- (In the revision, "abilities" was used instead of "talent(s)" because "talent" most often has the sense of natural aptitude for the arts. Thus, one would not normally speak of a "talented" philosopher, economist, politician, administrator, or the like.)]

Remote antecedent

14) A: In admitting these <u>persons</u> into the Party, we must neither lower our requirements nor take in everyone who is qualified. The Party organizations should not only examine whether <u>they</u> are qualified politically, but should consider whether admission benefits <u>their</u> revolutionary activities.

B: In admitting these persons into the Party, we must neither lower our standards nor take in everyone who is qualified. The Party organizations should consider not only whether *a candidate* is qualified politically, but also whether admission will help *him* in *his* revolutionary activities.

[- In A-version the pronoun "they," which is intended to refer to the "persons" mentioned in the preceding sentence, is so far away from its antecedent that the reader does not readily make the connection between the two.

- Rather, the pronoun is attracted to the intervening "Party organizations," which are close at hand and also in the

234

strong position of subject of the sentence.

- Both grammatically and logically, the pronoun "their" could refer either to the Party "organizations" or to the "persons" applying for membership. The reader has no way of knowing which is the intended antecedent.

- In B-version "they" has been replaced by "a candidate." That word matches the singular "everyone," and it leads to "him" and "his," singular pronouns that can only refer to the "candidate."

- (Review: In A-version "consider" is essentially only a second reference to "examine," so the reviser tightened the sentence by dropping "examine.")]

15) A: That is the test of whether you are truly carrying out the de-cisions or just going through the motions, dragging your feet and perhaps even deliberately misinterpreting them.

   B: That is the test of whether you are truly complying or just going through the motions, dragging your feet and perhaps even deliberately misinterpreting _decisions_.

   [- In A-version the inescapable reading is that you are misin-terpreting your feet. The true antecedent of "them," "de-cisions," is too far away to be associated with the pronoun.

   - In B-version "them" has been replaced by the noun it was intended to stand for, "decisions."

   - (Review: To avoid repeating "decisions," the reviser changed "carrying out decisions" to "complying," which did not require an object and, in this context, meant the same thing.)]

16) A: We should create an atmosphere in which everybody can discuss <u>questions</u> from a socialist standpoint, so that we can do a good job in literature and art and satisfactorily carry out the policy in this field. On <u>these</u>, we each have our own views, so why can't they be discussed?

B: We should create an atmosphere in which everybody can discuss *questions* from a socialist standpoint, so that we can do a good job in literature and art and satisfactorily carry out the policy in this field. We each have our own views on *these questions*, so why can't they be discussed?

[- In A-version the antecedent "questions" is so far back that readers have forgotten it by the time they reach the pronoun "these." The "these" seems to refer rather to the intervening "literature and art."

- In B-version the pronoun "these" was turned into an adjective modifying "questions," the noun to which the pronoun referred.]

17) A: The congress has, for the first time, made a systematic exposition of the basic guiding principle of the primary stage of socialism, <u>which</u> is of important immediate significance.

B: For the first time, the Congress has systematically set forth the basic guiding principles of the primary stage of socialism. *This statement* (*or* : explanation, *or* : clarification) is of immediate importance.

[- In A-version the antecedent of "which" is not clear. The relative pronoun is apparently meant to refer to the whole preceding idea — that the Congress has made a systematic exposition etc. But it is attracted to the specific nearby elements — both "the primary stage of socialism" and "the

236

basic guiding principle."

- As in the preceding example, in B-version the pronoun was discarded and replaced with a noun plus adjective: "this statement."

- (Review: "Of important immediate significance" was considered redundant and reduced to "of immediate importance." "Made a systematic exposition of" — an example of the unnecessary verb + noun construction — was replaced with a plain verb, "systematically set forth.")]

Disagreement between pronoun and antecedent

18) A: "Every top official should go and spend several days in a number of impoverished villages before they make decisions concerning poverty alleviation," said President Jiang Zemin.

B: "All top officials should go and spend several days in a number of impoverished villages before they make decisions concerning the alleviation of poverty," said President Jiang Zemin.

[- "Every" official is singular, as is clear from the singular form of the noun. (Cf. "each" official, "either" official, "any" official etc.) It therefore cannot be referred to, as in A-version, with a plural pronoun, "they."

- In B-version the antecedent was made plural to agree with the pronoun.

- It would also have been possible to make the pronoun singular to agree with the antecedent. But then, to avoid the suggestion that "every top official" is necessarily a man, the polisher would have had to use the formula "he or

237

she." As is often the case, it seemed less awkward to use the plural "they," which does not specify gender.

- (Review: "Poverty alleviation" was changed to "the alleviation of poverty" to avoid using a noun ("poverty") as an adjective in an unfamiliar combination.)]

19) A: <u>Someone</u> is bound to make trouble, but we must not let <u>them</u> cause serious disturbances.

B: *Some people* are bound to make trouble, but we must not let *them* cause serious disturbances.

[- "Someone" is plainly singular since it takes the singular verb "is." (Cf. most other indefinite pronouns: "somebody"/ "something"; " everyone"/"everybody"/"everything"; "anyone"/"anybody"/"anything"; "no one"/ "nobody"/ "nothing"; etc.)

- Accordingly, in A-version the plural pronoun "them" disagrees with its antecedent.

- In the revision the antecedent "Someone" was replaced by the plural "Some people" to match the plural pronoun.]

20) A: The national leadership of our country has been shifted to a new <u>generation</u>, and now <u>they</u> are dealing with state affairs.

B: The national leadership of our country has been shifted to *members* of a new generation, and it is now *they* who are dealing with state affairs.

[- In A-version the plural pronoun "they" refers to the singular antecedent "generation."

- In principle, the polisher could have corrected the agreement by replacing "they" with the singular pronoun "it."

238

But she felt that "it has begun to deal with state affairs" would be clumsy at best.

- Logically too, "it" seemed wrong: it was not an entire generation that was taking over the leadership but only certain members of that generation.

- For these reasons, the polisher introduced "members" as a plural antecedent for the pronoun "they." In other words, instead of changing the pronoun to match the antecedent, she changed the antecedent to match the pronoun. (Remember that this alternative solution sometimes produces a smoother version.)

- ("Now they are dealing with state affairs" was changed to "it is now they who are dealing with state affairs" to provide better emphasis in accordance with the meaning of the Chinese.)]

Twenty exercises

You may want to underline each pronoun and then check that the antecedent is correct, that it is plainly recognizable, and that the pronoun agrees with it.

1) The West really wants unrest in China. They want turmoil not only in China but also in the Soviet Union and Eastern Europe.

2) China is estimated to possess 69.4 billion tons of onshore oil reserves, but only 25 per cent of it has been verified.

3) Right now Korea is confronted with difficulties, but they are holding on courageously, fighting a guerrilla war in the south and putting up resistance in the north.

4) After a successful revolution each country must build socialism according to their own conditions.

5) No one would come here and invest without getting returns on their investment.

6) "The registered capital of the holding company is $ 30 million, so we have a commitment to more investments here," Wendin said. But he didn't elaborate on when the new joint projects will be launched. It reported sales averaging $ 50 million a year.

7) Old China was dependent on imperialism not only in the economic sphere but also in the spheres of culture and education; it was exploited economically and polluted ideologically. That was very dangerous. It is now time to expose and eradicate its evil influence.

8) During the peak season, peasants compete to sell their eggs, while during the off-season they are usually in short supply in the cities.

9) Foreign trade has been developing rapidly in Fuxin. It has been continuously growing in variety and volume. Many of its quality products are welcome in the international market.

10) During the Japanese and puppet regimes, most of these positions were held by Japanese. But after August 15, 1945, they were replaced by Chinese.

11) All these are problems left over from the past. They are acute now because the longstanding semi-colonial, semi-feudal economy has undergone radical changes. Although they bring some hardship with them, these changes in themselves are not

bad.

12) China's growth has peaked and is expected to slow down next year. Even so, it will remain one of the fastest developing economies in the world.

13) At present our government organs are overstaffed. They may not all have to stay on in government offices. Some of them can be transferred to enterprises.

14) Yesterday two friends from the former Whampoa Military Academy talked about the March 20th Incident and the Southern Anhui Incident. It was interesting to hear it, but I had to leave after one and a half hours because of other engagements.

15) It cannot be said that every paragraph of this speech I am making today has been discussed by the Party Central Committee. Of course, some of them have been discussed, but others are my personal opinions.

16) The problem now facing Shanghai is to obtain adequate rice and cotton supplies, and the key factor is whether they can muster adequate transport facilities to bring them in.

17) I spent one year in a university after my graduation from senior middle school. Yet I didn't learn very much because this coincided with the May 4th Movement.

18) Prosperity is the common objective of all our nationalities, which we must never lose sight of.

19) Following the Wuchang Uprising of 1911, the Hubei military government set forth the idea of changing the form of government by establishing a republic of five nationalities, which

was also advocated by Dr. Sun Yat-sen.

20) *Footnote identifying a text in a collection of works*:
Summary of a speech made at a national forum of representatives
of Customs personnel, which first appeared in *People's Daily*
on October 26, 1949.

IX. The Placement of
Phrases and Clauses

As you know from your study of the language, in English the changing grammatical function of certain words is represented by inflection — that is, by a change in form. The verb "read" becomes the noun "reader," the noun "blood" becomes the verb "bleed," the adjective "rapid" becomes the adverb "rapidly," and so on. We can tell at once what part of speech these words are.

But countless other words do not change in this way. "Plant" looks and sounds the same whether it is a noun or a verb, "clean" can be either a verb or an adjective, "daily" an adjective, an adverb, or a noun.

And even if we can tell from its inflection which general class a word belongs to, there may be no characteristic ending or vowel change to indicate how it is being used in a particular sentence.

"Student" is plainly a noun and could not be mistaken for any form of the verb "study." But there is no way to tell from its appearance or pronunciation how it relates to the words around it. Considered in isolation, it could be functioning as either the subject of a verb ("the student wrote a letter"), the direct object of a verb ("I addressed the student"), the indirect object of a verb ("I wrote the student a letter"), or the object of a preposition ("my letter to the student").

For this reason, the order in which words appear in English, like the order of Chinese characters, is of prime importance as an indicator of the relations between them and hence of meaning. This is especially true of the written language, which lacks the clues supplied by a situational context and by the speaker's voice.

Consider the following pairs. Within each pair the words are identical. It is only their order that tells us how they are related and consequently what the combination of words means:

- our forces overcame the enemy
  the enemy overcame our forces

- many high cadres will attend the meeting
  will many high cadres attend the meeting (?)

- an army private
  a private army

- the achievement of this purpose
  the purpose of this achievement

- we soon came to that conclusion too
  we came to that conclusion too soon

Clearly, if translators wish to communicate ideas, even on the most elementary level, they must order their words carefully, respecting the conventions of the language.

For any student of English who has advanced to the point of attempting translation, the placement of individual words, as in these pairs, generally presents no problem. He or she automatically uses the order subject-verb-object in a declarative sentence and auxiliary-subject-verb in the interrogative, places an adjective before the noun it modifies, and so on.

The translator is often less certain, however, where to put groups of words, that is, phrases or clauses. The proper placement of these longer units is important for two reasons.

The first is that logical order serves to prevent misunderstanding. If a group of words is in the wrong place logically, it can be confusing or ambiguous. Worse, it can make a sentence convey something quite different from what the writer had in mind or even reduce it to an absurdity.

The second reason is that the order of phrases and clauses in a sentence shows which of them the writer wishes to emphasize. It indicates the relative importance attached to the various ideas and makes plain the logical connections between them. Arranging the parts of a sentence to provide the correct emphasis gives readers indispensable help as they try to follow a narrative, exposition, or argument.

In this chapter we shall look at some Chinglish sentences in which words have been poorly arranged, either from the point of view of logic or from the point of view of emphasis. Often, if the order is wrong logically, it provides the wrong emphasis as well. Nevertheless, these are essentially two different problems, and we shall consider them separately.

Correct word order for logic

In this section we shall see how a phrase or clause that appears in the wrong place can mislead the reader as to the meaning of a sentence.

Misplaced phrases

The kind of phrase most likely to cause trouble is one that serves as an adjective or adverb. Such a phrase is misplaced when it modifies, or appears to modify, some element in the sentence other

245

than the one intended. For example:

A: In an article celebrating the 28th anniversary of the founding of the Chinese Communist Party in 1949, Mao Zedong said . . . .

B: *In 1949*, in an article celebrating the 28th anniversary of the founding of the Chinese Communist Party, Mao Zedong said . . . .

[In A-version, the phrase "in 1949" modifies not "anniversary," as the writer clearly intended, but "founding," which is the closer word. Thus, the sentence says that the Party was founded in 1949. Moved to the beginning, the phrase modifies "said," which restores the correct meaning.]

A: over the past decades he has devoted the greater part of his life to developing and spreading improved orange strains among fruit growers

B: over the past decades he has devoted the greater part of his life to *developing* improved orange strains *and spreading* them *among fruit growers*

[- In A-version, the adverbial phrase "among fruit growers" modifies both the developing and spreading of the improved strains. But logically, one cannot develop oranges among growers. The revision separates "developing" from "spreading" and restricts the modifying phrase to "spreading."

- (Review: The pronoun "them" was used to avoid a second reference to "improved orange strains.")]

A: Inside the grand Dacheng Palace in the middle of the

246

Confucius Temple, musicians will play tunes allegedly refined by Confucius, <u>using antique instruments</u> including
the stringed *guqin*.

B: Inside the grand Dacheng Palace in the middle of the
Confucius Temple, musicians *using antique instruments*,
including the stringed *guqin*, will play tunes allegedly refined by Confucius.

["Using antique instruments" is plainly meant to modify
"musicians," but in A-version its placement makes it
modify the immediately preceding "Confucius." In
B-version, the participle "using" is attached to the right
noun, "musicians."]

A: <u>After years of effort</u>, Gao said that soil erosion has been
brought under control in 16,700 square kilometers of the
affected land areas, or 58% of the total.

B: Gao said that *after years of effort*, soil erosion has been
brought under control in 16,700 square kilometers of the
affected land area, or 58% of the total.

[In A-version, the introductory phrase modifies not "has
been brought under control," but the principal verb,
"said." This makes it appear that Gao spent years trying
to speak. B-version establishes the logical connection between the parts of the sentence.]

It is true that readers who misinterpret sentences like these
probably will not be deceived for long. They may even grasp the intended sense intuitively, without having to retrace their steps. But
they will come to the right understanding in spite of, not because of,
the words on the page. That their confusion may be only momentary

does not relieve the translator of the obligation to write sentences which, when analyzed, actually say what they are supposed to mean.

Misplaced clauses

Logically misplaced clauses are less frequent in Chinglish than misplaced phrases. When they do appear, however, it is usually for the same reason: the clause in question acts as a modifier, and the translator has inadvertently made it modify the wrong element in the sentence. Here are two examples:

A: So long as we strictly implement the Government Administration Council's Decision on Unifying National Financial and Economic Work, <u>after we go through several months of difficulties</u>, we have every reason to expect that the financial situation will gradually improve.

B: So long as we strictly implement the Government Administration Council's Decision on Unifying National Financial and Economic Work, we have every reason to expect that *after a few difficult months* the financial situation will gradually improve.

[- The clause "after we go through several months of difficulties," is intended to function as an adverb modifying "will improve." But in A-version, coming before "we have every reason to expect," it modifies those words instead.

- The principle is the same as in the last example above, about Gao and soil erosion. There too, the adverb ("after years of effort") modified the wrong verb, and for the same reason: the translator had placed it on the wrong side of the relative pronoun "that."

248

- (Once the word order was corrected, it became clear that the clause "after we go through several months of difficulties" could be reduced to a simple phrase, "after a few difficult months.")]

A: We should also review our experience frequently and make adjustments in light of the actual conditions <u>when we find problems</u>.

B: We should also review our experience frequently and, *when we find problems*, make adjustments in light of the conditions.

[- The subordinate clause is intended to modify "make adjustments" (i. e., make adjustments when we find problems). In A-version, however, it attaches itself to the immediately preceding "conditions" instead (i. e., make adjustments in light of the conditions that exist at the time we find the problems). The difference in sense is not great, but B-version is preferable for both clarity and rhythm.

- (<u>Review</u>: "Actual" was dropped as a redundant intensifier.)]

Mistakes in logic like the ones we have been discussing can easily be corrected by a change of word order. The difficulty lies in recognizing them, but that is largely a matter of practice. When you reread your work, try to be on the alert for misplaced modifiers and make sure that what you have written means what you meant it to mean.

Word order for proper emphasis

On the question of how to arrange material in an English sentence to achieve a desired emphasis, writers on style are in general agreement. Jacques Barzun speaks for them all when he says [p. 154] "the emphatic places in a sentence are beginning and end, the end being the more so."

For this reason, the most important element in the writer's thought, the one on which he or she wishes to focus the reader's attention, usually appears at the end of the sentence. The idea next in importance will probably come at the beginning, while any incidental details are relegated to the middle.

Strunk and White [p. 32] even formulate this as a general principle: "The proper place in the sentence for the word or group of words the writer desires to make most prominent is usually the end."

In this section we shall examine the practical applications of that principle as it affects the work of the translator.

A misplaced phrase

Consider the following versions of the same sentence:

- After more than twenty days of exhausting marches and heavy combat, they reached the Dabie Mountains in late August.

- They reached the Dabie Mountains in late August, after more than twenty days of exhausting marches and heavy combat.

- In late August, after more than twenty days of exhausting marches and heavy combat, they reached the Dabie

Mountains.

The sentence consists of three basic elements: an independent clause ("<u>they reached</u> the Dabie Mountains") and two prepositional phrases ("<u>after</u> more than twenty days etc." and "<u>in</u> late August"), both of which function as adverbs modifying the verb "reached."

The arrangement of these three elements makes no difference to the plain meaning of the sentence. Unlike the misplaced modifiers discussed above, the two prepositional phrases here can be placed virtually anywhere — there are even further possibilities — without offense to logic.

The difference between the three arrangements is one of emphasis: each highlights a different aspect of the event. To choose which version to adopt, the translator must decide which aspect should be given most prominence — in other words, which element should come last.

This sentence occurred in a historical account of the War of Liberation. When the polisher came upon it in a draft translation, she went back over the whole passage, because she knew it was not enough to look at a single sentence in isolation.

Earlier paragraphs in the text made it clear that the PLA's drive on the Dabie Mountains in the summer of 1947 was of great strategic importance and as daring as it was dangerous. Then came a paragraph describing the PLA troops' surprise crossing of the Yellow River, their annihilation of a large enemy (KMT) contingent, and their heroic 500-kilometer march south, during which they had to cross rivers and marshes, fighting all the way. The sentence under consideration came at the end of that paragraph.

Plainly, in this context the main point of the sentence was that despite all hazards, the revolutionary forces had finally reached their destination. The time of their arrival and even the ordeals they had been through on the way were of secondary importance. The arrival of the troops, therefore, should be accorded the place of honor at the end of the sentence.

In the draft the polisher had before her, however, that was not the case. The original translator had used instead the first version cited above:

- After more than twenty days of exhausting marches and heavy combat, they reached the Dabie Mountains <u>in late August</u>.

The polisher thought that in last position, the adverbial phrase "in late August" distracted readers by drawing attention to a relatively unimportant fact and, worse, came as an anticlimax undercutting the dramatic effect of the account. It was, in short, as plainly "misplaced" as if it had been modifying the wrong word. Accordingly, she moved the phrase up to precede the main clause:

- After more than twenty days of exhausting marches and heavy combat, <u>in late August</u> they reached the Dabie Mountains.

That version emphasized the central point. But now it seemed to give too little consequence to the date. This was, after all, a narration of historical events in chronological order, and dates were of some importance. Suppose the shorter phrase were put first:

- <u>In late August</u>, after more than twenty days of exhausting marches and heavy combat, they reached the Dabie

Mountains.

At last, the polisher felt, the emphasis was right. The clause and the "August" phrase were in the positions of prominence, end and beginning, while the strong content and greater length of the "after" phrase ensured that it would not be lost in the middle.

As often happens, the right emphasis produced the right rhythm as well. Readers would be carried rapidly forward to the suspensefully delayed verb "reached," which would then come as the culmination of the sentence, just as it was the culmination of the events described. The form matched the content.

More misplaced phrases

Here are additional examples of phrases that are misplaced because they usurp the position normally reserved for the more important information:

A: The pro-Japanese Kuomintang group, headed by Wang Jingwei, vice-president of the KMT, chairman of the Central Political Council, vice-chairman of the Supreme National Defence Conference, and chairman of the People's Political Council of the Kuomintang, openly capitulated to the Japanese in December 1938.

B: *In December 1938*, the pro-Japanese Kuomintang group, headed by Wang Jingwei, vice-president of the KMT, chairman of the Central Political Council, vice-chairman of the Supreme National Defence Conference, and chairman of the People's Political Council of the Kuomintang, openly capitulated to the Japanese.

[The date is of secondary importance. The main point of the sentence is that the pro-Japanese group, headed by a man who held all these top-level positions in the KMT, capitulated to the Japanese. The whole sentence builds toward the dramatic predicate, "capitulated to the Japanese." Any detail that comes after that will inevitably seem incongruous, like a short tail on a large dog.]

A: It is estimated that our army will reach 5,500,000 <u>at its peak next year</u>.

B: It is estimated that *at its peak next year* our army will reach 5,500,000.

[The main clause here is less dramatic than in the preceding example, but it is still the one that deserves emphasis: our forces (at their peak) will reach this very large number.]

A: We have gained the initiative in Northern Manchuria <u>as a result of our work over the past eight months</u>.

B: *As a result of our work over the past eight months*, we have gained the initiative in Northern Manchuria.

[Never mind the modest self-congratulation, "as a result of our work." The important news is that we have finally gained the initiative in Northern Manchuria.]

A: Roughly speaking, the government will be in much better financial shape next year than this, <u>despite another enormous deficit</u>.

B: Roughly speaking, *despite another enormous deficit*, the government will be in much better financial shape next year than this.

[The fact to be emphasized here is not the negative one (there will again be an enormous deficit), but the positive one (we will be in much better shape).]

254

Misplaced clauses

For phrases, as we have seen, the relative importance of each determines their proper placement. But it does not affect their wording. "In late August" and "despite another enormous deficit" remain unchanged whether they are emphasized or not.

For clauses, however, relative importance governs not only their placement but their form. As you know from studying English, if two ideas are of equal importance, they will be expressed as coordinate clauses, whereas if one is more important than the other, they will be cast as a main (or "independent") clause and a subordinate (or "dependent") clause.

Coordinate clauses will be joined by a conjunction like "and," "but," "or," "so," etc. A subordinate clause, which cannot stand alone, will be linked to the main clause by some connecting word like "which," "when," "although," "because," "if," "after," "until," etc., plainly indicating its dependent nature.

Unfortunately for translators, subordination is not so plainly marked in Chinese. Chinese tends to juxtapose phrases and clauses without any connecting words to indicate the relations between them. As Professor Cheng Zhenqiu has pointed out [p. 62], "the various parts of a Chinese sentence often appear to be coordinate with one another without any grammatical indication of their relative importance." As a consequence, he warns translators against following the Chinese mechanically and treating every phrase or clause as if they all had equal weight.

Thus, when confronted with any Chinese sentence composed of two or more clauses, you must decide whether they are coordinate and, if not, which is the main one. Once that question is answered,

255

the further question of how to arrange the clauses for correct emphasis answers itself.

Logically, a subordinate clause should occupy a subordinate position in a sentence. And since, as we have seen, English normally reserves the final place for the most important idea, the subordinate clause should generally precede the main one.

The following sentences have been arranged in that pattern:

- But as we have often said, <u>although the road ahead is tortuous</u>, the future is bright.

- <u>As they marched</u>, the students shouted the slogans "Oppose hunger!" and "Oppose civil war!"

- It can be said that <u>ever since our two countries established diplomatic relations in the 1970s</u>, we have followed those principles to the letter.

- Then, <u>when they</u> [the skeptics] <u>saw that things were getting better in areas where the reform had been carried out</u>, they began to follow suit.

Try reversing the order of ideas in these examples:

- But as we have often said, the future is bright, <u>although the road ahead is tortuous</u>.

- The students shouted the slogans "Oppose hunger!" and "Oppose civil war!" <u>as they marched</u>.

- It can be said that we have followed those principles to the letter, <u>ever since our two countries established diplomatic relations in the 1970s</u>.

- Then they began to follow suit, <u>when they saw that things</u>

256

were getting better in areas where the reform had been carried out.

As can be seen in each case, when the order is reversed the emphasis is shifted to the wrong part of the sentence. The result is as flat and disappointing as when the phrase "in late August" appeared at the end of "they reached the Dabie Mountains."

The chief point to remember is that when there is more than one possible arrangement of an English sentence — and except for the simplest utterances, there always is — you must make an important choice: which element is to be emphasized?

That choice will depend on the meaning of the Chinese passage and on the emphasis, explicit or implicit, that you perceive in it. Professor Cheng Zhenqiu stresses this point with italics when he writes [p.64], "In translation, the important thing is . . . to determine which part of the sentence should, in accordance with the *meaning* of the original, be given prominence."

An added benefit of right emphasis

At the beginning of this chapter we noted that arranging the parts of a sentence to provide the desired emphasis has two virtues. First, as we have seen, it shows readers which idea the writer regards as most important. Second, it helps them follow the writer's line of thought. It is this secondary benefit that we shall consider briefly now.

When the elements of a sentence are presented in the right order for the desired emphasis, the readers' attention is directed to the core idea located at the end, the one that the writer is going to build on in the following sentence. The period that brings the sentence to a close gives them a pause during which they can absorb this idea. And since it is the one that has made the most recent impression on their minds, they are able to move on smoothly to the next sentence, following a logical progression of ideas.

To illustrate this point, we must use longer examples showing how two or three sentences work together:

A: We used to serve the old society, <u>although we didn't work directly for the Northern Warlords or for the Kuomintang</u>. So we cannot say we were not influenced by the old society.

B: *Although we didn't work directly for the Northern Warlords or for the Kuomintang*, we used to serve the old society. So we cannot say we were not influenced by it.

[- In the revision, the subordinate clause ("although we didn't work directly etc.") comes first, leaving the position of greater prominence to the main clause ("we used to serve etc.").

- This change in order also provides a natural sequence of ideas. The end of the first sentence now leads directly into the second: we used to serve the old society, so we cannot say we were not influenced by it.]

A: Self-practice is important for all of them [students of foreign languages], <u>no matter whether they will take up the career of teachers or serve as foreign relations personnel</u>. Don't interfere with them when they manage to find time for self-practice.

B: *Whether they are going to go into teaching or work in foreign affairs*, it is important for all of them to practice by

258

themselves. Don't interfere with them when they manage
to find time to do it.

[- Again the subordinate clause has been moved up to subordinate position. And again, the last idea in the first sentence now prepares readers for the idea that will be presented in the next: it is important for them to practice,
(so) don't interfere with them when they are practicing.

- (Note that "self-practice," unlike the similar "self-
study," is not accepted English.)]

A: We are going through a period of war and enemy blockade.
Nationwide victory, however, is now a foregone conclusion — and it will not be long in coming. . . . Of course,
we should not close our eyes to the present situation, <u>just
as we should not lose sight of the future</u>. At present, we
have yet to wipe out the remaining enemy forces.

B: We are going through a period of war and enemy blockade.
Nationwide victory, however, is now a foregone conclusion — and it will not be long in coming. . . . Of course,
although we should not lose sight of the future, we
should not close our eyes to the present situation either.
We still have to wipe out the remaining enemy forces.

[- In the revision, the usual change of order has been made
to draw attention to the main clause ("we should not close
our eyes to the present situation").

- The result is the same as before: related ideas are brought
together. The reference to the "present situation," now
coming at the end of the sentence, is immediately followed
by the statement of what, in the present situation, remains to be done ("We still have to wipe out etc."). In

259

A-version, the reference to what must be done "at present" followed the unrelated statement that we should be mindful of the future.]

Thus we see in these three examples that correcting the word order of a given sentence to achieve proper emphasis also serves to achieve a logical connection between that sentence and the one that follows. This is very often the case, as will be demonstrated in many of the further examples below.

Twenty more examples of revision

1) A: On November 12 and 25, 1947, the Federation of Comrades of the Three People's Principles, the KMT Association for Promoting Democracy, and the Democratic Revolutionary League, along with various democrats within the KMT, convened a Congress of Representatives of Democratic Factions of the Chinese Kuomintang in Hong Kong.

B: On November 12 and 25, 1947, *in Hong Kong*, the Federation of Comrades of the Three People's Principles, the KMT Association for Promoting Democracy, and the Democratic Revolutionary League, along with various (*or*: individual) democrats within the KMT, convened a Congress of Representatives of Democratic Factions of the Chinese Kuomintang.

[- In A-version the phrase "in Hong Kong" attaches itself to "the Chinese Kuomintang," which immediately precedes it. Thus, the Congress appears to include only members of the Hong Kong branch of the KMT.

- In B-version the phrase indicating the location of the

260

Congress has been moved up to the beginning where, like
the one indicating the date, it properly modifies the verb
"convened." (It could also have been placed directly after
"convened.")

- This change also corrects the emphasis. After the long and
impressive build-up to the Congress, the detail "in Hong
Kong" would be anticlimactic.]

2) A: The election of Xiang Zhongfa as the principal leader of the
Party was due to the influence of the Communist International, which put undue emphasis on the class status of a
worker in selecting cadres.

B: The election of Xiang Zhongfa as the principal leader of the
Party was due to the influence of the Communist International, which *in selecting cadres* put undue emphasis on
the workers' class status.

[- In A-version the prepositional phrase appears to modify the
preceding noun "worker," as if it were the worker who
was selecting cadres.

- The revision places the phrase next to the verb it is supposed to modify, "put emphasis on." (It is also nearer to
"the Communist International," which is doing the selecting.)

- This change also left the end of the sentence to the main
idea.

- ("Class status of a worker" was changed to "workers' class
status" for reasons of logic. A-version appears to mean
that the class status of anyone other than a worker would
not be taken into consideration. The intended meaning is
that the International emphasized "working-class

status."）

- （Review: Because of the distracting repetition of sound —
"due to" and "undue" — "undue" should have been
changed to "too much."）]

3) A: Hong Kong could contribute to filling part of the gap in the
mainland's financial infrastructure and assist China's drive
to invigorate State-owned enterprises <u>with its mature financial market</u>, officials and experts agreed yesterday.

   B: *With its mature financial market*, Hong Kong could help fill
the gap in the mainland's financial infrastructure and assist
in the drive to invigorate State-owned enterprises, officials
and experts agreed yesterday.

   [- A-version is misleading. At first, the "with" phrase seems
to be attached to the immediately preceding "enterprises":
the reader thinks for a moment that it should be "with
<u>their</u> mature financial market." But of course "its" must
have a singular antecedent.

   - Looking back, the reader finds "drive." But a drive cannot
have a financial market. Then for a moment he or she
tries to attach the market to "China's." Wrong again.

   - The problem is that the "with" phrase is too far removed
from the words it is logically attached to, "Hong Kong."

   - This is easily remedied in B-version. There, the phrase has
been put in the usual place for an adjective, directly before
the word or words it modifies. (It could also have been
placed directly after: "Hong Kong, with its mature financial market, could help etc.").

   - Note that this example is an exception to the rules of emphasis we have discussed. The most important element in

262

the sentence is clearly the clause telling how Hong Kong could help the mainland. That unnamed officials and experts agreed upon this is quite secondary. In principle, therefore, the sentence should have been rearranged to put the first clause last ("Officials and experts agreed yesterday that . . . .").

- But this sentence happened to be the lead in a newspaper story. For reasons that need not concern us here, in the matter of emphasis the practice of journalists is somewhat different from that of other writers, and for their purposes the order in A-version (important statement first, attribution last) was correct.

- (Review: In the revision, "part of" the gap was dropped because it is redundant with "contribute" or "help." "China's" was eliminated as self-evident.)]

4) A: Unifying control over national financial and economic work will not only help overcome today's financial difficulties, but also create the necessary preconditions for economic development <u>without loss of time</u> in the days to come.

B: Unifying control over national financial and economic work will not only help us overcome our present financial difficulties, but will also create the conditions *that will enable us to move on quickly* to economic development.

[- Again, A-version is misleading. At first, the phrase "without loss of time" appears to be attached to the immediately preceding noun "development," suggesting that the development will be rapid. But "development without loss of time" is not English: the phrase is plainly adverbial and needs to modify a verb.

263

- Looking back to find a verb expressing some action that will take place "without loss of time," the reader lights on "create": "will also create, without loss of time, the necessary preconditions . . . ." But that is not the right meaning either.
- The polisher of this sentence looked in vain for the word that "without loss of time" was supposed to modify. It was not on the page.
- Only by going back to the Chinese could he determine that the intended meaning was: "will also create the necessary preconditions that will enable us to undertake economic development without loss of time."
- With this understanding, it was possible to produce a revised version that conveyed the right sense in simple language: "the conditions that will enable us to move on quickly to economic development."
- (Review: The modifier "in the days to come" was eliminated as redundant with the future tense of the verb "will enable.")]

5) A: The SFCA (Sight First China Action) campaign, the chief purpose of which is to help Chinese people cure or prevent cataracts with $15 million funded by the Lions Club International and some special government funds, is being carried out by the China Disabled Persons' Federation and the Ministry of Public Health.

 B: The SFCA (Sight First China Action) campaign, the chief purpose of which is to help Chinese cure or prevent cataracts, is being carried out by the Chinese Federation of Disabled Persons and the Ministry of Public Health, *with*

264

> *$ 15 million provided by the Lions Club International and some special government funds.*

[- In A-version it is not clear what the prepositional phrase is supposed to modify. At first it seems to be attached to the preceding verbs "cure or prevent." But that is not logical: diseases are not cured or prevented by money but by the services and medicines that money can buy.

- Most probably, the phrase was intended to modify the "campaign." But it is so far removed from that word that without rereading the sentence carefully, no reader would make the connection.

- The polisher moved the floating phrase to the end of the sentence. In that position, it was securely and logically anchored to the preceding verb, "is being carried out."

- ("$ 15 million funded by" was changed to "$ 15 million provided by" for two reasons. First, for logic: it is not the money that is "funded" but the campaign. Second, for sound: "funded" and "funds" in the same phrase would make an annoying repetition like the ones we discussed in Chapter V.)

- (Review: "Chinese people" was reduced to "Chinese," which means the same thing. In the title of the China Disabled Persons' Federation, the noun "China," used to modify "Federation," was changed to the adjective "Chinese." Then the relations between the words were clarified by the addition of an "of": the "Chinese Federation of Disabled Persons.")]

6) A: It [the resolution of the Gutian meeting in 1929] answered the fundamental question of how to turn a revolutionary army

mainly composed of peasants into a people's army of a new type <u>in an environment of rural warfare</u>. Never in the history of China had there been such an army.

B: It answered the fundamental question of how to turn a revolutionary army *that was* mainly composed of peasants and *operating in an environment of rural warfare* into a people's army of a new type. Never in the history of China had there been such an army.

[- In A-version the phrase "in an environment of rural warfare" attaches itself to the immediately preceding "new type." This suggests that the new type of army will operate in a new environment, which is not true.

- In B-version both phrases — "in an environment etc." and "composed of peasants" — have been placed in a subordinate clause beginning with "that," immediately following the words they modify, "a revolutionary army."

- The change in word order also allowed the most important element, "an army of a new type," to take its rightful place at the end of the sentence.

- As an added benefit of correcting the emphasis, the end of the sentence now led directly into the following one, which expanded on the idea of a new type of army.

- ("Operating" was inserted for clarity and also to provide parallel structure with two participles — "composed of" and "operating in.")]

7) A: Don't assume that you no longer have the duty to think over the practicability of the reconstruction program <u>since it has been endorsed by the central authorities and approved by the State Planning Commission</u>. Very often our decisions

are flawed or not well thought through.

B: Don't assume that *once the reconstruction program has been endorsed by the central authorities and approved by the State Planning Commission* , you no longer have the duty to think whether it is feasible. Very often our decisions are flawed or not well thought through.

[- In B-version the subordinate clause was moved up to a subordinate position in the sentence.

- Again, the last idea in the sentence now led directly into the next material. The notion that the program might or might not be feasible was followed by an admission that the central authorities often made mistakes. One idea led to the next in logical progression.

- (Review: To combat the noun plague, "practicability" was changed to a verb + adjective construction, "whether it is practicable." Then a better word was substituted: "feasible.")]

8) A: "Although the world is complaining about the adverse consequences of the greenhouse effect, the farmers of Heilongjiang seem to benefit from it," Ma said. The climate of the province is ideal for farming. There have been no low temperatures and early frosts, which usually do great harm to crops, in the past seven years, largely due to the greenhouse effect.

B: "Although the world is complaining about the adverse consequences of the greenhouse effect, the farmers of Heilongjiang seem to benefit from it," Ma said. The climate of the province is ideal for farming. *In the past seven years* there have been no low temperatures or early frosts,

267

which usually do great harm to crops. This is largely thanks to the greenhouse effect.

[- In A-version, the adverbial phrase "in the past seven years" seems to modify the immediately preceding "do great harm to crops." In B-version it has been moved up to precede the words to which it is properly attached, "there have been no low temperatures or early frosts."

- So far as logic is concerned, the sentence could also have been revised to read: "Largely because of the greenhouse effect, in the last seven years there have been no low temperatures etc." But in this context it was important for correct emphasis to leave the "greenhouse effect" in the final position.

- ("There have been no low temperatures and early frosts" was changed to "no low temperatures or early frosts," because the two phenomena do not ∙ necessarily go together.)]

9) *Headline of a newspaper advertisement*:

A: Column of the latest room rates for hotels receiving foreign visitors <u>to be launched by China Daily Ad Department</u>.

B: Column *to be launched by China Daily's Advertising Department* will list latest rates of hotels receiving foreigners.

[- In A-version "to be launched" (intended as headline language for "is to be launched") appears to be a modifier attached to the immediately preceding noun. Unfortunately, that noun is not "column" but "visitors."

- The revision converts "to be launched" into a true modifier and places it directly after the correct noun, leaving the foreign guests safely on the ground.

268

- (Review: To clarify the ambiguous noun-as-adjective construction, "China Daily" was changed into a possessive
noun, "China Daily's." For the same reason, "Ad,"
which is normally an abbreviation for the noun "advertisement," was spelled out as the adjective "Advertising."
"Foreign visitors" was shortened to "foreigners," because
the reference to hotels made "visitors" self-evident.)]

10) A: This is because the national bourgeoisie adopted the neutral
and sympathetic and even cooperative attitude toward revolution <u>during the period of the democratic revolution, especially during the War of Resistance Against Japan and
the War of Liberation</u>, an attitude quite different from
that of landlord and bureaucrat-capitalist classes.

B: This is because *during the period of the democratic revolution, especially during the War of Resistance Against
Japan and the War of Liberation*, the national bourgeoisie took a neutral, sympathetic, or even cooperative
attitude toward revolution, an attitude quite different
from that of the landlord and bureaucrat-capitalist classes.

[- In A-version the subordinate phrase "during the period
etc." follows the main idea (the attitude adopted) rather
than preceding it and is thus misplaced for proper emphasis.

- Worse, the phrase comes between the first "attitude" and
the second. The two words have identical meaning — the
second is merely a repetition of the first, useful for the
structure of the sentence — and logically, they must not
be too far separated. But here the intervening phrase is so
long that by the time readers reach the second "attitude,"

they have forgotten the first one to which it refers.

- In B-version, both problems were solved simply by moving the prepositional phrase forward in the sentence.

- (For reasons of logic, "neutral and sympathetic and even cooperative" was changed to "neutral, sympathetic, or even cooperative," since the same attitude could scarcely be all three at once.)]

11) A: <u>For more than a hundred years</u>, the Anti-Japanese War was the first complete victory won by the Chinese people <u>among the wars they waged to fight against the invasion by capitalist and imperialist countries for their national liberation</u>. For the first time in modern history, China, which had always been defeated in its resistance to armed foreign invasion, was able to avenge all the national humiliation since the 1840s.

B: *Of all the wars the Chinese people had fought over more than a hundred years for national liberation from capitalist and imperialist invaders*, this was the first that had ended in complete victory. For the first time in modern history, China, which had always been defeated in its resistance to armed foreign invasion, was able to avenge all the national humiliation since the 1840s.

[- Like the Dabie Mountains example discussed in the text, this is a sentence summing up historical events. The most important idea is clearly that this was the first complete victory, and in the B-version that idea is given the most prominent place, at the end.

- As in the Dabie Mountains sentence, the delayed central statement ("this was the first") heightens the suspense and provides a dramatic conclusion to a long narrative.

- By placing the "complete victory" at the end, B-version has the further advantage of preparing the reader for the next sentence, which is its natural continuation.

- ("Invasion by capitalist and imperialist countries" was condensed to "capitalist and imperialist invaders.")

- (The plain past tense in A-version — among the wars "they waged" — was corrected to pluperfect — of the wars they "had waged," indicating that those other wars had preceded this one.)

- (Since a war cannot be a victory, the revision stated that the war "ended in" victory.)

- (Review: "Waged" was dropped because it was redundant with "fight.")]

12) A: I once said that we should anticipate the necessity of blowing up the great dam at Sanmenxia in case of an emergency, such as the occurrence of torrential rains, when the Sanmenxia reservoir, which is badly silted up, would overflow the Central China Plain and endanger the industrial areas around.

B: I once said that in an emergency — *if, for example, there were torrential rains, and the Sanmenxia reservoir, which is badly silted up, threatened to overflow the Central China Plain, endangering the surrounding industrial areas* — it might be necessary to blow up the great dam at Sanmenxia.

[- After the dramatic statement that it might be necessary to blow up the great dam, the long speculation about the circumstances that would constitute an emergency is distinctly anticlimactic. Placed first, as in the revision, these subordinate ideas all build to the climax of the sentence, the delayed main clause.

- (Review: The noun "occurrence" was changed to a structure using a verb, "if there were.")]

13) *The next sentence after the preceding example* :

A: I said this to encourage you to be bold in thinking, but not necessarily to urge you to burst the great dam.

B: I said this *not necessarily to urge you to blow up the dam* but to encourage you to think boldly.

[- Here too in A-version the emphasis is wrong. Clearly, what the speaker meant when he said something is more important than what he did *not* mean. Accordingly, it should come last.

- In B-version, the wrong interpretation of the remark is disavowed before the correct one is announced.

- Note that rearranging the preceding sentence (example 12) makes it logical to begin the present one with "I said this." The "this" is plainly meant to refer not to the description of the potential emergency, but to the words "it might be necessary to blow up the dam." In the revised version of example 12, those words appear at the end, where they will be immediately followed by "I said this."

- (Review: To reduce the incidence of the noun plague, "be bold in thinking" was changed to "think boldly," which was shorter, simpler and replaced a gerund with a verb.)]

14) A: We should look at the problem of language reform from the

stand of 600 million people, <u>rather than from the individ-</u>
<u>ual habits and temporary convenience</u>.

B: We should look at the problem of language reform *not in the*
light of our individual habits and temporary convenience
but from the point of view of 600 million people.

[- The way we should "look at a problem" is clearly more
important than the way we should *not* look at it. Thus,
in the revision the wrong point of view is disposed of before the right one is introduced.

- The principle here is the same as in the preceding
example: the positive statement is more important than
the negative one and should therefore come last. (This
principle generally applies to sentences on the pattern "I
meant <u>not</u> this <u>but</u> that," "<u>instead of</u> doing this, they did
that," "<u>rather than</u> rely on this, we should rely on that,"
and so on.)

- ("From the stand" of 600 million people was changed to
the more idiomatic "from the point of view." And since
one cannot look at something "from" habits and convenience, or even "from the point of view" of habits and
convenience, the phrase was changed to "in the light
of.")

- ("Our" was introduced to anchor the floating "habits"
etc. to identifiable persons indicated by the subject "we":
"We should look at the problem ... not in the light of our
individual habits and temporary convenience but ....")]

15) A: We should set up additional state trading agencies and supply
and marketing cooperatives, and organize private merchants to go into the mountains to establish commercial

273

networks so as to promote <u>interflow of commodities</u>.

B: *To promote the exchange of commodities*, we should set up additional state trading agencies and supply and marketing cooperatives, and we should organize private merchants to go into the mountains and establish commercial networks.

[- The order in A-version is wrong for reasons of logic. The adverbial phrase is intended to explain the purpose of both measures — that is, it is supposed to modify both "set up" and "organize." Positioned at the end, however, it modifies neither of these, applying rather to the nearest preceding verb "establish."

- The order is also wrong for reasons of emphasis. It places a subordinate idea (<u>why</u> we should do these things) in the place that should be reserved for the principal idea (<u>what</u> we should do).

- Again, the simple solution to both problems was to move the phrase to the beginning of the sentence.]

16) A: The government should also help the missionary schools since they have great difficulty in funds <u>after severing relations with foreign countries</u>. The Ministry of Education should make it a point to solve the problems of private schools.

B: Missionary schools, *having severed relations with foreign countries*, are in trouble financially, and the government should help them with their difficulties too. The Ministry of Education should make it a point to solve the problems of private schools.

[- Here there is nothing wrong with the word order in A-version from the point of view of logic. But again it places the subordinate idea (<u>why</u> the schools are in difficulty) in the place of emphasis that should be reserved for the main idea (<u>what</u> should be done about it).

- There are three ideas in this sentence. In order of descending importance, they are (a) that the government should help the missionary schools, (b) that the schools are in difficulty, (c) that the reason for this is that they have severed relations with foreign countries.

- The translator, no doubt following the Chinese, presented them in that order, inadvertently giving greatest prominence to the least important element, (c).

- The polisher remedied this by placing the central idea at the end of the sentence, the second most important at the beginning, and the least important in the middle. In other words, she followed the order: (b) the schools are in difficulty, (c) they are in difficulty for this reason, (a) the government should help them.

- This last notion then led smoothly to the next: "The Ministry of Education should . . . ."

- (The prepositional phrase "after severing relations" could be understood simply as an indication of the time sequence of events. To strengthen the notion that this was the <u>cause</u> of the schools' difficulties, the polisher tightened the connection between the two ideas, attaching them with a participle, "having severed.")

- (Note that "with their difficulties" could probably have been omitted as self-evident after " in trouble financially.")]

17) A: Developing township and village enterprises is essential <u>for the countryside to become moderately prosperous</u>. We

shall therefore continue to support such enterprises, especially in the central and western regions.

B: *If the countryside is to become moderately prosperous*, it is essential to develop township and village enterprises. We shall therefore continue to support such enterprises, especially in the central and western regions.

[- In A-version "for the countryside to become moderately prosperous" gives the reason for developing the township enterprises. But the point to be emphasized is that they must be developed, which should therefore come last. The principle is the same as in the two preceding examples: why before what.

-This consideration led to a change of order: "For the countryside to become moderately prosperous, developing township enterprises is essential." But since "For the countryside to become etc." seemed awkward, the polisher recast the idea as a subordinate clause, "If the countryside is to become etc."

- The change in word order, juxtaposing "township enterprises" at the end of the first sentence with "such enterprises" at the beginning of the next, made a tight logical connection between the two.

- (Review: Again, as in example 13, because of the noun plague, the construction with the gerund, "developing is essential," was changed to one with a verb, "it is essential to develop.")]

18) A: A Party organization can be regarded as consolidated if it is strong within and each and every member maintains a public position and is publicly acknowledged as a good

<u>person</u>. Only such an organization can fulfill the task assigned by the Central Committee: ....

B: *If a Party organization is strong within , if every member has a regular job , and if each is generally regarded as a good person* , that organization can be considered consolidated. Only such an organization can fulfill the task assigned by the Central Committee: ....

[- In the revision the conditions, expressed in a series of subordinate clauses, are all placed first, with the conclusion, expressed in the main clause, at the end.

- As usual, the change in order also creates a smooth transition from this sentence to the next: " such an organization" is plainly one that is "consolidated. "

- (The vague "a public position" was changed to the precise "a regular job. ")

- (<u>Review</u>: The redundant twins "each and every" were reduced to "every. ")]

19) A: In response to Bai's hint or under his influence, the KMT Hubei Provincial Political Council and the chairmen of the Henan and Hunan Provincial Governments recommended resumption of peace talks. They also demanded Chiang's resignation <u>in the interest of peace talks</u>.

B: In response to Bai's hint — or perhaps under his influence — the KMT's Hubei Provincial Political Council and the governors of Henan and Hunan provinces recommended resumption of peace talks. *To that end* , they also demanded Chiang's resignation.

[- For proper emphasis, the prepositional phrase was moved up to precede the important main clause. This produced:

277

"In the interest of peace talks, they also demanded Chiang's resignation."

- Again, the change of word order also established a logical connection — not with the next sentence, this time, but with the one before. The idea that these officials were promoting the "resumption of peace talks," which closed the preceding sentence, was now immediately picked up at the beginning of this one ("In the interest of peace talks, they also demanded.")

- (Review: To avoid a second reference to "peace talks" immediately after the first, the polisher replaced the phrase "In the interest of peace talks" with the summary expression "To that end." In "the KMT Hubei Provincial Political Council," "the KMT" — a noun used as an adjective — was changed to a possessive noun, "the KMT's." Cf. the change from "China Daily" to "China Daily's" in example 9.)]

20) A: With these thoughts in mind, Mao Zedong issued a great call to carry the revolution through to the end <u>in his New Year message</u> released <u>through the Xinhua News Agency</u> <u>on December 30, 1948</u>.

   B: With these thoughts in mind, *on December 30, 1948*, Mao Zedong issued *through the Xinhua News Agency a New Year's message* that was a great call to carry the revolution through to the end.

   [- By this time, you will no doubt recognize that the important element to be highlighted in this sentence is the "great call to carry the revolution through to the end."

   - In A-version, however, the "great call" is lost in a clutter of circumstantial details. Consequently, its dramatic potential fizzles out like a defective New Year's firecracker.

- Also, because it is not clear what "in his New Year message" is meant to modify, it seems at first that the revolution is to be carried through to the end of Mao's message.
- By this time, you will also recognize that the solution to both problems is to recast the sentence in such a way as to place the great call at the end. That is what was done in B-version.
- There are no less than four subordinate prepositional phrases in this sentence: "with these thoughts in mind," "in his New Year's message," "through the Xinhua News Agency" and "on December 30, 1948."
- These four elements can be arranged in different ways, and the order that appeared in print was not necessarily the best. Other versions might be equally valid, so long as they give Mao's stirring "call" the place of honor at the end.]

Twenty exercises

Here again, you might find it useful to underline subordinate phrases and clauses, as was done in the examples of revision, and then decide if they ought to be moved. Remember that other minor changes may need to be made as well, in accordance with the principles discussed in earlier chapters.

1) Zhou Enlai ... travelled to southern Anhui Province to discuss with the leaders of the New Fourth Army the strategic tasks for the army in February 1939.

2) Chinese Premier Li Peng emphasized the importance of reforming and expanding undertakings in science and technology, education, and culture in his government work report.

3) First, an appropriate speed was set for China's economic development after a review of the experience of the past seven years.

4) Soong Ching Ling is the sole person who champions revolution among the three brothers and three sisters in her family.

5) The local government of Taiwan will enjoy certain powers of its own which the governments of other provinces, municipalities, and autonomous regions do not possess, provided the national interests are not impaired.

6) In 1989 the provincial government called for a province-wide initiative to reforest Jiangxi Province. An ambitious goal was set to plant trees wherever it could be done by 1995.

7) In order to ensure achievement of the Party's political, military and economic objectives, Mao emphasized that the Party must first consolidate its ranks.

8) Our actions should be both beneficial to the national unity and suitable to local conditions, as stipulated in the Common Programme.

9) As the People's Liberation Army went over to the strategic offensive, the KMT authorities stepped up their oppression and exploitation of the people and their suppression of the patriotic democratic forces in an effort to maintain their tottering rule.

10) Should we be discouraged by these difficulties? No. We should recognize that our present difficulties are nothing very serious, compared to the difficulties we have faced over the last two

decades of struggle.

11) According to a survey, the forested region in the Northeast will be depleted completely in 10 to 25 years, unless our forestry work is improved.

12) It is obvious to all that, lording it over the Chinese people, the imperialists have used science as a means to exploit, oppress, and slaughter the Chinese people over the last more than one hundred years.

13) Now the situation is quite different from what it was in the early days of liberation, although there still exist remnant counter-revolutionaries and new ones will emerge in future.

14) Education Minister Zhang Xiro once recalled that he found some pupils in Xi'an speaking very good *putonghua* when he was on an inspection there.

15) Before the Long March he was wrongly dismissed from the post of chief of the general staff, because of his opposition to dog-matism in the military command and demoted to chief of staff of the Fifth Army Group of the Chinese Workers' and Peasants' Red Army.

16) At this time, different opinions appeared in the Fourth Red Army's Party organizations and leadership. On June 22nd, an argument regarding the establishment of an Army Committee broke out at the 7th Party Congress of the Fourth Red Army held in Longyan, Fujian.

17) Since the Red Army let slip this golden opportunity, Chiang was able to complete the all-round encirclement of the Central Soviet Area after having defeated the Fujian People's

Government.

18) The Provincial Party Committee decided to stage an uprising in the seven counties in central Hunan with Changsha as the center instead of an uprising in the whole province as originally planned.

19) These percentages were the outcome of the unequal treaties signed by the KMT government at the expense of national sovereignty, not the result of normal foreign investment and fair economic exchange.

20) He once fell on ground which was slippery after a rain, breaking two ribs while he was on the way to an orchard.

X. Dangling Modifiers

In the last chapter we talked about misplaced modifiers —
phrases that function as adjectives or adverbs and that are illogical because they are in the wrong place. As we saw, the usual way to deal
with them is simply to change the word order in the sentence.

There is another group of modifiers that are illogical not because
of faulty placement but because of faulty grammatical relations with
other elements in the sentence. A change in word order, therefore,
will not generally suffice to correct them; the translator has to deal
with them in other ways. It is modifiers of this sort, which are tradi-
tionally called "unattached" or "dangling," that we shall turn to
now.

The standard texts and handbooks for students, journalists, and
other writers who are native speakers of English list a number of different types of dangling modifiers. In this chapter we shall deal only
with those that appear frequently in the work of Chinese translators.
There are five of these: three phrases based on verb forms (participles, gerunds, and infinitives), plus prepositional phrases and individual adjectives.

1. Dangling participles

As you know from your study of English, participles are verb
forms that act as adjectives. In regular verbs, the present participle
ends in -ing (a <u>pleasing</u> child) and the past participle in -ed (a <u>pleased</u>
child).

Like any adjective, a participle (or participial phrase) needs to

283

be closely linked to the noun or pronoun it modifies. When it is not, it is said to "dangle." The dangling participle is one of the most common mistakes in the writing of native speakers of English, so we should not be surprised that it is frequently found in Chinglish as well.

In the last chapter we discussed a dangling participle, although we did not identify it as such:

- Inside the grand Dacheng Palace in the middle of the Temple of Confucius, musicians will play tunes allegedly refined by Confucius, <u>using antique instruments</u> including the stringed *guqin*.

In that sentence the participial phrase, which was intended to modify "musicians," attached itself instead to the immediately preceding noun, "Confucius." As you may recall, to make the right logical connection, the reviser moved the phrase to a position next to the noun it belonged to: "*musicians*, using antique instruments, including the stringed *guqin*, will play tunes . . . ."

This example was included in the category of misplaced modifiers because, to correct it, the reviser had only to change its place in the sentence. But as noted above, in most instances one cannot "fix" a dangling participle simply by repositioning it. Very often, it is not possible to move it next to the word it should modify, because that word is only implied and does not appear in the sentence. And even if the word is present, other grammatical changes are generally required to make the right connection.

Dangling participles at the beginning of a sentence

The difficulty presented by a participle arises most frequently when it stands at the beginning of a sentence. To satisfy the demands of logic, an opening participial phrase must modify the subject of the sentence (the subject of the main verb). That subject will normally be the noun or pronoun that comes immediately after the participial phrase.

Before considering examples of faulty construction, let us look at some examples of the correct, established pattern:

- Looking back over the past seventy years, the Chinese people are more convinced than ever that their choice of socialism as their goal has been correct.

[The present participle "looking" modifies the subject of the sentence: it is the Chinese people who are looking back.]

- Performed by the China Youth Art Theater, the play describes the different lifestyles, feelings, and concepts of two brothers, one a bricklayer and the other a painter.

[The past participle "performed" modifies the subject of the sentence: it is the play that is being performed.]

- Panicked by the flames and seeking a way out, residents found their escape blocked by iron-barred doors and windows.

[Both participles modify the subject of the sentence: it is the residents who were panicked and who were seeking an exit.]

Readers of sentences like these do not know at first what person or thing the opening participle refers to. But consciously or unconsciously, they expect that that person or thing will be named immediately after, as the subject of the sentence. When their expectation is fulfilled, as in the examples above, the sentence is logical.

Now let us consider two examples in which the word the participle is intended to modify — the word to which it logically refers — is *not* the subject of the sentence.

- Using either military or peaceful means, most of the remaining enemy forces were put out of action.

[- The subject of this sentence is "most of the enemy forces." But it was not they who were "using either military or peaceful means." Rather, it was "we" (the revolutionary forces) who used those means to put the enemy out of action.

- The word that the present participle "using" is intended to modify is "we," but "we" is not the subject of the sentence — indeed, it is nowhere to be found. So "using" attaches itself instead to the subject provided (the "enemy forces"), producing the wrong meaning.]

- Conveniently situated, traffic from Jin Hui Tower to Beijing International Airport takes only 1/2 hour via the Third Ring Road.

[- The subject of this sentence is "traffic." But it is not the traffic that is "conveniently situated."

- What the past participle "situated" is meant to modify is the new Jin Hui office building. The word it logically refers to is "Tower," but "Tower" is only the object of the preposition "from," not the subject of the sentence. Again, the participle attaches itself instead to the word that *is* the subject ("traffic"), this time producing nonsense.]

Sentences like these arouse expectations that they fail to meet. Readers assume that when they get to the subject of the sentence they will learn who is using military or peaceful means and what is conveniently situated. They do not. In the first example they are misinformed, and in the second they are presented with an absurdity.

It is as if the writer had begun with one subject in mind (the revolutionary forces, or the Jin Hui Tower) and then, without giving notice, changed to another (the enemy forces, traffic). Even readers who do get the right meaning will have the uncomfortable feeling that something is wrong. The train of thought that started out in one direction has suddenly switched to another track.

The way to keep the train running along the same track is to establish logical grammatical relations between one idea and the next. To do that, we could revise the two sentences as follows:

- *Using either military or peaceful means*, *we* put most of the remaining enemy forces out of action.

[The word to which the participle refers ("we") has been introduced and made the subject of the sentence. The subject is now consistent with the opening phrase, so the second idea follows logically from the first.]

- *The Jin Hui Tower is conveniently situated* (*or*: located), only 1/2 hour from Beijing International Airport via the Third Ring Road.

[The participial phrase has been abandoned and the idea restated as an independent clause. Again, the logic has been straightened out.]

These examples illustrate the two possible ways of recasting a sentence to eliminate a dangling participle. You can either:

- make the word that the participle logically modifies the subject of the sentence, or

- drop the participial phrase and express the idea in another
form.

In *Modern American Usage* [p. 117], Wilson Follett sums up
the case nicely in a single sentence:

The modern doctrine, which codifies the modern feeling, is that
a participle at the head of a sentence automatically affixes itself
to the subject of the following verb — in effect a requirement
that the writer either make his subject consistent with the participle or discard the participle for some other construction.

Dangling participles in other positions

As we noted at the outset, danglers are most often found at the
beginning of a sentence. But participles can also dangle when they
appear in other positions.

Here is an example in which the participial phrase comes at the
end of the sentence:

A: In recent years, China has introduced much technology and
equipment from abroad, playing an important role in improving its petrochemical technology.

B: In recent years, China has introduced much technology and
equipment from abroad, and *these imports have played* an
important role in upgrading its petrochemical industry.

[- The principle is the same as if the participial phrase came
at the beginning: "Playing an important role in improving
China's petrochemical technology, China has introduced
etc." Whether the participle comes at the beginning or the
end of the sentence, it attaches itself to the subject

("China").

- As a result, what A-version actually says is that China is playing an important role in improving its own technology. The intended meaning, however, is that the newly introduced technology and equipment are playing an important role.
- Here, the nouns to which the participle logically refers do appear in the sentence: "technology and equipment from abroad." The problem is that those words are not the subject of the verb, "introduced," but its object.
- The polisher found that there was no good way of moving "technology and equipment from abroad" into the position of subject. She therefore changed the participial phrase into an independent clause: "In recent years, China has introduced much technology and equipment from abroad, and the technology and equipment from abroad have played an important role etc."
- (Review: Then, to avoid repetition, she changed the second reference to "technology and equipment from abroad" into "these imports": "and these imports have played an important role etc.")
- (To avoid the self-evident statement that new technology improves "technology," she also changed "in improving its petrochemical technology" to "in upgrading its petrochemical industry.")]

Dangling participles that have become acceptable

Authorities on English agree that through long usage, certain unattached or dangling participles have become acceptable. Indeed, for practical purposes they have ceased to be participles and have acquired the status of prepositions, conjunctions, or adverbs. Such words have no obligation to cling to a particular noun.

For example, not even the strictest grammarian would object to idiomatic constructions like these:

- Generally speaking, cows are amiable creatures.
- Judging from the ripple of laughter that went through the hall, the delegates did not take the suggestion seriously.
- Our business should be concluded by the end of the week, barring unexpected delays.
- Owing to unforeseen circumstances, the administration has been obliged to cancel all music classes today.
- According to witnesses, it was after midnight when the accident occurred.
- Provided there are no objections, the committee will adjourn tomorrow.

These participles do not modify the subjects of their sentences. The cows are not speaking, the delegates were not judging their own response, our business is not barring delays, etc. Technically, therefore, the participles are dangling. But because they have been used so often in free-standing constructions, they have finally achieved independence. They no longer need to lean on nouns for support, and they display no tendency to attach themselves where they are not wanted. They stand alone, with no offense to logic.

In addition to these examples, certain other participles that have a general, abstract meaning — "concerning," "regarding," "assuming," "allowing for," "granted that," and the like — have achieved independent status. And since the language is constantly evolving, a

290

number of others are in transition.

There is no absolute test to determine whether a given participle has been transformed into another part of speech. It is largely a matter of opinion, and one writer might include in a list of "liberated" participles a word that another, who had stricter standards, might reject or regard as dubious.

In addition, even a participle that all writers would consider completely transformed may at the same time continue to function as a participle. A familiar example of a word that possesses this dual character is "considering." In one sentence it may be used as a preposition and in another as a participle.

For example:

- Considering the circumstances, the accused could hardly be blamed for her actions.
- Carefully considering the evidence, the accused was declared innocent.

In the first sentence, "considering" plainly functions as a preposition, the equivalent of "under," "in light of" or "in view of." It is not attached to the subject, and readers have seen and heard it used in this sense so often that they do not expect it to be.

In the second example, "considering" is perceived as a present participle that wrongly modifies "the accused." When the sentence abruptly changes direction after the comma, a critical reader will feel the jolt and reread, making a mental revision: "Carefully considering the evidence, *the jury* declared the accused innocent."

Thus, the treatment of participles calls for judgment. Translators, especially if they are not native speakers of English, would do well to be conservative in the matter and to restrict their notion of "acceptable" danglers to familiar expressions like the ones cited above. If the status of a participle is in doubt, it is best to assume that it is still a participle and must be firmly tied to an appropriate noun.

Dangling participles in the English of native speakers

The whole notion of what is acceptable and what is not in the usage of participles in English has evolved over time. Until perhaps the end of the nineteenth century, unattached participles were considered permissible, and examples can readily be cited from the work of even the most admired writers of that and earlier times.

But standards have become increasingly strict. It was nearly a hundred years ago that the brothers H. W. and F. G. Fowler [p. 119 ff.] called attention to the shift toward tighter construction. Since then, generations of English teachers have warned students against dangling participles, and the authors of countless handbooks on writing have offered cautionary examples.

For instructional purposes, these authors tend to select examples in which the participle, which lacks all sense of propriety in the choice of a mate, has formed a particularly deplorable attachment. Here are a few:

- Being in a dilapidated condition, I was able to buy the house very cheap. [Strunk and White, p. 14]

- Wondering irresolutely what to do next, the clock struck twelve. [Ibid.]

- Quickly summoning an ambulance, the corpse was carried to the mortuary. [Barzun, p. 64]

292

- Roasted to perfection, carved, and reheated in orange sauce,
  you can serve this duck to the boss. [Cook, p. 29]

Yet despite the manifest absurdity of such examples, the defenders of logic have not had much influence on the general public — or even on those persons who, making their living by the use of words, might be supposed to have a particular care for the language.

Here are some dangling participles produced by professional writers:

- *From the* Far Eastern Economic Review, *in a review of a book on China by the American journalist Harrison Salisbury*:
Written during the reign of Deng, Salisbury relies heavily on sources who support the new New China.
[It is not the author who was written at that time but the book.]

- *From the* International Herald Tribune:
Based on the moderate rate of inflation over the last year, many analysts expect an increase in social security benefits of about three percent.
[It is not the analysts that are based on the rate of inflation but their expectation.]

- *From a mail-order catalog, in a paragraph describing the origin of a special key case offered for sale*:
While visiting the German factory that makes some of our superb pens, our host put his car keys on the conference table.
[Our German host was not visiting his own factory; "we" were the visitors.]

<u>Knowing</u> of your interest in El Salvador and your concern over
U.S. policy in Central America, <u>you</u> will be interested to
know that Senator Kennedy and I have introduced [in
Congress] a bill which will cut off military and economic
aid to El Salvador.

[Naturally, the citizen knew of her own interest in El Salvador.
The staff member who drafted the letter for the Senator
meant to say that the Senator also knew of it.]

Of course, the very fact that dangling participles are so often
seen in print suggests that the grammarians are fighting a losing battle with native speakers of English. Nevertheless, Chinese
translators, who do not wish to be suspected of either ignorance or
negligence, should be careful to respect the rule.

2. Dangling gerunds

A gerund, you will recall, is the -ing form of a verb that acts as
a noun (<u>pleasing</u> a child is easy).

Unlike a participle, which can readily stand alone as an adjective
(a <u>pleasing</u> child, a <u>pleased</u> child), a gerund by itself rarely serves as
a modifier. But it is often part of a prepositional phrase that serves as
a modifier (<u>by pleasing</u> the child, <u>in trying</u> to please the child, etc.)

In phrases of this kind the subject of the gerund is not expressed
but only implied. (The person who is "pleasing" or "trying" to
please the child is not identified.)

Still, when the phrase stands at the beginning, that unexpressed
subject must be logically related to the expressed subject of the sentence. Otherwise, like an opening present participle, the gerund will

"dangle." The rule here is simple: the implied subject of an opening gerund must be the same as the subject of the sentence.

Again, it will be useful to begin with examples of correct structure:

- After occupying the county of Tongdao, on the southwest border of Hunan Province, the troops entered Guizhou.

[The implied subject of "occupying" is the same as the subject of the sentence: it was the troops who had occupied Tongdao.]

- In establishing special economic zones and implementing an open policy, we must make it clear that our guideline is just that — to open and not to close.

[The implied subject of the two gerunds is the same as the subject of the sentence: it is "we" (the Chinese government) who are establishing the SEZs and implementing the open policy.]

Now, two contrary examples:

- Fortunately, by cutting the number of employees, the annual debt of the firm has decreased.

[The implied subject of "cutting" is "the firm," but "the firm" is present only as object of the preposition "of." The subject of the sentence is "the annual debt." It is not the debt that has laid off workers.]

- After gaining some experience, these measures will gradually be introduced in other regions across the country.

[The implied subject of "gaining" is "we" (the government), but the subject of the sentence is "these measures." The

295

measures will not gain any experience.]

The objection to constructions like these is the same as the objection to dangling participles: readers expect a logical continuity of thought. They automatically assume that the writer will be consistent, that he or she will not launch a sentence with one (unspoken) subject in mind and then, without warning, switch to another. Thus, a dangling gerund gives readers the same disconcerting jolt as a dangling participle.

The two possible remedies are also the same: the translator can either make the subject of the sentence consistent with the opening phrase or replace the phrase with another construction:

- Fortunately, *by cutting* the number of employees, *the firm* has reduced its annual debt.
  [The implied subject of "cutting" ("the firm") has been made the subject of the sentence.]

- *After we have gained some experience*, these measures will be gradually introduced in other regions across the country.
  [The phrase with the gerund has been turned into a subordinate clause with its own expressed subject, "we."]

Like dangling participles, dangling gerunds are most often found at the beginning of a sentence. But they too may occur in other places. Here is an example:

- The Chinese Government and people will never accept violations of or interference in China's sovereignty by directly or indirectly including the Taiwan Straits in the scope of Japan-U.S. defense cooperation, Shen said.
  [Even in the middle of the sentence, when it follows the main

296

verb, the gerund phrase, which is adrift without a subject of its own, clings to the subject of the sentence. Thus, it is "the Chinese Government and people" who will never include the Straits in the defense arrangements of Japan and the U. S.]

A solution would be to change the gerund so that "the Chinese Government and people" would be its logical subject:

- *The Chinese Government and people* will never accept violations of or interference in China's sovereignty *by allowing* the Taiwan Straits to be included, directly or indirectly, in the scope of Japan-U. S. defense cooperation, Shen said.

Dangling gerunds in the English of native speakers

These are almost as common as dangling participles. Here are a few examples, drawn from sources that one might expect to be models of correct English:

- *From a form letter sent by the President of the United States to recently naturalized citizens*:

In adopting the United States of America as your homeland, I want to congratulate you as a new citizen of this nation we hold so dear.

[It was not "I" (President Reagan) who had just adopted a new homeland.]

- *From a form letter sent by the U. S. Department of Commerce to all citizens, asking them to fill out census forms and return the forms by mail*:

By doing so, a census taker will not have to visit your home.

297

[The implied subject of "doing so" is "you" (the recipient of the letter), not the census taker, who is the subject of the sentence.]

- *From the* Boston Globe, *in a feature story on real estate*:

After getting directions, at least five pairs of eyes watched me get back into my red sports car.

[Eyes can express many things, but they cannot ask for or receive driving directions.]

- *From the* International Herald Tribune, *in a political commentary by William Safire, the author of a regular column on language*:

In trying to conceal a blunder, real crimes have been committed.

[- It was not the crimes that were trying to conceal the blunder but the unnamed persons in the government who had allegedly committed them.

- (Presumably, if confronted with this dangling gerund, Mr. Safire — who is a recognized authority on English but was writing here in a different capacity — would acknowledge it as a "blunder" on his own part.)]

3. Dangling infinitives

Infinitives and infinitive phrases can also be modifiers. And although they generally give less trouble than participles and gerunds, they too can dangle.

The rule for infinitives is the same as for gerunds: the implied subject of an opening infinitive must be the same as the subject of the sentence. Since the correct pattern is the same as for gerunds, a single example will suffice:

- To guarantee the establishment and improvement of a socialist market system, we must have a complete legal system.

[The implied subject of "to guarantee" is the same as the subject of the sentence: it is "we" (the government) who must guarantee the establishment etc.]

As for the incorrect pattern, we have already seen an example in the last chapter. You may recall exercise 7:

- In order to ensure achievement of the Party's political, military and economic objectives, Mao emphasized that the Party must first consolidate its ranks.

In that exercise you were asked to recognize that the introductory phrase wrongly modified "emphasized." This suggested that it was Mao's words, rather than the Party's actions, that would ensure achievement of the goals. To attach the phrase to the right verb, "must consolidate," you had to reorder the sentence, moving the phrase into the subordinate clause introduced by "that" — the clause to which it logically belongs:

- Mao emphasized that *to ensure* achievement of its political, military and economic objectives, *the Party* must first consolidate its ranks.

Since a change of word order sufficed to correct the error, this example was classified as a simple misplaced modifier. But it is essentially a dangling infinitive, one that does not conform to the rule about the necessary consistency of subjects. In the original sentence, the implied subject of "to ensure" is "the Party," but the subject of the sentence is "Mao."

Although in that instance, all that was necessary was to

299

rearrange the words, dangling infinitives, like dangling participles, cannot usually be so easily brought to order. Here is a more typical example:

- <u>To lead</u> China into the 21st century, <u>efforts</u> must also be made to promote cultural and ethical progress, to consolidate the Party, to strengthen unity among China's various ethnic groups, and to maintain political stability.

[The implied subject of "to lead" is again "we," but the subject of the sentence is "efforts." Only people can lead China, not efforts.]

To correct this sentence, we would have to introduce a subject that would match the implied subject of the infinitive:

- *To lead* China into the 21st century, *we* must also promote cultural and ethical progress, consolidate the Party, strengthen unity among various ethnic groups, and maintain political stability.

[(<u>Review</u>: "Make efforts to" would be an unnecessary introductory phrase. "China's" can be taken for granted.)]

Dangling infinitives in the English of native speakers

These are not so common as dangling participles and gerunds. Still, there is one dangling infinitive phrase with which Americans, at least, are only too familiar. It is "in order to serve you better."

This phrase is typically used by banks, post offices, supermarkets, pharmacies, and similar establishments to announce that a burden of some sort is being laid on customers. They are instructed to fill out a form, punch in their 14-digit account number, return their shopping wagon to the designated location, take a seat and wait, or the like.

The phrase "in order to serve you better," intended to persuade customers that this inconvenience is actually in their own interest, is typically left unattached:

- *A notice posted in a bank regarding the procedure for depositing money*:

In order to serve you better, please fill out a deposit slip before
approaching the window.

[The implied subject of the infinitive "to serve" is the bank or,
more precisely, the bank teller at the window. But the
subject of the sentence (the unexpressed subject of the
main verb, "fill out") is "you," the customer.]

The faulty grammar disguises faulty reasoning. It is true that if you spend less time at the window filling out a form, the teller will be able to move on sooner to the next person in line. But the suggestion is that you yourself will save time, which is not the case. It is more likely that while you are making out the form before joining the queue, two or three people will line up ahead of you.

A revision of the notice might read:

To save time for the teller, please *fill out* a deposit slip before
approaching the window.

The subject of the infinitive "to save" would then match the subject of the main verb, "fill out" (both being an unexpressed "you"), and the message would be more candid. But the bank knows that if the request were thus plainly stated, it might arouse resistance.

- *From the instructions given by a mail-order company to customers wishing to return a purchase (the "return code"*

301

is a number indicating the reason the merchandise is un-satisfactory):

In order <u>to serve</u> you better, simply <u>write the return code</u> in the box provided.

[The implied subject of "to serve" is the company, while the (unexpressed) subject of the sentence is "you."]

Again, the logic behind the request is as obscure as the grammar. By taking the time to find and enter the code number on the form, you will be doing the company a service, not the other way around.

4. Prepositional phrases
(not based on verb forms)

Prepositional phrases based on gerunds ("<u>by cutting</u> the number of employees") and on infinitives ("<u>in order to ensure</u> achievement") are not the only ones that need to be related logically to the subjects of their sentences.

Any opening prepositional phrase that acts as an <u>adjective</u> will affix itself to the <u>noun or pronoun</u> that is the subject of its sentence, in the same manner as an opening participial phrase. And if that subject is not the word the phrase is intended to modify, the effect will be the same as that of a dangling participle.

Here is an example taken from promotional material for Jiangxi Province designed to attract foreign investors:

- <u>With a favorable environment</u> and preferential government policies, any <u>investment</u> is assured of healthy returns.

The prepositional phrase, which is meant to describe the province,

302

attaches itself instead to the subject of the sentence, "investment."

The two possible solutions for such a problem are the same as for a dangling participle: you can either find the word that the phrase actually modifies and make it the subject of the sentence, or you can convert the phrase into a separate clause:

- *With its favorable environment* and preferential government policies, *Jiangxi Province* ensures that any investment will bring healthy returns.

- *Because Jiangxi Province has a favorable environment* and offers preferential government policies, any investment there is assured of healthy returns.

In the same way, an opening prepositional phrase that acts as an adverb will affix itself to the main verb in the sentence. That was the problem in one of the examples of misplaced modifiers discussed in the last chapter:

- After years of effort, Gao said that soil erosion has been brought under control . . . .

In that sentence, you will recall, the introductory phrase attached itself to the verb in the main clause, "said." To connect it to the right verb, "has been brought," we had to move it into the subordinate clause introduced by "that":

- Gao said that *after years of effort*, soil erosion *has been brought* under control . . . .

Next to prepositional phrases containing gerunds, the ones that are most often left dangling in Chinglish are those introduced by "like" and "as." Following is an example of each, with a suggested revision:

303

From an advertisement for a Holiday Inn newly opened in Zhengzhou :

A: Just <u>like the Crowne Plaza</u> [in Beijing], <u>all rooms</u> feature an electronic door lock, a private safe, two telephones with IDD ....

B: *Like the rooms* in the Crowne Plaza, *all those* in the Holiday Inn feature an electronic door lock, a private safe, two telephones with IDD ....

 [- In A-version the opening phrase is not logically attached to the subject of the sentence. What is "like" the Crowne Plaza is not "all rooms" but the missing Holiday Inn.

 - Replacing "all rooms" with "the Holiday Inn" would have correctly matched the subject to the phrase, so that one hotel was being compared to another: "Just like the Crowne Plaza, the Holiday Inn ...." But that would have made it awkward to manage the rest of the sentence.

 - The easiest way to achieve the right match was to change not the subject but the introductory phrase, comparing rooms to rooms: "Just like the rooms in the Crowne Plaza, all those in the Holiday Inn ...."

 - ("Just" was omitted as unnecessary.)]

From the remarks of a high Party cadre :

A: <u>As leaders</u>, <u>it</u> is necessary to get a clear picture of the problems and work out measures to solve them.

B: *As leaders* , *we* must get a clear picture of the problems and work out measures to solve them.

 [In A-version, the opening phrase has no logical connection with the following "it. " Readers expect that the subject of the sentence will tell them who these leaders are — "we," "you," "they," "senior cadres," or whatever persons the term refers to. In the revision, the correct subject is provided.]

Dangling prepositional phrases in the English of native speakers

A few examples, taken from sources on both sides of the Atlantic:

- *From the British* Manchester Guardian Weekly, *in a review of a show of work by the American painter Andy Warhol* :

But like Rivera, one of his publicly exhibited works, "Thirteen Most Wanted Men," was sufficiently offensive to bourgeois tastes that it was painted over after being briefly exhibited at the 1964 New York World's Fair.

[As in the Crowne Plaza example above, the opening phrase is not logically attached to the subject of the sentence. What, in the opinion of the reviewer, was "like" the famous Mexican painter Diego Rivera was not one of Andy Warhol's works but the missing Andy Warhol himself. The comparison should have been either Rivera/Warhol or Rivera's work/Warhol's work.]

- *From a letter from a major U.S. credit card company to a cardholder* :

As a valued MasterCard Gold customer, we are pleased to inform you that we have increased the credit limit of your MasterCard Gold account to the amount shown above.

[On reading the opening phrase, the recipient of the letter confidently expected that she herself was to be named as the valued customer. Her expectation was disappointed.]

305

- From an advertisement in a publication of the American Association of Retired Persons:

As a pharmacist for many years, my customers appreciate the benefits of garlic. As a consumer for even longer, I also appreciate the benefits of saving money.

[In the first sentence the pharmacist confuses himself with his customers. Plainly, what he meant to say was, "*As a pharmacist* for many years, *I* have found that my customers appreciate etc.*" In the second sentence he got the construction right.]

- From an article in the Los Angeles Times *concerning women's fashions in Washington*, *D.C.*:

With little time to shop or even to think about her wardrobe, and the threat of social censure if she takes fashion risks, a universally acceptable uniform would be a blessing.

[Thanks to "her" and "she," throughout the long introductory phrase the reader is convinced that the subject of this sentence is the professional woman in need of something safe to wear on all occasions. At "uniform," the train of thought does not merely give a jolt, it is completely derailed. Logically, there is only one possible way to complete the sentence: "With little time to shop . . . and the threat of social censure if she takes fashion risks, *she* would consider a universally acceptable uniform a blessing."]

5. Individual adjectives

Lastly, individual adjectives in an initial position, ones that are not part of prepositional phrases, can also dangle when they do not modify the subject of the sentence.

This faulty construction is less common than the others we have discussed, but here is an example from a Chinese publication:

- <u>Tall and shy</u>, Diana's stylish <u>gowns</u> were recently auctioned off for $ 5.7 million.

[The adjectives, meant to describe Diana, attach themselves instead to the subject of the sentence, "gowns."]

Since the word the adjectives are intended to modify appears in the sentence, we could simply change the word order:

- The stylish gowns of *tall* , *shy* Diana were recently auctioned off for $ 5.7 million.

Another solution would be to put the adjectives in a separate subordinate clause:

- The stylish gowns of Diana, *who was tall and shy*, were recently auctioned off for $ 5.7 million.

Both of these versions are grammatically correct but have little else to recommend them. The basic difficulty is that in this context the Princess's height and alleged shyness are irrelevant, and the revisions only make this more apparent. The only way to make such a sentence truly logical is to drop the adjectives entirely:

- Diana's stylish gowns were recently auctioned off for $ 5.7 million.

Twenty more examples of revision

Present participles

1) A: <u>The procuratorate</u> handled 744 cases of dereliction crimes and

1,119 major accidents in the first half of this year, <u>rising</u> respectively by 23 per cent and 30 per cent over the same period in 1986.

B: In the first half of this year, the procuratorate handled 744 crimes of negligence and 1,119 major accidents, *an increase of* 23 per cent and 30 per cent respectively over the same period in 1986.

[- In A-version, the participle ("rising"), even though it is not in opening position, attaches itself to the subject of the sentence ("the procuratorate"). This produces a meaning that contradicts common sense: what has risen is not the procuratorate but the number of crimes investigated.

- In the revision the participle has been replaced by "an increase of" (an abbreviated form of "which is an increase of").

- ("Dereliction crimes" was replaced by the standard English term, "crimes of negligence.")

- (<u>Review</u>: "Cases of" was eliminated as an unnecessary category-noun.)]

2) A: <u>Boasting</u> the world's third largest bank of energy resources, after the United States and Russia, China's <u>output</u> of coal in the 1990s leads the world, while its crude oil output ranks fifth and electricity second.

B: In the 1990s *China*, *which boasts* the world's third largest energy reserves after the United States and Russia, ranks first in output of coal, second in output of electricity, and fifth in output of crude oil.

[- In A-version there are two clauses with two separate subjects: a main clause, the subject of which is "China's output of coal," and a subordinate clause introduced by "while," the subject of which is "crude oil output."

- In such a case, the participle must modify not the subject of the sentence (since there are two of them) but the subject of <u>the clause to which it belongs</u>.

- The word the participle ("boasting") should logically modify is "China," but the subject of the clause to which it belongs is "China's output of coal." It is not the output of coal that is "boasting."

- In the revision, the subject of the main clause has been changed from "China's output" to "China." This gave "boasting" the right noun to modify, but the polisher still thought it better to convert the participial phrase into a subordinate clause ("which boasts").

- ("Leads the world" was changed to "ranks first" in order to put the three figures in comparable form. They were then rearranged in a logical descending order: China ranks first in x, second in y, fifth in z.)]

3) A: Many scattered <u>liberated areas</u> were linked up, <u>enabling</u> the people's armed forces to take the initiative militarily.

  B: Many scattered liberated areas were linked up, *which enabled* (*or*: which made it possible for) the people's armed forces to take the initiative militarily.

  [- A-version seems logical enough at first, but it does not bear close examination. The participle ("enabling") does not refer to the subject of the sentence ("liberated areas"). It is not the "scattered liberated areas" that enabled the people's armed forces to take the initiative but the linking of those areas.

- In B-version the participial phrase has been turned into a subordinate clause introduced by "which."
- (<u>Review</u>: Here the relative pronoun "which" plainly refers to the entire main clause immediately preceding: "Many scattered liberated areas were linked up.")]

4) *The next sentence after the preceding example*:

A: Gradually, <u>guerrilla warfare</u> was turned into mobile warfare, <u>creating</u> the conditions necessary for a full-scale counter-offensive.

B: Gradually *they* turned guerrilla warfare into mobile warfare, *creating* the conditions necessary for a full-scale counter-offensive.

[- This sentence, like the preceding one, is understandable, but it does not actually say what it means.
- Again, the participle ("creating") does not refer to the subject of the sentence ("guerrilla warfare"). It is not "guerrilla warfare" that created the conditions for a counter-offensive but the change of tactics on the part of the revolutionary army — the gradual transition from guerrilla warfare to mobile warfare.
- This time the main verb was changed to active voice and given a subject that the participle could logically refer to. In B-version it is "they" (the people's armed forces, mentioned at the end of the preceding sentence) who have created the necessary conditions by turning guerrilla warfare into mobile warfare.
- (<u>Review</u>: Since "the people's armed forces" appears at the end of the immediately preceding sentence, the pronoun "they" has a clear antecedent.)]

310

5) A: The Liaoxi-Shenyang campaign lasted 52 days, and 472,000 enemy troops were wiped out. From this time onward, the PLA was superior to the KMT in numbers, bringing the Chinese revolution to another turning point.

B: During the 52 days of the Liaoxi-Shenyang campaign, 472,000 enemy troops were wiped out. From this time onward, the PLA was numerically superior to the KMT, *a change that marked* another turning point in the Chinese revolution.

[- In A-version the participle ("bringing") wrongly attaches itself to the subject of the sentence ("the PLA"). It was not the PLA that brought the revolution to another turning point but the change in the relative strength of the two opposing forces.

 - The polisher first introduced the missing word for the participle to modify: ". . . the PLA was numerically superior to the KMT, a change bringing another turning point in the Chinese revolution."

 - Then, because that version was awkward, she replaced the participial phrase with a subordinate clause introduced by "that": "a change that brought another turning point in the Chinese revolution."

 - Lastly, considering that this was neither idiomatic nor logical (nothing "brings" a turning point), she substituted "a change that marked another turning point etc."

 - (Review: In A-version the two ideas in the first sentence — the length of the campaign and the number of enemy troops wiped out — are presented in two coordinate clauses, as if they were of equal importance. But since in this

311

context the length of the campaign is only of secondary interest, in the revision it was relegated to a prepositional phrase — "During the 52 days etc.")]

6) A: The expansion of the productive forces was ignored, and <u>policies</u> were formulated <u>neglecting</u> the realities of the primary stage of socialism.

B: No attempt was made to expand the productive forces, and *the policies we formulated were too ambitious* for the primary stage of socialism.

[- In A-version the participle ("neglecting") belongs to the second clause, introduced by "and." The subject of that clause is "policies," and it is "policies" that the participle appears to modify. Logically, however, it was not the "policies" that were "neglecting" the realities but the unmentioned policy-makers.

- To revise the sentence, the polisher first replaced the participle ("neglecting") with a prepositional phrase ("without regard for the realities"), at the same time changing the clause to active voice: "we formulated policies without regard for the realities of the primary stage of socialism."

- (That version was grammatically acceptable, but it was still vague. A second polisher, after studying the Chinese again for context, was able to make a further improvement. She changed the general statement "we formulated policies without regard for the realities," which says only that the policies were unsuitable, to the more specific "the policies we formulated were too ambitious," which explains why they were unsuitable.)

- (<u>Review</u>: "The expansion ... was ignored" was changed

312

to "no attempt was made to expand," in order to get rid of an abstract noun.)]

Past participles

7) A: <u>Suffocated</u> by huge debts and overstaffing, more than 25,000 <u>workers</u>, one quarter of the firm's total, have been persuaded by decision-makers in the enterprise to give up their original jobs in the mines.

B: *Since the enterprise was suffocated* by huge debts and overstaffing, its decision-makers have persuaded more than 25,000 workers, one quarter of the total, to give up their original jobs in the mines.

[- Plainly, in A-version the participial phrase ("suffocated by huge debts etc.") is intended to modify either "the firm" or "the enterprise." But since neither of those nouns is the subject of the sentence, the phrase attaches itself to the one that is: "workers." Thus, readers are led to believe that it is the 25,000 workers who are "suffocated by huge debts."

- This erroneous interpretation is all the more plausible because workers in a failing enterprise might indeed be heavily in debt. Readers are well into the sentence before they realize they have been misled.

- In the revision, the participial phrase was simply discarded and replaced by a subordinate clause introduced by "Since." (This had the further advantage of putting the verb in active voice.)

- (<u>Review</u>: "The firm's" in the phrase "of the firm's total" was dropped as a self-evident modifier.)]

313

8) A: "Based on the current situation, we chose apartments as our first property investment here," said Benson Lam, executive director of Dynamic Holdings Co.

B: "*On the basis of* the current situation, we *chose* apartments as our first property investment here," said Benson Lam, executive director of Dynamic Holdings Co.

[- In A-version the participial phrase "based on" is used as if it had already become a prepositional phrase. It has not, and the result of treating it as independent is an illogical statement: it is not the company ("we") that is based on the current situation but the company's decision.

- In B-version the participial phrase has been replaced by a true prepositional phrase, "on the basis of," which acts as an adverb correctly attached to the main verb, "chose."

- (Note that a number of other expressions could also have been used: "in view of," "in light of," "considering," etc. "Based on" could even have been replaced by another past participle. "Having studied," for example, would have been perfectly acceptable, because it would have logically modified the subject, "we.")]

9) A: Compared with the pace at which the financial and economic work was unified in a liberated area when it was separated from others, it may indeed seem too soon to exercise unified management of financial and economic work at present.

B: *If we consider* the length of time it took for financial and economic work to be unified within each separate liberated area, it may indeed seem too soon to try to unify it nationwide.

314

[- In A-version the opening participle ("Compared") does not modify the subject of the main clause, to which it belongs ("it," representing "to exercise unified management"). "Compared" is floating unattached because it has nothing to modify — no other "pace" is compared with the pace at which the work was unified.

- In B-version the participial phrase "Compared with etc." has been converted to a subordinate clause ("If we consider etc.").

- ("Nationwide" was added to clarify the sense by underlining the contrast between unification in a single liberated area and unification throughout the country.)

- (Review: "Exercise unified management," an unnec. verb + noun structure, was reduced to "unify." The second reference to "financial and economic work" was replaced by the pronoun "it." "At present" was eliminated as redundant with the present tense of the verb "it may seem.")]

Gerunds

10) A: A country's revolution and construction depend on the practice of the people of that country. Only by integrating the universal truths of Marxism-Leninism with the actual realities of the country can Marxism-Leninism be enriched and developed.

B: A country's revolution and construction depend on the practice of the people of that country. Only *if the universal truths of Marxism-Leninism are integrated* with the realities of the country can Marxism-Leninism be enriched and developed.

[- In A-version it is not clear just who is supposed to be the subject of "by integrating" — an implied "we" in general or "the people of each country."

- The subject of the sentence is "Marxism-Leninism," and the gerund tries to attach itself to that subject. But "Marxism-Leninism" cannot integrate its own truths.

- In the revision the gerund phrase "by integrating" has been turned into a subordinate clause ("if the universal truths are integrated"). The verb was deliberately left in passive voice to keep the subject vague, as it was in the Chinese.

- (Review: "Actual" was omitted as a superfluous intensifier.)]

11) A: The world is vast and things are complicated, but <u>after analyzing</u> the situation, there are only <u>a few people</u> who support war, and most people want peace and oppose war.

B: The world is vast and complex, but *if you analyze* the situation you will find there are only a few people who support war; most people want peace.

[- In A-version the sentence has no one subject, because there are several clauses, each with its own subject.

- In such a case, the rule for gerunds is the same as the one for participles in sentences having more than one clause (see example 2 above): the implied subject of the gerund must be the same as the subject of <u>the clause to which it belongs</u>.

- Here the gerund phrase "after analyzing" belongs to the second independent clause, introduced by "but." The unexpressed subject of "analyzing" ("you," meaning the persons being addressed) should therefore be the same as the subject of the second clause. That subject, however, is "a few people." It is not "a few people" who are "analyzing the situation."

- First the polisher changed the gerund phrase to a different construction — a subordinate clause with its own subject: "but if you analyze the situation, there are only a few people who support war."

- But that version did not seem quite right: she felt there was an element missing. She therefore spelled out the meaning in full: "but if you analyze the situation you will find there are only a few people who support war."

- (Review: "There are only a few people who support war, and most people want peace and oppose war" is a classic example of saying the same thing twice — indeed, three times. "And oppose war" was eliminated as plain redundancy, but "most people want peace" was allowed to stand for emphasis.)]

12) A: In reforming and restructuring, upgrading quality should be the focus for technological renovation.

B: *In reforming and restructuring, we* should concentrate on technological renovation to upgrade quality.

[- In A-version, the implied subject of "reforming and restructuring" is "we" (the government), while the subject of the sentence is "upgrading."

- In B-version, the correct subject of the sentence has been introduced ("we"), to match the implied subject of the gerunds.

- (Also, in A-version the relation between "reforming and restructuring" and "the focus for technological renovation" is vague at best. In the revision, the logical connections between the various elements of the sentence have been clarified. The structure now is: in doing x, we should concentrate on y, in order to achieve z.

- (Review: At the same time, this revision changed an abstract noun, "focus," to a verb, "should concentrate.")]

13) *The next sentence after the preceding example*:

A: In so doing, techniques and equipment should be upgraded, testing and experimental facilities should be improved . . . .

B: *In so doing*, *we* should upgrade techniques and equipment, improve testing and experimental facilities . . . .

[- "In so doing" is a handy device for subordinating one idea to another and at the same time avoiding repetition, but it is often left dangling in Chinglish.

- Here, "In so doing" stands for "in concentrating on technological renovation." Its implied subject is therefore the same "we" as in the preceding sentence ("we should concentrate on"). In A-version, however, the subject of the clause in which the phrase appears is not "we" but "techniques and equipment."

- The solution is the same as in example 12: the implied subject of the gerund ("we") has been made the expressed subject of the clause.]

14) A: In late May 1989 I said that we should boldly choose for the new leadership persons who were generally recognized as

318

adhering to the line of the reform and the opening up and who had scored some achievements in reform and the opening up. By so doing, people will see that we are wholeheartedly carrying out the reform and the opening up.

B: In late May 1989 I said that we should boldly choose for the new leadership persons who were generally recognized as adhering to the line of reform and opening up and who had some achievements in that respect to their credit. *This would convince the people* that we were wholeheartedly committed to that line.

[- The problem in A-version is exactly the same as in the example just above. "By so doing" stands for "by boldly choosing etc., " so its implied subject is the same "we" as in the preceding sentence ("we should boldly choose"). But the subject of the main clause in which the phrase appears is not "we" but "people."

- This time, the reviser chose to drop the gerund phrase ("By so doing") and replace it with a clause introduced by "this," referring to the whole preceding sentence: "This would convince the people that etc."

- Another solution would have been to make the implied subject of the gerund the expressed subject of the clause it belonged to, as was done in the last two examples: "By so doing, we would show the people that etc."

- (Review: To avoid intolerable repetition, the polisher changed the second reference to "reform and opening up" to "in that respect" and the third to "that line.")]

15) A: In the course of examining our work, certain persons' views may not be totally correct.

B: *In the course of examining* our work, certain *persons* may express views that are not totally correct.

[- In A-version the implied subject of the gerund "examining" is "we" (Party members), while the subject of the sentence is "certain persons' views." "Views" cannot examine our work.

- In the revision the possessive adjective "persons'" has been converted into a noun, "persons," and made the subject of the main clause. Since the "certain persons" are some of the Party members participating in the examination, the subject of the clause is now consistent with the subject of the gerund.]

16) A: A person's ideological problems can be solved only by gradually raising his political consciousness and through studying and thinking by himself and remolding himself.

B: The only way *a person can solve* his ideological problems *is to* gradually *raise* his political consciousness and *remold* himself through studying and thinking.

[- In A-version it is not clear who or what is the subject of the first gerund, "by raising." Plainly, it is not the "problems" (the subject of the sentence), but is it the person in question or his comrades who are trying to help him?

- To clarify the meaning, the reviser turned "by raising" into an infinitive whose subject is the "person" himself: "the only way a person can solve his ideological problems is to gradually raise his political consciousness etc."

320

- The last gerund, "remolding," was then converted to an infinitive parallel to the first: "to gradually raise ... and remold ...."]

Infinitives

17) A: <u>To reach</u> a more objective conclusion, he said, historical, cultural, and other <u>backgrounds</u> of the ethnic groups should be considered when <u>studying</u> religion in China.

   B: *To reach* a more objective conclusion, he said, *people studying* religion in China should consider the history and culture of the various ethnic groups and other aspects of their background.

   [- In A-version the unspoken subject of the infinitive phrase ("To reach a more objective conclusion") is the people studying religion in China. But those people are never mentioned.

   - Readers expect that when they reach the subject of the sentence they will learn who it is that wants to reach a more objective conclusion. Instead, they find "backgrounds."

   - The word that the participle "studying" should modify is also the absent "people." Having nothing sensible to attach itself to, the participle is adrift just like the infinitive.

   - In B-version the polisher has introduced the missing word "people" and made it the subject of the sentence. That subject now conforms to the implied subject of "To reach" and also serves as a logical anchor for "studying."

   - ("Historical, cultural, and other backgrounds" was

changed to "history and culture . . . and other aspects of their background" because a group does not have plural "backgrounds.")]

18) A: From the military point of view, in order to carry the War of Liberation to a victorious conclusion, Mao analyzed the methods used by the PLA.

B: From the military point of view, Mao analyzed the *methods* that the PLA had been using and *that would enable it to carry* the War of Liberation to a victorious conclusion.

[- In A-version the implied subject of the infinitive phrase is "the PLA," but the subject of the sentence is "Mao." The phrase is intended to indicate the reason for the PLA's choice of methods, not the reason for Mao's analysis. That is, it should modify "used by," not "analyzed."

- To make the right logical connection, the polisher had only to move the phrase to the end of the sentence: "From the military point of view, Mao analyzed the methods used by the PLA to carry the War of Liberation to a successful conclusion."

- (Referring back to the Chinese, he then decided that a further change was needed to accurately convey the meaning of the original. "The methods used by the PLA to carry the War of Liberation to a victorious conclusion" became "the methods that the PLA had been using and that would enable it to carry the War of Liberation to a successful conclusion.")]

Prepositional phrases (not based on verb forms)

19) A: As a veteran Party member and citizen, who has worked for

322

decades for the communist cause and for the independence, reunification, development, and reform of the country, <u>my life</u> belongs to the Party and the country.

B: *Since I am a veteran Party member and citizen* who has worked for decades for the communist cause and for the independence, reunification, development, and reform of the country, my life belongs to the Party and the country.

[- In this passage, the "veteran Party member" is speaking about himself. Readers of A-version work their way through the introductory prepositional phrase, with its long subordinate "who" clause, in the confident expectation that the subject of the sentence, when it eventually appears, will inevitably be "I."

- When they reach "my life" — jolt. The speaker has apparently started with one subject in mind and then suddenly switched to another.

- Since the opening prepositional phrase ("As a veteran Party member etc.") does not accord with the subject of the sentence ("my life"), it dangles just as a participle would in the same position ("Being a veteran Party member . . . my life belongs to the Party etc.").

- In B-version the prepositional phrase has been abandoned in favor of a subordinate clause: "Since I am a veteran Party member etc."

- An alternative solution would have been to introduce the anticipated word as the subject of the sentence: "As a veteran Party member . . . I feel that my life belongs to the Party and the country."]

20) A: Once <u>on a trip to Shandong</u>, <u>my host</u> announced that he was treating us to a special flavor.

B: Once *when I was on a trip to Shandong*, my host announced that he was treating us to a special dish.

[- Although we are dealing here with a prepositional phrase, the principle is the same as in the example of a dangling participle cited earlier (from a native speaker): "While visiting the German factory ... our host put his car keys on the conference table."

- In both instances, despite grammatical appearances, the host was on home ground and only the speaker was traveling.

- In B-version the abbreviated prepositional phrase has been fully spelled out as a subordinate clause ("when I was on a trip"), which allows of no misunderstanding.

- (The "special flavor" turned out to be steamed cornbread and was therefore changed to the more idiomatic "a special dish.")]

Twenty exercises

Each of the following exercises contains at least one dangling modifier. If you first identify the suspect phrase — usually at the beginning of the sentence — and the subject of the clause in which it appears, you will be well on the way to solving the problem.

As we have seen, it is usually easiest to correct a dangling modifier by changing the subject of the clause. If that is not practical, consider changing the dangler itself into some other construction — a subordinate clause introduced by "since," "if," "which," or the like, or perhaps a prepositional phrase. (In one of the exercises, you have

324

only to delete the unattached participle.)

Often, a sentence can be revised in more than one way, and the versions offered in the key do not necessarily exhaust the possibilities.

1) Compared with the developed countries, China's per capita national income is still very low.

2) As a developing country with more than 1.2 billion people, he noted, China's hydrocarbon resources will not be able to meet the fast-growing demand.

3) Set to the music of Rachmaninoff's "Second Piano Concerto" played by the Central Ballet Theater Orchestra, the dancers depict Anna [Karenina] during the turbulent social transition in Russia at the turn of the 19th century.

4) While deepening reform and quickening the pace of economic development, efforts to build a clean and honest government should be strengthened.

[Hint: see Chapter III, page 78, revision 1.]

5) Disciplinary action must be taken against those Party members who refuse to correct their errors, but in doing so no "Left" mistakes of resorting to summary measures and subjecting too many people to criticism should be repeated.

6) He [an orchestra conductor] reduced the number of string players in an attempt to keep a balance with the brass and woodwind sections. By doing so, the sound quality of the orchestra could be likened to that of a chamber music ensemble.

7) Living in a city among crowded cement "matchboxes," my eyes have become insensitive to the architecture around me.

8) Peasants in the Border Region have increased the output of millet and wheat by more than 20 million kg. When added to the output of army units, government departments, Party organizations, and schools, the total increase will come to more than 40 million kg.

9) By choosing Hong Kong as the venue [for the 52nd annual meetings of the World Bank and the IMF], it indicates that the international community has given a vote of confidence to Hong Kong as an important financial center.

10) In February 1949, acting on instructions from the Military Commission of the CPC Central Committee to standardize the designations of the entire Chinese People's Liberation Army, the Central Plains Field Army was renamed the Second Field Army.

11) Affected by bourgeois ideas, there exists a lot of waste in our diplomatic work.

12) Only by carrying out this policy can cultural undertakings contribute more to our socialist construction.

13) In getting more than 90 per cent of the people to join the mass organizations, women merit our special attention.

14) However, China is short of some minerals crucial to economic development, leaving Chinese geologists with a tough task.

15) Failing to draw lessons from the uprisings in Nanchang and Guangzhou, the political line at that time still encouraged insurrections everywhere.

16) Covering an area of 1.3 square kilometers, construction of the new project is expected to start within this year and will be

completed in five stages over the next eight years.

17) As a non-profit, non-governmental mass organization, Wang and her colleagues have been working to make the center [the Maple Women's Psychological Counseling Center] do more than just help women with their troubles.

18) Based on this analysis, production of motorcycles for 1995 is expected to hit six million, with over 400 different models and 14 types of engine displacement.

19) Some time ago in Shanghai, in streamlining administration the size of staff was reduced.

20) In studying *putonghua*, you can't just rely on your ears and tongue, because it is easy to forget what you have learned. To be more efficient, there must be books printed in a phonetic alphabet and dictionaries giving the phonetic transcription for each character . . . .

XI. Parallel Structure

Parallel structure — that is, the expression of matching ideas in matching form — is one of the most basic and valuable stylistic devices in English. Not only does it satisfy the desire for order and balance, but at its best, by highlighting the connection between ideas, it can give the reader a fresh perception of them, summed up with great economy and force.

Many of the most memorable lines in English, from the humblest folk sayings to the most highly polished literary passages, owe their enduring power to the parallel statement of parallel thoughts. Some of the following examples will no doubt be familiar to Chinese students of English (they are identified in the numbered footnotes below):

- A penny saved is a penny earned. [1]

- Where there's a will there's a way. [2]

- To be, or not to be: that is the question .... [3]

- Early to bed and early to rise, makes a man healthy, wealthy, and wise. [4]

- Annual income twenty pounds, annual expenditure nineteen nineteen six, result happiness. Annual income twenty pounds, annual expenditure twenty pounds ought and six,

---

[1] Anonymous.

[2] Anonymous.

[3] William Shakespeare, *Hamlet*, act III, scene 1 (1600 – 1601).

[4] Benjamin Franklin, *Poor Richard's Almanack* (1735).

result misery. [5]

- Is life so dear or peace so sweet as to be purchased at the price
  of chains and slavery? Forbid it, Almighty God. I know
  not what course others may take, but as for me, give me
  liberty or give me death! [6]

- We hold these truths to be self-evident; that all men are created equal; that they are endowed by their creator with certain unalienable rights; that among these are life, liberty,
  and the pursuit of happiness . . . . [7]

- It is rather for us to be here dedicated to the great task remaining before us — that from these honored dead we take increased devotion to that cause for which they gave the last
  full measure of devotion; that we here highly resolve that
  these dead shall not have died in vain; that this nation,
  under God, shall have a new birth of freedom; and that
  government of the people, by the people, and for the people shall not perish from the earth. [8]

- To have and to hold from this day forward, for better for
  worse, for richer for poorer, in sickness and in health, to
  love and to cherish, till death us do part. [9]

- Blessed are the poor in spirit: for theirs is the kingdom of
  heaven.

---

[5] Charles Dickens, *David Copperfield*, chapter 12 (1849 – 1850).
[6] Patrick Henry, speech in Virginia Convention (1775).
[7] Thomas Jefferson, Declaration of Independence (1776).
[8] Abraham Lincoln, Address at Gettysburg (1863).
[9] Solemnization of Matrimony, the American *Book of Common Prayer* (1789, re-
    vision of 1928; derived from the *English Prayer Book* of 1549).

Blessed are they that mourn: for they shall be comforted.

Blessed are the meek: for they shall inherit the earth. [10]

To native speakers of English most of these proverbs and quotations are so well known that their form is taken for granted, as if it were inevitable. Yet in each case it would be perfectly possible to express the same meaning in a different way. For example:

- A penny saved is the same as if you had earned it.

- To be, or to cease living: that is the question . . . .

- . . . that among these are the rights to life, liberty, and to pursue happiness . . . .

- . . . that government of the people, exercised by themselves and for their own benefit, shall not perish from the earth.

- Blessed are the poor in spirit: for theirs is the kingdom of heaven.
People who are in mourning are blessed, because comfort will be given them.
Meek people are blessed too, for they shall inherit the earth.

In these alternative versions the sense remains intact. Nothing is missing except parallel structure — nothing, that is, except the conciseness, the energy, the rhythm, and the symmetry that have imprinted the originals on the minds of countless generations.

These few examples will suffice to indicate the grace and strength that the use of parallel structure brings to speech and writing

---

[10] Bible, The Gospel According to St. Matthew, chapter 5, verses 3 – 5; opening of the "Beatitudes" from Jesus' Sermon on the Mount (85 or 90; Authorized [or King James] Version in English, 1611).

of the most varied kinds. But in addition to the eloquence it can sometimes achieve, parallel structure has another virtue, one that is probably of greater everyday utility to Chinese translators: it is a wonderful aid to clarity.

When two or more matching elements in a sentence are presented in matching grammatical form, it is easier for the reader to recognize the logical relations between them.

As can be seen from the examples above, this principle applies equally to elements of any length or grammatical category:

- words: healthy, wealthy, and wise. A series of three single adjectives, all modifying "man."

- phrases: of the people, by the people, and for the people. Three prepositional phrases of equal length, all modifying "government," the parallelism being reinforced by the repetition of the same word ("people") as the object in each.

- clauses: Where there's a will there's a way. A pair of short independent clauses constructed on the same pattern ("there's an x"/"there's a y"), the parallelism being underlined by alliteration ("will"/"way").

- sentences: Annual income twenty pounds, annual expenditure nineteen nineteen six, result happiness. Annual income twenty pounds, annual expenditure twenty pounds ought and six, result misery. Two sentences of almost the same length and exactly the same pattern ("if annual income is x and annual expenditure is y, the result is z"). The parallelism between the two is heightened by the use of

331

identical words ("Annual income twenty pounds," "annual expenditure," "result") and opposite words ("happiness"/"misery").

In each of these examples, what Wilson Follett [p. 211] calls "putting like thoughts into like constructions" ensures that the form of the utterance illuminates its content. A pair or a series of elements that are to be understood as parallel in meaning are presented to the reader in parallel grammatical form. Their structural similarity brings out their logical similarity, inviting ready comprehension.

In Chapter IX, The Placement of Phrases and Clauses, we saw how a translator could clarify the logic and emphasis of a sentence by placing certain elements in the right order. Parallelism is a way of achieving that same lucidity by placing certain elements in the right structure.

Difficulties in using parallel structure

In his *Handbook of Good English* [p. 15], the experienced American book editor Edward Johnson declares that "[c]orrecting faulty parallelism occupies more of an editor's attention than correcting all other grammatical faults put together."

That is not true for editors of Chinglish texts, which — understandably — contain more grammatical errors than would normally be found in manuscripts submitted to a New York publishing house. Still, the remark calls attention to the ease with which even native speakers of English can make mistakes when attempting (or neglecting) parallel structure.

Parallelism is either required, desirable, or possible in a great variety of situations, each affording opportunities for error. Follett [p. 211] warns of "a labyrinth of ways to go wrong," and not all of those ways are easy to recognize.

We shall not attempt to survey here the entire terrain of parallel structure and all the pitfalls with which it is riddled. For our purposes, it will suffice to concentrate on those areas in which parallelism is virtually mandatory and on those potential missteps that have proved most hazardous to Chinese.

The constructions we shall consider are those in which:

1. sentence elements are linked by one of the <u>coordinating con-junctions</u> ("and," "or," etc.)

2. elements are linked by one of the so-called <u>correlative con-junctions</u> ("both ... and," "not only ... but also," etc.)

3. items appear in the form of <u>a list or a series of headings</u> (e.g., subtitles in a report)

4. elements are linked in <u>comparisons</u>

1. Elements linked by coordinating conjunctions

The chief coordinating conjunctions, you will remember, are "and," "or"/"nor," and "but." (The others — "for," "so," and "yet" — have more limited uses and are far less common.) These conjunctions connect words or groups of words that perform the same grammatical *function* in the sentence.

For example:

- On Mount Emei it starts snowing in late October <u>or</u> early November, <u>and</u> it does not stop until April.

333

"Late October" and "early November," connected by "or," both serve as objects of the preposition "in." The two parts of the sentence connected by "and" are both independent clauses.

A more complex example:

- Li said that China and [1] the Netherlands shared many common views on safeguarding world peace, promoting economic development, and [2] enhancing cooperation and [3] exchanges, despite differences in historical and [4] cultural background and [5] level of development.

Of the five "and"s in this sentence, #1 joins two subjects of the dependent "that" clause; #2 joins three objects of the preposition "on"; #3 joins two objects of the gerund "enhancing"; #4 joins two modifiers of the noun "background"; and #5 joins two objects of the preposition "in."

The elements linked by a coordinating conjunction are necessarily parallel in *meaning*. (Here, of course, "parallel" does not mean "the same": the two clauses in "give me liberty or give me death" have quite different meanings, but the meanings are parallel.) In the example just given, "China" is parallel to "the Netherlands; "safeguarding world peace," "promoting economic development" and "enhancing cooperation and exchanges" are all parallel; and so on.

Since the function and meaning of coordinate elements are parallel, it follows that, for logic and clarity, they should be expressed in parallel *form*. There are degrees of parallelism, and perfect symmetry is both rarely achieved and rarely necessary. But at a minimum, parallel form means that the words or groups of words in a pair must belong to the same grammatical category.

To begin with, single words should not be paired with phrases or clauses. In addition, if the elements joined are words, they must both be the same part of speech — nouns, adjectives, etc.; if phrases, both of the same type — infinitive, participial, etc.; if clauses, both of the same rank — independent (main) or dependent (subordinate). The same is true when there are three or more items in a series: all must be of the same kind.

If we return to our second example, we find that this rule has been observed. Each pair or series consists of items in the same grammatical category:

- Li said that China and [1] the Netherlands shared many common views on safeguarding world peace, promoting economic development and [2] enhancing cooperation and [3] exchanges despite differences in historical and [4] cultural background and [5] level of development.

In the pair joined by "and" #1, both words are nouns ("China"/"the Netherlands"). In the series joined by #2, all three elements are gerund phrases ("safeguarding ..."/"promoting ..."/"enhancing ..."). The pair joined by #3 are both nouns ("cooperation"/"exchanges"), the pair joined by #4 are both adjectives ("historical"/"cultural") and the pair joined by #5 are again both nouns ("background"/"level"). Form matches function, and both are matched to meaning.

Examples of mismatched elements

In the A-versions of the following sentences, the parallelism is faulty because the elements linked by the coordinating conjunctions belong to different grammatical categories. In other words, we have parallel function and parallel meaning, but not parallel form.

Consciously or unconsciously, readers expect a sequence of comparable terms, and when their expectation is disappointed, the effect is jarring. The B-versions, by making the terms grammatically consistent, smooth out the bumps in the road.

A: Also to be coordinated [between Hong Kong and Guangdong] are <u>water supply</u>, <u>security</u>, and <u>how to move people</u> and trucks across the border more efficiently. (Noun + noun + infinitive phrase.)

B: Also to be coordinated are *water supply*, *security*, and efficient *movement* of people and trucks across the border. (Three nouns.)

A: Whether reunification can be brought about smoothly will be determined by two factors. One is the <u>result</u> of the practice of "one country, two systems" in Hong Kong, and the other is <u>whether we can make a breakthrough</u> in economic development. (Noun + dependent clause.)

B: Whether reunification can be brought about smoothly will be determined by two factors. One is *how well the* "*one country, two systems*" *formula is applied* in Hong Kong, and the other is *how successful we are* in developing the economy. (Two dependent clauses.)

A: Timber is needed <u>for construction</u> and <u>to withstand</u> floods. (Prepositional phrase + infinitive phrase.)

B: Timber is needed *to provide* material for construction and *to help withstand* floods. (Two infinitive phrases.)

A: They [mainland educators] also expect their Taiwan counterparts in education to edit textbooks to follow the principle of <u>seeking</u> truth from facts, <u>being</u> responsible for the

336

young and for the future of the Chinese nation, and safe-
guard the unification of the motherland. (Gerund phrase
+ gerund phrase + verb.)

B: They also expect their Taiwan counterparts to edit textbooks
in accordance with the principles of *seeking* truth from
facts, *being* responsible for the young and for the future
of the Chinese nation, and *safeguarding* the unification of
the motherland. (Three gerund phrases.)

A: Adhering to the principles of integrating Marxism-Leninism
with the realities of the Chinese revolution, seeking truth
from facts, and the mass line, the Party skillfully wielded
the two weapons — the United Front and armed struggle.
(Gerund phrase + gerund phrase + noun.)

B: Adhering to the principles of *integrating* Marxism-Leninism
with the realities of the Chinese revolution, *seeking* truth
from facts, and *following* the mass line, the Party skillfully wielded two weapons: the united front and armed
struggle. (Three gerund phrases.)

In each of these examples, one of the disparate elements has
been changed to conform to the other(s). That is the usual remedy
for mismatched elements and the first you should try.

Sometimes, however, the items in a pair or series cannot readily
be made compatible. If you find that reducing them to the same
grammatical form produces a sentence that is awkward and
unnatural, it may be that they are not logically comparable after all.
In that case, it is best to abandon the attempt at parallelism and try
another construction.

A note about mixing nouns and gerunds

In the last example above — "<u>integrating</u> Marxism-Leninism with the realities of the Chinese revolution, <u>seeking</u> truth from facts and the <u>mass line</u>" — we had two gerunds followed by a noun. In this instance, a third gerund is plainly needed: readers expect one, and without it there would be nothing but an easily ignored comma to prevent them from thinking that the Party was seeking truth from facts and from the mass line.

But because gerunds and ordinary nouns are so closely related, they can sometimes work together without creating the jarring effect of more obvious mismatches. In the following sentence, for example, although the series is noun + gerund + noun, the reader is not aware of any discrepancy between the terms:

- Local financial and economic departments throughout the country were demanding that the <u>regulation</u>, <u>planning</u> and <u>administration</u> of many matters be centralized as well.

This means that when nouns and gerunds are mixed, the combination may or may not be acceptable. Once again, a matter of judgment.

2. Elements linked by correlative conjunctions

The so-called correlative conjunctions are connectives that work together in pairs. The following are the most common:

- both . . . and
- either . . . or
- neither . . . nor
- not . . . but
- not only . . . but also

In these combinations, the first word announces what is coming next: two equivalent terms joined by a coordinating conjunction. By specifically drawing attention to the parallelism ahead, it sets up in the reader's mind an inevitable expectation. In effect, that first word is an implied commitment to the reader that whatever element comes after will be followed by a suitable mate.

Wilson Follett puts it unequivocally. Speaking of the constructions "either ... or" ("neither ... nor") and "not only ... but also" [p. 212], he says, "If any two verbal formulas are hard-and-fast promises of parallel construction, [these] are such promises." And referring to "both ... and" [p. 91], he warns, "If what follows *and* is not the logical and rhetorical equivalent of what follows *both*, the result is disappointment or shock."

Thus, when correlative conjunctions are used, it is particularly important that the terms they connect be strictly parallel. The grammatical construction following the second conjunction must correspond exactly to the one following the first.

Here are two examples of sentences that violate the rule, together with proposed revisions:

A: The delegates [to a conference on meat production] agreed that these are vital issues for the next century, both <u>for</u> <u>people's quality of life</u> and <u>for saving</u> the environment. (Preposition/noun + preposition/gerund.)

B: The delegates agreed that these are vital issues for the next century, affecting both *the quality of people's lives* and *the preservation of the environment*. (Two nouns, each modified by a matching prepositional phrase.)

A: This will help the authorities set prices that are appropriate not only <u>for</u> their own localities but also <u>in relation to</u> prices throughout the country. ("For x" + "in relation to y.")

B: This will help the authorities set prices that are appropriate not only *in relation to* their own local conditions but also *in relation to* prices throughout the country. ("In relation to x"/"in relation to y.")

3. Items in a list or a series of headings

Another formula that some authorities include in lists of correlative conjunctions is "first ... second ... third." "First" is certainly a promise of at least a "second" to come, and that second item and any others following must be in matching form. Here is an example of the expected pattern:

- Socialism has two major requirements. First, <u>its economy must be dominated by public ownership</u>, and second, <u>there must be no polarization</u>. (Two independent clauses; in addition, both are based on the verb "must be.")

The same principle applies when the items are presented not in a single sentence but in the form of a list. Here, however, is a list in which not one of the three items matches either of the others:

- Jiang said that ... the Party should now concentrate on the following three aspects:

First, the whole <u>Party must keep</u> its ideological and political unity. ...

Second, the <u>unity</u> of the Party in organization and action <u>to be enhanced</u> through implementing democratic centralism.

340

Third, strengthen further the close relationship between the Party and the people, putting the struggle against corruption at the top of the agenda.

The first item in this series is an independent clause with an ordinary indicative verb in active voice ("must keep"). The second is not a clause at all but a "headline" having no verb except an infinitive ("to be"), which cannot stand alone. The third is again an independent clause, but this time the verb is in the imperative ("strengthen").

The translator's uncertainty is reflected in the introductory statement. We are told that according to Jiang, the Party should concentrate on three "aspects," but the question "aspects of what?" remains unanswered. Admittedly, it is hard to know just what a free-floating "aspect" is and what form it should take. Still, whatever form is decided upon must be used consistently.

Here is a tentative proposal for a revision:

- Jiang said that ... the Party should now concentrate on the following three tasks (endeavors? goals?):

First, *it must maintain* its ideological and political unity ....

Second, *it must enhance* its unity in organization and action by implementing democratic centralism.

Third, *it must strengthen* its close relations with the people, placing the struggle against corruption at the top of its agenda.

Instead of being introduced by "first," "second," "third," etc., the successive points may be marked "1 ... 2 ... 3" or "a) ... b) ... c)," or they may appear without any indication of sequence at all. But even if the numbering is only implied, logic

341

demands that all the points be cast in similar constructions.

Like items in a list, a series of subtitles in a document or of chapter headings in a book are essentially coordinate and should be parallel in form. Even if they are not numbered, and even if they are widely separated, the reader expects them to be consistent and finds it disconcerting and confusing if they are not.

For instance, if one section of a government report is entitled "Seizing the Opportunity to Speed up Economic Development" (gerund phrase), corresponding later sections should not be headed "Accelerate the Reform and Open Wider to the Outside World" (independent clause with imperative verbs), or "We must Create a Better Social and Political Environment for Economic Development" (independent clause with indicative verb). Once the pattern is set, it should be followed: "Seizing the Opportunity ...," "Accelerating the Reform and Opening Wider ...," and "Creating a Better Social and Political Environment ...."

4. Elements linked in comparisons

Items that are being compared (or contrasted) are linked not by conjunctions but by such words as "like" or "unlike," "as much as," "the same as," "different from," "greater than," "less desirable than," "more rapidly than," and so on. By definition, elements in a comparison should be parallel *logically*; otherwise, the comparison is false.

For example, in the last chapter (page 304) we cited the following sentence:

A: Just like the Crowne Plaza, all rooms feature an electronic door lock, a private safe, two telephones with IDD ....

B: *Like the rooms* in the Crowne Plaza, *all those* in the Holiday
Inn feature an electronic door lock, a private safe, two
telephones with IDD . . . .

The error here was identified as a dangling prepositional phrase
("like the Crowne Plaza") that was not logically attached to the subject of the sentence ("all rooms"). But it can also be described as a
failure of parallelism. The two elements are similar from the point of
view of grammar (they are both nouns), but not from the point of
view of logic (you cannot compare a hotel with rooms in another
hotel). In the revision rooms were compared with rooms.

When comparisons are faulty, it is usually, as in this instance,
because the items involved are not parallel logically. Consequently,
the meaning of the sentence is obscured or perverted. But it can also
be a problem when the items are not parallel grammatically. The
meaning generally survives, but again, the reader's expectations are
frustrated.

By way of illustration of the correct structure, following are
some typical comparisons in which the two elements in question are
expressed in the anticipated matching form:

- She did not like revising as much as translating.
- She thought it was more creative to translate than to revise the
  work of others.
- She was less willing to take on a revision than a translation.
- She was no more able to give up working than to stop eating.
- She was transferred from another unit rather than promoted
  from inside. (Not, as is often written: rather than being
  promoted.)
- No sooner had she arrived at her new post than she set to

343

<u>work</u>.

Note that parallel structure is not equally essential in all these patterns. For example, in the first one, if the gerund "revising" were matched not with another gerund but with a noun, "translation," the reader might slide over the discrepancy without any sense of a disappointed expectation.

In the last one, however, the opening formula, "<u>No sooner had x happened</u>," commits the writer to one particular, predictable course. It can be completed *only* by "<u>than y happened</u>." If it were followed by any other construction, the writer would be guilty of a broken promise, and the reader would feel betrayed.

Further refinements

As stated at the outset of this discussion, the matching of grammatical categories in a pair or series is only a minimal requirement of parallel structure. If the meaning calls for it, further refinements can create a closer, more effective parallelism.

Consider, for example, the following sentence:

- <u>Should we follow a policy that will</u> not help us shake off poverty and backwardness, or <u>should we</u>, on the basis of those four principles, <u>choose a better policy that will</u> enable us to rapidly develop the productive forces?

The two elements linked by the coordinating conjunction "or" are both independent clauses, as required by the rule of matching categories. Both are interrogative. (It would be impossible to construct an English sentence beginning with a question followed by "or" in which the second clause was not also a question.) This much is essential.

344

But other aspects of the sentence are also matching:

- the two clauses have the same subject ("we")
- each is based on a verb in active voice ("follow"/"choose"), so
    that each has the same internal pattern ("should we do
    x?"/ "should we do y?")
- each verb has an object, and the two objects are the same
    ("policy")
- each object is modified by a dependent clause beginning with
    "that"
- the two dependent clauses have contrasting but similar patterns
    ("that *will* not help us do x"/"that *will* enable us to do
    y")

These additional likenesses of form and language create a tighter parallelism than is strictly necessary, but one that is highly effective. It clarifies the speaker's thought — the comparison of two possible courses of action — and despite the reference to the four cardinal principles, which somewhat breaks the rhythm, it is satisfying to the ear.

We shall look first at ways of enhancing parallel structure beyond the minimum, in places where parallelism is clearly required. Then, at ways of introducing parallelism in places — between two sentences, for example — where it is desirable even if not obligatory.

Nouns

Nouns in a pair or series will work better together if they are of the same order of ideas — either abstract or concrete. For example:

- In the protracted struggle against ruthless oppression by impe-
    rialism, Kuomintang bandits and feudal landlords, the

345

> people in the old base areas made the greatest contributions to the revolution . . . .

The sentence is clear and grammatical, and the series of nouns satisfies the basic demand of parallel structure. But it mixes an abstraction ("imperialism") with two concrete nouns representing persons ("bandits" and "landlords"). The series would be smoother — more "parallel" — if all three were of the same nature:

> - In the long struggle against ruthless oppression by *imperialists*, Kuomintang *bandits*, and feudal *landlords*, the people in the old base areas made the greatest contributions to the revolution . . . .

Another example:

> - Since the end of July the amount of money in circulation has increased, owing to factors such as the <u>expansion</u> of the territory under our control, the <u>diversion</u> of more bank notes to the countryside, increased farm <u>produce</u>, and the <u>recovery</u> of industry and commerce.

At first sight the series seems unobjectionable. But a careful reader will notice that the items are not of the same order. "Expansion," "diversion" and "recovery" are abstract terms, but "produce" ("increased" or not) is concrete. Better to make the four items match more closely:

> - Since the end of July the amount of money in circulation has increased, owing to such factors as the *expansion* of the territory under our control, the *diversion* of more bank notes to the countryside, an *increase* in farm production, and the *recovery* of industry and commerce.

346

Verbs

Two verbs in the same sentence will be more symmetrical if they are both in the same voice. The following sentence, for example, meets the minimum standard, because the two elements joined by "and" are both independent clauses:

- China's foreign policy is known to all, and it will remain unchanged.

But from the point of view of parallel structure, the sentence would be improved if both verbs were either passive or active:

- China's foreign policy *is known* to all, and it *will not be changed*. Or:
- Everyone *knows* China's foreign policy, and it *will remain unchanged*.

Phrases

Phrases will be better balanced if each of the pair or series follows the same internal pattern. For example, the following series is acceptable because each of the items is a noun:

- Simultaneous with that is the allocation of land, rent reduction, and wage increases . . . .

But a closer match can be achieved by giving the three word groups the same structure:

- Simultaneous with that is the *allocation of land* , *reduction of rents* , and *increase in wages* . . . .

[Review: A translator mindful of the noun plague might prefer to recast the sentence using verbs, with no loss of parallelism: "At the same time, land *is being distributed* , rents *are being reduced* and wages *are being increased* ."]

347

As we saw above in the opening example ("Should we follow a policy..."), another means of heightening parallelism between word groups is repetition of wording. For instance:

- From their point of view [that of the local authorities], many projects for meeting local needs are primary, but in view of the overall interest, they are often regarded as secondary and can be postponed.

Again, the sentence is tolerable (barely), but a neater and stronger version can be produced by repeating the same wording:

- *From their point of view* many projects designed to meet local needs are of primary importance, but *from the overall point of view* it is quite possible that they are secondary and can be postponed.

Clauses

The same principles apply to clauses. Consider again the example of a mismatched noun and clause given above:

- Whether reunification can be brought about smoothly will be determined by two factors. One is the result of the practice of "one country, two systems" in Hong Kong, and the other is whether we can make a breakthrough in economic development.

In principle, to match the two elements it would have been sufficient to change the noun "result" to another dependent clause:

- Whether reunification can be brought about smoothly will be determined by two factors. One is how well the "one country, two systems" formula is applied in Hong Kong, and the other is whether we can make a breakthrough in economic development.

But we can achieve greater clarity and a more satisfying balance by repeating the pattern of the first clause in the second:

- Whether reunification can be brought about smoothly will be determined by two factors. One is *how well the "one country, two systems" formula is applied* in Hong Kong, and the other is *how successful we are* in developing the economy.

Here is another example of two clauses whose parallel meaning can be better brought out if they are given the same structure:

- In late 1948 Shanghai had a population of 5.05 million, according to statistics, and the figure rose to 5.5 million <u>by the end of last May</u>.

A simple change of word order will bring the two phrases into alignment so that they occupy the same position in their respective clauses:

- According to statistics, *in late 1948* Shanghai had a population of 5.05 million, and *by the end of last May* the figure had risen to 5.5 million.
[Review: Moving "by the end of last May" to the beginning of its clause has the further advantage of leaving the emphatic end-position to the main point — the new higher figure.]

Sentences

So far we have looked at examples of parallel structure only within single sentences. But sometimes you may wish to introduce a degree of parallelism into two separate but consecutive sentences.

The means are the same as those just described: to emphasize the correspondence between significant phrases or clauses, you can repeat the same pattern and language in both sentences.

Following is an example in which two key phrases virtually cry out for parallel form:

- <u>Only by resisting</u> the Japanese for a long time <u>could the people</u> in the occupied areas gain a better understanding of the war and enhance their sense of organization and the need to gradually expand their forces. <u>Without waging</u> an extensive people's war in the rear areas of the enemy, <u>it would be impossible for China</u> to win the final victory in the war against Japan.

Here the patterns of the two sentences are:

- only by doing x could the people do y
- without doing x it would be impossible for China to do y.

To make the sentences parallel we have only to change the second to match the pattern of the first:

- only by doing x could the people do y
- only by doing x could China do y.

These changes produce:

- *Only by resisting* the Japanese for a long time *could the people* in the occupied areas gain a better understanding of the war and become fully aware of the need to organize themselves and gradually expand their forces. And *only by waging* a large-scale people's war in the enemy's rear areas *could China* win final victory.

[Review: "Enhance their sense of organization" was spelled out

350

as "become fully aware of the need to organize themselves." Thus a vague structure based on two abstract nouns, "sense" and "organization," was turned into a plain statement based on an adjective, "aware," and a strong verb, "organize." "In the war with Japan" was dropped as self-evident.]

Now an example in which two sentences would make the speaker's point more effectively if they were couched in the same language:

- The Central Government certainly will not intervene in the day-to-day affairs of the Special Administrative Region, nor is that necessary. But is it not true that something could occur in the region that might jeopardize the fundamental interests of the country? Couldn't such a situation arise? If this happens, should Beijing interfere? Is it not possible that something could happen in Hong Kong that would harm the fundamental interests of Hong Kong itself?

In this instance the two patterns are already the same:

- is it not true that something could occur in the region that might jeopardize the fundamental interests of x?

- is it not possible that something could happen in Hong Kong that would harm the fundamental interests of y?

But the difference in wording only diminishes the intended parallel between the two situations. It is easy enough to make identical pairs out of "true"/"possible," "occur"/"happen" and "jeopardize"/ "harm." This is the result:

- The Central Government certainly will not intervene in the day-to-day affairs of the Special Administrative Region, nor is that necessary. But *isn't it possible that something could happen* in the region that might *jeopardize* the fundamental interests of the country? Couldn't such a situation arise? If that happened, should Beijing intervene or not? *Isn't it possible that something could happen* there that would *jeopardize* the fundamental interests of Hong Kong itself?

[Review: In the last sentence "in Hong Kong" was replaced by "there" to avoid an unnecessary duplication. Unlike the deliberate repetitions, a second mention of "Hong Kong" would add nothing to parallel structure.]

Misleading parallel structure

Follett tells us [p. 212] that "[w]hat is fatal is to arouse an expectation of matched constructions and then to frustrate it." But what is equally fatal is to use matched constructions for elements that do not, in fact, match. Either failing gives the impression of a disorderly mind at work.

When parallel structure is imposed on elements that are not logically parallel, the result is always startling (e.g., "Just like the Crowne Plaza, all rooms ... "). Sometimes it can be deliberately humorous. Johnson [p. 9] cites the false parallels "He took his hat and his leave" and "He bolted his door and his dinner." He implies that no one, without comic intent, would write, "He keeps fit, sheep, and his word."

But most often a logical mismatch is inadvertent. H. Ramsey

352

Fowler and Jane E. Aaron [p. 354] quote a misleading construction in which a writer has unwittingly suggested a similarity where there is none:

- The painting has subdued tone, great feeling, and a length of about three feet.

And Claire Cook [p. 67] offers this thought-provoking parallel, which could hardly have been intentional:

- The police found no alcohol in his bloodstream but a loaded gun in his car.

Jacques Barzun and Henry F. Graff [p. 275], insisting, like Follett, that a parallel construction once begun should always be carried through, nevertheless emphasize that the construction should not be entered upon in the first place unless it is logically justified. "Parallelism," they say, "is so important a device in writing that its use must be kept pure. Do not give parallel forms to disparate ideas . . . ."

If you remember that bit of advice, you will avoid the mistake made by the French veteran of the Napoleonic wars who recounted that he had been wounded three times: once in an ambush, once in the leg, and once in the Netherlands.

Twenty more examples of revision

1) A: Economically, we are struggling for the democracy of distribution of food grain, reduction of rent and interest, increase of wages, getting rid of unemployment and developing production.

B: Economically, we are struggling to *ensure* the democratic distribution of grain, *reduce* rents and interest rates, *increase* wages, *eliminate* unemployment and *develop* production.

[- In A-version we have a series of three nouns and two gerunds connected by the coordinating conjunction "and." The combination is disconcerting, especially because the verb cannot be followed by a gerund (e.g., "we are struggling for getting rid of" is not English).

- In the revision "for" was replaced by "to," and all five elements were converted to infinitives: "we are struggling to ensure ... reduce ... etc." These changes not only produced acceptable parallel structure but eliminated the three nouns and two gerunds.

- (Review: "Food" was deleted as an unnecessary adjective: it can be taken for granted that unless otherwise stated, grain is for human consumption.)]

2) *From the back of a ticket to a performance of Peking opera*:

A: After renovation Hu Guang Guild Hall has been turned into Beijing Traditional Operas Museum, which is a cultural center with multifunction such as opera <u>performing</u>, <u>exhibition</u>, <u>shopping</u> and <u>restaurant</u>, etc.

B: After renovation, the Hu Guang Guild Hall has been turned into the Beijing Museum of Traditional Opera, a multi-functional cultural center including *an opera hall*, *exhibition space*, *shops*, *restaurants*, etc.

[- In A-version we have another series connected by "and" in which nouns and gerunds are mixed.

- In addition, the first three elements ("performing," "exhibition," "shopping") are abstract words representing activities, while the fourth ("restaurant") is a concrete

354

word designating a place. (If the last word had matched the first three — "dining," for example — the combination of nouns and gerunds might have been tolerable.)

- In the revision all four elements have been made concrete nouns naming various places.

- (Review: The "Beijing Traditional Operas Museum" was spelled out as the "Beijing Museum of Traditional Opera" to avoid a pileup of nouns and adjectives before the noun "Museum.")]

3) A: The forces were greatly reduced in number because of persistent <u>march</u> under the heat of the midsummer sun, <u>fatigue</u>, plus <u>deaths</u> and <u>the wounded</u> in battles and <u>deserters</u> during the march.

B: Their numbers were now greatly reduced because of battlefield *casualties*, *desertions*, and the *exhaustion* of constant marching under a blazing midsummer sun.

[- This time, in A-version the series is composed entirely of nouns, if we include the past participle "wounded," which can act as a noun (cf. "the injured," "the unemployed," etc.). But the nouns are not comparable.

- The first two — "march(ing)" and "fatigue" — are not parallel, because the second is not a separate hazard but a consequence of the first.

- The last three — "deaths," "the wounded," and "deserters" — should logically be either "deaths"/ "wounds"/"desertions" (three causes of loss) or "the dead"/"the wounded"/"the deserters" (three types of people). And so on.

- In B-version "march" and "fatigue" were combined in a

single phrase showing the relation between them ("the exhaustion of constant marching"). "Deaths" and "the wounded" were collapsed into one word ("casualties").

- The causes enumerated were thus reduced from five mismatched terms to three that were relatively consistent: "casualties," "desertions," and "exhaustion."]

4) A: Most public grain has already been collected; standardized tax regulations, tax items and tax rates have been promulgated; and because the mainland has been liberated, tax receipts have been greater than last year.

B: Most public grain has already been collected; standardized tax *rates* and *regulations*, and *lists of taxable items* have been promulgated; and because the mainland has been liberated, tax receipts have been greater than they were last year (*or*: than last year's).

[- The three subjects of the second clause in A-version are again all nouns, but again they are not of the same order.

- "Regulations" and "rates" are abstract, but taxable "items" (physical objects, like salt or vehicle licenses) are concrete and, unlike the other two, cannot be "promulgated" (i.e., announced or proclaimed).

- In B-version the abstract word "lists" was introduced to solve this problem.

- (In the last clause, "tax receipts" are inadvertently compared with "last year," instead of with the tax receipts of last year. The error was corrected in the revision: "tax receipts have been greater than they were last year.")]

5) A: But even so, it will be hard to prevent expenditure from exceeding revenue and a fall in revenue, and there may be such factors as a grain shortage that will contribute to price rise.

B: But even so, it will be hard to *prevent expenditure from exceeding.* revenue and to *keep revenue from falling*, and other factors, such as a grain shortage, may also drive prices up.

   [- In A-version the two objects of "prevent" are not of the same grammatical category: the first ("expenditure from exceeding revenue") is a whole phrase, while the second ("a fall") is a single noun.

   - In the revision the two objects were separated and given separate verbs. That made it possible to establish a new and exact parallel between "prevent expenditure from exceeding" and "keep revenue from falling."

   - (Review: In the interest of replacing a weak noun construction with a strong verb, "contribute to price rise" was changed to "drive prices up.")]

6) A: Last month I went to Tingzhou and did the following with regard to contract negotiations [for the grocery workers there]:

   1. Studying first of all where the enterprises concerned really stand, whether the contract already negotiated has been observed, and what the demands of the workers are....

   2. Relying on the Party branch, strengthening its leadership and consolidating its organization ....

   3. The negotiated contract should be realistic and flexible, as required by the actual conditions of the grocery trade in

Tingzhou.

B: Last month I went to Tingzhou and did the following with regard to contract negotiations:

    1. First of all, *I tried to find out* where each enterprise actually stood, whether the contract already negotiated was being observed, and what the demands of the workers were ....

    2. *I relied on* the Party branch, strengthening its leadership and consolidating its organization ....

    3. *I made sure* that the negotiated contract was realistic and flexible and in keeping with the conditions in the grocery trade in Tingzhou.

[- The three items listed were separated by several pages of intervening text. That made it all the more important to present them in parallel form, so as to help the reader keep track of the speaker's argument and remember that these were all things he had done in Tingzhou.

- In A-version, however, the three coordinate points are inconsistent in form: (1) gerund (" studying "); (2) gerunds (" relying, " " strengthening, " " consolidating "); (3) verb (" should be "). Worse, none of those constructions can logically come after "I did the following. "

- In the revision all three were cast in the same form, as active verbs with the same subject ("I tried to find out, " "I relied on, " "I made sure").

- (Review: " Actual " was eliminated as superfluous with " conditions. ")]

7) A: Some intellectuals complain that our personnel contact them only on three things: namely, a <u>transfer</u> of work, a

358

review of personal history, and <u>when a mistake is committed</u>.

B: Some intellectuals complain that our people talk to them on only three occasions: *when they are to be transferred* to another job, *when their personal history is being reviewed*, and *when they make a mistake*.

[- In this sentence we have what is essentially an unnumbered list of three items linked by "and." Each item, therefore, should belong to the same grammatical category, but in A-version the series is: noun + noun + subordinate clause.

- In the revision, all three elements are subordinate clauses. The parallelism is reinforced by the repeated use of the same conjunction ("when") and the same pattern ("when x happens").

- The parallelism was also increased by the change from "when a mistake is committed" to "when they make a mistake," which corresponds more closely to the shape of the two preceding clauses ("when they," "when their," "when they").

- ("Make a mistake" was used instead of "commit a mistake" because the latter is not an idiomatic combination in English.)

- (<u>Review</u>: The change in construction also served to convert two abstract nouns — "a transfer," "a review" — to verbs. Changing "when a mistake is committed" to active voice, which requires a stated subject, "they," had the further advantage of clarifying who made the mistake.)]

8) A: You have not only <u>met</u> Chairman Mao and <u>visited</u> our capital, but also <u>have witnessed the power</u> of our army and <u>how</u>

the people love our Party and the leader.

B: You have not only *met* Chairman Mao and *visited* our capital but (also) *witnessed the power* of our army and *the love* the people bear our Party and our leader.

[- In A-version the constructions following "not only" and "but also" do not match exactly. After the first we find "met" and "visited," after the second "have witnessed." The pattern is "You have not only x and y but also have z."

- To create the exact parallelism required by correlative conjunctions, the polisher deleted the "have." Thus the pattern became "You have not only x and y but also z."

- In A-version the two objects of "witnessed," linked by the coordinating conjunction "and," are not parallel either: a noun ("power") is matched with a noun clause ("how the people love"). In the revision the phrase was changed to another noun ("love").]

9) A: This shows on the one hand that China's vehicle and component industries are still highly fragmented, but on the other hand it is indicative of the enthusiasm displayed by manufacturers in trying to tap into China's rapidly expanding automotive market.

B: *This shows* , *on the one hand* , *that* China's vehicle and component industries are still highly fragmented but, *on the other hand* , *that* many manufacturers are eager to tap into the rapidly expanding automotive market.

[- Here the elements linked by the coordinating conjunction "but" are both independent clauses. But an attentive reader will still find A-version unsatisfactory.

360

- The prepositional phrase "on the one hand" is like the first segment of a correlative conjunction in that it sets up the expectation of a partner phrase to follow. And as in the "not only ... but also" example above, the element that comes after the second segment should match the one that comes after the first.
- In A-version that is not the case. "On the one hand" is followed by a dependent clause ("that China's vehicle and component industries are etc."), whereas "on the other hand" is followed by an independent clause ("it is indicative of etc.").
- In the revision the second clause was changed to a dependent clause to match the first ("that many manufacturers are ...").
- An alternative solution would be to change the first clause to an independent clause to match the second. That would produce: "On the one hand this shows that ... but on the other hand it indicates (*or*: shows) that ...."]

10) A: They unanimously suggested that <u>more funds should be injected</u> into scientific development, that <u>a more flexible system be introduced</u> to help the transfer of talent between economic sectors and scientific institutes, and that <u>more efforts are needed</u> to accelerate the transfer of the fruit of scientific research into industrial and agricultural production.

B: They unanimously suggested that *more funds should be allocated* for scientific development, that *a more flexible system should be introduced* to facilitate the exchange of highly trained people between economic enterprises and

361

scientific institutes, and that *more efforts should be made* to ensure that the results of scientific research are rapidly applied in industry and agriculture.

[- Here again the basic requirement of matching grammatical categories has been met in A-version: all three elements linked by "and" are subordinate "that" clauses.

- But again, a critical reader will still be uncomfortable, because in other respects the three clauses are not parallel constructions. They all have different patterns: "that x should be done"/"that y be done"/"that efforts are needed to do z."

- In B-version the second and third clauses exactly match the pattern of the first: "that x should be done." The tighter parallelism is easy to achieve and more satisfying both to the mind and to the ear.

- "Economic sectors" was changed to "economic enterprises" so as not to draw a parallel between an abstract noun ("sectors") and a concrete one ("institutes").

- ("Talent" was changed to "highly trained people" because, as mentioned in Chapter VIII, page 234, revision 13, the word is seldom used in English in a context like this. In particular, outside of show business, even "talented" people are not referred to as "talent.")]

11) A: If state revenue is not centralized, if state expenditure is not determined <u>in accordance with the same regulations</u> and <u>in observation of the principle of austerity</u> ... the inevitable result will be a waste of financial resources and aggravated inflation.

B: If control of state revenue is not centralized, and if decisions

362

regarding state expenditures are not made *in accordance with a uniform set of regulations* and *a consistent principle of austerity* ... the inevitable result will be a waste of financial resources and aggravated inflation.

[- A-version is adequate, because the "and" links two prepositional phrases, but it can be tightened and improved.

- "In accordance with" and "in observation of" mean the same thing and serve the same function (modifying the verb "determined"), so they can be condensed into one expression. In B-version they became a single phrase, "in accordance with."

- "In accordance with the same regulations" raised the question "the same as what?" (presumably the same as in other places, i. e., the same everywhere, but that was not stated). The polisher therefore substituted "a uniform set of regulations."

- "Consistent" was then introduced ("a consistent principle of austerity"). This was done partly to clarify the meaning — which is that everything should be done everywhere in the same way, according to the same rules — and partly to heighten the parallelism by balancing "uniform" ("a uniform set of regulations").

- (At the beginning of the sentence "state revenue" was changed to "control of state revenue" for better logic: it is not money that is to be "centralized" but control over money.)]

12) A: The purpose of struggling against the KMT was not to overthrow its rule but <u>to hinder it from capitulating</u> to the Japanese invaders and <u>from fighting</u> against the Communist

Party and <u>to keep it</u> in the anti-Japanese united front.

B: The purpose of struggling against the KMT was not to over-throw its rule but *to prevent it from capitulating* to the Japanese invaders, *fighting* the Communists and *abandoning* the anti-Japanese united front.

[- Here the correlative construction "not ... but" is in good order, each segment being followed by an infinitive ("not to overthrow ... but to hinder ...").

- The coordinate construction with "and" is likewise acceptable, since the two elements joined are also both infinitives ("to hinder ... and to keep"). Still, with a little revision it is possible to do better.

- In A-version two elements are governed by "hinder it from" ("capitulating to the invaders" and "fighting against the CP"). In B-version the third element ("to keep it in the united front") has been cast in the same form as the first two: "to hinder it from capitulating ... fighting ... and abandoning."

- As in the preceding example, the result of this condensation is not only a stronger parallelism but a neater, more concise statement.

- ("Hinder" was changed to "prevent" simply because "prevent" was the more appropriate word.)]

13) A: At this meeting it was decided that <u>a part of the Red army led by Peng Dehuai and Teng Daiyuan should stay</u> to defend the Jinggang Mountains and that <u>Mao Zedong, Zhu De and Chen Yi should lead the main forces of the Fourth Army</u>, numbering 3,600, <u>to march</u> toward southern Jiangxi to launch an attack.

B: At this meeting it was decided that *a part of the Red Army, led by Peng Dehuai and Teng Daiyuan, should stay* to defend the Jinggang Mountains, while *the main forces of the Fourth Army*, numbering 3,600, *led by Mao Zedong, Zhu De, and Chen Yi, should march* to southern Jiangxi to launch an attack there.

[- In A-version the minimal demand of parallel structure is met, since the two elements joined by the coordinating conjunction "and" are both dependent clauses. It would be more satisfying, however, and easier to follow, if the missions of the two forces were expressed in more closely matching form.

- The pattern of the first clause is: "x troops, led by y, should do z"; the pattern of the second is: "y should lead x troops to do z." In the revision, the second clause was rearranged to match the first: "the main forces of the Fourth Army, led by Mao et al., should march . . . ."

- (This revision had the further advantage of correcting the classic Chinglish construction "lead the main forces to march." In English you can lead people to a <u>place</u>, whether it is literal, like the "gate" or the "other side of the river," or metaphorical, like "victory" or a "conclusion." But, except when "lead" has the sense of "induce" or "persuade," you cannot lead them to <u>do</u> something — to "cross the river," to "win a victory" or to "march to southern Jiangxi.")

- (To emphasize that the two forces were to act simultaneously, the logical connective between the clauses was changed from "and" to "while.")

14) A: The environment in which we find ourselves invariably has
limitations, so we should examine things from various an-
gles. Everyone inevitably has limits in his cognition,
therefore we should pay great heed to different views.

B: *The environment* in which we find ourselves *is necessarily
limited*, *so* we should examine things from *different* an-
gles. *Our knowledge* too *is necessarily limited*, *so* we
should pay attention to *different* views.

[- The two statements are plainly parallel in meaning.
A-version is grammatical, but it fails to provide parallel
form and is awkward as well.

- In the revision both sentences have the same pattern and
are based on the same key words ("x is necessarily
limited"/"y is necessarily limited"), making the logical
similarity clear.

- The incidental words in the two sentences have also been
made consistent to heighten the parallelism: "invariably"/
"inevitably," "so"/"therefore" and "various"/"different"
have all been reduced to matching pairs.

- ("Too" was added to express the logical connection between the two sentences.)

- (Review: The change in structure — from "has limits" to
"is limited" — has also made it possible to dispense with
three abstract nouns: "limitations," "limits,"
"cognition.")]

15) A: The purpose of our meeting is to end the past and open up a
new era. By ending the past, I mean we can leave it aside
and concentrate on the future.

B: The purpose of our meeting is to put the past behind us and

366

open up a new era. By *putting* the past behind us I mean *ceasing* to talk about it and *focusing* on the future.

[- In this example the wording itself suggests the need for parallel structure. The formula "by x I mean y" indicates that x and y are equivalent in the speaker's mind; accordingly, they should be expressed in equivalent form.

- In A-version we have a gerund phrase ("by ending the past") on one side of "I mean" and two verbs ("we can leave ... and concentrate") on the other. In B-version, the sequence was changed to three gerund phrases ("by putting ... I mean ceasing ... and focusing ... ").

- ("Ending the past" was changed to "putting the past behind us" not because the second expression is any more logical than the first, but because it has become idiomatic.)]

16) A: One-sidedness means <u>thinking</u> in terms of absolutes, that is, a metaphysical <u>approach</u> to problems.

B: One-sidedness means *thinking* in terms of absolutes, that is, *taking* a metaphysical approach to problems.

[- Here again, as in the preceding example, the wording of the sentence indicates the need for parallelism. The formula "x, that is, y" (or "x, in other words, y") is another way of telling the reader that x and y are logically equivalent.

- In A-version we have on one side of the equation a gerund phrase ("thinking in terms of absolutes"), and on the other a noun ("a metaphysical approach"). In the revision, a gerund was added to the second element to match the one in the first ("taking a metaphysical

367

approach").

- Commenting on this example in his lectures [pp. 80 – 81], Professor Cheng Zhenqiu remarks that the addition of "taking" "makes the sentence more balanced."]

17) A: During the whole period of the War of Resistance Against Japan there existed contradictions which had an important bearing on the destiny of the Chinese nation: first, the contradiction between the Chinese and the Japanese nations, which determined the survival of the Chinese nation; second, the class contradiction which determined whether we could carry through to the very end the nationwide War of Resistance Against Japan and build a new China after the war.

B: Throughout the period of the War of Resistance Against Japan there were contradictions that had an important bearing on China's destiny: first, the *national contradiction between China and Japan*, which *determined whether* the Chinese nation would survive; second, the *class contradiction between the Communist Party and the Kuomintang*, which *determined whether* the people would be able to carry the War of Resistance through to the end and afterwards build a new China.

[- In this sentence there is a "list" of two contradictions labeled "first" and "second"; plainly the two should be expressed in matching form. But in A-version "the ·contradiction between the Chinese and Japanese nations" is paired with "the class contradiction."

- In the revised version, material was added to each of these "contradictions" to make them match. "National"

368

(justified by the reference to "the Chinese and Japanese nations") was added to the first, to correspond to "class" in the second.

- Then " between the Communist Party and the Kuomintang" (the meaning of "class" contradiction, as made clear by the context) was added to the second to correspond to "between China and Japan" in the first.
- To enhance the parallelism between the two items, the patterns of the two subordinate clauses ("which determined ...") were also made to match.
- "Which determined the survival of the Chinese nation" in the first was changed to "which determined whether the Chinese nation would survive," corresponding to "which determined whether the people would be able to ..." in the second.
- (Review: As usual when a verb is introduced, the elimination of an abstract noun was a side benefit: "would survive" replaced "survival.")]

18) *Summation of a long passage describing the political maneuvering of the U.S. government and the KMT in the early 1940s :*

A: American <u>imperialism</u> and <u>Chiang Kai-shek's threats and deceit</u> could not obstruct the advance of the Chinese people in their effort to strive for independence, democracy, and liberation.

B: *Neither the machinations of the* U.S. *imperialists nor the threats and deceit of Chiang Kai-shek could halt the advance of the Chinese people in their drive for independence, democracy, and liberation.*

369

[- A-version is minimally correct (the "and" links a noun with two other nouns), but it has little else to recommend it. The content of this strong summary statement calls for symmetry and force — precisely the qualities that can be provided by greater parallelism.

- In B-version the two elements in the compound subject have been recast in matching form. "The machinations" of the U.S. have been introduced to balance "the threats and deceit" of Chiang; abstract "imperialism" has been changed to concrete "imperialists" (persons) to balance "Chiang Kai-shek" (a person).

- The symmetry is emphasized by the "neither ... nor" construction, which promises a tight parallelism.

- (Review: "In their effort to strive for" — an empty phrase that means only "in their effort to make efforts" — was replaced with "in their drive for," which was both shorter and stronger.)]

19) A: The Chinese Communist Party <u>put forward a proposal that we should establish</u> a new China which would be, in the words of Mao Zedong, "independent, free, democratic, united, prosperous, and powerful." While the Chiang Kai-shek clique <u>stuck to the point that the Chinese society should still be kept</u> in a semi-feudal, semi-colonial status, under the rule of the big landlords and the big bourgeoisie <u>with policies against Communists and the people pursued. And the Chinese people would have to face poverty and split of the nation.</u>

B: The Communist Party *was proposing the establishment of a new China* that would be, in the words of Mao Zedong, "independent, free, democratic, united, prosperous, and powerful." The Chiang Kai-shek clique, on the other hand, *was insisting on the perpetuation of the old China* — semi-feudal, semi-colonial, ruled by the big landlords and the big bourgeoisie, a China in which *the people would remain sunk in poverty, Communists would be persecuted, and the nation would be split*.

[- These sentences contrast two different visions of the future of the Chinese people after their victory in the War of Resistance Against Japan, one put forward by the Communists, the other by the Chiang Kai-shek clique. Another classic instance where parallel structure is wanted — but in A-version there is none.

- The polisher first tightened the opening clause and corrected the tense, so that the Communist Party "was proposing the establishment of a new China."

- Then, to make the parallel clause match, she changed the wordy "stuck to the point that the Chinese society should still be kept ..." to the same pattern: "was insisting on the perpetuation of the old China."

- (To emphasize the contrast — and because an independent clause cannot begin with "while" — she substituted "on the other hand" for "While.")

- In the draft version everything after "the big bourgeoisie" is again awkward and disorderly. To introduce some clarifying parallelism into this part of the sentence as well, the polisher rearranged the various elements into three subordinate clauses all following the same pattern ("the people would remain" "the Communists would be" and "the

371

nation would be").]

20) A: It should be recognized that <u>all streams and rivers</u> <u>have their</u> <u>source of origin</u>, while <u>trees</u> <u>depend on their roots for</u> <u>growth</u>.

B: We should recognize that *every river has its source* and *every tree grows from its roots*.

[- In context, this was a double metaphor indicating that Mao Zedong Thought originated in Marxism-Leninism. In A-version the lack of parallel structure (and the presence of superfluous words) destroys any potential rhythm and undermines the force of the imagery.

- In the revision the polisher did everything possible to reduce each of the two complementary images to its concise essence and to emphasize their similarity of meaning.

- First, the unnecessary words were eliminated: "streams," because it was the redundant twin of "rivers" and to match the single word "trees"; "of origin," because it was redundant with "source."

- Next, the patterns of the two clauses ("all rivers have their source"/"trees depend on their roots for growth") were brought into closer conformity ("every river has its source"/"every tree grows from its roots").

- Lastly, the subordinate conjunction "while" was changed to the coordinate "and," again to stress the equivalence of the two ideas.

- (The weak and unnecessary passive voice — "It should be recognized"— was changed to active — "We should recognize.")]

372

Twenty exercises

Once again, before revising each sentence you may find it helpful to underline the parts that you think should be made parallel.

1) "The three most important tasks for the Liberated Areas," the Central Committee declared, "are the training of soldiers, the reduction of rents, and increasing production."

2) In the past the Political Consultative Conference has concentrated its work mainly on political study, on international activities, and on collecting historical accounts of past events.

3) Lei Fachun, an ethnic Tu farmer from Huzhu County in Qinghai Province, felt hopeless about the prospect of feeding his three sons after getting divorced and the death of his parents.

4) In this way every unit can avoid the mistakes of departmentalism and exclusively relying on the state alone and will make the greatest possible contributions in its field.

5) Yao said that to ensure continued and steady growth of agricultural production, "we need a long-range plan for agricultural development and to adopt certain basic measures."

6) Senior cadres of the various departments and organizations are not familiar with the current financial difficulties and how to overcome them.

7) Consequently, some workers are becoming jobless and need relief or to turn to other trades.

8) The difference of opinion was not only over the issue of the special economic zones, but also included the larger issues, such as the rural reform that introduced the rural household

contract responsibility system . . . .

9) He fell in love with automotive design not because he foresaw the rise of the auto industry as one of the country's "pillar" industries, but because of his belief that auto design represented the highest level of industrial design.

10) *Headings in a speech on the financial and economic situation in 1949* :
   1) To share the burden
   2) To restore production
   3) Broaden sources of income and reduce expenditures
   4) Have a good grasp of policies

11) These are vital questions for the next century, both for people's quality of life and for protecting the environment.

12) But over the past year we have seen leading manufacturers of automobiles joining hands with farm vehicle producers in trying to tap into this market.

13) However, by 1978 the average monthly salary for our workers was still only 45 yuan, and most of our rural areas were still in poverty.

14) In face of the Japanese imperialists' aggression one party in China was for resistance and the other party was for making concessions.

15) Production during the first eight months of this year was 54,000 units, and 52,000 were sold.

16) Even at the time when our army had only millet to eat and the only weapons at its disposal were rifles, he began to consider combined operations of the various services.

17) Only through this process can a man's thinking develop, a party formulate a complete set of policies, and an organization improve its work.

18) The dictatorship was to be based ... mainly on the alliance of workers and peasants, because those two classes were the main force in overthrowing the rule of imperialism and feudalism and in the transition from new-democracy to socialism.

19) Since its implementation, the law has won broad support from the people, and excellent results have been achieved.

20) Probably they [certain minority nationalities] migrated to far away, distant regions out of the country. There is also the possibility that they were assimilated and became identical with the Han or other ethnic groups.

XII. Logical Connectives

In the last four chapters we have been dealing with different aspects of a single, fundamental requirement of English prose: the need for logical connections between ideas.

The kinds of revision we have been studying — matching a pronoun to its antecedent, putting an emphasized point at the end of a sentence so that it leads into the next, correcting a misplaced or dangling modifier, introducing parallel structure — all these are simply means of ensuring clear and rational connections between the elements of a sentence or between successive sentences.

There is one additional means of achieving logical coherence that we should now consider. This means cannot replace the others, but it is called into play more often than any of them. It is the use of words and phrases such as these:

- "also" and "in addition"
- "but" and "on the contrary"
- "because" and "as a consequence"
- "meanwhile" and "at that time"

Expressions of this kind show the reader how two adjacent ideas are related, smoothing the transition from one to the next. In other words, they indicate the direction the writer's thought is about to take, making it easy for the reader to follow.

Chinese translators working into English do not always use these expressions correctly. The reason is simple: the equivalent characters are often lacking in the original. More than once in these pages we have noted that the Chinese language freely omits some elements that in English are considered essential. Chinese readers understand a text without these clues, but native speakers of English need and expect more help from the writer. For them, as we have seen, the translator must make explicit certain terms that in the original are only implied.

Nowhere is this more important than in the domain of logical connectives. Most often, when relations between ideas have only to be suggested in Chinese, they must be plainly stated in English. Barzun and Graff make the point succinctly when they advise writers [p. 261] that "to be heard and heeded you must do more than lay your ideas side by side . . . you must *articulate* them."

The many words and phrases that serve to "articulate" ideas — that is, to join them together in a meaningful way — include some of the shortest and simplest in English: "and," "but," "if," "also," "too," "since," "then," and so on. But their frequent appearance in any piece of prose demonstrates that, like the modest but indispensable prepositions, they are among the most valuable words in the language.

In this chapter we shall examine some of these words and phrases that translators need to provide. They offer one of the principal means of achieving continuity, coherence, and clarity in writing of any kind. They are the glue that holds English discourse together. Without them, an otherwise well constructed sentence or series of sentences will appear to the reader as no more than "a plate of loose sand."

Examples of logical connectives

The conjunctions that link clauses grammatically are also the primary means of linking them logically. "And," "but," "because," "after," "although," "until," "so that," and the others, both coordinating and subordinating, are our keys to meaning.

Almost any sentence that is composed of more than a single independent clause requires a conjunction to make a grammatical connection between the two clauses and, at the same time, to express the logical relation between them. Two examples will suffice:

- Forty-two thousand refugees will be short of food in the coming months, and 3,000 houses need to be restored.
(Grammatical connection: two independent clauses, joined by coordinating conjunction. Logical relation: second statement gives additional information related to the first.)

- Since most of Hunan's coal mines are located in remote, hilly land, the province has encouraged laid-off workers there to switch to agriculture to earn a living.
(Grammatical connection: dependent clause + independent clause, joined by subordinating conjunction. Logical relation: second statement is a consequence of the first.)

Although two sentences are by definition separate structures that are not connected grammatically, they still need to be connected logically. Sometimes the logical relation is self-evident, but often a word is needed to make it explicit. In that case, a coordinating conjunction may serve the purpose. "But," for example, can make a logical connection not only between two independent clauses in the same sentence but also between two sentences:

- Luo's art is based on traditional techniques, but he does not allow himself to be restricted by tradition.

378

- Luo's art is based on traditional techniques. <u>But</u> he does not allow himself to be restricted by tradition.

More often, however, the logical link between two sentences is provided not by a conjunction but by an adverb. The function of adverbs, as you know, is simply to modify a verb, an adjective, another adverb, or sometimes a sentence as a whole.

Unlike conjunctions, such adverbs as "therefore," "however," "consequently," "nevertheless," "besides," and so on contribute nothing to the grammatical structure of a sentence. But like conjunctions, they contribute a great deal to its meaning. They show how the thought or action expressed in a given sentence is related to the thought or action in the preceding one.

They do this with admirable precision and economy. William Zinsser remarks, for example [p. 114], that in the sentence, "<u>Nevertheless</u> he decided to go," a single word "can replace a whole long phrase that summarizes what the reader has just been told: '*Despite the fact that all these dangers had been pointed out to him*, he decided to go.'"

Zinsser goes on to cite other short adverbs that are equally efficient at conveying complex meaning: "'<u>Instead</u> I took the train.' '<u>Still</u> I had to admire him.' '<u>Thus</u> I learned how to smoke.' 'It was <u>therefore</u> easy to meet him.' '<u>Meanwhile</u> I had talked to John.'" And he gratefully concludes, "What a vast amount of huffing and puffing these pivotal words save!"

Examples of these "pivotal" adverbs can be found on any page, linking the meanings of sentences and sometimes of independent clauses. Here are two examples from Chinese publications:

- In New China, men and women — especially women, who suffered most from feudal oppression — have gained freedom of marriage and equal rights. <u>Thus</u>, in our new society they are taking a greater part in all kinds of political activities and in all fields of construction.

- We should not be dissuaded by the minor difficulties this will cause; <u>otherwise</u>, we shall have major difficulties that will affect the national economy and the people's well-being.

A large number of adverbial phrases, though a little longer than single adverbs, are no less useful indicators of logical connections. "In reality," "at the same time," "for instance," "in other words," "in the first place," "in the same way," "to summarize," "for this reason" — these and many more perform the same function. Here, for example, are two of them in action, bridging the gap between ideas.

- According to local statistics, the province now has green areas averaging 3.2 square meters per person. <u>In addition</u>, there are 29 scenic spots and nature reserves, covering a total area of 3,088 square kilometers.

- The Shanghai Housing Reform Office has granted 47 million yuan ($ 872 million) to more than 300 enterprises and work units for housing construction. <u>As a result</u>, a total of 7,644 families who previously had a per capita floor space of less than 2.5 square meters moved into new houses last year.

It should be noted that just because they are so useful, these ready-made connectives can be overworked. Jacques Barzun, for one, warns against excessive reliance on them and recommends that they be reduced to a minimum. "Ideally," he says [p. 165] "the perfect composition would consist of sentences so formed that the transition to the next would occur, without a word, in the reader's mind."

This is shrewd advice, and to the extent that writers of English have the skill to compose such sentences, we should all try to follow it. But Chinese translators run less risk of sprinkling a text with too many "however"s and "moreover"s than of failing to insert enough of them to provide coherence.

In the following sections we shall look first at various types of connectives and then at some passages in translations where they are missing but should have been supplied.

Types of logical connectives

The countless words and phrases that link ideas can be classified according to the different relations they express. Following are some of those relations with a few examples of each category:

- addition or amplification: and, moreover, in addition
- contrast or opposition: but, on the contrary, instead
- cause or effect: because, thus, hence
- similarity: likewise, similarly, in the same way
- purpose: in order that, to this end, for this purpose
- time sequence: after, then, meanwhile
- logical sequence: in the first place, next, finally
- illustration: for instance, as an example, specifically
- concession: granted, to be sure, of course
- intensification: indeed, in fact, surely
- restatement: that is, in other words, as has been said
- conclusion: to sum up, in short, in conclusion

There is little to be said about any of these expressions beyond recommending that translators be alert to the need for them. To establish the principle of when and why they are required, we have only to consider some examples of the first three types listed, which are among the most useful. It is the connectives that express these relations that are most likely to be missing from translations where they are wanted.

Examples of missing links

1. *Addition or amplification*

The simplest and doubtless the most common sequence of ideas in expository prose is one in which a statement is followed by another statement that adds something to the first. The second statement will offer more information on the subject, supporting evidence for the argument, further development of the idea, the next event in the narrative, or the like.

Although this simple relation of addition or amplification can often be taken for granted, a connecting word — "and," "also," "too," "moreover," "besides," "furthermore," etc. — may be required to express it.

Consider this passage from the draft translation of an account of the War of Resistance Against Japanese Aggression:

- As for the Chinese, in the stage of strategic defensive, the Kuomintang troops staged one retreat after another in front-line battlefields. Although the people's anti-Japanese forces had expanded, they were far from being able to carry out a strategic counter-offensive; before they were ready to do that they would still have a long, hard

382

struggle to go through.

These two sentences together tell readers that at this stage of the war the Chinese position as a whole was weak. The first states that the KMT forces were continually retreating, the second that the revolutionary forces were not yet ready to mount an offensive. The second sentence adds information that reinforces the first, and readers should be made aware of that before they come to it. A simple "and" will serve the purpose:

- As for the Chinese, in the stage of strategic defensive, the Kuomintang troops had retreated time after time from front-line battlefields. *And* although the people's anti-Japanese forces had expanded, they were far from being able to carry out a strategic counter-offensive; before they were ready to do that they would still have a long, hard struggle to go through.

[Review: In the first sentence, "staged one retreat after another" was changed to "retreated time after time." This revision substituted a plain verb ("retreat") for an unnec. verb + noun construction ("stage a retreat"). It also eliminated the rhyming sound of "stage"/"staged," which immediately calls attention to itself and suggests that the two words are somehow related in meaning, when in fact they are not.]

In the revision "and," which usually serves to connect two words, phrases, or clauses, is used to connect two sentences. Although it was long considered impermissible to begin a sentence with "and" (or "but"), that notion is now discredited. Barzun expresses the consensus when he says [p. 159] that while both words "have

383

suffered from ignorant prohibition ... it is plain from American and English literature that the most exacting writers use them without hesitation as normal openers."

Here is another passage from the same text, this time from a paragraph describing the weaknesses of the KMT:

- As a result of successive defeats, it lost large numbers of men, and morale continued to sink. The mood among the officers and men was defeatist and war-weary. The people in the KMT areas rose up in struggle, making the KMT army's rear area insecure.

The first sentence tells readers of the KMT's loss of men and its deteriorating morale. The second sentence is so clearly an extension of the first that the two might as well be joined into one. The third sentence cites yet another, perhaps more important factor hastening the KMT army's disintegration. It amplifies what readers have just been told, and they should be given a signal of that in advance.

These considerations led to the following revision:

- As a result of successive defeats, it had lost large numbers of men, and morale continued to sink: the mood among the officers and men was defeatist and war-weary. *Moreover* (*or*, *stronger*: What is more), the people in the KMT areas rose up in struggle, making the KMT army's rear insecure.

Minor changes thus turned three choppy, disjointed sentences into a smooth, coherent whole.

2. *Contrast or opposition*

Another common sequence of ideas is one in which the second

opposes or qualifies the first. The content of the two successive clauses or sentences is not cumulative but contradictory.

There are a great many words and phrases that can express this relation: "but," "yet," "although," "however," "nevertheless," "on the other hand," "in spite of," and so on.

It is more important to use these, where appropriate, than it is to use words expressing addition or amplification. Although the lack of an "and" or a "furthermore" may make sentences seem jerky and disconnected, readers will still be able to follow the writer's line of thought. But if there is no "but" or "on the contrary" to signal that the writer is changing direction, readers will be misled, at least until they are well into the second sentence.

Zinsser [p. 114] makes this point very strongly. "I can't overstate," he says, "how much easier it is for readers to process a sentence if you start with 'but' when you're shifting direction, or, conversely, how much harder it is if they must wait until the end to realize that you're now in a different gear."

The following passage illustrates the pertinence of that remark:

- During the next six months, because the British side stuck to its position on the question of sovereignty over Hong Kong, there was no progress in the negotiations. In March 1983 Mrs. Thatcher wrote to the Chinese Premier promising that at a certain stage she would propose to the British Parliament that sovereignty over all of Hong Kong be returned to China.

The first sentence states that negotiations were stalemated because the British were intransigent. With nothing to indicate the contrary, readers assume that the next sentence will support the first. On learning that Prime Minister Thatcher wrote to Premier Zhao, they automatically expect to be told that her letter expressed a continuing refusal to compromise, and they proceed almost to the very end of the sentence with that understanding in mind. It is only when they reach the crucial words "be returned to China" that they realize they were mistaken.

The addition of a single word was all that was needed to prevent this misunderstanding. In the revision readers were given notice early on in the second sentence that the content of the letter, when they came to it, would represent a change in the British position:

- During the next six months, because the British side stuck to its position on the question of sovereignty over Hong Kong, there was no progress in the negotiations. In March 1983, *however*, Mrs. Thatcher wrote to the Chinese Premier promising that at a certain stage she would propose to the British Parliament that sovereignty over all of Hong Kong be returned to China.

The "however" could also have been put at the beginning of the sentence, but many advisers on writing think that in that position it is too obtrusive. Unless the word is to be given special emphasis, it is probably best to place it as in this revision, not at the very beginning but near it, between commas.

Here is another example of contrasting ideas that lack a connecting link:

- I am a layman in natural science. As my trip to Shanghai coincides with your discussion of a ten-year plan for science, I'd like to avail myself of this opportunity to touch on a

386

few questions.

Here again, the first sentence leads readers to anticipate something different from what follows. Logically, if a person begins by saying he is a layman, one expects his next remark to be that he hesitates to address this conference of learned scientists, or perhaps that he hopes to listen and learn — at any rate, something consistent with his preliminary admission that he has no special knowledge of the subject under discussion. Instead, he says something contradictory: that he wants to talk about it. Readers have the uncomfortable sense that somewhere they missed a turn in the road.

They missed the turn because the translator failed to post a sign informing them that the second idea would stand in opposition to the first. Again, all it would have taken to set them on the right path was a single word:

- I am a layman in natural science. *But* as my trip to Shanghai
  coincides with your discussion of a ten-year plan for science, I'd like to avail myself of this opportunity to touch
  on a few questions.

3. *Cause or effect*

This type of connective includes such expressions as "because," "since," "so that," "as a result," "for this reason," "therefore," "accordingly," etc. They are needed when one clause or sentence shows the consequence of another.

These connectives are even more essential to readers' understanding than are those that express contrast. So fundamental is the concept of cause and effect that if readers fail to perceive that relation where the writer intended it, they will miss a crucial element of meaning.

Here is a simple example from a draft translation:

- Private schools are in difficulty now because they can no longer
  rely on warlords and bureaucrat-capitalists for financial resources as they used to. Their school farmland was distributed to peasants during the agrarian reform. The government should show concern for these difficulties.

In this passage three ideas are simply "laid side by side" without
"articulation," as three independent and seemingly unrelated statements. The first sentence tells readers that the private schools are in
trouble because their source of funds has dried up. The second sentence states that they have lost their farmland, but the loss is not
identified as another reason for their difficulties. The third sentence
does indeed seem to follow from the first (the schools are in
difficulty, and the government should show concern), but the intervening sentence destroys the connection.

The polisher decided the way to pull all these ideas together was
to provide the missing link between the first sentence and the second
— the relation of cause and effect:

- Private schools are having difficulties now, because they can no
  longer rely on warlords and bureaucrat-capitalists for financial support, *and because* their farmland was distributed to peasants during the agrarian reform. The government should concern itself with these difficulties.

[Review: In the first sentence "in difficulty" was changed to
  "having difficulties" to provide an antecedent for "these
  difficulties" in the last sentence.]

Once the first two sentences were logically related, the third flowed from them as a natural conclusion.

In the following example from another draft translation, the two sentences are longer and more complex than in the preceding one, but the need for a logical connective between them is no less plain:

- However, the Party had not had time for the entire membership to make a systematic review of its historical experience and, in particular, it had not thoroughly analyzed the kinds of thinking that were at the root of the "Left" and Right mistakes of the past. There were still differences of opinion with regard to the Party's guiding ideology, and these continued to be damaging to the revolutionary cause at certain times and places and in certain respects.

The author, it seemed clear, was making the point that because the Party had not thoroughly analyzed the mistaken thinking of the past, there were still damaging ideological differences at this time. But as in the preceding example, the cause-and-effect relation was only implied.

The polisher made it explicit:

- However, the Party had not had time for the entire membership to make a systematic review of its historical experience and, in particular, it had not thoroughly analyzed the kinds of thinking that were at the root of the "Left" and Right mistakes of the past. *Accordingly* (*or*: thus, *or*: as a result), there were still differences of opinion with regard to the Party's guiding ideology, and these continued to be damaging to the revolutionary cause at certain times and places and in certain respects.

Dubious logical connectives

There are two frequently used connectives that merit particular attention because they are often vague or ambiguous. They are "while" and "with."

1. *While*

The subordinating conjunction "while" is a slippery word that can be used in several senses, some of which are more acceptable than others. Its primary meaning is "at the same time as":

- While Mother read the letter aloud, the family listened in silence. ("While" = "during the time that.")

Most language critics recommend that the word be restricted to this use, linking two simultaneous events.

Still, there is widespread, if sometimes grudging, acceptance of "while" used to represent a contrast without any reference to time, in the sense of either "although" or "whereas":

- While everyone was astonished by the news, no one said a word until she had finished. ("While" = "although.")

- Not all the listeners had the same reaction. The children were delighted at the prospect of meeting their Taiwan cousins at last, while Grandfather maintained a frosty reserve. ("While" = "whereas" = "but, by contrast.")

What all authorities agree on is that "while" should not be used merely as an elegant substitute for a plain "and":

- As he turned the pages of the album, Grandfather took a keen interest in the photographs of his brother and sister-in-law, <u>while</u> the whole family eagerly examined the pictures of Taipei. ("While" = "and," which should replace it.)

It is also generally agreed that "while" should not be used for "although" or "whereas" if its meaning is ambiguous — that is, if the reader cannot tell immediately in what sense the word is to be understood:

- The visitors were offered tea in the courtyard, <u>while</u> dinner was served indoors. ("While" = "whereas"? or "at the same time as"?)

Leaving this little family drama, we can now turn to two examples of "while" that have appeared in the work of Chinese translators.

Here is one that conforms to the generally approved usage — "while" has its original meaning of "at the same time":

- When the congress opened, the leaders of the Communist Party organization in Guangdong were in favor of attacking the Right wing of the Kuomintang, isolating the middle-of-the-roaders and expanding the Left wing, <u>while</u> preparing to repel Chiang's attack.

Here is another in which "while" is ambiguous:

- As all of us lack experience in diplomacy, we should carry forward democracy. Three cobblers with their wits combined equal Zhuge Liang, the mastermind. <u>While</u> soliciting everybody's opinion, we should stress centralism. Efforts must be made to make democracy prevail in our embassies. Stress only on centralism without democracy will lead to bureaucracy. Advocating democracy can help us get rid of bureaucracy.

Does "while" here mean "at the same time" (= while we are asking their opinions we should talk to them about the importance of centralism)? Or does it mean "although" (= although we should ask their opinions, we should remember that centralism is primary)?

And what is the logical connection between the last three sentences, all of which express the importance of democracy, and this one saying "we should stress centralism," which they seem to contradict? Just what point is the speaker trying to make?

Since no reader should have to struggle with such questions, the polishers tried to prevent them from arising:

- Since none of us is experienced in diplomacy, we should cultivate democracy. As the old saying goes, "Three cobblers with their wits combined match Zhuge Liang, the mastermind." *Of course*, *while* it is necessary to solicit everybody's opinion, we should stress centralism. *But* we must establish democracy in our embassies. Stressing centralism to the neglect of democracy will lead to bureaucratism, *while* promoting democracy can help us get rid of it.

Now it was clear that the first "while" was being used in the sense of "although." Also, that the following sentences were a return to the main point presented at the beginning (the need for democracy), the intervening remark ("we should stress centralism") being only parenthetical. The second "while" plainly meant "whereas."

But, you might argue, if "while" used in the sense of "although" or "whereas" can be ambiguous and requires such care, why not just put one of those words and be done with it? In the revision, the first "while" could easily be replaced with "although" and the second with "whereas." Wouldn't that be simpler and perhaps clearer as well? Your argument would have merit, and it would be applauded by all those who recommend that "while" be reserved for expressing time relations.

2. *With*

Unlike all the words we have considered so far in this chapter, "with" is a preposition. But it is so often used as a logical connective — and so often in a vague or confusing manner — that it is worth considering alongside the conjunctions, adverbs and adverbial phrases that usually serve to tie ideas together.

A moment's reflection will show that "with" can be used in a great variety of senses. The following are only a few of the relations that this versatile word can express:

- accompaniment: he went with the children to see their teacher
- agency: with a nail and some twine she was able to repair the latch
- characterization: the girl with most courage spoke up first
- manner: with dogged persistence, they trudged on through the snow
- possession: the man with the key is not here

These and many other uses of "with" are entirely legitimate: in each example the connection made is clear and specific.

The difficulty arises when "with" is used in such a vague sense that it gives no precise indication of the relation between the two elements it joins.

For example:

- <u>With</u> the rapid increase of automobile production and import starting from the early 1980s, Chen was promoted as the director of the newly formed Automotive Office in the Ministry.

The connection between the two events is foggy at best. The "with" suggests that Chen was promoted <u>because of</u> the increase in the number of automobiles. But that is by no means clear, and in any event it is not logical: someone else might have been appointed just as well, for the same reason.

The polisher decided that the true connection was simply one of timing. She therefore substituted for "with" a conjunction that would make that plain:

- *When* the production and import of automobiles began to increase rapidly in the early 1980s, Chen was promoted to the post of director of the newly formed Automotive Office in the Ministry.

Another example:

- <u>With</u> professionals familiar with the country's laws and proficient at foreign languages, these offices will save the time and energy of foreign trademark registrants.

Again "with" is too vague and general to express the relation between the two elements it is asked to connect. The professionals may be familiar "with" the laws, but what does it mean to say that the offices are "with" professionals?

It was not hard for the polisher to find a specific replacement:

- *Staffed by* professionals familiar with the country's laws and proficient at foreign languages, these offices will save time and energy for registrants of foreign trademarks.

One last example:

- With wide streets and a small population, the city is filled with gas stations and karaoke bars.

Here the difficulty is not that the relation between the ideas is vague but that it is non-existent. There is no logical reason why a city with wide streets and a small population should have many gas stations or karaoke bars. The writer has simply used "with" as a means of tacking onto his or her main clause some additional information about the city.

We can make the faulty logic a little less evident by consigning the irrelevant information to a subordinate clause:

- The city, *which has wide streets and a small population* , is filled with gas stations and karaoke bars.

Or, we could arrange the elements in two independent clauses, as a coordinate series of unrelated details:

- The city has wide streets and a small population, *and* it is filled with gas stations and karaoke bars.

Two separate sentences might be even better:

- The city has wide streets and a small population. It is filled with gas stations and karaoke bars, and ...

The several revisions we have just cited represent the two ways for polishers to deal with a sentence that hinges on an inadequate "with." You can either:

> - substitute another, more precise expression that clarifies the logical relation between the two terms in question ("<u>when</u> the production of automobiles," "<u>staffed by</u> professionals")

or, if there is no logical relation to be expressed:

> - abandon the attempt to make an arbitrary connection and content yourself with two independent statements.

To conclude this discussion of dubious connectives, we need only refer to the list of "Fifty Forbidden Words" that Barzun and Graff [p. 255] suggest the "self-critical writer" will want to deny himself. Under the heading "Feeble Connectives," their list includes "while (apart from time relations)" and "with (as a universal joint)."

Wrong logical connectives

Sometimes a translator recognizes the need for a connective in English but supplies the wrong one. The commonest mistake of this kind is to put an "and" or an "also" where logic requires a "but" or a "however." Here is an example from a draft translation:

> - In our system the public sector is the major sector of the economy <u>and</u> there are also other sectors.

The second statement does not support the first but, rather, reduces its force. The sense is: yes, it's true that in our system the public sector is the major sector of the economy, but it is not the only one. The word needed to express the connection between the two ideas is not an "and" but a "but," and the reviser changed it accordingly:

> - In our system the public sector is the major sector of the

economy, *but* there are also others.

Here is another example, this time one that appeared in print in a Chinese English-language publication:

- Efforts will be made to introduce pensions, medical insurance, and housing systems, <u>and</u> the best way to get laid-off workers out of poverty is to help them find jobs, Li stressed.

Again the second clause stands in opposition to the first. The intended meaning is: yes, we will take these other measures to make things easier for the unemployed, but the most important thing we can do is to help them find jobs. The sentence should have been revised to make that relation clear:

- Efforts will be made to introduce pensions, medical insurance, and housing systems, *but* the best way to get laid-off workers out of poverty is to help them find jobs, Li stressed.

Sometimes a translator makes the opposite mistake and puts a word indicating contrast or opposition where the sense demands one expressing addition or amplification. Here is an example from the draft translation of an editorial published in March of 1950. (The "public grain" referred to was a portion of the harvest collected by the central government as a tax in kind.)

- In most of these new areas last autumn's public grain, which constitutes the greater part of national revenue, was collected only in January and February of this year. <u>However</u>, in many localities it has not yet been collected; tax collection in newly liberated areas has not been organized very quickly.

The first sentence tells readers that in most of the newly liberated areas there is a problem: taxes in grain were collected late. The second sentence says that in some places the problem is even more serious: taxes in grain have not been collected at all. Thus, the second idea, instead of contrasting with the first, as "however" indicates, expands upon it.

The polisher noticed the logical inconsistency in the draft translation and corrected it as follows:

- In most of these new areas last autumn's public grain, which constitutes the greater part of national revenue, was collected only in January and February of this year, *and* in many places it has *still* not been collected. It has taken time to organize tax collection in newly liberated areas.

"And" and "or" are often confused as well. In Chapter IX we have already seen two examples of sentences in which "and" was used when logic demanded "or." In revision 8 (pages 267 – 268) "low temperatures <u>and</u> early frosts" was changed to "low temperatures *or* early frosts," because the two did not necessarily coincide. And in revision 10 (pages 269 – 270) "the national bourgeoisie adopted the neutral <u>and</u> sympathetic <u>and</u> even cooperative attitude toward revolution" was changed to "neutral, sympathetic, *or* even cooperative" because these were three different attitudes.

Here is another example:

- Yunnan Province will also build <u>and</u> upgrade the highways leading from Kunming to such areas as Sichüan Province, the Guangxi Zhuang Autonomous Region, and Myanmar,

398

Laos, and Vietnam.

Plainly, the same highway cannot be both built and upgraded. What the writer meant to say was:

> - Yunnan Province will also build *or* upgrade highways leading from Kunming to such areas as ....

> [Note the absence of the definite article "the": we cannot speak of "the highways" leading from one place to another if some of them do not yet exist.]

There are no formal rules to help Chinese translators avoid mistakes of this kind in English. The best advice is probably the simplest: pay attention to the connectives you use, and before you choose one, give some thought to the logical relation between the ideas you are expressing.

Twenty more examples of revision

1) A: We hold countless meetings, and our articles and speeches are too long and too repetitious, in both content and language. Reiteration in speech is needed, but one must be concise.

B: We hold countless meetings, and our articles and speeches are too long and too repetitious, in both content and language. *Of course*, some words have to be repeated, but we should try to be concise.

> [- In the first sentence the speaker tells Party leaders that when they speak or write they are too repetitive. In the second he concedes that repetition is sometimes necessary but urges them to try to reduce it.

> - This notion ("I grant that ..., but ...") was only

399

implied in the draft version. In the revision it was made explicit by the phrase "Of course," meaning "of course, I know that ...."

- (Review: To eliminate a formidable abstract noun, the reviser changed "reiteration is needed" to the plain-English construction "some words have to be repeated.")]

2) A: After the downfall of the Gang of Four, the Party Chairman, Hua Guofeng, who was in charge of the work of the Central Committee, clung to the erroneous notion of the "two whatevers" and reaffirmed the wrong theories, policies, and slogans of the "cultural revolution." On April 10, 1977, Deng Xiaoping wrote a letter to the Central Committee, proposing that to guide the work of the Party, the Central Committee should use a correct understanding of Mao Zedong Thought as an integral whole.

B: After the downfall of the Gang of Four, the Party Chairman, Hua Guofeng, who was in charge of the work of the Central Committee, clung to the erroneous notion of the "two whatevers" and reaffirmed the wrong theories, policies, and slogans of the "cultural revolution." On April 10, 1977, Deng Xiaoping wrote a letter to the Central Committee, proposing that to guide the work of the Party, it should use *instead* a correct understanding of Mao Zedong Thought as an integral whole.

[- These two sentences present two contrasted alternatives. Deng was proposing that the Party be guided by a "correct understanding" of Mao Zedong Thought rather than by Hua Guofeng's "erroneous notion." In A-version this relation is only implied.

- In the revision "instead" was added to underline the contrast between Deng's "understanding" and Hua's, and also to make it clear that one was to replace the other.
- (Review: To avoid a third reference to "the Central Committee," the polisher substituted the pronoun "it.")]

3) A: This fact tells us that the policies pursued by the feudal rulers were intended to weaken certain nationalities. This was <u>particularly</u> true of imperialist policies.

B: This fact tells us that the policies of the feudal rulers were intended to weaken certain nationalities. This was *also and particularly* true of the policies of the imperialists.

[- The structure of A-version implies that the imperialists were part of the group of feudal rulers. (For example, if the statement were, "All his new colleagues were friendly; this was particularly true of Chen," the reader would understand that Chen was one of the group of colleagues.)
- In other words, "particularly" by itself gives a false indication of the logical connection between the two sentences.
- In the revision "also" was introduced to show that the two groups — foreign imperialists and domestic feudal rulers — were separate, although alike in their policies.
- Since "particularly" had to be retained for the meaning, the result was the somewhat unusual double connective, "also and particularly."
- (Review: "Imperialist policies" was changed to "the policies of the imperialists" to create parallel structure with the preceding "the policies of the feudal rulers.")]

4) A: They [local governments] bear full responsibility for collecting public grain and taxes, for storing and transporting grain, and for supervising the local enterprises and helping them carry out the tasks assigned by the parent ministries. If local governments do not help in this connection, it will be impossible for these enterprises to fulfill their tasks according to plan.

B: They bear full responsibility for collecting public grain and taxes, for storing and transporting grain, and for supervising the local enterprises and helping them carry out the tasks assigned by the parent ministries. *Indeed*, without such assistance from local governments, it will be impossible for these enterprises to fulfill their tasks according to plan.

[- The second sentence adds an idea that not only supports but intensifies the first. The sequence of ideas is: (1) local governments have certain responsibilities that they must fulfill; (2) it is absolutely essential for them to fulfill those responsibilities, because otherwise ....

- In the revision this reinforcement was neatly indicated by "Indeed."]

5) A: This led to a disparity between the purchasing and selling prices [of grain], so the state had to make up the difference. This is contrary to the law of value. On the one hand, we cannot arouse the enthusiasm of the peasants for production, and on the other hand the state bears a heavy burden — that is, every year it must use dozens of billions of yuan for subsidies. It is impossible for the state to use many funds for economic development and for education,

science, and cultural undertakings.

B: This led to a disparity between the purchasing and selling prices, so the state had to make up the difference. This is contrary to the law of value. On the one hand, we cannot arouse the enthusiasm of the peasants for production, and on the other hand the state bears a heavy burden — that is, every year it must use tens of billions of yuan for subsidies. *Consequently*, the state doesn't have enough money for economic development, *let alone* for educational, scientific, and cultural undertakings.

[- In the first two sentences the speaker says the state spends enormous amounts of money on grain subsidies; in the third he says the state is short of funds needed for other purposes. The relation between the two ideas is one of cause and effect, but in A-version that is only implied.

- The polisher made it explicit by adding "Consequently."

- There was nothing in A-version to indicate the relative importance of the several alternative uses for funds mentioned in the last sentence (economic development, education, science, culture).

- The polisher knew, however, that at the time when these words were spoken (1988), economic development was to take precedence over everything else. She therefore changed the "and" in the draft version, which indicated the equality of the following items, to "let alone," which indicated the primacy of economic development over the other three.

- It is instructive to note that the polisher in this instance happened to be a foreigner who could not read the Chinese

403

original. Accordingly, she based her proposed revisions solely on the implied logic of the English version and on her knowledge of the period.

- But when a second, Chinese polisher later reviewed the work, comparing it with the original, she found that the notions introduced by the foreigner — "consequently" and "let alone" — were indeed expressed in the Chinese and had been omitted by the first translator only through error.

- Thus, either method would have sufficed to discover the faults in the A-version: a thoughtful analysis of the English or a careful comparison with the Chinese.

- ("Dozens of billions of yuan" was changed to "tens of billions of yuan" because when it is a question of money, English-speakers habitually count in units of ten, not twelve. Since the figure mentioned here was only a rough estimate, the discrepancy between the English version and the Chinese made no difference. Naturally, where exact numbers are important, "tens" cannot be substituted for "dozens.")]

6) A: It [the newly formed Central Advisory Commission] is aimed at lowering the average age of members of the Central Committee <u>and</u> making it possible for some elderly comrades who have retired from the forefront of affairs to continue to play a certain role.

B: The purpose of establishing this commission is to lower the average age of members of the Central Committee *and at the same time* to make it possible for some elderly comrades who have retired from the forefront of affairs to continue to play a certain role.

[- "And" is basically the right conjunction here, because it
   expresses the addition of a second aim to the first.

 - The Central Advisory Commission, however, was formed
   for two separate though complementary purposes, and
   "and" alone does not suffice to bring this out.

 - In B-version "at the same time" was added to make a clearer separation between the two purposes.

 - (Review: The polisher changed "aimed at" primarily because a commission is not "aimed at" anything. Another
   consideration, however, was her desire to resist the noun
   plague. "It is aimed at" had to be followed by gerunds
   ("lowering" and "making"), whereas "The purpose is"
   led to verbs (the infinitives "to lower" and "to make").]

7) A: We should appreciate it if all enterprises in your country
      [Japan] — large, medium-sized and small — strength-
      ened their cooperation with us. We hope the Japanese
      government will encourage them to take a longer-range
      view. China lacks funds and has many resources that have
      yet to be developed. If they are developed, China will be
      able to supply more of Japan's needs. If it invests in China
      now, Japan will benefit greatly in future.

   B: We should appreciate it if all enterprises in your country —
      large, medium-sized and small — strengthened their coop-
      eration with us. We hope the Japanese government will
      encourage them to take a longer-range view. China is
      short of funds *and for that reason* has been unable to de-
      velop many of its resources. If they are developed, we
      shall be able to supply more of Japan's needs. *So*, if Japan

invests in China now, it will benefit greatly in future.

[- The key sentence in this series is the third one: "China lacks funds and has many resources that are yet to be developed." But that sentence is not clear. To the speaker, the connection between the two statements it contains is obvious, but that does not mean it is obvious to the reader.

- The logical relation between the ideas — China lacks funds; China has many undeveloped resources — is one of cause and effect. "And," the connective in A-version, cannot convey that relation.

- In B-version the meaning was spelled out in "for that reason."

- The polisher thought that a connective was needed between the last two sentences as well. Judging that the intended relation was again one of cause and effect, she put, "So, if Japan invests in China now . . . ."]

8) A: In 1978 we held the Third Plenary Session of the Eleventh Central Committee, and in a few days we shall convene the Third Plenary Session of the Twelfth Central Committee, which will have its own special features. The first Third Plenary Session focused on rural reform, and this Third Plenary Session will center on urban reform, including the reform of industry, commerce, and other sectors.

B: In 1978 we held the Third Plenary Session of the Eleventh Central Committee, and in a few days we shall convene the Third Plenary Session of the Twelfth Central Committee, which will have its own special features. The first Third Plenary Session focused on rural reform, *whereas* this Third Plenary Session will focus on urban reform, including the reform of industry, commerce, and other sectors.

[- In these two clauses the second idea is not consistent with the first but in contrast to it: "the first meeting focused on x, but this one will focus on y." Here again, the "and" in A-version fails to indicate the right connection.

- To mark the contrast, the polisher changed "and" to "whereas."

- (Review: In the second sentence, "centre on urban reform" was changed to "focus on urban reform" to mark the parallel structure of the two clauses by repeating the word "focus.")]

9) A: While fighting corruption, we must demonstrate our will not to change the policies of reform and opening to the outside world and our resolve to deepen the reform and open even wider to the outside world.

B: While fighting corruption, we must demonstrate our resolve not to change the current policies *but*, *on the contrary*, to deepen the reform and open even wider to the outside world.

[- This sentence presents two ideas: "our resolve to deepen the reform and open even wider" and "our will not to change" those policies. The "and" that connects them in A-version seems quite reasonable, and it is grammatically correct because it joins two equal notions: "we must demonstrate our will . . . and our resolve."

- Nevertheless, "and" does not express the intended relation between the two objects of "demonstrate." In reality, the

407

second idea ("our resolve to deepen") is meant not as a simple addition to the first ("our will not to change") but as a contradiction of it. The meaning is: far from changing the policies, we intend to do just the opposite.

- To express that meaning, the polisher changed "and" to "but, on the contrary."

- (Review: This example has already been cited in Chapter V, page 131, as revision 8. There it was offered to show that the repetition of the long formula "reform and opening to the outside world" could be avoided by use of the single word "current.")]

10) A: We can't expect to participate in many events in the next Olympic Games in 1956. Six years later, by 1960, many top athletes will emerge if our sports activities are undertaken along the correct path.

B: We can't expect to participate in many events in the next Olympic Games in 1956. *But* by 1960, six years *from now*, many top athletes will emerge if our sports program is carried out correctly.

[- "Later" can be a useful connective indicating a time sequence, but here it is the wrong one and therefore confusing. Coming after the reference to 1956, "six years later" means 1962, not 1960. The speaker, who made this remark in 1954, meant "six years from now." The change was made in the revision.

- With this correction, the two ideas were clear enough, but they were simply "laid side by side" without any apparent logical connection. Even an inattentive reader would feel that something was missing.

- In the revision "But" was inserted as a link showing that the second idea was in contrast to the first.]

11) A: This policy of completely decentralized management was appropriate for the separated liberated areas, <u>so</u> we accomplished a great deal. Last year we made rapid progress in the War of Liberation: in that one year, all of China's mainland was liberated, except for Tibet, to form a continuous liberated area. Under these circumstances, much of our financial and economic work had to be unified.

B: This policy of completely decentralized management was appropriate *at a time when* the liberated areas were separated geographically, *and it enabled us* to accomplish a great deal. *But* last year we made rapid progress in the war: in that one year we took over the entire mainland, except for Tibet, making it one continuous liberated area. Under these *new* circumstances, much of our financial and economic work had to be unified.

[- The point of this paragraph (from a 1950 editorial) is that the situation has changed and that the policy has had to change in consequence. Most of the revisions in the draft version, particularly those relating to logical connectives, were made to bring this out.

- "Appropriate for the separated liberated areas" was spelled out for greater clarity and, especially, to underline the time element: "appropriate at a time when the liberated areas were separated geographically."

- "So we accomplished a great deal" was changed to "and it enabled us to accomplish a great deal." This strengthened the connection between the policy of decentralization and

409

the accomplishments, emphasizing that the policy had been useful at that time.

- In the second and third sentences, starting at "Last year we made rapid progress," the writer expresses an opposing idea: that good as it was, this policy is no longer appropriate. "But" was inserted to prepare the reader for the change of direction.

- "Under these circumstances" was changed to "under these new circumstances" to stress the writer's point that the situation is different now.

- (Review: "All of China's mainland was liberated . . . to form a continuous liberated area" was changed to active voice. "We took over" was used instead of "we liberated" to avoid three appearances of the same word in so short a passage. "China's" was dropped because it was obvious.)]

12) A: It is very important for us to launch projects in the order of their importance and urgency; otherwise we shall lose sight of the overall situation. You comrades must have acquired some understanding of this point after your study tour. Likewise, it is wrong for us to consider only the most important and urgent projects to the neglect of others.

B: It is very important for us to launch projects in the order of their priority; otherwise we shall lose sight of the overall situation. You comrades must have learned that from your study tour. *On the other hand*, it would be wrong for us to consider only the most important and urgent projects to the neglect of others.

[- The first two sentences stress the importance of undertaking high-priority projects first. The third ("Likewise, it is wrong etc.") says we must not neglect the others. Plainly, the third sentence provides not a supporting idea that amplifies the first one but an opposing idea that reduces its force.

- To express the opposition between the two ideas, the polisher changed "likewise," an indicator of similarity, to "on the other hand," an indicator of difference.

- (Review: In the first sentence, "importance and urgency" was changed to "priority" partly to avoid using "important" and "importance" in the same sentence and partly to express the idea more concisely.)]

13) A: However, it is not possible to train intellectuals of working class and peasant origins all at once. That calls for planned steps and long-term effort. The difficulty is especially great because our workers and peasants have long suffered from exploitation and oppression, and many of them are illiterate. Difficult as it is, university educators should pay more attention to it.

B: However, it is not possible to train intellectuals of working class and peasant origins all at once. That calls for planned steps and long-term effort. The difficulty is especially great because our workers and peasants have long suffered from exploitation and oppression, and many of them are illiterate. Precisely *because this problem is so difficult*, university educators should pay more attention to it.

[- The third sentence in A-version ("The difficulty is especially great") says that the problem is particularly difficult

411

and explains why. The fourth ("educators should pay more attention") is the conclusion drawn from the preceding statement.

- The implied meaning is: "the problem is particularly difficult; therefore you should pay more attention to it." In short, the relation between the ideas is one of cause and effect.

- The connective in A-version, however — "Difficult as it is" — means not "because it is difficult" but rather "although it is difficult."

- To make the right logical connection, expressing what she perceived to be the speaker's intention, the polisher changed "Difficult as it is" to "Precisely because this problem is so difficult."

- In both versions the first sentence refers to "intellectuals of working class and peasant origins." The "and" is not wrong, but the same idea might have been better expressed as "intellectuals of working class or peasant origin."]

14) A: As CPC General Secretary Jiang Zemin said in his report delivered to the 15th congress, the battle against corruption is vital to the very existence of both the Party and the country. Besides, ordinary people will lose confidence in the government if graft among officials cannot be eliminated. Though the sentiments of disgust toward corruption are almost the same in every corner of the world, East Asian people, especially the Chinese, usually set high moral criteria for the government.

B: As CPC General Secretary Jiang Zemin said in his report to the 15th congress, the battle against corruption is vital to the very existence of both the Party and the country. If graft among officials cannot be eliminated, ordinary people will lose confidence in the government. *Though* people in every corner of the world have almost the same feeling of disgust for corruption, East Asian people, especially the Chinese, usually set *particularly* high moral standards for government officials.

[- The first sentence in A-version states that "the battle against corruption is vital to the very existence of both the Party and the country." The next one says that if that battle is lost, ordinary people will lose confidence in the government.

- The "Besides" that introduces the second idea suggests that it is almost an afterthought — a separate and lesser potential consequence of unchecked corruption.

- It seems, rather, that this second idea is of prime importance and an integral part of the first. It would be precisely because people had lost confidence in the government that "the very existence" of the Party and the country would be threatened.

- The polisher decided that the tight logical connection between the two sentences was evident without additional words and simply deleted the misleading "Besides."

- In the last sentence of A-version, the two clauses state: (1) people everywhere despise corruption; (2) East Asian people set high standards for government. Those two ideas are entirely consistent. Consequently, the opening "Though," which sets up in the reader's mind the

413

expectation of a contradiction, is misleading, and the sentence makes no sense.

- To make it logical, the polisher had only to insert the word "particularly." "Though" now introduced a reasonable contrast: between people everywhere, who all despise corruption, and East Asians, who set particularly high standards for officials and therefore (presumably) despise it more than most.

- (Review: The order of clauses in the second sentence — "people will lose confidence ... if graft cannot be eliminated" — was reversed to put the subordinate idea first and the main one at the end. Note that in the last sentence — "Though the sentiments of disgust ... East Asian people" — the order of clauses was already correct in A-version.)]

15) A: The Chinese Communist Party put forward a proposal that we should establish a new China which would be, in the words of Mao Zedong, "independent, free, democratic, united, prosperous, and powerful." While the Chiang Kai-shek clique stuck to the point that the Chinese society should still be kept in a semi-feudal, semi-colonial status, under the rule of the big landlords and the big bourgeoisie ....

B: The Communist Party was proposing the establishment of a new China that would be, in the words of Mao Zedong, "independent, free, democratic, united, prosperous, and powerful." The Chiang Kai-shek clique, *on the other hand*, was insisting on the perpetuation of the old China — semi-feudal, semi-colonial, ruled by the big landlords and the big bourgeoisie . . . .

[- "While" is a subordinating conjunction that introduces a subordinate (dependent) clause. By definition, such a clause cannot stand independently as a complete sentence. (Cf. clauses introduced by "although," "until, "when," etc.)

- For that reason, and to emphasize the contrast between Chiang's position and that of the CPC, the polisher substituted "on the other hand."

- (Review: You may recall that this passage was quoted in the last chapter as an example of one requiring parallel structure. An explanation of the other changes will be found there, on page 371, in revision 19.)]

16) A: Being in the position of leadership, the central authorities, including the Party Central Committee and the State Council, view the general situation more comprehensively but are liable to ignore some immediate interests of the masses, while the local authorities can easily get close to the masses so that they know more about local concerns, particular problems, and the immediate interests of the masses.

B: Being in the position of leadership, the central authorities, including the Central Committee and the State Council, have a better overall view of the general situation, but they are liable to ignore certain immediate interests of the masses. *On the other hand*, the local authorities, who can easily get close to the masses, know more about local concerns, particular problems, and the immediate interests of the people.

[- The first problem with A-version is that it is all one sentence. English-readers cannot absorb so much information at one time without a pause; by the time they get to the end of the sentence they have forgotten the beginning. Mindful of this, the polisher's first concern was to break the sentence in two.

- The logical point for the break was at "while." But this posed a grammatical problem: as we have just seen, a "while" clause cannot stand alone as a separate sentence.

- "While" was plainly being used here in the sense of "whereas." But "whereas" was ruled out as a possible replacement because it too is a subordinating conjunction that can only introduce a subordinate clause.

- The polisher's solution was to start the new sentence with — again — "On the other hand." This overcame the grammatical difficulty and at the same time made a sound logical connection between the two ideas: the central authorities may ignore local interests; local authorities, on the other hand, will not.

- (Review: "Party" Central Committee was omitted as a self-evident modifier. The third reference to "the masses" was changed to "the people" to avoid repetition.)]

17) A: Such an open statement of strategy and tactics <u>when</u> fighting was still going on is unusual in world history of wars. Mao <u>also</u> pointed out that because the PLA's strategy and tactics were based on a people's war, no army opposed to the people could use them or cope with them.

B: Military leaders in world history have seldom made such an open statement of their strategy and tactics *while* fighting

416

was still going on. *But* Mao pointed out that because the PLA's strategy and tactics were based on a people's war, no army opposed to the people could either adopt them or defeat them.

[- The statement was issued at the same time that the fighting was going on; indeed, that is the central point of the passage.

- "When" is not a wrong connective here, but there is another conjunction that better conveys precisely this relation of simultaneity: "while." The polisher therefore put "while" in the revision, confident that in this usage, for once, it was irreproachable.

- The first sentence says that it was unusual for a military commander to reveal his strategy and tactics while a war was still in progress. The second tells why Mao felt free to do so: the enemy could not take advantage of the knowledge. The logical relation between the two sentences is that such a statement was unusual, but Mao could make it without risk.

- With this understanding, the polisher changed the translator's "Also," which was confusing, to a "But."

- (Review: She also changed "Such an open statement is unusual" to "Military leaders have seldom made such an open statement." By introducing action and actors, she not only made the sentence stronger but provided some other leaders to stand parallel to, and in contrast with, Mao.)]

18) A: After the founding of the People's Republic, in the rural areas we initiated agrarian reform and launched a movement

417

for the cooperative transformation of agriculture, <u>while</u> in the cities we conducted the socialist transformation of capitalist industry and commerce. We were successful in both. From 1957 on, China was plagued by "Left" ideology, which gradually became dominant.

B: After the founding of the People's Republic, in the rural areas we initiated agrarian reform and launched a movement for the cooperative transformation of agriculture, *while* in the cities we conducted the socialist transformation of capitalist industry and commerce. We were successful in both. *However*, from 1957 on, China was plagued by "Left" ideology, which gradually became dominant.

[- The "while" in A-version might have been replaced by "and," but it is acceptable here in its primary sense of "at the same time." The transformation of agriculture and the transformation of industry and commerce were close enough in time that from this distance — the remarks were made in 1985 — they can be considered to have taken place simultaneously.

- In A-version, although the last sentence ("From 1957 on") expresses a contrast to the preceding statement, there is no transition between them to make that clear.

- In B-version "However" was added to alert the reader to a turn in the road.]

19) A: It was <u>with</u> her leadership and negotiation skills that the customers were eventually compensated with 5 billion yen by the Japanese company.

B: It was *thanks to* her leadership and negotiating skills that the customers eventually received 5 billion yen in compensation from

418

the Japanese company.

[- A-version is understandable, but that is in spite of the all-purpose "with," which is not logical here. As it stands, it suggests that the customers were compensated with her leadership and 5 billion yen.

- In the revision "with" was replaced by a more precise term that accurately expressed the relation between her leadership and the compensation.]

20) *The following passage is taken from a pre-Liberation document. The speaker is addressing the question of how many bonds the people's government should issue in the territory under its control. The proportion of private enterprise in the different areas is important because it is mainly in that sector that potential purchasers of the bonds are to be found.*

A: With China's vast territory, government bonds to the value of 120 million silver dollars do not represent a big sum. In comparison, Chiang Kai-shek wants to issue 200 million silver dollars' worth of government bonds in the shrinking area still under his control. He always did this in the past whenever he was at the end of his tether. Northeast China, with its 40 million people, has a much lower proportion of private enterprise than areas south of the Great Wall. It decided to issue, in two installments, government bonds amounting to a value of 12 million silver dollars, and the first installment has already been sold on schedule. With a much greater proportion of private enterprise, areas south of the Great Wall can set a higher target for bond issues.

B: (1) *Considering* China's vast territory, 120 million silver dollars' worth of government bonds is not a large amount. *For purposes of comparison*, Chiang Kai-shek wants to issue 200 million silver dollars' worth of bonds (2) *just* in the shrinking area still under his control. That's what he has always done when he was at the end of his tether. Northeast China, (3) *for all* its 40 million people, has a much lower proportion of private enterprise than areas south of the Great Wall. (4) *Yet* the authorities there have decided to issue, in two installments, government bonds amounting to a value of 12 million silver dollars, and the first installment has already been sold on schedule. (5) *Thus*, in areas south of the Great Wall, (6) *where* there is a much greater proportion of private enterprise, higher targets can be set for bond issues.

[- In A-version this long and closely reasoned passage has only four logical connectives to help the reader follow the argument. One is the useful "in comparison"; the other three are vague "with"s.

- As a result, the reader is faced with what seems to be a string of unrelated, or only loosely related, facts from which it is hard to draw any understanding of the speaker's point.

- In B-version half a dozen changes were made to clarify the relations between ideas. They were the following:

- (1) The opening "With" had no clear meaning. It was therefore changed to the more precise "Considering."

- (2) "Just" was added to indicate that the large amount of bonds that Chiang wanted to issue would be sold only in a relatively small area.

- (3) "With" its 40 million people simply gives a fact without telling the reader its significance. The logical connection between the high population and the relatively low proportion of private enterprise is one of contrast: "for all its 40 million people" (= in spite of having 40 million people, even though it has 40 million people).

- (4) The preceding sentence tells readers that there is relatively little private enterprise in Northeast China. This one says that Northeast China has decided to issue bonds in the amount of x. In A-version the two facts are simply juxtaposed without explanation. The intended sense is that even though there is not much private enterprise, a large number of bonds have already been issued and sold there. In B-version "Yet" was inserted to announce the contradiction.

- (5) In A-version there is nothing to show readers that they have come to the conclusion of a line of argument. In the revision this was signaled by "Thus."

- (6) In A-version "with" makes only a loose connection between the "areas south of the Great Wall" and the "much greater proportion of private enterprise." In the revision the prepositional phrase was replaced by a clear subordinate clause: "where there is a much greater proportion."

- (In the last sentence, although active voice is generally preferable to passive, "areas south of the Great Wall can set higher targets" was changed to "in areas south of the Great Wall higher targets can be set." This was done to avoid personifying "areas." People — officials, authorities, etc. — can set targets, and so can political or administrative entities — a province, for example, or Northeast China, as above. But in English mere geographical "areas" cannot make decisions of any kind.)]

Twenty exercises

A number of the examples in this set of exercises are necessarily longer than usual. This means that the draft versions often presented many errors in addition to wrong or missing logical connectives. These other errors have been corrected, so that you can concentrate. exclusively on the meaning of each passage and the logical relation of its parts.

Also because of the length of the examples, words added or changed in the proposed revisions in the key have been italicized. This will make it easier for you to compare the revisions with your own versions.

As always, the revisions offered are not necessarily the only "right answers." Where you find a "however," a "but" might do just as well; a "therefore" might be substituted for an "accordingly," and so on.

1) The vast majority of workers, city dwellers, and even members of the middle and lower petty bourgeoisie were brought to the brink of disaster. The rural economy went into a sharp recession.

2) If the North-South problem is not solved, it will hinder the development of the world economy. The solution, of course, lies in North-South dialogue, and we support dialogue. But

dialogue alone is not enough; cooperation among Third World countries — in other words, South-South cooperation — should be stepped up.

3) There is no doubt that the system of management described above is much more centralized than the one that was in effect last year. If we were asked how many undertakings will still be under decentralized management, we would have to answer, a great many.

4) At first, the Yangtze Automotive Chassis Plant will be able to assemble 60,000 chassis a year for one- and two-ton trucks. With the completion of construction, it will have an annual capacity of 100,000 chassis.

5) It is not necessary to launch such a movement [against the "five evils"] now. In Shanghai 160,000 cases of tax evasion have been uncovered, and most of them are medium or minor ones. These cases of tax evasion vary in seriousness, and there are also defects in our tax system. These things have to be addressed and rectified, but there is no need for a lesser movement against the "five evils."

6) Not much progress has been made in the talks on control of nuclear arms and of weapons in outer space. That's why for many years we emphasized the danger of war. Recently, there have been some changes in our views. We now think that although there is still the danger of war, the forces that can deter it are growing, and we find that encouraging.

7) Some people think that since China is emphasizing the importance of ideals, that means it is going to close its doors again. That is not true. We are soberly aware of the possible

negative effects of the open policy and will not ignore them. Our principle is not to close but to continue to open. We may open even wider in the future.

8) At that session [the Third Plenary Session of the Eleventh Central Committee], we criticized the "two whatevers" and put forward the slogan, "We must emancipate our minds and put our brains to work."

9) All local authorities and departments should make the improvement of the performance of large and medium-sized state enterprises an important item on their agendas, taking practical measures to create a favorable environment for their production and operation and to help them reduce losses and increase profits. Basically, state enterprises must rely on their own efforts to extricate themselves from their predicament. While actively carrying out the reform, they should adjust their mix of products to conform to the demands of domestic and international markets, produce readily marketable goods, keep developing new products, and enhance their ability to adapt to the market and compete.

10) Changchun has now reached an annual production capacity of 400,000 automobiles with over 100 models of medium trucks, light vehicles, and sedans.

11) As late as May 1926 he [Chiang Kai-shek] still stated, "Not only am I not opposed to Communism, but I very much approve of it." For the time being, the KMT continued to cooperate with the CPC. The fact that command over the Northern Expeditionary Army was largely in Chiang's hands made it clear that while the revolution was progressing rapidly, it was

already in a serious crisis.

12) If China, with its one billion people, took the capitalist road, it would be a disaster for the world. It would be a retrogression of history, a retrogression of many years. If China, with its one billion people, abandoned the policy of peace and opposition to hegemonism or if, as the economy developed, it sought hegemony, that would also be a disaster for the world, a retrogression of history. If China, with its one billion people, keeps to socialism and adheres to the policy of peace, it will be following the right course and will be able to make greater contributions to humanity.

13) "Graft, bribery, and other corruption cases have become quite serious, while crimes involving the exchange of power for money are spreading among some government departments and officials," Liang told a national conference of provincial procurators on Wednesday. "So, we must focus attention on such developments, but not underestimate the seriousness of the threat posed by corruption."

14) Shen says that research and production of friction materials for motor vehicles in China had always been based on asbestos, which is both cheap and plentiful in the country. At present there are close to 30 manufacturers with a total annual production of more than 20,000 tons of friction materials, most of which are made from asbestos. Realizing that asbestos was a hazardous substance and that international manufacturers were no longer using it, Shen made up her mind to develop China's own non-asbestos materials.

15) Zhou announced at the reception that he had asked Hu Zongnan

personally if he had sent his troops defending the Yellow River west to prepare an attack on the Shaanxi-Gansu-Ningxia Border Region. "Deputy Commander Hu told me," he said, "that he had no intention of attacking the Shaanxi-Gansu-Ningxia Border Region and that the troops under his command would take no such action. I was very happy to hear this, and I believe everyone else will be happy, too." Hu's scheme to attack the region was made known to the public.

16) With a 30-year history, the museum is dedicated to the collection of items related to ancient China, Chinese paintings and calligraphy, historical pictures, and contemporary Hong Kong art.

17) If the CPC [in 1937] were to give up its proletarian stand of independence and initiative [as recommended by the Comintern], make no distinction between the proletariat and the bourgeoisie, refrain from arousing the masses, and try to appease the bourgeoisie in all matters so as to maintain the united front, it would only weaken the position of the proletariat, put the united front at the mercy of the bourgeoisie, and eventually bring about China's defeat. After he arrived in Yan'an, Wang Ming did everything possible to carry out this "new policy" of the Communist International.

18) The objective reasons [for the revival of the CPC after the failure of the Great Revolution of 1924 - 1927] were as follows.... Many of the troops that had previously been engaged in attempts to encircle and suppress the Workers' and Peasants' Red Army were moved to other battlefields to take part in [the warfare between the new rival warlords], leaving a

426

vacuum in certain areas and an opportunity for the Red Army
to grow. Under the rule of the KMT government, the national crisis was aggravated. Every one of the fundamental
contradictions in Chinese society became intensified, and the
Nanjing government grew increasingly fascist.... Discontent
was growing even among those who had cherished illusions
about the KMT.

19) The principal contradiction in Chinese society in the present stage
is the one between the growing material and cultural needs of
the people and the backwardness of production. To promote
the all-round progress of society, we must give priority to the
growth of the productive forces and make economic development our central task.

20) The venture, named Huazhong-Warner Transmission Co.,
Ltd., has a total investment of 255 million yuan ($30.72
million), with Borg-Warner contributing 60 percent.

XIII. Summing it All Up

Like Chapter VI, which was a review of Part One on unnecessary words, this final chapter will be a review of Part Two on questions of sentence structure. It will offer no new material but only additional revisions and exercises representing the problems we have studied in this second part of the Guide.

Twenty more examples of revision

As in Chapter VI, the explanation of the revisions will show the order in which the various faults in each example were dealt with. Usually the polisher started with the ones that were most obvious and easiest to correct — unnecessary words.

In your own work, you may prefer to reverse the order, starting with the major problems and then cleaning up the minor ones. In the course of practice you will settle on the procedure that suits you best. But a narrative account of the polisher's approach to each of the following passages will demonstrate one method of reaching an acceptable revision and, it is hoped, help demystify the editing process.

The Noun Plague

1) A: This decision is a <u>measure</u> of vital <u>importance</u> to do a good <u>job</u> of our financial and economic <u>management</u>.

   B: This is a very *important* decision that will enable us to *manage* our financial and economic affairs *more effectively*.

   [- A-version of this short sentence was weighed down with five abstract nouns, of which only the first, "decision," appeared to be essential.

- The polisher first deleted "measure" as an empty word that added nothing to "decision."
- She then changed "importance" to an adjective ("an important decision").
- Next she changed "management" to a gerund: "to do a good job of managing our financial and economic affairs."
- This left the vague and endlessly repeated noun-formula "do a good job." It could not be simply eliminated, because it contained an element of meaning, but it could be easily replaced. The polisher had only to change "managing" to "to manage" and add "more effectively."]

2) A: Rational <u>scale</u> of investment is an important condition for maintaining economic stability and enhancing the sustaining <u>power</u> of development. The <u>scale</u> of construction projects now under way is large enough and the <u>scale</u> of planned investment for this year is not small either, so no further expansion can be permitted.

B: An important condition for maintaining economic stability and *continued* development is that *investment must be restricted to a rational scale*. *Enough* construction projects are already under way, and *considerable* investment is planned for this year, so no further expansion can be permitted.

[- The first problem the polisher noticed in A-version was the repetition of the abstract noun "scale": three appearances in two sentences — at least two too many. She examined them in turn.
- The first "scale," she thought, was useful and should be retained. But "rational scale of investment" was too

429

condensed for easy comprehension. Accordingly, she introduced a verb to spell out the idea: "investment must be restricted to a rational scale."

- This change also had the effect of correcting the word order: the important idea was now at the end of the sentence, where it led naturally into the next one.

- The two "scale"s in the second sentence, however, contributed nothing to meaning. The polisher found it was not hard to eliminate them both, using more concrete language and simpler constructions: "enough projects are already under way" and "considerable investment is planned."

- There remained the awkward circumlocution "enhancing the sustaining power of development." This, she decided, meant no more than "maintaining continued development," which eliminated another abstract noun, "power."]

3) A: China has continuously broadened its scope of undertakings in the field of multilateral diplomacy ....

B: China has *taken an active part in more and more* multilateral diplomatic *forums* ....

[- First, recognizing "the field of" as an unnec. "category" noun, the polisher eliminated the phrase. That left "China has continuously broadened its scope of undertakings in multilateral diplomacy ...."

- The polisher considered that this language was too vague, abstract, and general to convey anything specific to the reader. Studying the original in context, he decided that to "broaden the scope" of diplomatic "undertakings"

430

meant, in plain terms, to undertake more diplomacy —
that is, to participate in more international forums.

- Accordingly, he dispensed with both "scope" and "undertakings," spelling the meaning out with the help of the
relatively concrete "forums" and the simple "more and
more."

- (It might even have sufficed to say: "China has taken an
increasingly active part in multilateral diplomacy.")]

4) A: The <u>tendency</u> toward <u>indifference</u> [to intellectuals] is characterized by the <u>underestimation</u> of the <u>significance</u> of the
tremendous progress made in the political and academic
<u>studies</u> by the intellectuals and of the important role
played by the intellectuals in our socialist cause . . . .

B: *Certain comrades* are *indifferent* to intellectuals, because
they *underestimate* the tremendous political and academic
progress that intellectuals have made and the important
role they have played in our socialist cause. . . .

[- In approaching A-version, the polisher's first act was to replace the abstract "tendency" with some real people:
"Certain comrades." This naturally led to a verb + adjective ("are indifferent") instead of the noun
"indifference."

- She next considered what could be done with the abom-
inable "characterized by." (That expression, like "conducive to," "aimed at," "resulting in," and countless others ending in prepositions, inevitably leads to a cottony
mouthful of abstract nouns or gerunds.)

- She soon realized that in this case the words were not even
logical: the cadres' indifference was not "characterized

431

by" the underestimation etc.; rather it was the result of it. This perception led to the revision, "because they underestimate."

- "Significance" seemed to add nothing useful, especially in the presence of "tremendous" and "important." The polisher simply deleted it. She likewise dispensed with "studies."

- To avoid a third reference to "intellectuals" in the same sentence, she substituted the pronoun "they" for the last one ("the important role they have played").

- Although earlier "they" had been used to represent "Certain comrades," she thought there would be no confusion in this instance.

- "Intellectuals" would be automatically understood as the antecedent, because it was nearer than "comrades," and especially because it was grammatically parallel to the pronoun: "the progress intellectuals have made"/"the role they have played."

- (It is not certain that one can "play a role" in a "cause." It might have been better to put, "the important contributions they have made to our socialist cause.")]

Pronouns and Antecedents

5) A: Some countries have suffered serious setbacks, and socialism has seemingly been weakened. But the people will have tempered themselves and drawn lessons from it, and that will make socialism develop in a healthier direction.

B: Some countries have suffered major setbacks, and socialism appears to have been weakened. But the people have been tempered by *the setbacks* and have drawn lessons from *them* , and that will make socialism develop in a healthier direction.

[-The first thing that struck the polisher about A-version was that the translator had clearly paid no attention to the sound of what he or she had written.

- To the ear of a native speaker of English, the sequence "Some - suffered - serious - setbacks - socialism - seemingly" called attention to itself as an intolerable repetition. Indeed, it suggested a deliberate "tongue-twister," on the order of "Peter Piper picked a peck of pickled peppers."

- Accordingly, her first act was to break up the pattern by substituting "major" for "serious" and "appears" for "seemingly."

- Next, her attention was drawn to the vague "it," which had no antecedent. Presumably what the people had "drawn lessons from" was the "setbacks." But (1) to agree with the plural "setbacks," "it" would have to become "them," and (2) even if that change were made, "setbacks" would still be too far away to be immediately recognized as the antecedent.

- The solution was simply to repeat "setbacks": "But the people have tempered themselves and drawn lessons from the setbacks."

- Then it occurred to the polisher that it was those same "setbacks" that had "tempered" the people. Perhaps a tighter logical connection could be made between the two elements: "But the people have been tempered by the setbacks and have drawn lessons from the setbacks." That

433

was clearly the intended sense.

- All that remained was to avoid the third appearance of "set-backs." It could easily be replaced by the pronoun "them," which now had a clear and nearby antecedent that agreed in number: "But the people have been tempered by the setbacks and have drawn lessons from them."]

6) A: The Russians built the Chinese Eastern Railway in China's Northeast after the Qing Dynasty government concluded a secret pact with czarist Russia in 1896. *It* was operated by Russia until a 1924 Sino-Soviet agreement brought *it* under joint management. After the Kuomintang reactionary regime was established in 1927, it pursued a pro-imperialist and anti-Soviet foreign policy and created a series of anti-Soviet incidents.

B: The Russians built the Chinese Eastern Railway in Northeast China after the Qing Dynasty government concluded a secret pact with czarist Russia in 1896. *It* was operated by Russia until 1924, when a Sino-Soviet agreement brought *it* under joint management. *The reactionary KMT regime* established in 1927 pursued a pro-imperialist and anti-Soviet foreign policy and created a series of anti-Soviet incidents.

[- The first time the polisher read A-version she understood that the Eastern Railway pursued a pro-imperialist foreign policy.

- On a second reading she saw why she had been led astray: in the three successive uses of "it," the translator had switched antecedents without warning. The first two

434

times the pronoun represented the railroad, but the third
time it stood for the KMT regime.

- The change of antecedents was particularly misleading because the third pronoun ("it pursued"), like the first ("It
was operated"), was the subject of its sentence. Since the
two words had the same function as well as the same
form, the reader tended to assume that they also had the
same meaning.

- To prevent misreading, the polisher simply dropped the
third "it" and substituted the words the pronoun was
meant to represent: "the reactionary KMT regime."]

7) A: The news that Wang Baosen, Vice-Mayor of Beijing, had shot
himself to death when faced with charges of "economic
crimes" created quite a stir among Beijing residents, not
only because he was the highest government official who
had committed suicide since the Cultural Revolution and
that he was using a gun, <u>which</u> is strictly forbidden in
China, but also because of the potential political ramifica-
tions of his act.

B: The news that Wang Baosen, Vice-Mayor of Beijing, had shot
himself when faced with charges of "economic crimes"
created quite a stir among Beijing residents. They were
shocked not only because Wang was the highest government official who had committed [*or*: to commit] suicide
since the Cultural Revolution and because he had used a
gun, *private possession of which* is strictly forbidden in
China, but also because of the potential political ramifica-
tions of his act.

[- Reading A-version, the polisher first understood that in
435

China people are forbidden to use guns to commit suicide. The relative pronoun "which" was correctly attached, referring to the immediately preceding clause ("that he was using a gun"). The problem was that that clause did not express the intended meaning.

- In the revision the polisher spelled out the true antecedent of "which." What is "strictly forbidden" in China is private possession of firearms.

- Rereading her revision, the polisher thought that the sentence was too long, presenting too much information for the reader to swallow at one gulp. Accordingly, she broke it into two, beginning the second sentence with "They were shocked," which under the circumstances seemed a justifiable addition.]

The Placement of Phrases and Clauses

8) A: [There is no doubt that the system of management described above is much more centralized than the one that was in effect last year. But if we were asked how many undertakings will still be under decentralized management, we would have to answer, a great many.] For example, agricultural production must be organized and led by local governments, after the Ministry of Agriculture of the Central People's Government has laid down the general principles.

B: For example, *after the Ministry of Agriculture has laid down the general principles*, agricultural production still has to be organized and led by local governments.

[- Before doing anything else, the polisher deleted "of the Central People's Government" as a self-evident modifier.

There is only one "Ministry of Agriculture," and it is by
definition a ministry of the central government.

- She then turned her attention to the question of emphasis.
The point of the passage (from a speech given in the early
1950s) was that even though many government functions
were to be centralized, local governments would still have
an important role to play.

- But in A-version the placement of the subordinate clause
("after the Ministry of Agriculture . . . has laid down")
undercut the main message.

- To correct this, the polisher moved the subordinate clause
up, leaving final place in the sentence to the affirmation of
the continuing responsibilities of local governments.

- Lastly, she clarified the logic of the argument by inserting
"still."]

9) A: It seems almost a rule that an organization, no matter how intelligent and capable its leading members may be, will
mostly be affected by bureaucratism <u>so long as it has an
overextended structure and is staffed by too many people</u>.
The reason is that when an organization has become overstaffed due to its over-expansion, quite a number of its
personnel will spend their time doing nothing but in-
dulging in idle talk . . . .

B: It seems to be a rule that no matter how intelligent and capable its leading members may be, *if an organization is
overexpanded and consequently overstaffed*, it will be
affected by bureaucratism. That is because in such an
organization many people will spend all their time in idle
talk . . . .

437

[- On reading A-version, the polisher first became aware of
the qualifiers "almost" and "mostly." Neither one seemed
necessary, so she deleted them both.

- Next, she was troubled by the repetition of ideas. "When
an organization has become overstaffed due to its over-expansion" seemed to be only a thinly disguised restatement
of the immediately preceding "so long as it has an overextended structure and is staffed by too many people."

- She therefore condensed the two clauses into one: "if an organization is overexpanded and consequently overstaffed,"
followed by "such an organization."

- It was only after this tightening that the polisher considered the order of clauses in the first sentence. She saw
that the revised subordinate clause ("if an organization is
overexpanded etc."), coming at the end of the sentence,
usurped the place of the main clause ("it will be affected
by bureaucratism").

- Accordingly, she reversed the order of the two clauses.
This change placed the emphasis on the important point
and, at the same time, made a better logical connection
between the two sentences. "It will be affected by bureaucratism" was now directly followed by "That is
because. . . ."]

10) *From* Asiaweek:

A: China's leaders have made their intentions clear. "China will
not devalue the yuan <u>for the sake of its own economic development and economic stability in Asia</u>," premier-in-
waiting Zhu Rongji said last month.

B: China's leaders have made their intentions clear. "*Both for*

438

the sake of its own economic development and for the sake of economic stability in Asia ," premier-in-waiting Zhu Rongji said last month, "China will not devalue the yuan."

[- The translation of Zhu Rongji's remarks that appeared in the magazine was plainly made by a person who did not recognize that the word order was faulty from the point of view of both logic and emphasis.

- The statement, "China will not devalue the yuan for the sake of its own economic development," suggests at first that China will devalue the yuan for some other reason. There is nothing in the sentence to correct this impression.

- In addition, the crucial announcement that China will not devalue its currency is buried by the long explanation that comes after it.

- As indicated in B-version, a careful editor could have solved the problem of logic by moving the prepositional phrase ("for the sake of etc. ") to the beginning of the sentence, where its meaning would have been unmistakable.

- That change would also have solved the problem of emphasis. The important news would have been left to the end of the quotation and, indeed, to the end of the sentence, with nothing following to diminish its impact.]

Dangling Modifiers

11) A: Gao also stated that his office had finished drafting a document entitled Administrative Measures for the

Implementation of the Patent Law and Regulations, which has been presented to the State Council for review. Once adopted, patent violators will face tougher administrative penalties, and patent enforcement bodies will have more power in law enforcement.

B: Gao also stated that his office had finished drafting a document entitled Administrative Measures for the Implementation of the Patent Law and Regulations, which has been presented to the State Council for review. *Once these measures are adopted*, patent violators will face tougher administrative penalties, and the bodies that enforce the patent laws will have more power.

[- Seeing the past participle at the beginning of the second sentence in A-version ("Once adopted"), the polisher immediately looked for the word it modified, which should have been the subject of the clause. It was not. What she found instead was "patent violators will face etc.," with no mention anywhere of what was to be "adopted."

- She solved this problem easily by converting the participial phrase to a separate clause with its own subject, "measures," the word that "adopted" was intended to modify. (To avoid repeating the long title of the document, she used the demonstrative adjective "these.")

- The polisher hesitated over the noun-used-as-adjective construction "patent enforcement bodies," which was perhaps acceptable, but decided it would be more readily understood if it were spelled out as a clause: "bodies that enforce the patent laws."

- Lastly, considering that if these law enforcement bodies

were given more power, it could only be more power to
enforce the law, she deleted "in law enforcement" as
self-evident.]

12) A: Based on data gathered at the epicenter [of an earthquake in
Hebei], construction experts should finish designs for the
buildings by the end of next month.

   B: Construction experts expect that the building *designs*,
which are based on data gathered at the epicenter, will be
finished by the end of next month.

   [- The polisher saw that in A-version the opening participial
phrase ("Based on") attached itself to the subject of the
sentence ("experts"), which, however, was not the word
it logically modified. It was not the "construction experts"
that were based on the seismological data but the
"designs" for the new quake-resistant houses.

   - To eliminate the dangling participial phrase she discarded
it and substituted a subordinate clause: "Construction experts should finish designs for the buildings, which are
based on data gathered at the epicenter, by the end of
next month."

   - That solved one problem, but it created another: the
"which" attached itself not to the "designs," as she had
intended, but to the intervening "buildings." Thus, it
was no longer the "experts" that were based on the data
but the "buildings," a reading that was just as wrong.

   - The solution, she saw, was to place the true antecedent of
"which" — the "designs" — immediately before the pronoun, so that the connection between them would be unmistakable: "Construction experts should finish the

building designs, which are based on data gathered at the epicenter, by the end of next month."

- The sentence now said what the Chinese author meant it to say, but the polisher thought it would be easier to read if "by the end of the month" were not so far removed from the verb it modified, "should finish."

- To bring the two related elements closer, she made a slight change of wording: "Construction experts expect that the building designs, which are based on data gathered at the epicenter, will be finished by the end of next month."]

13) A: The draft report was printed and distributed to 135 work units at central and local levels <u>soliciting</u> their opinions <u>based on</u> a decision made by the Political Bureau of the CPC Central Committee on July 10 this year.

B: *In accordance with* a decision made by the Political Bureau of the CPC Central Committee on July 10, *the drafting group* printed the draft report and distributed it to 135 work units at central and local levels, *soliciting* their comments.

[- The polisher saw at once that in A-version the present participle "soliciting" was afloat without an expressed subject: it was not the draft report that solicited opinions on itself. To solve this problem she introduced "the drafting group" to be the subject of "soliciting."

- "Based on" plainly had no true subject to lean on either and consequently attached itself to the wrong one. Thus, it appeared to be the work units' opinions that were based on the decision of the Politburo.

- The polisher dropped the participial construction "based on" and replaced it with a simple and appropriate prepositional phrase, "In accordance with."
- Then, to put the main point (that comments were solicited) in the place of emphasis at the end of the sentence, she moved the subordinate idea (the decision on which this action was based) to the beginning.]

14) A: "By employing state-of-the-art building techniques, it is expected that newly built houses in the quake-devastated areas will be able to withstand earthquakes of eight degrees of seismic intensity," Tian [a spokesman for the Ministry of Construction] said.

B: "*By employing* state-of-the-art building techniques," Tian said, "*we* expect to make the new houses in the quake-devastated areas able to withstand eight degrees of seismic intensity."

[- As soon as she saw the introductory gerund "by employing," the polisher looked for its implied subject. It was nowhere to be found. The subject of "employing" could not be "it is expected," far less "newly built houses."
- The people employing the advanced techniques could only be the builders or planners at the Ministry of Construction for whom Tian was speaking. The polisher therefore introduced the pronoun "we" to represent them.]

Parallel Structure

15) A: The volume of money in circulation and credit will be kept at a level beneficial to stabilizing the value of the renminbi

and to economic <u>growth</u>.

B: *The volume of money in circulation* and *the amount of credit available* will be kept at a level that will *stabilize* the value of the renminbi and *encourage* economic growth.

[- The polisher first noticed that in A-version the two subjects joined by the coordinating conjunction "and" were out of balance: "the volume of money in circulation" and "credit."

- To achieve greater parallelism, as well as greater clarity, she expanded the second term to "the amount of credit available."

- She then found that "beneficial to" was followed by two objects also joined by "and" but also ill-matched: "stabilizing the value of the renminbi" (a gerund with its own object) and "economic growth" (a noun without an object).

- In the interest of parallel structure, she again changed the second term to match the first: "stabilizing the value of the renminbi and encouraging economic growth."

- She then realized that "beneficial to" was as objectionable as "characterized by" and for the same reason: it trapped the writer into following with a noun or gerund.

- Accordingly, she replaced it with a verb structure that expressed the same idea more directly and with equal parallelism: "a level that will stabilize x and encourage y."]

16) A: Mutual <u>resentment</u>, <u>monopolizing</u> everything in one's own hands, <u>going</u> it alone and <u>refusing</u> to cooperate with others, mutual <u>contempt</u> and worse still, <u>engaging</u> in splittist activities — all such behavior must be prevented

444

among the cadres.

B: *Resenting* other cadres, *monopolizing* everything in one's own hands, *acting* independently and *refusing* to cooperate, *holding* other nationalities in contempt or, worse still, *engaging* in splittist activities — all such behavior must be prevented.

[- The polisher saw that A-version was based on an awkward and haphazard mixture of nouns and gerunds connected by the coordinating conjunction "and." In this case, she felt, it would be better to stick to one or the other.

- She also saw that the translator had not decided whether to talk about one person or two. "Mutual resentment" and "mutual contempt" could only refer to the reciprocal attitude of two persons, whereas "monopolizing everything in one's own hands" and "going it alone" plainly referred to the behavior of a single individual. Thus, readers were repeatedly asked to change their point of view.

- The polisher changed the nouns to gerunds, producing a series of parallel items that was both more satisfying to the ear and easier to understand.

- At the same time she introduced further consistency by making all the items refer to the behavior of one person only. "Mutual resentment" readily became "resenting other cadres," and "mutual contempt" became "holding other nationalities in contempt," an interpretation justified by preceding material.]

17) A: In short, <u>making</u> concessions on our part will only alleviate the internal contradictions among the enemy, whereas our <u>intervention</u> will bring about an aggravation of their

contradictions.

B: In short, *if we make concessions*, it will only alleviate the internal contradictions among the enemy, whereas *if we intervene*, it will aggravate those contradictions.

[- The polisher first changed "bring about an aggravation" (an unnec. verb + noun) to the plain-verb equivalent, "aggravate." With that detail out of the way, she turned to the structural problem.

- The two clauses compared alternative courses of action — a classic construction calling for parallelism. In A-version, however, the first clause had a gerund for a subject ("making") and the second a noun ("intervention"), a combination that was tolerable but scarcely satisfactory.

- The polisher converted both subjects to verbs ("we make," "we intervene"). These changes not only enhanced the parallelism but also, by avoiding the noun plague, substituted two easy and natural expressions for two stiff and awkward ones.

- She also tried to avoid the repeated reference to "contradictions," by replacing the second mention with a pronoun. This produced "if we make concessions, it will only alleviate the internal contradictions among the enemy, whereas if we intervene, it will aggravate them."

- But she abandoned that version as soon as she reread it. The pronoun "them," intended to refer to "contradictions," tried to attach itself instead to the nearer plural noun, suggesting the meaning "it will annoy the enemy." Better to repeat the noun than to substitute a potentially misleading pronoun.]

446

18) A: The third phase of the campaign lasted from December 15, 1948, to January 10, 1949. The chief objective now was to wipe out Du Yuming's forces. In order to coordinate this action with the Beiping-Tianjin campaign, in the beginning of this phase the PLA troops on the front line of the Huai-Hai campaign were ordered to stop their attack on Du's army for two weeks to give Fu Zuoyi's army on the North China front a false sense of security.

B: The third phase of the campaign lasted from December 15, 1948, to January 10, 1949. The chief objective now was to wipe out Du Yuming's forces. *However*, in order to coordinate this action with the Beiping-Tianjin campaign, in the beginning of this phase the PLA troops on the front line of the Huai-Hai campaign were ordered to stop their attack on Du's army for two weeks to give Fu Zuoyi's army on the North China front a false sense of security.

[- The second sentence in A-version said that the chief objective of this phase of the campaign was to wipe out Du Yuming's forces. With no notice to the contrary, the polisher assumed that the next sentence would tell her how this operation was set in motion.

- Instead, it said that for tactical reasons, the PLA troops in Du's area were, on the contrary, ordered to halt their attack on him.

- To prepare readers for this seeming contradiction, the polisher introduced a "However."]

19) A: It can be seen from the planned levying and expenditures for

public grain that there will be a surplus of 10.5 billion *jin*, or the equivalent of RMB 1,023 billion. Cash expenditures are expected to total 3,062 billion yuan. Using the tax receipts and surplus public grain to defray this expense, we will still have a deficit of 288.8 billion yuan.

B: It can be seen from the planned receipts and expenditures of public grain that there will be a surplus of 5.25 billion kg., or the equivalent of ¥1,023 billion. *But* cash expenditures are expected to total ¥3,062 billion. *So even* using the tax receipts and surplus public grain to defray this expense, we will still have a deficit of ¥288.8 billion.

[- After scanning A-version, the polisher first made the easy changes of form. She converted *jin* to kilograms, a more familiar measure in English. (This is not always necessary; it depends on the style preferred by the publication you are writing for.)

- Next she made "RMB" and "yuan" consistent. She changed both to the standard "¥" corresponding to the symbols used in English for dollars and pounds — " $ " and " £ ." (This also is a question of house style, but whatever form is chosen, it should be used consistently.)

- Turning then to the substantive problems of A-version, the polisher found that the three sentences appeared to state three unrelated facts. To tie them together and thus clarify the point being made, she introduced words that expressed the logical connections that were only implied in the original: "But" and "So even."]

20) A: The guiding general principle of national economic development — <u>with</u> agriculture as the foundation and industry as
the leading factor — must be applied to obtain better
results.

B: We must do better in applying the guiding principle of [na-
tional] economic development, *namely*, *that* agriculture
is the foundation and industry the leading factor.

[- The polisher thought the "with" in A-version was so
vague that the phrase it introduced seemed merely incidental. At the end of the sentence the reader still didn't know
just what the "with" was attached to or what the guiding
principle was.

- He therefore changed "with" to a precise word,
"namely," that made the relations between the elements
unmistakable and nailed down the meaning.]

- He also changed the sentence from passive voice — "The
principle must be applied" — to active —"We must do
better in applying the principle."]

Twenty more exercises

Many of the following exercises are more complex than those offered in preceding chapters, because they contain more than one element needing revision. This, of course, is very often the case in
"real-life" polishing.

Consequently, you must keep a sharp lookout not only for examples of the structural faults discussed in Part Two but also for examples of the unnecessary words studied in Part One. If you proceed
methodically, rereading your work after each revision to see if you
can make further improvements, you will be able to solve first one

problem and then another, until you are satisfied with your version.

You will note that this time, after each exercise there is a mention in parentheses of the title(s) of one or more chapters of the Guide. These indicate the nature of the errors that appear in the exercise and should help you identify them.

1) The situation in the Northeast is still characterized by the enemy's strength and our weakness.
   (*Noun Plague*)

2) This has been conducive to the aggravation of the internal contradictions in the capitalist camp, to the consolidation and expansion of the camp of peace and democracy, and to the growth of the forces of the national and democratic movements in the various countries of the capitalist world.
   (*Noun Plague + Unnec. Nouns and Verbs + Unnec. Modifiers*)

3) As our technical people are far from sufficient, the training of such people constitutes a very important task.
   (*Noun Plague + Repeated References to the Same Thing*)

4) "Running an operation in China is a great challenge and requires a lot of patience and long-term planning," says Kuang-Ming Lin, president of Dana China. "However it is a fast growing economy with some good business opportunities."
   (*Pronouns and Antecedents*)

5) There is nothing to fear if the imperialists refuse to do business with us. Their past invasions turned China into a colonial and semi-colonial country. The Chinese people rose up to make revolution because that was the only way they could survive.

We certainly cannot rely on them now.

(*Pronouns and Antecedents*)

6) Non-staple foods are daily necessities for people living in the cities and in industrial and mining areas, and indeed they consume more non-staple foods than staple ones.

(*Pronouns and Antecedents*)

7) A legal aid organization for young people was opened in Guangzhou on Wednesday, China News Service reported. It launched Jibuhuan Yunlai Legal Aid Fund the same day.

(*Pronouns and Antecedents + Placement of Phrases and Clauses*)

8) The Government Administration Council of the Central People's Government issued a Decision on the Unification of the National Financial and Economic Work on March 3.

(*Placement of Phrases and Clauses + Noun Plague*)

9) A senior financial official reaffirmed yesterday that to keep currency values stable remains the ultimate objective of Chinese monetary policy, despite the fact that China's economy has achieved a "soft landing."

(*Placement of Phrases and Clauses + Noun Plague*)

10) Li, who arrived in Hong Kong on Saturday afternoon to attend the annual World Bank Group and International Monetary Fund meeting, said China hoped to strengthen cooperation with the World Bank during a meeting with World Bank President James Wolfensohn.

(*Placement of Phrases and Clauses + Noun Plague + Repeated References*)

451

11) Entering the town, what first appears to visitors is a spread of green bamboo and lawns dotted here and there with beautifully designed houses, clearly showing the wealth and taste of the homeowners.

(*Dangling Modifiers*)

12) Compared to a regular automobile, it costs much less to operate a farm vehicle.

(*Dangling Modifiers*)

13) As an outstanding strategist, Bocheng's strategic insight was demonstrated not only in directing battles, but also in his consideration of building modernized and regularized army forces.

(*Dangling Modifiers + Parallel Structure + Noun Plague + Repeated References*)

14) To better distribute water among provinces along the river and utilize the precious water efficiently more water conservancy facilities should be constructed.

(*Dangling Modifiers + Parallel Structure + Repeated References*)

15) Encouraged by the strong market demand, Beijing Jeep Corporation has set a sales target of 80,000 units for this year and 100,000 for next year. Production during the first eight months of 1995 was 54,000 and 52,000 were sold.

(*Parallel Structure + Noun Plague*)

16) The required training period for a car driver is six months, that for a farm vehicle only three months.

(*Parallel Structure + Noun Plague*)

17) We should not only know how to use the modern equipment but

also its functions and mechanism.

(*Parallel Structure* + *Redundant Twins*)

18) With the construction of more apartment houses, the people [in your city] will be able to live in a better environment.

(*Logical Connectives* + *Noun Plague*)

19) The loans [to college and university students] will be awarded on a zero-interest basis. Guarantees will also be required before the loan is granted.

(*Logical Connectives* + *Noun Plague* + *Repeated References*)

20) At that time I was in charge of the work of the Central Committee and the government, and I introduced a series of measures for straightening things out. We had quick results and indeed excellent results in every area. These measures for straightening things out actually ran contrary to the "cultural revolution" and irritated the Gang of Four. So once again I was ousted from office.

(*Logical Connectives* + *Repeated References* + *Unnec. Modifiers*)

Part Three:
Supplementary Examples

In Part Three you will find 40 additional examples of Chinglish that you can use to review all the material covered in this Guide.

Because it is both more important and more difficult to correct mistakes of sentence structure than to eliminate unnecessary words, these examples include more of the faults discussed in Part Two than those discussed in Part One. But each of the eleven major categories of problems we have considered is represented at least five or six times, and some of them — notably the eternal noun plague — a great many more.

Unlike most of the examples provided elsewhere in the book, these 40 are not sorted into separate categories and arranged by type or by degree of difficulty. That, of course, only reflects reality. In "real life," problems of translation do not appear in isolation or conveniently grouped in some logical way. On the contrary, they often present themselves in tangled clumps, and always in random order.

Nevertheless, as we have seen, and as these examples will confirm, even a long and intimidating passage, full of intertwined problems, can be taken apart and reworked piece by piece.

You may wish to try your hand at editing these examples two or three at a time, and then to check your versions against the revisions provided at the end of the list. (As in chapters VI and XIII, the revisions are accompanied by detailed explanations describing the changes in chronological order.)

Most of the examples contain at least two or three errors, and a few as many as eight or nine. All told, there are some 150 trouble spots in want of attention. And as Jacques Barzun [p. 185] assures writers who are rereading their work, "[t]he sharper your judgment, the more trouble you will find."

It is equally true that the greater your patience, the more trouble you will find. The surest way to catch remaining elements of Chinglish in a translation is to read it over and over, and then, if possible, over again after a lapse of time that enables you to view it afresh.

In Professor Barzun's handbook *Simple and Direct* [p. 201], the last of 20 basic principles he sets forth for writers makes exactly this point: "Read and revise, reread and revise, keep reading and revising until your text seems adequate to your thought." That is, for translators, until your text seems adequate to your author's thought.

Do not be discouraged if, on comparing your version with the one provided, you find that you have not identified every problem and come up with the best solution for it. After all, many of these A-versions were selected precisely because they required extensive and difficult revision.

Remember too that revising is hard work even for native speakers of English. Like any other complex skill, it is acquired by degrees and largely through practice. No one ever mastered the craft of editing all at once — certainly not just by taking a course on the subject or by reading a book about it.

There is, however, one piece of practical advice, offered by Barzun and by many other experienced writers, that may prove helpful. It is that after you have "finished" a piece of work, you reread what you have written two or three times from different critical points of view, to see if it meets certain tests.

Addressing American writers, Barzun lists ten questions they should ask themselves about the text, including many relating to content and organization. For Chinese translators, who are not responsible for those aspects of a piece, we can propose a list of just three:

- First, is my version <u>clear</u> (no pronouns without plain antecedents, no misplaced or dangling modifiers, no expressions so vague or so highly condensed as to be incomprehensible)?

- Second, is my version <u>logical</u> (right emphasis, parallel structure where appropriate, logical connectives where needed)?

- Third, is my version as <u>tight</u> and as <u>light</u> as possible (no unnecessary or repetitive words and an absolute minimum of abstract nouns)?

If you can answer Yes to those three questions, you can be confident that you have turned Chinglish into English.

Forty final exercises

1) It is an important political task of the Party during the transition period to continue to provide assistance to the intellectuals for their self-reform.

2) Our basic ideas, ranging from the development strategy to the principles and policies, including the policies of reform and opening to the outside world, are correct. If there is any inadequacy, it lies in the fact that the efforts we have made along the line of reform and opening are inadequate.

3) They [the KMT reactionaries] send or buy over traitors, who hide themselves in the Party, to spy on Party leaders and worm their way into leading Party organs, so that they can wipe out local Party organizations from top to bottom at one fell swoop when they give the order.

4) The most significant policy change is the ongoing process of shifting to national treatment for foreign investors in China from the practice of offering tax privileges and other preferential treatment to foreign investors, as in the first few years after the open policy was introduced.

5) The better you do your work and the more achievements you have, the better the people throughout the country will understand the value of knowledge, thus encouraging the people to respect and acquire knowledge.

6) In 1928 when the revolution was suffering serious setbacks, it was easy to see that the "Left" tendencies that appeared in the Party were wrong and to quickly put an end to putschist mistakes. But after the outbreak of the wars between the KMT

warlords of different factions and at the time of apparent revival of the revolutionary movement, many comrades in the Party unrealistically overestimated revolutionary developments, giving rise to more intense and sustained growth of "Left" impetuosity.

7) The Party's Seventh National Congress was held two or three years after the rectification movement began which strengthened the unity of the Party and enabled our Party to achieve tremendous growth after Japan's surrender and to further demonstrate its strength during the War of Liberation.

8) Thus, the August 7th Meeting [of the Central Committee, in 1927] pointed out a new road for the CPC ... making a great contribution to saving the Party and the revolution. It was the historic turning point from the failure of the Great Revolution to the rise of the agrarian revolutionary war. [new paragraph] Owing to the "Left" ideas of the Communist International and its representatives and the "Left" tendency within the CPC, "Left" mistakes were not prevented while opposing Right mistakes at this meeting. On the contrary, adventurism and commandism were allowed and encouraged.

9) For example, if some of them who live in the cities with their families are not suited to work in the countryside, we should not force them to move, instead, allow them to remain in the cities.

10) The transfer of surplus labor force from rural areas to non-agricultural trades or its rational flow from one place to another is an objective requirement and inevitable trend of economic development.

458

11) In face of the butcher's policy of the reactionaries to kill all the revolutionaries, there was only one choice for the Communist Party of China: hold high the revolutionary banner and carry out armed resistance. Otherwise, it was like waiting for death and allowing the whole country to fall into darkness. The question remained: under such difficult conditions, how to continue to hold high the revolutionary banner and how to carry out armed resistance.

12) Finally, Party organizations at all levels in the anti-Japanese base areas and guerrilla zones should analyze their work on small guerrilla groups to learn how to coordinate their development with that of larger guerrilla units and the self-defense corps and what the relations should be among the three.

13) Third, the swollen organization of many private enterprises, their irrational methods of operation, their high costs and low profits or even losses, have also given rise to the phenomenon that many industrial and commercial enterprises are reducing their scale of business or even closing down.

14) By showing the injustice Xu suffers during the "cultural revolution," movie-goers are shown that women's status and dignity will continue to suffer as long as old-fashioned marriage and family concepts are kept.

15) We must do our best to mobilize the people if we want them to render assistance to the army wholeheartedly and ceaselessly; otherwise, such assistance will not be forthcoming. Only through immense efforts to get the masses organized can the Party widely motivate them to aid the army in the anti-Japanese base areas in North China today.

16) Upon their first entry into the country's heartland areas, they [the Manchus] had only a population of several hundred thousands. This figure rose to somewhere between four and five millions during the years when the Qing dynasty reached the apex in development.

17) Encouraged by new oil finds across the country, the long-term strategy for China's petrochemical industry is to double its crude oil processing capacity and chemical production by the end of the century to meet the rising domestic demand.

18) We must do our best to employ diversified means to use foreign funds to accelerate China's economic development . . . .

19) The general calls issued by the Comintern were not in conformity with the realities of different countries, and it made concrete arrangements for various parties instead of giving them overall guidance, resulting in interfering with the internal affairs of various Communist parties . . . .

20) Keeping a basic balance of international payments is an important condition for achieving sustained and smooth economic development. . . . Last year China's import increased considerably and its growth of export was relatively slow, thus resulting in a fairly huge trade deficit.

21) Revitalization and further development of agricultural production represents the central task in our current efforts to adjust the national economy.

22) Fourth, Ma discussed reform steps and measures. He said that China's reform has unprecedented and unique characteristics. Reform is carried out gradually in a planned and step-by-step

way.

23) *From a paragraph dealing with the implementation of state capitalism in the early 1950s :*

To the reactionary classes coercion must be applied and when dealing with matters within the ranks of the democratic classes, the principle of voluntariness must be observed, because it is a cooperative undertaking and cooperation admits of no coercion.

24) It is a major reform in our Party leadership system from the situation in which the responsibilities of the Party have not been separated from those of the government to that of the separating of the Party and the government.

25) Nationwide surprise inspections are expected to take place next month to ensure sanitary conditions in restaurants, unit canteens and roadside food stands. It is one of the activities that the Ministry of Health has scheduled to publicize the Food Hygiene Law in the first week of November.

26) As the simplification of Chinese characters is in the interest of the broad masses, we intellectuals should actively support it instead of taking a passive attitude toward it.

27) These four activities carried out by the Communist groups gave a powerful impetus to the dissemination of Marxism and to its integration with the workers' movement. Those intellectuals who had just fostered their belief in communism gradually had profound changes in their thinking and their feelings while they were integrating themselves with the workers; a number of workers had learned something about Marxism and raised their class consciousness, both becoming advanced elements of.

the proletariat.

28) We have to pay attention to lowering the average age of members of the leading bodies and selecting Marxists as leaders.

29) Secretary for Constitutional Affairs Michael Suen said at a luncheon yesterday that an independent Electoral Affairs Commission will be established, which will present plans on geographical constituency demarcation, voter registration and election procedures to the chief executive before the end of October.

30) The Leftist adventurism in this resolution [of the Political Bureau] found its expression first in the totally incorrect assessment of the situation, maintaining that the great decisive battle was just round the corner for both the Chinese and the world revolution. It wrote, "the fundamental political and economic crisis in China continues to sharpen in totally identical manner in each and every part of the country without the slightest essential difference."

31) It would be very difficult to accomplish the task of reclaiming as much as 140 million *mu* of land in a period of twelve years . . . .

32) In March the same year [1920], Li Dazhao, after repeated consultations with Deng Zhongxia and others, set up at Beijing University a society for the study of Marxist theories. This was the first body established in China for learning and studying Marxism, the first attempt made by Li Dazhao to assemble "those who are interested in the study of theories of the Marxist school and those who are willing to study Marxist theories."

33) In order to build a new democratic country, the Congress put forth again the slogan of abolishing the Kuomintang one-party dictatorship and forming a democratic coalition government. It also expounded in detail the programs on such aspects as politics, economy and culture, which would be carried out in the new democratic country. In view of the fact that the Kuomintang ruling clique pursued policies of betraying our country, staging civil war and exercising dictatorship, the Congress called on the whole Party to be prepared for another eventuality, that is, the breakout of the civil war while striving for the establishment of a coalition government. If the KMT waged a civil war, the people would respond by waging a revolutionary war to overthrow the reactionary regime and build a new China.

34) We are working to build a great socialist community in which all nationalities will enjoy a thriving and affluent life ....

35) A landslide caused 12 deaths in Lushui County, Yunnan Province, on Friday. *China Daily* learned yesterday that 13 others were missing and 11 houses still buried under the earth last Sunday. Heavy rain resulted in a 750-meter-wide, 300-meter-high mass of earth, with a volume of 60,000 cubic meters, sliding about 20 meters downhill. The landslide damaged 182 households, affecting 1,100 people. But a danger remains, as 1.5 million cubic meters of earth are still moving, said the report.

36) This gradual transformation must be undertaken in a planned way and leadership exercised over that so that success will be assured when conditions are ripe.

37) *From a talk by a senior Party leader urging the necessity of sep-*
    arating the functions of the Party and the government and of
    delegating powers to lower levels :
    We uphold the Party's leadership, but the problem is whether
    the Party is doing a good job of leading. It should give effec-
    tive leadership and not intervene in too many matters. The
    Central Committee should take the lead in this regard. This is
    not meant to weaken the Party's leadership. Too much inter-
    vention and mishandling of things will actually weaken the
    Party's leadership.

38) That same day Mao Zedong, Zhu De, Peng Dehuai and other
    leaders of the Red Army cabled Chiang Kai-shek to indicate
    that the officers and men of the Red Army wished to "deal
    with the enemy for the purpose of defending the land and
    country and to save the life of the nation."   •

39) In doing economic work in 1992, we shall, under the guidance
    of the Party's basic line, step up the pace of reform, broaden
    the scope of opening to the outside, pay close attention to
    readjustment of the economic structure and improvement of
    efficiency, lay stress on improving agriculture and large and
    medium-sized state-owned enterprises, and promote
    sustained, stable and harmonious development of the national
    economy.

40) The focus of work for this year is to exert efforts to resolutely
    overcome unhealthy practices and to push forward the building
    of clean and honest government.

Forty final revisions

1) A: It is an important political task of the Party during the transition period to continue to <u>provide assistance</u> to the intellectuals for their <u>self-reform</u>.

B: One of the Party's important political tasks during the transition period is to continue *helping* intellectuals *reform themselves*.

[- First, the polisher noted that "provide assistance to" was only the unnec. verb + noun form of "assist" or "help." She replaced it with the plain verb: "to continue to help intellectuals with their self-reform." Then, not liking the repeated "to" in "to continue to help," she substituted "to continue helping."

- To combat the noun plague, she changed "with their self-reform" to a construction with a verb instead: "reform themselves," which was more natural and easier to understand.

- (Note that a similar conversion from noun to verb often helps clarify or correct a "self-" compound, e.g.:

to enjoy self-management = to manage one's own affairs

to have time for self-practice = to have time to practice by yourself

because of self-pay tuition = because students must pay their own tuition.)]

2) A: Our basic ideas, ranging from the development strategy to the principles and policies, including the policies of <u>reform and opening</u> to the outside world, are correct. <u>If there is any inadequacy, it lies in the fact that the efforts we have</u>

made along the line of reform and opening are inadequate.

B: Our basic ideas, from the development strategy to the principles and policies, including the policies of *reform and opening* to the outside, are correct. *If our efforts have fallen short in any respect, it is that we have not done enough to implement those policies.*

[- The first thing that caught the polisher's eye was the useless expression "the fact that," so strongly condemned by Professor Strunk. She promptly edited it out: "If there is any inadequacy, it is that the efforts we have made . . . ."

- Her next thought was to get rid of the abstract noun "inadequacy," especially in view of the "inadequate" farther on. "If there is any inadequacy" became "if we have failed in any respect."

- This brought her to the end of the sentence: "the efforts we have made along the line of reform and opening are inadequate." She decided that was only a weak and wordy circumlocution for "we have not done enough to implement the reform and opening."

- The second sentence now read: "If we have failed in any respect, it is that we have not done enough to implement the reform and opening."

- Not bad by itself, she thought, but following the first sentence it presented an annoying repetition of "reform and opening." That could be easily remedied: she changed the second mention to "those policies."

- Rereading the new version, the polisher thought the word "failed" was perhaps too strong. She changed "if we have failed" to "if our efforts have fallen short."]

466

3) A: They send or buy over traitors, who hide themselves in the Party, to spy on Party leaders and worm their way into leading Party organs, so that they can wipe out local Party organizations from top to bottom at one fell swoop when they give the order.

B: *They* send *their* agents or bribe traitors to hide in the Party, spy on Party leaders, and infiltrate leading Party organs, so that *once they give the order*, the local Party organizations can be wiped out from top to bottom at one fell swoop.

[- It took the polisher two or three readings of A-version to recognize the cause of her confusion: the pronouns "they" and "their" were used in two different senses, and the antecedent kept changing.

- The first " They " represented the reactionary KMT; "their" and the following "they" referred to the traitors hiding in the Party; the final "they" again stood for those who employed the traitors.

- The polisher revised the sentence so as to use "they" and "their" consistently. In B-version the pronouns refer only to the KMT planners who "send agents," "bribe traitors" and "give the order" to wipe out CP branches.

- The polisher then noticed that the subordinate clause "when (once) they give the order" came at the end of the sentence as an anticlimax. To remedy this, she moved the clause up in the sentence, placing full emphasis on the devastating "wiped out from top to bottom at one fell swoop."

- (Note that for educated readers of English the expression

467

"at one fell swoop" — a quotation from Shakespeare's play
Macbeth — has a particularly chilling connotation of sudden, ruthless, politically motivated murder. In this context, the words are entirely appropriate, but they are
sometimes wrongly used in Chinglish to mean simply "all
at once" or "all of a sudden.")]

4) A: The most significant policy change is the <u>ongoing process of</u>
<u>shifting</u> to <u>national treatment</u> for <u>foreign investors</u> in
China from <u>the practice of</u> offering tax privileges and other
preferential <u>treatment</u> to <u>foreign investors</u>, <u>as in the first</u>
<u>few years after the open policy was introduced</u>.

B: The most significant policy change is the *gradual shift* from
offering foreign investors tax privileges and other preferential *treatment* , *as in the first few years after the open*
policy was introduced , to *treating them in the same way*
as Chinese nationals .

[- The polisher's first impression of A-version was that it was
loose and wordy. She set about tightening it.

- "The practice of," being only a category noun, was the
first candidate for elimination. "The process of" was likewise a category noun, so she changed "the ongoing process
of shifting" to "the ongoing shift" and then to "the gradual shift."

- The double reference to "foreign investors" offered another
opportunity for shortening: for the second mention she
substituted the pronoun "them."

- The sentence on the page now was: "The most significant
policy change is the gradual shift to national treatment for
foreign investors in China from offering them tax

privileges and other preferential treatment . . . ." But that
was not a natural word order. Logically, a change is from
x to y, not to y from x. Also, the more important idea,
the new policy, should come last.

- The polisher reversed the order of the two phrases: "The
most significant policy change is the gradual shift from offering tax privileges and other preferential treatment to
foreign investors in China to national treatment for them,
as in the first few years after the open policy was introduced."

- But that change clearly entailed another: "as in the first
few years etc." now modified "national treatment for
them" which made the wrong sense.

- To correct the logic she moved the phrase to the right
place: "the gradual shift from offering foreign investors in
China tax privileges and other preferential treatment, as in
the first few years after the open policy was introduced, to
national treatment for them."

- Now it was plain that parallel structure was wanted. The
two elements in the comparison had to be of the same
grammatical category, not "offering tax privileges" and
"national treatment" (a gerund and a noun) but "offering
tax privileges" and "giving national treatment" (two
gerunds).

- These changes produced a new version: "The most significant policy change is the gradual shift from offering foreign investors in China tax privileges and other preferential
treatment, as in the first few years after the open policy
was introduced, to giving them national treatment."

469

- The sentence was now in good shape, clear and concise, but one thing still bothered the polisher: "national treatment." First, "treatment" was an abstract noun; second, it had just been used ("preferential treatment"); third and most important, it was hard to tell what "national treatment" meant.
- She abandoned the phrase and spelled out the meaning, being careful to use another gerund to match "offering": "treating them in the same way as Chinese nationals."]

5) A: The better you <u>do your work</u> and the more <u>achievements you have</u>, the better the <u>people</u> throughout the country will understand the value of <u>knowledge</u>, thus <u>encouraging</u> the <u>people</u> to respect and acquire <u>knowledge</u>.

B: The better you *work* and the more you *achieve*, the better the *people* throughout the country will understand the value of *knowledge* and *the more they will be encouraged* to respect and acquire *it*.

[- The first thing the polisher noticed about A-version was the dangling participle. Having been given no noun to modify, "encouraging" attached itself to the subject of its clause.
- The principle was the same as if the participle had come before the subject instead of after: "Encouraging the people to respect and acquire knowledge, the people throughout the country will understand etc." Thus, "the people" appeared to be encouraging themselves to respect knowledge.
- To solve this problem, the polisher converted the participial phrase into a separate clause: "and thus the people will be

470

encouraged to respect and acquire knowledge."

- Then, to avoid repeating nouns that had just been used, she immediately substituted "they" for "the people" and "it" for "knowledge."

- The sentence now read as follows: "The better you do your work and the more achievements you have, the better the people throughout the country will understand the value of knowledge, and thus they will be encouraged to respect and acquire it."

- The polisher saw that she could enhance the parallel structure by repeating in the second half of the sentence the pattern of the first: "the better x and the more y, the better x and the more y." Accordingly, she changed the last clause to read "and the more they will be encouraged to respect and acquire it." That version reinforced the logic and satisfied the ear.

- As final improvements, she reduced the two unnec. verb + noun constructions to plain verbs. "The better you do your work" became "The better you work," and "the more achievements you have" became "the more you achieve." These changes not only tightened the sentence but also heightened the parallelism.]

6) A: In 1928 when the revolution was <u>suffering serious setbacks</u>, it was easy to see that the "Left" tendencies that appeared in the Party were wrong and to quickly put an end to putschist mistakes. But <u>after the outbreak of the wars</u> between the KMT warlords of different factions and <u>at the time of apparent revival</u> of the revolutionary movement, many comrades in the Party <u>unrealistically</u> overestimated

revolutionary developments, <u>giving rise</u> to more intense and sustained growth of "Left" impetuosity.

B: In 1928, when the revolution was *suffering grave setbacks*, it had been easy to see that the "Left" tendencies in the Party were wrong and to quickly put an end to putschist mistakes. But *at this time*, *when the KMT warlords* of different factions *were fighting* among themselves, *and when the revolutionary movement appeared to be reviving*, many Party members overestimated revolutionary developments, *and this fostered* a more intense and sustained growth of "Left" impetuosity.

[- This passage compared Party members' understanding of the revolutionary situation in 1928 and in 1930. The polisher saw that the contrast between the two attitudes would be clearer and stronger if the two sentences had parallel structure.

- To achieve this, she changed the pattern of the second sentence to match that of the first.

- First she introduced "at this time" (i.e., in 1930) to balance "In 1928." Then she changed the prepositional phrases "after the outbreak of the wars" and "at the time of apparent revival" to subordinate clauses ("when the KMT warlords were fighting" and "when the revolutionary movement appeared to be reviving") to match the subordinate clause of the first sentence ("when the revolution was suffering").

- (Note that these latter changes would have been desirable in any event because they replaced abstract nouns with verbs.)

472

- Proceeding with the second sentence, the polisher came upon another structural difficulty: "giving rise to" was a dangling participle. It was not the "comrades," the subject of the clause, who gave rise to the growth of "impetuosity" but their overestimate of revolutionary developments.

- To correct this error, she converted the participial phrase into a separate clause: "and this gave rise to." Then she thought of a more appropriate word: "fostered."

- Rereading her new version, the polisher made two more minor improvements. In the first sentence, to avoid the obtrusive repetition of "s" sounds in "suffered serious setbacks," she changed "serious" to "grave." In the second, she deleted "unrealistically" as redundant, since an "overestimate" is unrealistic by definition.]

7) A: The <u>Party</u>'s Seventh National Congress was held <u>two or three years after the rectification movement began</u> which strengthened the unity of the <u>Party</u> and enabled our <u>Party</u> to achieve tremendous growth after Japan's surrender and to further demonstrate its strength during the War of Liberation.

B: *Two or three years after the rectification movement began*, the *Party* held its Seventh National Congress. *That* strengthened the unity of the *Party* and enabled *it* to achieve tremendous growth after Japan's surrender and to further demonstrate its strength during the War of Liberation.

[- First noticing the three references to the "Party," the polisher replaced the third with the pronoun "it."

473

- She then studied the relative pronoun "which." Apparently it was meant to refer to the whole idea just expressed: "The Party's Seventh National Congress was held." But the long intervening modifier ("two or three years after the rectification movement began") separated the pronoun from its intended antecedent and — especially in the absence of a comma after "began" — tempted it to attach itself instead to the nearby "rectification movement."
- To bring the pronoun nearer its antecedent, the polisher moved the subordinate phrase up to the beginning: "Two or three years after the rectification movement began, the Party's Seventh National Congress was held, which strengthened the unity of the Party etc." That also served to correct the emphasis.
- Then she recast the verb in active voice: "the Party held its Seventh National Congress."
- The "which" now had a clear antecedent, but it still made a very long sentence. The polisher discarded it, broke the sentence in two and made a fresh start with the demonstrative pronoun "That."
- Located at the end of the first sentence, the statement that the Congress was held now led directly into the second and provided a plainly recognizable antecedent for "That."]

8) A: Thus, the August 7th Meeting pointed out a new road for the CPC ... making a great contribution to saving the Party and the revolution. It was the historic turning point from the failure of the Great Revolution to the rise of the agrarian revolutionary war. [*new paragraph*] Owing to the "Left" ideas of the Communist International and its

representatives and the "Left" tendency within the CPC, "Left" mistakes were not prevented while opposing Right mistakes at this meeting. On the contrary, adventurism and commandism were allowed and encouraged.

B: Thus, the August 7th Meeting pointed out a new road for the CPC . . . making a great contribution to saving the Party and the revolution. It was the historic turning point from the failure of the Great Revolution to the rise of the agrarian revolutionary war. [*new paragraph*] *Nevertheless*, owing to the "Left" ideas of the Communist International and its representatives and to the "Left" tendency within the CPC, *although the Central Committee criticized Right mistakes* at this meeting, *it did nothing to prevent "Left" mistakes*. On the contrary, adventurism and commandism were allowed and *even* encouraged.

[- Even though there was a paragraph break after the remarks in praise of the August 7th Meeting, the polisher was well into the next sentence before she realized that it was critical of the meeting.

- To signal to the reader that the new material would contrast with what had preceded, she introduced a "Nevertheless" at the beginning of the paragraph.

- The remainder of the sentence posed several problems. First the polisher dealt with the dangling participle, "opposing," which had no subject to modify. She gave it one: "The Central Committee did not prevent 'Left' mistakes, while opposing Right mistakes at this meeting."

- She then became aware that the order of ideas was wrong: the point to be underlined here was not what the Central

475

Committee had done but what it had failed to do. To correct the emphasis, she reversed the two clauses: "While opposing Right mistakes at this meeting, the Central Committee did not prevent 'Left' mistakes."

- Having made these modifications, she reread her version: "Nevertheless, owing to the 'Left' ideas of the Communist International and its representatives and to the 'Left' tendency within the CPC, while opposing Right mistakes at this meeting, the Central Committee did not prevent 'Left' mistakes."

- She was troubled by the awkward sequence of two participial phrases ("owing to . . . , while opposing . . ."). In particular, she was reluctant to burden the reader with such long modifiers before the subject of the sentence ("the Central Committee") was even announced.

- Accordingly, she decided to drop the second participle, "opposing," even though it was now correctly attached. The result was: ". . . while the Central Committee opposed Right mistakes at this meeting, it did not prevent 'Left' mistakes."

- Now that the sentence structure was satisfactory, she took a closer look at the wording. Considering that "opposed" was not quite right with "mistakes," she changed it to "criticized." And wishing to strengthen "did not prevent," she changed it to "did nothing to prevent."

- Then, as a concession to the strict grammarians who recommended that "while" be used only to indicate a relation of time, she replaced it with "although."

- When the polisher read the next sentence, she felt that

something was lacking. The point was that adventurism and commandism were not only tolerated but, worse, encouraged. However, the notion that "encouraging" was a more serious mistake than "allowing" was only implied. She expressed it by adding "even" — again, a question of making logical connections plain.]

9) A: For example, if some of them who live in the cities with their families are not suited to work in the countryside, we should not force them to move, instead, allow them to remain in the cities.

B: For example, if some of them who live with their families in the cities are not suited to work in the countryside, *we should allow them to remain* in the cities.

[- A-version was a simple example of saying the same thing twice in the mirror-image form (we should not do this; instead, we should do the opposite). Plainly, if we should not force them to move, we should allow them to remain. The polisher saw no reason to retain both statements.

- She tried dropping the second statement of the idea. This produced: "For example, if some of them ... are not suited to work in the countryside, we should not force them to move."

- But a second polisher pointed out that this might mean "we should not force them to move but only try to persuade them." To avoid any ambiguity, they decided to drop the first statement instead: "For example, if some of them ... are not suited to work in the countryside, we should allow them to remain in the cities."]

10) A: The <u>transfer</u> of surplus labor <u>force</u> from rural <u>areas</u> to non-agricultural <u>trades</u> <u>or</u> its rational <u>flow</u> from one place to another <u>is an objective requirement and inevitable trend</u> of economic development.

   B: *It is an objective requirement and inevitable trend* of economic development for surplus labor to *transfer* from *farming* to non-agricultural *occupations and* to *move* from one place to another in a rational manner.

[- On reading A-version the polisher was aware of the heavy weight of abstract nouns and modifiers at the end: "an objective requirement and inevitable trend of economic development." There seemed to be no other way of expressing that idea, but perhaps she could lighten the rest of the sentence.

- To change the nouns "transfer" and "flow" to verbs, she changed the order of ideas: "It is an objective requirement and inevitable trend . . . for surplus labor force to transfer . . . or to flow . . . ." This new structure also improved the emphasis, drawing attention to the two key verbs, "transfer" and "flow."

- The polisher then saw that she could dispense with a third noun, "force." "Surplus labor force" meant nothing more than "surplus labor," so "force" could be deleted as redundant.

- The sentence was now easier to understand, but it still did not seem logical. For one thing, the surplus labor was transferring from "rural areas" to "non-agricultural trades," two terms that were not comparable (places and occupations). To make them parallel, the polisher changed them to "farming" and "non-agricultural occupations."

- Another illogical element was the conjunction "or." Since the second term was not an alternative to the first but a supplement to it, the connection wanted was not "or" but "and." She made that change too.

- Lastly, feeling vaguely uncomfortable about the metaphor "flow" modified by "in a rational manner," she substituted the straightforward "move."]

11) A: In face of the butcher's policy of the reactionaries to kill all the revolutionaries, there was only one choice for the Communist Party of China: hold high the revolutionary banner and carry out armed resistance. Otherwise, it was like waiting for death and allowing the whole country to fall into darkness. The question remained: under such difficult conditions, how to continue to hold high the revolutionary banner and how to carry out armed resistance.

B: Faced with the reactionaries' policy of *butchering* all revolutionaries, the *Communists* had only one choice. *If they were not simply to wait for death and allow the whole country to be plunged into darkness*, they must *hold high the revolutionary banner and carry out armed resistance*. *But* the question remained: under such difficult conditions, *how was that to be done*?

[- First, to tighten the first sentence the polisher combined the "butcher's policy" and "to kill" — essentially a double reference to the same idea — into a single word: "the reactionaries' policy of butchering."

- Next she considered the second sentence. If the

479

"Otherwise it was like" had been not a new sentence following a period but a subordinate clause following a semicolon, she would have unhesitatingly moved it up to precede the main point, that the Party must "hold high the revolutionary banner and carry out armed resistance."

- Seeing that that would be an improvement, and judging that in this instance the punctuation in A-version made no difference, she combined the two clauses into one sentence and changed their order.
- This produced: " . . . there was only one choice for the Communist Party of China. If it was not simply to wait for death and allow the whole country to be plunged into darkness, it must hold high the revolutionary banner and carry out armed resistance."
- That was stronger and more dramatic, and it emphasized what the Party had to do, not what would happen "otherwise." Also, the end of this sentence now led directly into the question posed in the next: how could the Party hold high etc.
- A logical connective was needed, however, to warn the reader that what followed would be in opposition to what had just been said. The polisher inserted "But" to signal that a problem was about to be stated.
- Reaching the end of the sentence, she found "hold high the revolutionary banner" and "carry out armed resistance" again. To avoid the repetition, she replaced both terms with a simple demonstrative pronoun: "how was that to be done?" ("Continue to" seemed unnecessary in context and was simply dropped.) Along with the other

revisions, this tightening reduced the length of A-version by 20%.

- Rereading the new version, the polisher thought of one more small improvement. To introduce some concrete actors, she replaced "the Communist Party of China" with "the Communists." That version presented to the reader's imagination not an impersonal abstraction (the "Party" or "it") but real people (the "Communists" or "they") who had to choose between waiting for death and taking up arms to combat repression.

- (With regard to the expression "hold high the revolutionary banner," note that normal English word order would place the object directly after the verb: "hold the revolutionary banner high." However, because the given word order has a certain poetic ring, and because it has been consecrated by long usage, it was allowed to stand.)]

12) A: Finally, Party organizations at all levels in the anti-Japanese base areas and guerrilla zones should analyze <u>their</u> work on small guerrilla groups to learn <u>how to coordinate</u> their development with that of larger guerrilla units and the self-defense corps and <u>what the relations should be</u> among the three.

B: Finally, Party organizations at all levels in the anti-Japanese base areas and the guerrilla zones should analyze *their* work in relation to small guerrilla groups. *They should consider how to coordinate* the development *of such groups* with that of larger guerrilla units and of the self-defense corps and *how to establish* correct relations among the three.

481

[- The polisher had to read A-version twice before she understood that the pronoun "their" had two different antecedents. The first time it represented "Party organizations"; the second time it stood for "small guerrilla groups." She solved this problem by substituting "of such groups" for the second "their."

- Then, since the sentence contained too many ideas to be absorbed without a pause, she broke it in two and started over with the pronoun "They." This "They," like the preceding "their," clearly stood for "Party organizations."

- The skeleton of the second sentence now read: "They should consider how to coordinate the development ... and what the relations should be ...." The statement was clear and correct, but the polisher saw that it could be strengthened and clarified by parallel structure.

- She therefore changed the second element to match the first: "They should consider how to coordinate the development ... and how to establish correct relations ...."]

13) A: Third, the swollen organization of many private enterprises, their irrational methods of operation, their high costs and low profits or even losses, have also given rise to the phenomenon that many industrial and commercial enterprises are reducing their scale of business or even closing down.

B: Third, *because of overstaffing*, irrational methods of operation, high costs, and low profits or even losses, *many privately owned factories and stores* are *having to cut back their business* or even close down.

[- The first thing that struck the polisher on reading A-version was the wordy and awkward construction that was the heart of the sentence: "x, y, and z have also given rise to the phenomenon that many . . . enterprises etc."

- Her first act was to jettison "give rise to" in favor of a simpler construction with "because": "because of x, y, and z, many . . . enterprises etc."

- This produced: "because of the swollen organization of many private enterprises, their irrational methods of operation, their high costs and low profits or even losses, many industrial and commercial enterprises are reducing etc." That was distinctly better than giving rise to the "phenomenon" that something was happening.

- Next the polisher became aware of the two references to "enterprises." Clearly, the "many private enterprises" with the swollen organization etc. were the same as the "many industrial and commercial enterprises" that were reducing their scale of business. There was no necessity for both, so she eliminated the first mention.

- Then, to retain the sense of "private," which had disappeared along with the first "enterprises," she reinstated it with the second mention: "many privately owned industrial and commercial enterprises." (Thanks chiefly to these two major revisions, B-version turned out to be some 30% shorter than A-version.)

- Satisfied with the structure of the sentence, the polisher looked more closely at the wording.

- "Swollen organization," she thought, was a somewhat dubious metaphor for plain "overstaffing," which she used instead. "Industrial and commercial enterprises" could be simplified to everyday "factories and stores." And

483

"reducing their scale of business" was just the noun-style version of "cutting back their business."

- Lastly, she decided the meaning would be clearer if for "are cutting back their business or even closing down" she substituted "are having to cut back their business or even close down."]

14) A: <u>By showing</u> the injustice <u>Xu suffers</u> during the "cultural revolution," <u>movie-goers are shown</u> that women's status and dignity will continue to <u>suffer</u> as long as <u>old-fashioned marriage and family concepts are kept</u>.

B: *By showing* the injustice *to which Xu is subjected* during the "cultural revolution," *the film demonstrates* that women's status and dignity will continue to *suffer* as long as *people cling to old-fashioned concepts of marriage and the family*.

[- When the polisher looked for the subject of "showing" at the head of the main clause in A-version, she found only "movie-goers" — the people who were "shown" the injustice and plainly could not be "showing" it.

- She therefore made "the film" the subject of the sentence, matching the implied subject of the introductory gerund. This change not only corrected a dangling modifier but also had the advantage of changing passive voice ("movie-goers are shown") to active ("the film shows").

- To continue in active voice, she also changed "as long as old-fashioned marriage and family concepts are kept" to "as long as people cling to old-fashioned marriage and family concepts."

- Then, not liking the two nouns used as adjectives in this

last phrase, she broke up the sequence with a preposition: "old-fashioned concepts of marriage and the family."

- The revision now stood as follows: "By showing the injustice Xu suffers during the 'cultural revolution,' the film shows that women's status and dignity will continue to suffer as long as people cling to . . . ." The structure of the sentence was satisfactory, but the polisher was bothered by the repetitions "showing"/ "shows" and "suffers"/ "suffer."

- To vary the sound, she changed "the film shows" to "the film demonstrates" and "the injustice Xu suffers" to "the injustice to which Xu is subjected."]

15) A: <u>We must do our best to mobilize the people if we want them to render assistance to the army</u> wholeheartedly and ceaselessly; <u>otherwise, such assistance will not be forthcoming.</u> <u>Only through immense efforts to get the masses organized can the Party widely motivate them to aid the army</u> in the anti-Japanese base areas in North China today.

B: *If we want the people to give the army their* wholehearted *assistance*, and to keep on giving it, *we have to mobilize them. We must make every effort to organize the masses: that is the only way to secure their help* in the anti-Japanese base areas in North China today.

[- After rereading this passage several times, the polisher realized that in essence it said the same thing not twice but three times: (1) we must mobilize the people if we want them to help us; (2) otherwise, they will not help us; (3) only if we organize them will they be willing to help us.

485

- She decided to retain the first and third statements of the idea for emphasis, but to drop the second (the mirror-image "otherwise such assistance will not be forthcoming").
- First she rewrote the first statement, making it a separate sentence and ending with the main point. This produced: "If we want the people to give the army their wholehearted assistance and to keep on giving it, we must do our best to mobilize them."
- Then she considered the third statement: "Only through immense efforts to get the masses organized can the Party widely motivate them to aid the army." She wanted to tighten it and also to make it less repetitive of the first sentence.
- After some false starts, she rearranged and varied the elements: "We must make every effort to organize the masses: that is the only way to secure their help."
- Rereading the two new sentences, she saw that "we must do our best to mobilize them" at the end of the first was now immediately followed by "We must make every effort to organize the masses" at the beginning of the second.
- In this context, "do our best" was not just an empty cliché, but thinking that the idea was adequately conveyed in "make every effort," she decided to omit it anyway. The end of the first sentence thus became simply "we have to mobilize them."]

16) A: Upon their first entry into the country's heartland areas, they [the Manchus] had only a population of several hundred thousands. This figure rose to somewhere between four and five millions during the years when the Qing

dynasty reached the apex in development.

B: *When they first entered* the heartland of China, they *numbered only* a few hundred thousand. *But during the years when the Qing dynasty was at its height*, their *population* rose to between four and five million.

[- Spotting the noun phrase at the beginning of A-version, the polisher changed it at once to a construction with a verb: "When they first entered."

- Then she deleted "areas" as redundant with "heartland."

- Next she changed "had only a population of" to "numbered only," a version that was shorter and eliminated another abstract noun.

- The second sentence seemed to be the statement of just another, unrelated fact. To make the connection between the two, she inserted "But."

- Then she moved "during the years when the Qing dynasty etc." out of the final position so as to end with the main clause giving the new and much larger figure. At the same time she reduced "reached the apex in development" to "was at its height."

- As a last improvement, she changed "this figure rose" to "their population rose," the second word, although still an abstraction, being more concrete than the first.]

17) A: Encouraged by new oil finds across the country, the long-term strategy for China's petrochemical industry is to double its crude oil processing capacity and chemical production by the end of the century to meet the rising domestic demand.

B: *Encouraged* by new oil finds across the country, *and hoping*

487

to meet the rising domestic demand , China's petrochemi-cal industry has established the long-range *goal* of dou-bling *its capacity to process crude oil* and *its production of chemicals* by the end of the century.

[- Noting the past participle at the beginning of A-version, the polisher looked for the noun it modified. The noun was present ("industry"), but it was not the subject of the sentence; in its place she found "strategy."

- To correct this error she rearranged the elements: "En-couraged by new oil finds across the country, China's petrochemical industry has adopted a long-term strategy of doubling . . . ."

- When she came to "crude oil processing capacity," she recognized the dense modifier as a manifestation of the noun plague and broke it up into its logical components: "its capacity to process crude oil."

- "Chemical production" was not so objectionable, since "chemical" was not a noun but a genuine adjective. Still, in the interest of parallel structure, she broke that down too: "the production of chemicals."

- The revision now stood as follows: "Encouraged by new oil finds across the country, China's petrochemical indus-try has adopted a long-term strategy of doubling its capacity to process crude oil and its production of chemi-cals by the end of the century to meet the rising domestic demand."

- That version was grammatically correct and easier to com-prehend, but the polisher thought it could be further im-proved.

- For purposes of emphasis, the subordinate phrase "to meet the rising demand" should be moved out of its final position. And to make a tighter logical connection and increase the parallelism, she could convert it to a participial phrase matching "Encouraged by."
- This produced: "Encouraged by new oil finds across the country, and hoping to meet the rising domestic demand, China's petrochemical industry . . . ."
- Only then did the polisher realize that "strategy" was not the logical word here. Doubling production was not a "strategy" the industry had adopted but a "goal" it had established. When she had made that change, she was content with the revision.]

18) A: We must <u>do our best</u> to <u>employ diversified means</u> to use foreign funds to accelerate <u>China's</u> economic development . . . .

   B: We must use foreign funds *in different ways* to accelerate economic development . . . .

   [- The polisher decided that "do our best" had no special meaning here but was only the conventional introductory phrase. She therefore edited it out.
   - The statement obviously referred to China, so she deleted "China's" as superfluous.
   - She then decided that "employ diversified means to use foreign funds" was only a pretentious way of saying "use different means to use foreign funds," which itself was none too clear. She expressed the idea simply: "use foreign funds in different ways."]

19) A: The general calls issued by the Comintern were not in conformity with the realities of different countries, and it made concrete arrangements for <u>various parties</u> <u>instead of giving</u> <u>them overall guidance</u>, <u>resulting in interfering</u> with the internal affairs of <u>various Communist parties</u> . . . .

B: The general calls issued by the Comintern were not in conformity with the realities of different countries, and *instead of giving individual parties overall guidance*, it made concrete arrangements for them, *thus interfering* in *their* internal affairs . . .

[- The polisher started by eliminating the obvious repetition: "various parties" and "various Communist parties."

- "Various," she thought, was unnec. in both places and could be usefully replaced in the first instance with "individual." The second reference to the parties ("the internal affairs of various Communist parties") could be easily replaced with the possessive pronoun "their" ("their internal affairs").

- Next she addressed the more serious problem of the dangling participle. "Resulting in" had nothing in particular to modify and tried vainly to attach itself to the subject of its clause, "it" (= the Comintern), which, however, was not resulting in anything.

- The easiest solution seemed to be to change the participle to one that could logically modify the subject: "it made concrete arrangements for individual parties instead of giving them overall guidance, thus interfering in their internal affairs." The new participle, "interfering," was now sensibly attached to "it" (the Comintern): "it" was

490

interfering in the internal affairs of the individual parties.
- At this stage the revision read: "The general calls issued
by the Comintern were not in conformity with the realities
of different countries, and it made concrete arrangements
for the individual parties instead of giving them overall
guidance, thus interfering in their internal affairs."
- Rereading this version, the polisher realized that the subordinate phrase "instead of giving them overall guidance"
was in the wrong place. For proper emphasis it should
come first, leaving the main point (what the Comintern
did do) to the end: "... and instead of giving individual
parties overall guidance, it made concrete arrangements
for them, thus interfering ...."
- She made that change, noting with satisfaction that it
placed the participle ("thus interfering") in a more logical
position. Now it directly followed the action to which it
referred — making concrete arrangements for individual
parties.]

20) A: <u>Keeping a basic balance</u> of international payments <u>is an im-</u>
<u>portant condition for achieving</u> <u>sustained and smooth</u> eco-
nomic development.... Last year <u>China's import in-</u>
<u>creased considerably and its growth of export was relative-</u>
<u>ly slow</u>, thus <u>resulting</u> in a <u>fairly</u> huge trade deficit.

B: *An important condition for achieving steady* economic
development *is to maintain* a basic balance of international payments .... Last year *imports increased consider-*
ably while exports grew relatively slowly, *with the result*
that there was a huge trade deficit.

[- This was an example of the frequent Chinglish
491

construction beginning with a gerund: "doing x is an important condition for doing y." The polisher reversed the order to put the main point at the end, and in the process changed the gerund "Keeping" to an infinitive, "to keep."

- Now the sentence read: "An important condition for achieving sustained and smooth economic development is to keep a basic balance of international payments."

- Then she made minor changes that she thought improved the wording: "sustained and smooth" became " steady," which implied both; "to keep" became "to maintain."

- Turning to the second sentence, the polisher first eliminated the superfluous modifiers: "China's" and "its" because they were obvious, and "fairly" because it was an unnecessary qualifier that only undercut the force of "huge."

- Next she studied "import increased considerably and growth of export was relatively slow." The two elements linked by "and" were minimally parallel, in that both were independent clauses. But "import" was aligned with "growth," and "increased" with "was slow," neither pair being a good match.

- To enhance the parallelism she balanced "imports" with its natural mate "exports" and "increased" with its synonym " grew ": "imports increased considerably and exports grew relatively slowly." (She was pleased to note that this revision also converted a noun, "growth," into a verb, "grew.")

- On rereading, the polisher decided that although "and" was not a wrong connective, "while" would be more precise. She made that change too.

- Finally, she paused over "thus resulting in." On first reading she had not found the phrase objectionable, but on closer inspection she saw that the participle was dangling without an expressed subject. It was not either "imports" or "exports" that had resulted in the deficit, but the combination of circumstances described.

- She thought briefly about supplying the true subject: "imports increased considerably while exports grew relatively slowly, a combination of circumstances resulting in a huge deficit." But that seemed wordy and complicated.

- How about "imports increased considerably while exports grew relatively slowly, which resulted in a huge deficit"? But the "which" would not have a clear antecedent.

- She decided the best solution was to replace "resulting" with "with the result that."]

21) A: <u>Revitalization and further development</u> of agricultural production <u>represents the central task</u> in our <u>current efforts to adjust</u> the <u>national</u> economy.

   B: *Our central task in adjusting* the economy is to *revitalize and expand* agricultural production.

   [- The polisher first eliminated the superfluous modifiers "further" and "national," because the sense of both could be taken for granted.

   - Next she turned the abstract nouns "revitalization" and "development" into verbs: "To revitalize and develop agricultural production represents the central task in our current efforts to adjust the economy."

   - Then, considering that "current" was obvious and

493

"efforts" added nothing but another noun, she reduced "in our current efforts to adjust the economy" to "in adjusting the economy."

- The revision now stood as follows: "To revitalize and develop agricultural production represents our central task in adjusting the economy."

- In accordance with the principle that the main point should come last, the polisher moved "in adjusting the economy" to the beginning of the sentence: "In adjusting the economy, our central task is to revitalize . . . ."

- But strictly speaking, this version left the introductory gerund "adjusting" dangling. The implied subject of "adjusting" was "we," but the subject of the sentence was "our task."

- In the presence of "our," which made it clear that "we" were doing the adjusting, the point was arguable. Still, the polisher judged it best to move the gerund to a safer position: "Our central task in adjusting the economy is to revitalize . . . ."

- As a final slight improvement, she then changed the vague and overworked "develop" to "expand."

- Note that the structural change here is the same as in the preceding example. Here "Revitalization . . . represents the central task" became "Our central task is to revitalize . . . ." In example 20 "Keeping a basic balance . . . is an important condition for achieving . . ." became "An important condition for achieving. . . is to maintain a basic balance . . . ."]

22) A: Fourth, Ma discussed <u>reform steps and measures</u>. He said
that <u>China's reform</u> <u>has unprecedented and unique charac-</u>
<u>teristics</u>. <u>Reform</u> is carried out <u>gradually in a planned and</u>
<u>step-by-step way</u>.

B: Fourth, Ma discussed *measures* to be taken. He said that
the reform, *which was an unprecedented enterprise*, had
to be carried out *one step at a time*, *according to a plan*.

[- The polisher's attention was first drawn to the three sets
of redundant twins, "steps and measures," "unprecedented and unique," and "gradually"/"in a step-by-step way."
She eliminated one of each set.

- While she was dealing with this last pair, she considered
what could be done to change the entire modifier. The familiar formula "step-by-step and in a planned way," of
which this was a variant, was by now a tiresome cliché to
which the reader would probably pay no attention.

- She recast the idea in a somewhat fresher — and more
idiomatic — form: "one step at a time, according to a
plan."

- Next, she decided that since Ma was now well into a
lengthy discussion of the economic reform in China — he
was making his "fourth" point, after all — there was no
need at this stage to specify that he was talking about "reform" measures in "China." She deleted both modifiers.

- The third "reform" she replaced with the pronoun "it."

- After these changes the revision read as follows: "Fourth,
Ma discussed measures to be taken. He said that the reform has unprecedented characteristics. It is carried out
one step at a time, according to a plan."

495

- The polisher thought she had now eliminated as many un-necessary words as possible, but the new version sounded choppy, and it still didn't make much sense. The logical connections between the three ideas were not clear; in particular, the second sentence had no apparent relation to either of the others.
- Studying the passage in context, she determined what the intended relation was: because we have no precedents to go by, we have to proceed carefully, taking measures one at a time in an orderly way.
- The notion of cause and effect had not been spelled out in the Chinese, and apparently it had not been well under-stood by the translator. Accordingly, he or she had simply said that reform "is carried out gradually etc. ," whereas the sense was that for this reason it "must be carried out gradually etc."
- To suggest the logical connection between ideas without adding too much to the original, the polisher converted the second sentence into a subordinate clause and changed the tense of the third: ". . . the reform, which was an un-precedented enterprise, had to be carried out one step at a time, according to a plan."]

23) A: To the reactionary classes coercion must be applied and when dealing with matters within the ranks of the democratic classes, the principle of voluntariness must be observed, because it is a cooperative undertaking and cooperation admits of no coercion.

   B: *When dealing with the reactionary classes, we must use coercion, but when dealing with* matters within the ranks

496

of the democratic classes, *we must observe* the principle of voluntariness, because *with them the implementation of state capitalism* is a cooperative undertaking, and cooperation admits of no coercion.

[- The polisher had to read A-version several times before she began to grasp its meaning. As a first step toward clarifying the sentence, she changed the verbs to active voice.

- This produced: "To the reactionary classes we must apply coercion, and when dealing with matters within the ranks of the democratic classes, we must observe the principle of voluntariness." That was easier to understand, and the introduction of the subject "we" served to anchor the dangling participial phrase "when dealing with etc."

- Then she realized that another source of her confusion was the "and" — it was the wrong logical connective and consequently misleading. The second clause stood in contrast to the first, a relation that should be indicated by "but."

- Next, she considered the question of parallel structure. The speaker was contrasting two different approaches to the same problem, so it would help the reader if the two were expressed in matching form.

- To make the two approaches more nearly parallel, she repeated in the first clause the phrase "when dealing with," which was used in the second clause: "When dealing with the reactionary classes, we must use coercion, but when dealing with matters within the ranks of the democratic classes, we must . . . ."

- So much for the first part of the sentence. Moving on to

497

the second, she saw at once that the pronoun "it," which at first seemed to represent "the principle," had no antecedent.

- Checking the preceding text to review the line of argument, she found that the paragraph as a whole dealt with the implementation of state capitalism. It was that phrase, which had appeared two sentences earlier, that the translator's "it" was supposed to stand for. She made the change accordingly: "because the implementation of state capitalism is a cooperative undertaking."

- But plainly, that applied only to the democratic classes; the reactionary classes were by no means cooperative, which was precisely why they had to be coerced. To make this distinction clear, the polisher added "with them": "because with them (= the democratic classes just mentioned) the implementation of state capitalism is a cooperative undertaking."]

24) A: It is a major reform in our Party leadership system from the situation in which the responsibilities of the Party have not been separated from those of the government to that of the separating of the Party and the government.

B: *Separating the functions of Party and government is a major reform* in the *system of Party leadership*.

[- It was only after the polisher had read A-version two or three times that she grasped what the writer was trying to say.

- Analyzing why she had had so much trouble, she noted first that the pattern of the sentence — "it is a major reform from x to y" — was not English. It was not a "reform" from x to y but a "change" from x to y.

- She started the revision by introducing that word: "A major reform in our Party leadership system is the change from the situation in which . . . ."

- Then she backed up to eliminate "situation": "A major reform in our Party leadership system is the change from not separating the responsibilities of the Party from those of the government to separating the Party and the government."

- But the intended meaning was clearly "the change from not separating the responsibilities of the Party from those of the government to separating the <u>responsibilities</u> of the Party and the government" — or, to avoid repeating the long phrase, "the change from not separating the responsibilities of the Party from those of the government to separating <u>them</u>."

- But then she realized that a change from "not separating" to "separating" was only a restatement of the same idea, first in negative form then in positive.

- Seeing that the repetition was inevitable so long as she retained the "change from x to y," she abandoned that formula: "It is a major reform in our Party leadership system to separate the functions of the Party from those of the government."

- To avoid using two nouns as adjectives, she changed "Party leadership system" to "the system of Party leadership."

- Only a few minor changes still had to be made. She corrected the order of ideas to emphasize the importance of

499

the reform and at the same time tightened the wording:
"Separating the functions of Party and government is a
major reform in the system of Party leadership."
- That, she thought, was a sentence that could be understood on the first reading ... and it was less than half as
long as A-version.]

25) A: Nationwide <u>surprise</u> inspections are <u>expected</u> to take place
<u>next month</u> to ensure sanitary conditions in restaurants,
unit canteens and roadside food stands. <u>It</u> is one of the activities that the Ministry of Health has <u>scheduled</u> to publicize the Food Hygiene Law <u>in the first week of</u>
<u>November</u>.

B: *In the first week of November* nationwide *surprise* inspections are *scheduled* to take place to ensure sanitary conditions in restaurants, unit canteens and roadside food
stands. *These* are among the activities that the Ministry of
Health has *planned* to publicize the Food Hygiene Law.

[- The first thing that caught the polisher's attention was
the seeming contradiction between "surprise" inspections
and their being "expected." But that was a small matter,
and she moved on, making a mental note to return to it
later.

- Next she found that the pronoun "It" at the head of the
second sentence had no antecedent. Or rather, it had a
logical antecedent, "inspections," but the antecedent was
plural whereas the pronoun was singular. To make them
agree she changed "It is one of the activities" to "These
are among the activities."

- Then, seeing that the second sentence ended in a

prepositional phrase ("in the first week of November"), she considered whether the phrase was in the right place. Deciding it was not, she moved it up, making it modify "has scheduled" rather than "to publicize."

- The result was: "These are among the activities that the Ministry of Health has scheduled for the first week of November to publicize the Food Hygiene Law." That seemed somewhat more logical, and it gave more prominence to the important element, "the Food Hygiene Law."

- But on rereading the revised version she noticed that there were two mentions of dates: "for the first week of November" in the second sentence and "next month" in the first. Presumably both referred to the time of the inspections and other activities.

- To avoid two references to the same thing, she deleted "next month" and moved "in the first week of November" to the beginning.

- Satisfied that the two sentences were now grammatical and concise, she returned to the question of the "surprise" inspections that were "expected" to take place. To make sure that other readers were not distracted by the apparent contradiction, she simply changed "expected" to "scheduled."

- Then, to avoid repeating the word in the second sentence, she changed "has scheduled" to "has planned."]

26) A: As the simplification of Chinese characters is in the interest of the <u>broad</u> masses, we intellectuals should <u>actively support</u> it instead of taking a passive attitude toward it.

B: As the simplification of Chinese characters is in the interest of the masses, we intellectuals should *not just passively accept it but actively support it*.

[- The polisher first deleted "broad," since the notion of "broad" was implicitly contained in the word "masses."

- That done, she addressed the main problem, "actively support it instead of taking a passive attitude toward it." She recognized this as an example of the mirror-image construction in which the same thing is stated twice, first in the positive then in the negative.

- Her first impulse was to delete the negative statement, since it added nothing to the meaning. But this sentence appeared in a speech by Premier Zhou Enlai, and she was reluctant to take liberties with it.

- As an alternative, she looked for a way to change the wording of the negative statement so that it would not seem so empty. Since "instead of taking a passive attitude toward it" was vague at best, she tried spelling the phrase out to give it more content: "instead of just passively accepting it."

- Now the second clause read "we intellectuals should actively support it, instead of just passively accepting it." That was an improvement not just because the double statement now made a discernible point, but also because the two elements were cast in parallel form.

- The sentence was still not satisfactory, however, because the order of the two statements was wrong, giving prominence to what intellectuals should *not* do. To correct the emphasis the polisher reversed the order, putting the negative statement first: "we intellectuals should not just passively accept it but actively support it."]

27) A: These four activities carried out by the Communist groups gave a powerful impetus to the dissemination of Marxism and to its integration with the workers' movement. Those intellectuals who had just fostered their belief in communism gradually had profound changes in their thinking and their feelings while they were integrating themselves with the workers; a number of workers had learned something about Marxism and raised their class consciousness, both becoming advanced elements of the proletariat.

B: These four activities of the Communist groups gave a powerful impetus to the dissemination of Marxism and to their integration with the workers' movement. In the process, those intellectuals who had only recently come to believe in communism gradually underwent profound changes in their thinking and in their attitude toward workers. At the same time, a number of workers learned something about Marxism and raised their class consciousness, so that both groups became advanced elements of the proletariat.

[- The polisher first deleted the empty words "carried out by," replacing them with a simple "of": "These four activities of the Communist groups."

- Next she made some minor corrections of wording: "those intellectuals who had just fostered their belief in communism" became "those intellectuals who had just come to believe in communism." "Had profound changes in their thinking" became "underwent profound changes in their

503

thinking."

- After those easy changes, she was somewhat at sea. She had to read A-version several times before she understood the basic point of the passage — that through these activities the intellectuals became integrated with the workers and that both parties were changed by the process.

- Once she reached that understanding, she saw what revisions were necessary to make it clear to the reader.

- First, it was not Marxism that was integrated with the workers' movement but the Communist groups. Therefore, "its" integration should become "their."

- Second, the vague and general "feelings" of the intellectuals (the nature of which was only implied in the original) should be spelled out precisely as their "attitude toward workers."

- Third, it should be made plain that what the workers learned was another result of this same process of integration. That could be done with the introduction of a logical connective, "At the same time." And this was a good point at which to break a sentence that was too long.

- The revised version now stood as follows: "These four activities of the Communist groups gave a powerful impetus to the dissemination of Marxism and to their integration with the workers' movement. Those intellectuals who had just come to believe in communism gradually underwent profound changes in their thinking and in their attitude toward workers while they were integrating themselves with the workers. At the same time, a number of workers learned something about Marxism and raised their class consciousness, both becoming advanced elements of the proletariat."

- But now the "both" at the end, which was already none too clear in A-version, was even farther removed from "those intellectuals," which it was intended to include. To make the meaning plain, she spelled it out with the help of another logical connective: "... raised their class consciousness, so that both groups became advanced elements of the proletariat."

- Rereading this version, the polisher thought that the sense was clear and the language idiomatic. But she now saw that the subordinate "while" clause at the end of the second sentence should go at the beginning, leaving the final position to the main point, the statement that the intellectuals had undergone profound changes.

- She moved the clause and reread once more: "These four activities of the Communist groups gave a powerful impetus to the dissemination of Marxism and to their integration with the workers' movement. While they were integrating themselves with the workers, those intellectuals who had just come to believe in communism ..."

- When she reached that point she became aware that she was repeating herself. Now that "While they were integrating themselves with the workers" immediately followed "their integration with the workers' movement," she could see that they were two references to the same idea.

- To eliminate the repetition, she replaced the second reference, "While they were integrating themselves," with a

505

summary phrase, "In the process."]

28) A: We have to <u>pay attention to</u> <u>lowering the average age</u> of <u>members of the leading bodies</u> and <u>selecting</u> Marxists as <u>leaders</u>.

B: We have to *select as members of the leading bodies younger people* and Marxists.

[- The empty introductory phrase "pay attention to" was the first to go: "We have to lower the average age ... and select ....".

- Next, "members of the leading bodies" were plainly the same as "leaders," so one of them could be dispensed with. The first expression recommended itself to the polisher as being more specific, so she deleted "as leaders."

- The sentence now read: "We have to lower the average age of members of the leading bodies and select Marxists." That, she thought, could be simplified and condensed: "We have to select as members ... younger people and Marxists."]

29) A: Secretary for Constitutional Affairs Michael Suen said at a luncheon yesterday that an independent Electoral Affairs Commission will be established, <u>which will present</u> plans on <u>geographical constituency demarcation</u>, voter registration and election procedures <u>to the chief executive</u> <u>before the end of October</u>.

B: Secretary for Constitutional Affairs Michael Suen said at a luncheon yesterday that an independent Electoral Affairs Commission will be established. *By the end of October the commission will present to the chief executive* plans for the *demarcation of geographical constituencies*, voter registration and election procedures.

[- The polisher's first concern was the "which": instead of coming immediately after the noun it referred to ("Commission") in the normal way, it was separated from its antecedent by the intervening verb "will be established." The sense was clear enough, but the word order was nevertheless illogical and disconcerting.

- The simplest solution seemed to be to abandon the "which" clause and start over with a new sentence. (Such a break was indicated in any event because A-version presented too much information for the reader to swallow in one mouthful.)

- This left the question of where to put the two prepositional phrases "to the chief executive" and "before the end of October," both of which were far removed from the verb they were logically attached to, "will present."

- The first found its normal place as indirect object immediately after the verb ("present to the chief executive"). The second was moved to the beginning of the sentence, where it plainly modified the same verb ("By the end of October the Commission will present").

- The changes introduced for reasons of logic also achieved the proper emphasis: the place of prominence at the end was now occupied by the plans themselves.

- Lastly, the polisher broke up the daunting noun-as-adjective construction "geographical constituency demarcation" with the preposition "of." She allowed "voter registration" and "election procedures" to remain, however, because they would be familiar to readers and hence readily understandable.)]

30) A: The Leftist adventurism <u>in this resolution</u> <u>found its expression</u> first in the <u>totally</u> incorrect assessment of the situation, <u>maintaining</u> that the <u>great</u> decisive battle was just round the corner for both the Chinese and the world revolution. <u>It</u> wrote, "the fundamental political and economic crisis in China continues to sharpen in <u>totally</u> identical manner in <u>each and every</u> part of the country without the slightest essential difference."

B: *In this resolution* "Left" adventurism *manifested itself in several ways*. First, *the Political Bureau* made a totally incorrect assessment of the situation, *maintaining* that the decisive battle not only for the Chinese revolution but for the world revolution was just around the corner. "The fundamental political and economic crisis in China," *the Bureau* wrote, "continues to sharpen in an identical manner in every part of the country without the slightest essential difference."

[- On reading A-version, the polisher was brought to a halt as soon as she reached "maintaining." The participle was adrift with nothing to modify ("adventurism" cannot hold an opinion). Consequently, her first concern was to anchor it to a subject.

- She knew from the preceding sentence that the proper subject was the Political Bureau of the Central Committee, which had adopted the resolution in question, so she used that: "The 'Left' adventurism in this resolution found its expression first in the totally incorrect assessment that the

Political Bureau made of the situation, maintaining that the decisive battle etc. " ("Great" was an unnec. intensifier.)

- She was soon stopped again by "It wrote." The pronoun had no antecedent ("adventurism" cannot write anything either). Happily, the introduction of the Political Bureau solved that problem too — she could now put "the Bureau wrote."

- Next the polisher deleted "totally." The word had just been used ("totally incorrect"), but more important, it was a redundant intensifier. Things that are "identical" are exactly (i. e. , "totally") the same; otherwise they would merely be "similar."

- Immediately after, she deleted "each" from the pair of twins "each and every."

- These faults, and the appropriate corrections, had suggested themselves to the polisher at once, on her first reading. Now she went back to see if there were any less obvious ones that she had missed.

- The second time around, the prepositional phrase "in this resolution" struck her as a misplaced modifier. "Adventurism" was not "in this resolution"; if anywhere, it was in the Politburo. It only "found its expression" — or, better, "manifested itself" — in the resolution.

- To make this clear, she moved the phrase to the beginning of the sentence: " In this resolution ' Left' adventurism manifested itself first in the totally incorrect assessment . . . . "

- Satisfied with her revision, the polisher moved on. But

when she read the next few paragraphs, she found that they cited other manifestations of adventurism in the Politburo's resolution — indeed, they began "Second," "Third" and "Fourth." She therefore returned to this passage to make one further revision.

- To clarify the logic, she rewrote the first sentence: "In this resolution 'Left' adventurism manifested itself in several ways. First, the Political Bureau made a totally incorrect assessment ...."

- Adding "in several ways" indicated that more than one "way" would be cited. Making "first" the beginning of a new sentence prepared the reader for a series of points to be expressed in matching form.]

31) A: It would be very difficult to <u>accomplish the task of reclaiming</u> as much as 140 million *mu* of land in <u>a period of</u> twelve years ....

B: It would be very difficult to *reclaim so great an area as* 140 million *mu*) in *just* twelve years ....

[- The polisher saw at once that "accomplish the task of reclaiming" was the familiar Chinglish construction, unnec. verb + unnec. noun + third word that expresses the real action. She deleted the unnec. words and converted the third word (in this case a gerund) to a verb: "to reclaim."

- Coming to "a period of," she recognized that used in this way, it was only a superfluous category noun introducing "twelve years." She edited it out.

- Then, to underline the logic of the statement, she added "just." This word told the reader that what followed would be a short period of time, considering the magnitude of the task.

- Rereading the new version, the polisher was not satisfied with "as much as," especially followed by *mu* , which a foreign reader might not immediately recognize as a unit of land measure. She substituted the more specific phrase "so great an area as" and omitted "of land" as unnec.]

32) A: In March the same year, Li Dazhao, after repeated consultations with Deng Zhongxia and others, set up at Beijing University a society for the study of Marxist theories. This was the first body established in China for learning and studying Marxism, the first attempt made by Li Dazhao to assemble "those who are interested in the study of theories of the Marxist school and those who are willing to study Marxist theories."

B: In March the same year Li Dazhao, after repeated consultations with Deng Zhongxia and others, set up at Beijing University a society *for the study of Marxist theories*. This was the first *such* body established in China and the first attempt by Li Dazhao to assemble "people *who have some interest in Marxist theories* and *those who want to study them* ."

[- The chief problem in this passage was clearly that it was so repetitive. The study of Marxism was mentioned no less than four times in two successive sentences.

- First the polisher replaced "the first body established in China for learning and studying Marxism" with a simple "such": "This was the first such body established in China." (This revision also eliminated the redundant

511

twins "learning" and "studying.")

- The rest of that sentence was the simplest possible example of the same thing said twice — the second clause
("those who are willing to study etc.") was only a restatement of the first ("those who are interested in the
study etc.") in virtually identical terms. The polisher
deleted the second, leaving only "... to assemble 'those
who are interested in studying the theories of the Marxist
school.'"

- It was a second polisher who, comparing this version with
the Chinese, objected to the omission on the grounds that
the original text referred to two different groups of
people. The difficulty was that A-version made no clear
distinction between them and was therefore merely redundant.

- To remedy this failing, the two polishers agreed on a
third version: "... to assemble 'people who have some
interest in Marxist theories and those who want to study
them.'"]

33) A: In order to build a new democratic country, the Congress put
forth again the slogan of abolishing the Kuomintang one-
party dictatorship and forming a democratic coalition government. It also expounded in detail the programs on such
aspects as politics, economy and culture, which would be
carried out in the new democratic country. In view of the
fact that the Kuomintang ruling clique pursued policies of
betraying our country, staging civil war and exercising
dictatorship, the Congress called on the whole Party to be
prepared for another eventuality, that is, the breakout of

the civil war while striving for the establishment of a coalition government. If the KMT waged a civil war, the people would respond by waging a revolutionary war to overthrow the reactionary regime and build a new China.

B: To build a new democratic country, the congress again *called for the abolition* of the Kuomintang's one-party dictatorship and the *formation* of a democratic coalition government. It also expounded in detail the *political, economic, and cultural programs* to be carried out. *However, since the policy of the Kuomintang ruling clique was to betray* the country, *launch* civil war, and *maintain* its dictatorship, the congress called on the entire Party membership, *while striving for the establishment of a coalition government*, to prepare for another eventuality: the outbreak of civil war. If the KMT waged a civil war, the people would respond by waging a revolutionary war to overthrow the reactionary regime and build a new China.

[- The polisher first made two minor improvements that suggested themselves almost at once. To reduce the population of nouns and gerunds, she (1) changed "put forth the slogan of abolishing ... and forming" to "called for the abolition ... and formation" and (2) replaced "In view of the fact that" with "Since."

- Then she addressed the main problem: A-version was hard to follow. On rereading, she saw that in the first two sentences the congress was envisioning the formation of a coalition government, but that in the last two it spoke of the opposite possibility, the outbreak of civil war.

513

- The difficulty was that the reader was given no indication of the change and therefore assumed that the third sentence would continue along the same line of thought as the first two.
- To give the reader notice that the content of the third sentence would contrast with that of the preceding ones, she inserted a "However."
- Another confusing element in A-version (third sentence) was the placement of the participial phrase "while striving for the establishment of a coalition government." It was far removed from the noun it was intended to modify: "the whole Party," or, as she now thought better, "the entire Party membership."
- To make a clearer logical progression, the polisher moved the subordinate phrase up in the sentence: "... the congress called on the entire Party membership, while striving for the establishment of a coalition government, to prepare for another eventuality: the outbreak of civil war."
- This rearrangement left "the outbreak of civil war" at the end of the sentence, where it led without interruption directly into the next idea: "If the KMT waged a civil war etc."
- Equally important, the change of order placed the emphasis on the dramatic words "the outbreak of civil war." In A-version their impact had been dissipated in the subordinate phrase ("while striving etc."), which came as a feeble anticlimax.
- After these clarifications, the polisher reread the new

version to see if any more changes needed to be made. "Programs on such aspects as economy, politics and culture" had bothered her from the beginning. It was the familiar Chinglish construction with free-floating "aspects" — aspects of <u>what</u> was not stated.

- The "aspects" were in any event superfluous, since one could simply say, "political, economic, and cultural programs." She made that change and at the same time eliminated "in the new democratic country" as evident from the context.

- One other point caught her attention: "the KMT ruling clique pursued policies of betraying our country, staging civil war and exercising dictatorship." A simpler and more natural structure would be "the policy of the KMT ruling clique was to do x, y, and z." That version also recommended itself because it replaced three gerunds with verbs. She revised the clause accordingly.]

34) A: We are working to build a great socialist community in which all nationalities will <u>enjoy a thriving and affluent life</u> . . . .
    B: We are working to build a great socialist community in which all nationalities will *thrive and prosper* . . . .
    [- "Enjoy a thriving and affluent life" was another unnec. verb + unnec. noun + third word construction. The polisher deleted the unnec. words and changed the ones bearing the content (in this case two adjectives) into verbs: "to thrive and prosper."

    - It could be argued that "thriving" and "affluent" ("thrive" and "prosper") are redundant twins. It might have been sufficient to say: "in which all nationalities will

enjoy a high standard of living (*or*: a life of
abundance)."]

35) A: A landslide caused 12 deaths in Lushui County, Yunnan
Province, on Friday. *China Daily* learned yesterday that
13 others were missing and 11 houses still buried under
the earth last Sunday. Heavy rain resulted in a 750-meter-
wide, 300-meter-high mass of earth, with a volume of
60,000 cubic meters, sliding about 20 meters downhill.
The landslide damaged 182 households, affecting 1,100
people. But a danger remains, as 1.5 million cubic meters
of earth are still moving, said the report.

B: A landslide caused 12 deaths in Lushui County, Yunnan
Province, last Friday. *China Daily* learned yesterday that
on Sunday 13 *people* were *still* missing and 11 houses
remained buried under the earth. Heavy rain had *caused
a mass of earth 750 meters wide*, *300 meters high* and
with a volume of 60,000 cubic meters to *slide* about 20
meters downhill. The landslide damaged 182 households,
affecting 1,100 people. *And according to the report* the
danger remains, as 1.5 million cubic meters of earth are
still moving.

[- A-version appeared in print, but a careful reviser might
have improved upon it.

- First, "others" has the wrong antecedent. It is intended
to refer to "other persons," but the antecedent on the
page is "deaths." It is not other "deaths" that are
missing.

- Second, the placement of "last Sunday" makes it unclear
what the phrase modifies. Moved up to precede the verb,

516

it would apply to both the missing persons and the buried
houses. The sense could be made clearer by the addition of
"still" missing ("still" buried being changed to
"remained" for variety).

- Third, an awkward construction with a gerund could be
  smoothed out by changing "resulted in a mass of earth
  sliding" to "caused a mass of earth to slide."
- Fourth, the pileup of nouns and adjectives before "mass of
  earth" could be avoided by giving the dimensions afterward.
- Fifth, "But" is misleading. The logical connection between the description of the damage and the statement
  that danger remains is not "but" but rather "and,"
  "moreover," or "furthermore."
- Lastly, the final sentence would be stronger if the subordinate reference to the report were moved to the
  beginning: "And according to the report the danger remains . . . ."]

36) A: This gradual transformation must be <u>undertaken in a planned
way</u> and <u>leadership exercised over that</u> so that success will
be assured <u>when conditions are ripe</u>.

B: This gradual transformation must be *well planned* and
properly led, so that *when conditions are ripe* success
will be assured.

[- As soon as the polisher had read this sentence, she read it
over again, mentally supplying the missing verb: "This
gradual transformation must be undertaken in a planned
way and leadership <u>must be</u> exercised over that . . . ." At
the same time she automatically changed "over that" to

517

"over it." Having made those revisions for a start, she considered what other changes were needed.

- "Must be undertaken in a planned way" was just a wordy version of plain "must be planned." That substitution produced: "This gradual transformation must be planned and leadership must be exercised over it . . . ."
- But "leadership must be exercised over it" was again only a clumsy version of "it must be led" ("to exercise leadership over" = unnec. verb + unnec. noun for "to lead"). Thus, the version became: "This gradual transformation must be planned and led."
- That was much better — neater and with a greater degree of parallelism. But the implied sense was surely "must be well planned and properly led." The polisher added the two adverbs.
- Lastly, she moved the subordinate clause "when conditions are ripe" to precede the independent clause that made the important point: "success will be assured."]

37) A: We uphold the Party's leadership, but the problem is whether the Party is doing a good job of leading. It should give effective leadership and not intervene in too many matters. The Central Committee should take the lead in this regard. This is not meant to weaken the Party's leadership. Too much intervention and mishandling of things will actually weaken the Party's leadership.

B: We uphold *Party leadership*, but the problem is whether the Party is doing a good job of leading. It should give effective leadership and not intervene in too many matters. The Central Committee should take the lead in this regard. *What I am proposing will not weaken leadership by the Party. On the contrary, its leadership will be weakened if it tries to take responsibility for too many areas.*

[- When the polisher reached the fourth sentence of A-version, she saw that the demonstrative pronoun "This" had no antecedent. Even if it was supposed to represent not just a particular word but an entire preceding idea, the reader could not tell what that idea was.

- She considered the context. The passage was part of a talk in which a senior leader was urging the necessity of separating the functions of the Party and the government and of delegating powers to lower levels. Clearly the implied subject of the sentence was this idea that he was putting forward. Accordingly, for "This" she substituted "What I am proposing."

- The polisher also thought the verb and tense were wrong. No Party leader would make a proposal that was "meant" to weaken the Party's leadership. The speaker was not explaining the intention of his proposal but predicting its result, hence: what I am proposing "will not weaken" the Party's leadership.

- Then she came to the last sentence: "Too much intervention and mishandling of things will actually weaken the Party's leadership." She found it unsatisfactory for several reasons. First, because it was based on a noun and a gerund ("intervention" and "mishandling"); second because it was vague (intervention in what? mishandling of what sort of things?); third because the point it was

519

making was not clear.

- In view of these objections, she rewrote the sentence entirely. First she discarded both "intervention" and "mishandling" and spelled out what she perceived to be the meaning with a verb: "if it (= the Party) tries to take responsibility for too many areas."
- Then, to direct the reader's attention to the speaker's point, she placed the real danger, now expressed in the subordinate "if" clause, at the end: "Its leadership will be weakened if it tries to take responsibility for too many areas."
- That version, she thought, was an improvement, but rereading once more, she became aware of another problem: there was nothing to indicate the logical relation between the last two sentences.
- To make it easier for the reader to follow the speaker's line of argument, and at the same time to strengthen and clarify his assertion, she introduced "On the contrary."
- On a final rereading, she noticed that "the Party's leadership" was ambiguous. It could be understood as meaning "the leaders of the Party," which was not the intended sense. To avoid that possibility, she changed the first reference to "Party leadership" and the second to "leadership by the Party." Having made this last clarification, she thought the immediately following "its leadership" would be correctly understood.]

38) A: That same day Mao Zedong, Zhu De, Peng Dehuai, and other leaders of the Red Army <u>cabled</u> Chiang Kai-shek to indicate that the officers and men of the Red Army wished

to "deal with the enemy for the purpose of defending the land and country and to save the life of the nation. "

B: That same day Mao Zedong, Zhu De, Peng Dehuai, and other leaders of the Red Army *sent a telegram* to Chiang Kai-shek saying that the officers and men of the Red Army wished to "*engage* the enemy *to defend* the *country* and save the nation. "

[- The polisher's first move was to fix a detail: she changed "cabled" to "sent a telegram to. " Only messages that are transmitted over the wires of an underwater cable are "cabled, " and at this point Chiang was still on the mainland.

- Then she considered the possible twins "land and country. " One could make a distinction between the "country" (meaning the territory, or the people) and the "nation" (meaning the state, the political entity). But in this context, at any rate, she could find no significant difference between the "country" and the "land. " Accordingly, she considered them redundant twins and deleted one of the pair.

- Next she changed "deal with" to "engage, " partly because it was the more precise military term and partly to avoid ambiguity. "Deal with" can have many meanings in English. In this particular context, it might have been interpreted as meaning to "negotiate with" the enemy, to "make a deal. "

- Lastly, the polisher changed "for the purpose of defending" to a simple infinitive, "to defend, " thereby eliminating a noun and a gerund.]

39) A: In doing economic work in 1992, we shall, <u>under the guid-</u>
<u>ance of the Party's basic line</u>, <u>step up the pace of</u> reform,
<u>broaden the scope of opening</u> to the outside, <u>pay close at-</u>
<u>tention to readjustment</u> of the economic structure and <u>im-</u>
<u>provement</u> of efficiency, <u>lay stress on improving</u>
agriculture and large and medium-sized state-owned enterprises, <u>and promote sustained, stable, and harmonious de-</u>
<u>velopment of the national economy</u>.

B: In our economic work in 1992, *we shall follow the Party's*
basic line. *To promote steady and harmonious develop-*
ment of the economy, we shall *accelerate* the reform,
open wider to the outside, and *concentrate on readjust-*
ing the economic structure and *raising* efficiency, *partic-*
ularly in agriculture and in large and medium-sized state-
owned enterprises.

[- This long and difficult sentence occurred in the draft
translation of a report by Premier Li Peng to a session of
the National People's Congress. Because it was an important document, the translation was reviewed by several
polishers, each of whom made contributions to the final
version. Consequently, it is hard to say in what order the
changes were made. They are therefore listed here not
necessarily in chronological order but in order of importance.

- The prepositional phrase "under the guidance of the
Party's basic line" was converted to a separate clause: "we
shall follow the Party's basic line."

- That change not only broke up a long sentence but clarified the logic. It gave more importance to the Party's basic

522

line and indicated that all the tasks to be named afterward were aspects of that line. (The revision had the added advantage of eliminating an abstract noun, "guidance.")

- A second structural change was also made in the interest of logic. Studying the original, the polishers decided that the last element in the series ("and promote sustained, stable, and harmonious development of the national economy") was not intended to be coordinate with the others. Rather, it was the overarching purpose of all the other endeavors. In other words, the appropriate logical connective was not "and" but "in order to."

- As a result of this understanding the last phrase, which now expressed a subordinate idea, was moved up to the beginning of the sentence: "To promote sustained, stable, and harmonious development of the national economy, we shall ...." There it governed everything that followed, and at the same time it left the end of the sentence to the main clause, "we shall step up the pace etc."

- A third change of structure was made for reasons of logic as well. The polishers considered that the vague "lay stress on improving agriculture and large and medium-sized state-owned enterprises" was not a separate item in the list. Rather, it was a part of "readjustment of the economic structure and improvement of efficiency."

- This meant that the better translation was not "lay stress on" but "laying stress on": "we shall ... pay close attention to readjustment of the economic structure and improvement of efficiency, laying stress on improving agriculture and large and medium-sized state-owned enterprises."

- A number of unnecessary nouns and verbs were eliminated. "Step up the pace of reform" became "accelerate reform"; "broaden the scope of opening" became "open wider"; "pay close attention to readjustment ... and improvement" became "concentrate on readjusting ... and improving"; and "laying stress on improving agriculture" became "particularly in agriculture."

- These simple changes did much to lighten the sentence and shorten it. In the final version, the net saving of words was 20%.

- "Sustained" and "stable" were identified as redundant twins, and both were replaced by "steady."

- "National" economy was deleted because it could be taken for granted.

- "Improving" efficiency was changed to the more precise term "raising."]

40) A: The focus of work for this year is to exert efforts to resolutely overcome unhealthy practices and to push forward the building of clean and honest government.

B: This year *we must concentrate on overcoming* unhealthy practices and *on building* (*or*: strengthening) *clean* government.

[- As soon as she read this sentence, the polisher knew that her chief task would be to clear away the underbrush that nearly obscured the meaning. It was not hard to do. In rapid succession she made the following revisions.

- She changed the unnec. verb + noun construction "to exert efforts" to its plain-verb equivalent, "to try": "The

524

focus of work for this year is to try to resolutely overcome. . . ." Then, seeing that "to try" added nothing but more words, she deleted it.

- She deleted the all-purpose adverb "resolutely," which added nothing useful.
- She replaced the static abstraction "The focus of work is to overcome" with a strong verb, "we must concentrate on overcoming."
- Since in this context· "push forward the building of" meant no more than "build," she dispensed with "push forward."
- "Clean" and "honest" being redundant twins (one word was only a metaphor for the other), she deleted "honest."
- Thus, she reduced 26 words to 14, highlighting the sense.]

Key to Exercises

Following are revisions of the examples of Chinglish that appear in the twenty exercises at the end of each chapter.

Remember that we are not dealing with problems in mathematics, which have a single correct solution that can be proved. In matters of translation there can be no "proof," and the versions decided on by the revisers may not always be the best in your opinion.

In a given example you may think the reviser was wrong to eliminate or retain a particular element of the draft sentence. Or, confronting the same problem of structure, you may have found a different way of turning the sentence that is equally acceptable or, perhaps, preferable.

In short, you are not obliged to accept the versions proposed below. You should, however, be able to defend your own.

I. Unnecessary Nouns and Verbs

1) the new state we have just inaugurated is unusual, entirely different from the empire of the Qing dynasty

2) throughout this period there was a severe shortage of a great variety of goods (*or*: of many kinds of goods)

3) Comrade Chen Yun constantly analyzed his experience

4) it is only by discussion, criticism, and reasoning that we can really foster correct ideas

5) At first they worked slowly, so as to achieve the best possible results in the agrarian reform.

526

6) the only correct policy for us is to mobilize the people

7) we must stop supplying materials in an unplanned way

8) This waste of the state's most precious resource must be eliminated.

9) the Army must increase efficiency

10) Chiang Kai-shek, for his part, ceaselessly expanded the war

11) to date, some 1,900 enterprises in 27 provinces and municipalities have separated (or: begun separating) taxes from profits

12) the government departments concerned should draw up (sound) plans for development of the special economic zones

13) we should regulate patterns of consumption so as to adapt them to China's (or: our) agricultural resources

14) we should strengthen all facets of public security

15) we shall further reform the banking system by controlling total supply and demand for currency and credit

16) it is of paramount importance to have a sober understanding of our basic conditions

17) our policy is to (try to) ensure that not a single person dies of starvation

18) Sun Yat-sen's firm support for cooperation between the two parties thwarted the efforts of the KMT Right-wingers to split the KMT

19) enterprises should be granted the power to make decisions about foreign trade

20) we should invigorate agriculture by applying scientific and

technological advances

II. Unnecessary Modifiers

1) we discovered this long ago but were never able to solve the problem

2) the General Secretary pointed out that to speed up construction of the new economic system it is imperative to resolve several key problems

3) Beijing plans to make greater efforts to improve sanitation

4) the spread of bourgeois liberalization may have grave consequences (*Or*, *better* : bourgeois liberalization, if allowed to spread, may have grave consequences)

5) I am convinced that these policies will not be changed

6) the reform and opening must be carried out in light of the particular conditions in each country, because countries differ from one another in many respects

7) first, every year we must solve some of the intellectuals' problems, producing genuine (*or* : practical) results

8) we should recognize that there are still many defects to be eliminated

9) we shall continue to crack down on smuggling

10) we shall unswervingly follow a policy of opening to the outside world and increase our exchanges with foreign countries on the basis of equality and mutual benefit

11) I am certain that the unhealthy practices that can now be found in society will gradually decrease and eventually disappear

12) the decree forbids the import and export of rhinoceros horns, tiger bones, and ready-made traditional Chinese medicines that contain them

13) you can suggest to the departments concerned that the time be extended

14) China will work to implement the Uruguay Round of accords, a Beijing representative said on Wednesday

15) I hope you will sit down together to study this question

16) however, it will be hard to avoid an occasional delay of ten to fifteen days

17) at its Third Plenary Session the Eleventh Central Committee defined the central task for the Party and the country (*or*: for the Party and for the country as a whole) as development of the productive forces

18) while there has been a phenomenal increase in output, it has not solved the problem of fragmentation of production

19) in this way, we can seize the opportunity to raise the economy to a new level

20) agricultural growth remains the foundation for the development of the economy as a whole

III. Redundant Twins

1) Since the publication of the Automotive Industrial Policy last July, the "family car" has been one of the hottest topics of discussion in the Chinese press.

2) the drafting of important documents has been completed ahead of

schedule

3) we should improve the overall balance of the economy

4) this will convince the people that you are sincere in carrying out (*or* : that you are wholeheartedly committed to) the policies of reform and opening to the outside world

5) in the final analysis, the growth of the CPC, the achievement of national independence, and China's advance toward strength and prosperity were closely linked to (*or*, *better* : were largely made possible by) the drive to liberate and expand the forces of production

6) The last decade of this century will be crucial for laying a foundation and creating good conditions for economic development in the first half of the next.

7) as long as the ranks of the Party are closely united and remain vigorous, the cause of socialism is bound to prosper

8) if the reform is successful, it will lay a solid foundation for stable development (in China) over the next few decades

9) the purpose of political reform is to improve and revitalize China's socialist system

10) actually, as means of developing the productive forces, different managerial forms can serve both capitalism and socialism

11) when we have dealt with those problems, our established principles and policies will only be carried out more smoothly and perseveringly

12) What obstacles are we going to run into? As I see it, there are two or three problems that might hold up the growth of our

economy . . . .

13) Mou Xinsheng, Vice-Minister of Public Security, urged public security organs to cooperate closely with banks in cracking down on white-collar crime.

14) Leading comrades of Party committees and governments at all levels should often visit schools, listen to what the teachers and students have to say, and help them overcome their difficulties.

15) We are not rich and cannot offer you much financial help, but we can share our experience with our friends, and that too is a kind of help.

16) It was then that Mao Zedong showed his outstanding ability to learn from both positive and negative experience.

17) So China must not allow itself to get out of control; we have that responsibility to ourselves and to all mankind.

18) We must therefore continue to uphold Mao Zedong Thought and enrich it with new principles and new conclusions corresponding to reality.

19) Of course, the report reflects my views, but in the main it embodies collective opinions.

20) After years of study, the State Bureau of Cultural Relics has agreed to unearth the much-talked-about No. 2 vault of terracotta soldiers, Yuan Zhongyi, President of the Terra-cotta Museum, said recently at Lintong, where the museum is located.

IV. Saying the Same Thing Twice

1) Enterprises with exclusively foreign investment should abide by China's laws (and regulations).

2) we should try our best (*or*: do everything possible) to keep prices from rocketing

3) The initiative in the war has shifted from the enemy to us.

4) there will be a great many economic imbalances, which it will take a long time to remedy

5) people who have made mistakes should be allowed to compensate by performing good deeds, provided they quickly come to realize their mistakes and make up their minds to mend their ways

6) industrial enterprises should manufacture products for both military and civilian use

7) We must expand and accelerate the production of import substitutes.

8) although the campaign is necessary, it should not go beyond these three months

9) We should expand the patriotic health campaign and improve the system of primary health care and the training of health workers at the grass roots.

10) We veterans should take advantage of this opportunity to read and increase our knowledge; if we let it slip, we may regret it when it's too late.

11) Family planning should be combined with efforts to help poor

areas become prosperous.

12) cadres should adopt an active attitude toward this work

    (*Or*, *better*: cadres should take an active interest in this work)

13) Promoting socialist cultural and ideological progress.

    (*Or*, *better*: Promoting progress in socialist culture and ideology.)

14) There will be full employment.

15) Our policy is firm, and we are not going to change it.

16) friendly contacts and trade relations between the Chinese and Japanese peoples have steadily developed (*or*: expanded)

17) To promote democracy at the village level and to advance rural development, governments at different levels must implement the Organic Law of Villagers' Committees, ensuring that villagers manage their own affairs.

18) This does not mean, however, that we can concentrate (exclusively) on industrial development to the neglect of agriculture, which now represents nearly 90 per cent of the economy.

19) We must, in particular, put a stop to the unauthorized use of arable land and the destruction of forests, and promote the planting of trees and grass in both town and country.

20) This year we hope to make great progress in this regard.

V. Repeated References to the Same Thing

1) Our present standard of living is still very low, and we have a long way to go to attain a relatively high one.

2) We have just held the Twelfth National Congress of the Party.

Since the Congress, our country has been more stable politically than ever before.

3) For two consecutive years, production of passenger cars has failed to reach the target, says Lu Fuyuan, Vice Minister of Machinery Industry, who is in charge of day-to-day administration of the automotive sector. Last year it was 80,000 short of the expected total.

4) If you want to find out whether the present policy is here to stay, you should first examine whether the policy is correct, whether it is right for the country and the people, and whether the life of the people is gradually improving under it. I believe that the people are discerning. If the present policy is altered, their standard of living will (definitely) fall.

5) Wang Ming was criticized at the Sixth Plenary Session of the Sixth Central Committee, and as many cadres raised their political consciousness he gradually became isolated. Even Chiang Kai-shek rejected him, refusing to appoint him a minister.

6) Party branches should regularly transfer good cadres to higher-level Party committees, so long as their own work does not suffer as a consequence.

7) Local governments are bound to encounter difficulties in the early days of centralized management. But those difficulties and their consequences will be far less serious than the ones that would result from the sharp fluctuations in monetary value and prices that would occur under a system of decentralized management.

8) The central task of the congress was to accelerate and deepen the reform. It expounded the theory of the primary stage of socialism in China and defined the Party's basic line for building socialism with Chinese characteristics during that stage.

9) We failed to attach equal importance to both types of work, and there was no proper coordination between them.

10) The principles our Party has laid down since the Third Plenary Session of its Eleventh Central Committee can be summed up in two points.

11) China must have a leading collective with the image of people who favor the policies of reform and opening to the outside world. I hope you will pay special attention to this point. We cannot abandon these policies.

12) Lin believes that it is important for a foreign company to keep its negotiating team intact from beginning to end and that it would be a good idea for the Chinese partner to do the same (*or*: to do likewise).

13) At the beginning of this year, the CPC Central Committee and the State Council called a meeting on nationality work. At the meeting, general experience in such work was analyzed, and major tasks and policies for the 1990s were put forward.

14) In 1995, 42 percent of the automotive manufacturers operated at a loss, a 42 percent increase over the previous year. Their total losses increased by 41 percent, and their inventory, which came to 200,000 units, by 14.2 percent.

15) Despite the stern measures taken by officials of the automotive industry and central government to combat smuggling,

transfer there large numbers of such personnel from North, East and Central-South China.

13) Analysts expect that the demand for Jeeps in China will reach 240,000 units by 2000 and 560,000 by 2010.

14) The cotton mills must make sure that their products are up to the standards set by the State Cotton Textile Company.

15) He added that reforming the old economic system means removing the obstacles to the development of the productive forces.

16) Even for champions of reform, it is good to be a bit skeptical.
   (Or: Even among champions of reform a little skepticism is a good thing.)

17) we must do all we can to prevent and treat serious diseases

18) In accordance with the principles of separating the functions of the government from those of enterprises and separating ownership from management, government departments should continue to change their functions and strengthen macro-economic control.

19) we shall ... improve the performance of investments using foreign funds and make more efficient use of such funds

20) both industrial and agricultural production have greatly increased, so that their total value is expected to be more than 60 per cent higher in 1957 than it was in 1952

VII. The Noun Plague

1) we do not have the facilities necessary to produce alloy steel

2) Unless you master essential skills, you will prove unequal to this

538

kind of job.

3) we must make them understand that the struggle in the Northeast will be protracted (*or*: long)

4) One reason is that we don't have a correct understanding of certain theories and principles, which is why we need to study
more theory.

5) At the same time, the U.S. government announced that it was
severing its diplomatic relations with the Taiwan authorities,
terminating the U. S.-Taiwan Joint Defense Treaty, and
withdrawing American troops from Taiwan.

6) The principal criteria for judging the success of reform and the
open policy are whether they help develop the productive
forces of our socialist society, increase our country's overall
strength, and raise the people's living standards.

7) these different sectors of the economy will have to be transformed
in different ways and at different speeds

8) Cadres are being trained for the land reform and for the people's
tribunals, and peasants' associations are being reorganized and
expanded.

9) "Zhang is always ready to help the farmers, who usually don't
know how to plant and care for fruit trees," says Cai Lihong,
a doctoral student under Zhang's tutorship.

10) To implement general policies in the transition period and to
build socialism, we have to improve the health of our people.

11) In order to stabilize currency and prices, we had to balance national expenditures and revenues and guarantee sufficient

supplies of goods.

12) We shall abolish this class by utilizing, restricting, and transforming the capitalist economy.

13) In the nine months since the Third Plenary Session of the Twelfth Central Committee, practice has proved that it was correct to reform prices.

14) We estimate that once the money supply in the localities has been reduced, prices throughout the country will become stabilized by November 25.

15) unless these problems are handled satisfactorily, our policies cannot be successfully implemented (*or*: carried out)

16) The Asian Development Bank on Wednesday approved two loans, totaling $256 million, to finance projects to alleviate water shortages and reduce air pollution.

17) "It is to our advantage to have an efficient system for developing and managing residential property," said Tan Kian Siew, executive deputy general manager of BJ Minghua Properties.

18) He made these remarks during a talk with Sakurauchi Yoshio and other leading members of the delegation from the Japanese Association for Promotion of International Trade.

19) This practice has helped ensure that no needy students will drop out because they are unable to pay their own tuition.

20) "The authorities in charge of (*or*: responsible for) administering State assets should help promote the process," said Zhang at a seminar organized by the Chinese Institute for Management of State Property.

VIII. Pronouns and Antecedents

1) The West really wants unrest in China. It wants turmoil not only in China but also in the Soviet Union and Eastern Europe.

2) China is estimated to possess 69. 4 billion tons of onshore oil reserves, but only 25 per cent of them have been verified.

(*Or*: It is estimated that China possesses 69. 4 billion tons of
onshore oil reserves, but only 25 per cent of that amount has
been verified.)

3) Right now the Korean people are confronted with difficulties,
but they are holding on courageously, fighting a guerrilla war
in the south and putting up resistance in the north.

4) After a successful revolution each country must build socialism
according to its own conditions.

5) No one would come here and invest without getting (*or*: unless
he got) returns on his investment.

6) "The registered capital of the holding company is $ 30 million,
so we have a commitment to more investments here," Wendin
said. But he didn't elaborate on when the new joint projects
will be launched. The company reported sales averaging $ 50
million a year.

7) Old China was dependent on imperialism not only in the economic sphere but also in the spheres of culture and education; it
was exploited economically and polluted ideologically. That
was very dangerous. It is now time to expose and eradicate
the evil influence of imperialism.

8) During the peak season, peasants compete to sell their eggs,

while (*or* , *better* : whereas) during the off-season eggs are usually in short supply in the cities.

9) Foreign trade has been developing rapidly in Fuxin. It has been continuously growing in variety and volume. Many of Fuxin's quality products are welcome on the international market.

10) During the Japanese and puppet regimes, most of these positions were held by Japanese. But after August 15, 1945, the Japanese were replaced by Chinese.

11) All these are problems left over from the past. They are acute now because the longstanding semi-colonial, semi-feudal economy has undergone radical changes. Although these changes bring some hardship with them, they are not bad in themselves.

12) China's growth has peaked and is expected to slow down next year. Even so, China's economy will remain one of the fastest developing in the world.

13) At present our government organs are overstaffed. Not all employees have to stay on in government offices; some of them can be transferred to enterprises.

14) Yesterday two friends from the former Whampoa Military Academy talked about the March 20th Incident and the Southern Anhui Incident. It was interesting to hear (*or* : I was interested in) what they had to say, but I had to leave after an hour and a half because of other engagements.

15) It cannot be said that every paragraph of this speech I am making today has been discussed by the Central Committee. Of course, some of the ideas (*or* : the views I am expressing)

have been discussed, but others are my own opinions.

16) The problem now facing the authorities in Shanghai is to obtain adequate supplies of rice and cotton, and the key question is whether they can mobilize enough transport facilities (to bring them in).

   (*Or*: The problem now facing Shanghai is to obtain adequate supplies of rice and cotton, and the key factor is the availability of transport facilities.)

17) I spent a year in a university after I graduated from senior middle school. But I didn't learn very much there, because it was the time of the May 4th Movement.

18) Prosperity is the common objective of all our nationalities, and we must never lose sight of it.

   (*Or*: Prosperity is the common objective of all our nationalities, an objective (that) we must never lose sight of.)

19) Following the Wuchang Uprising of 1911, the Hubei military government set forth the idea of changing the form of government by establishing a republic of five nationalities, an idea (*or*: a proposal) that was also advocated by Dr. Sun Yat-sen.

20) Summary of a speech made at a national forum of representatives of Customs personnel. It first appeared in *People's Daily* on October 26, 1949.

IX. The Placement of Phrases and Clauses

1) In February 1939 Zhou Enlai ... travelled to southern Anhui Province to discuss with the leaders of the New Fourth Army the strategic tasks for the army.

2) In his report on the work of the government, Premier Li Peng emphasized the importance of reforming and expanding undertakings in science and technology, education, and culture.

3) First, after a review of the experience of the past seven years, an appropriate rate of speed was set for China's economic development.

4) Of the three brothers and three sisters in her family, Soong Ching Ling is the only one who champions revolution.

5) Provided the national interests are not impaired, the local government of Taiwan will enjoy certain powers that the governments of other provinces, municipalities, and autonomous regions do not possess.

6) In 1989 the provincial government called for a province-wide initiative to reforest Jiangxi. An ambitious goal was set to plant trees by 1995 wherever it could be done.

7) Mao emphasized that to ensure achievement of its political, military and economic objectives, the Party must first consolidate its ranks.

8) As stipulated in the Common Programme, our actions should be both beneficial to national unity and suited to local conditions.

9) As the People's Liberation Army went over to the strategic offensive, the KMT authorities, in an effort to maintain their tottering rule, stepped up their oppression and exploitation of the people and their suppression of the patriotic democratic forces.

10) Should we be discouraged by these difficulties? No. We should recognize that compared to the difficulties we have faced over the last two decades of struggle, they are nothing very

serious.

11) According to a survey, unless our forestry work is improved, in 10 to 25 years the forested region in the Northeast will be totally depleted.

12) It is obvious to all that for the last hundred years the imperialists, lording it over the Chinese people, have used science as a means to exploit, oppress, and slaughter us.

13) Although there are still some remaining counterrevolutionaries and new ones will emerge in future, the situation is quite different now from what it was in the early days of liberation.

14) Education Minister Zhang Xiro once recalled that when he was on an inspection tour in Xi'an, he had found some pupils there speaking very good *putonghua*.

15) Before the Long March, because of his opposition to dogmatism in the military command, he was wrongly dismissed from the post of chief of the general staff and demoted to chief of staff of the Fifth Army Group of the Chinese Workers' and Peasants' Red Army.

16) At this time, a difference of opinion appeared in the Fourth Red Army's Party organizations and among the leaders. On June 22 at the 7th Party Congress of the Fourth Red Army, held in Longyan, Fujian, an argument broke out regarding the establishment of an Army Committee.

17) Since the Red Army let slip this golden opportunity, Chiang, having defeated the Fujian People's Government, was able to complete the encirclement of the Central Soviet Area.

18) The Provincial Party Committee decided that instead of staging

an uprising in the whole of Hunan Province as originally planned, it would do so only in the seven counties around Changsha.

19) These percentages were the result not of normal international investment and fair economic exchange but of the unequal treaties signed by the KMT government at the expense of national sovereignty.

20) Once, while on his way to an orchard after a rain, he slipped and fell, breaking two ribs.

X. Dangling Modifiers

1) Compared with the developed countries, China still has a very low per capita national income.

(*Or*: Compared with the per capita national income of the developed countries, China's is still very low.)

2) As a developing country with more than 1.2 billion people, he noted, China does not have enough hydrocarbon resources to meet the fast-growing demand.

3) Set to the music of Rachmaninoff's "Second Piano Concerto" played by the Central Ballet Theater Orchestra, the dance depicts Anna during the turbulent social transition in Russia at the turn of the 19th century.

4) While deepening reform and accelerating economic development, we should strengthen efforts to build a clean government.

5) We must take disciplinary action against those Party members who refuse to correct their errors, but in doing so we must not repeat the "Left" mistakes of resorting to summary

measures and subjecting too many people to criticism.

6) He reduced the number of string players in an attempt to keep a balance with the brass and woodwind sections. By doing so, he made the sound quality of the orchestra resemble that of a chamber music ensemble.

7) Living in a city among crowded cement "matchboxes," I no longer notice the architecture around me.

8) Peasants in the Border Region have increased the output of millet and wheat by more than 20 million kg. When this amount is added to the output of army units, government departments, Party organizations, and schools, the total increase will come to more than 40 million kg.

9) By choosing Hong Kong as the venue, the international community has given a vote of confidence to Hong Kong as an important financial center.

10) In February 1949, on instructions from the Military Commission of the CPC Central Committee to standardize the designations of the entire Chinese People's Liberation Army, the Central Plains Field Army was renamed the Second Field Army.

11) Affected by bourgeois ideas (*or*, *better*: values), we are quite wasteful in our diplomatic work.
   (*Or*: Because we are affected by bourgeois values, there is much waste in our diplomatic work.)

12) Only by carrying out this policy can we ensure that cultural undertakings will contribute more to socialist construction.
   (*Or*: Only if we carry out this policy can cultural undertakings contribute more to socialist construction.)

13) If we want to get 90 per cent of the people to join mass organizations, we must pay special attention to women.

14) However, China is short of some minerals crucial to economic development, and this means that Chinese geologists are facing a tough task.

15) Because the Party failed to draw the lesson of the uprisings in Nanchang and Guangzhou, the political line at that time still encouraged insurrections everywhere.

16) Construction of the new project, which will cover an area of 1.3 square kilometers, is expected to start this year and to be completed in five stages over the next eight years.

17) Wang and her colleagues have been working to make the center, which is a non-profit, non-governmental mass organization, do more than just help women with their troubles.

18) On the basis of this analysis, production of motorcycles for 1995 is expected to hit six million, with over 400 different models and 14 types of engine displacement.

19) Some time ago in Shanghai, in an effort to streamline administration the staff was reduced.

20) In studying *putonghua*, you can't just rely on your ears and tongue, because it is easy to forget what you have learned. For more efficient study there must be books printed in a phonetic alphabet and dictionaries giving the phonetic transcription of each character . . . .

    (*Or*: . . . . To study more efficiently, students must have books printed in a phonetic alphabet and dictionaries giving the phonetic transcription of each character . . . .)

XI. Parallel Structure

1) "The three most important tasks for the Liberated Areas," the Central Committee declared, "are training soldiers, reducing rents, and increasing production."

(*Or*, *better*: "The three most important tasks for the Liberated Areas," the Central Committee declared, "are to train soldiers, reduce rents, and increase production.")

2) So far the Political Consultative Conference has concentrated mainly on political study, international activities, and the collection of historical records.

3) After his divorce and the death of his parents, Lei Fachun, an ethnic Tu farmer in Huzhu County, Qinghai Province, felt hopeless about the prospect of feeding his three sons.

4) In this way every unit can avoid departmentalism and exclusive reliance on the state and will make the greatest possible contributions in its field.

5) Yao said that to ensure continued and steady growth of agricultural production, "we need to draw up a long-range plan for agricultural development and to adopt certain basic measures."

6) Senior cadres of the various departments and organizations are not familiar with our current financial difficulties and the means to overcome them.

7) Consequently, some workers are losing their jobs and need to receive relief or to turn to other trades.

8) The difference of opinion was not only over the special economic

zones but also over the larger issues, such as the rural reform that introduced the household contract responsibility system . . . .

9) He fell in love with automotive design not because he foresaw the rise of the auto industry as one of the country's pillar industries, but because he believed that auto design represented the highest level of industrial design.

10) 1) Sharing the burden
2) Restoring production
3) Broadening sources of income and reducing expenditures
4) Having a good grasp of policies
(*Or* , *better* : Understanding policies)

11) These are vital questions for the next century, both for enhancing people's quality of life and for protecting the environment.

12) But over the past year we have seen leading manufacturers of automobiles joining hands with producers of farm vehicles in an attempt to tap into this market.

13) Nevertheless, by 1978 the average monthly salary for our workers was still only 45 yuan, and the people in most of our rural areas were still mired in poverty.

14) When faced with aggression by the Japanese imperialists, one party in China was for resisting while the other party was for making concessions.

15) During the first eight months of this year, 54,000 units were produced and 52,000 were sold.

16) Even at the time when our army had only millet to eat and only rifles to fight with, he began to envisage combined operations

of the various services.

17) Only through this process can a man develop his thinking, a party formulate a complete set of policies, and an organization improve its work.

18) The dictatorship was to be based ... mainly on the alliance of workers and peasants, because those two classes were the main force in overthrowing imperialism and feudalism and in making the transition from new-democracy to socialism.

19) Since this law went into effect, it has won broad support from the people and has achieved excellent results.

20) Perhaps they migrated to distant regions outside China; perhaps they were assimilated with the Han or other ethnic groups and lost their separate identity.

XII. Logical Connectives

1) The vast majority of workers, city dwellers, and even members of the middle and lower petty bourgeoisie were brought to the brink of disaster. The rural economy *also* went into a sharp recession.

2) If the North-South problem is not solved, it will hinder the development of the world economy. The solution, of course, lies in North-South dialogue, and we support dialogue. But dialogue alone is not enough; cooperation among Third World countries — in other words, South-South cooperation — should be stepped up *as well*.

3) There is no doubt that the system of management described above is much more centralized than the one that was in effect

last year. *But* if we were asked how many undertakings will still be under decentralized management, we would have to answer, a great many.

4) At first, the Yangtze Automotive Chassis Plant will be able to assemble 60,000 chassis a year for one- and two-ton trucks. *When construction is completed*, it will have an annual capacity of 100,000 chassis.

5) It is not necessary to launch such a movement now. In Shanghai 160,000 cases of tax evasion have been uncovered *but* most of them are medium or minor ones. These cases of tax evasion vary in seriousness, and there are also defects in our tax system. These things have to be addressed and rectified, but there is no need for a lesser movement against the "five evils."

6) Not much progress has been made in the talks on control of nuclear arms and of weapons in outer space. That's why for many years we emphasized the danger of war. Recently, *however*, there have been some changes in our views. We now think that although there is still the danger of war, the forces that can deter it are growing, and we find that encouraging.

7) Some people think that since China is emphasizing the importance of ideals, that means it is going to close its doors again. That is not true. We are soberly aware of the possible negative effects of the open policy and will not ignore them. *Nevertheless*, our principle is not to close but to continue to open. We may open even wider in the future.

8) At that session we criticized the idea of the "two whatevers" and put forward *instead* the slogan, "We must emancipate our minds and put our brains to work."

9) All local authorities and departments should make the improvement of the performance of large and medium-sized state enterprises an important item on their agendas, taking practical measures to create a favorable environment for their production and operation and to help them reduce losses and increase profits. Basically, *however*, state enterprises must rely on their own efforts to extricate themselves from their predicament. While actively carrying out the reform, they should adjust their mix of products to conform to the demands of domestic and international markets, produce readily marketable goods, keep developing new products, and enhance their ability to adapt to the market and compete.

10) Changchun has now reached an annual production capacity of 400,000 automobiles, *including* over 100 models of medium trucks, light vehicles and sedans.

11) As late as May 1926 he still stated, "Not only am I not opposed to Communism, but I very much approve of it." For the time being, the KMT continued to cooperate with the CPC. *But* the fact that command over the Northern Expeditionary Army was largely in Chiang's hands made it clear that *although* the revolution was progressing rapidly, it was already in a serious crisis.

12) If China, with its one billion people, took the capitalist road, it would be a disaster for the world. It would be a retrogression of history, a retrogression of many years. If China, with its

one billion people, abandoned the policy of peace and opposition to hegemonism or if, as the economy developed, it sought hegemony, that would also be a disaster for the world, a retrogression of history. *But* if China, with its one billion people, keeps to socialism and adheres to the policy of peace, it will be following the right course and will be able to make greater contributions to humanity.

13) "Graft, bribery, and other cases of corruption have become (quite) serious, *and* crimes involving the exchange of power for money are spreading among some government departments and officials," Liang told a national conference of provincial procurators on Wednesday. "So, we must focus attention on such developments, *and* not underestimate the seriousness of the threat posed by corruption."

14) Shen says that research and production of friction materials for motor vehicles in China had always been based on asbestos, which is both cheap and plentiful in the country. At present there are close to 30 manufacturers with a total annual production of more than 20,000 tons of friction materials, most of which are made from asbestos. Realizing, *however*, that asbestos was a hazardous substance and that international manufacturers were no longer using it, Shen made up her mind to develop China's own non-asbestos materials.

15) Zhou announced at the reception that he had asked Hu Zongnan personally if he had sent his troops defending the Yellow River west to prepare an attack on the Shaanxi-Gansu-Ningxia Border Region. "Deputy Commander Hu told me," he said, " that he had no intention of attacking the

Shaanxi-Gansu-Ningxia Border Region and that the troops under his command would take no such action. I was very happy to hear this, and I believe everyone else will be happy, too." *Thus* Hu's scheme to attack the region was made known to the public.

16) The museum, *which has* a 30-year history, is dedicated to the collection of items related to ancient China, Chinese paintings and calligraphy, historical pictures, and contemporary Hong Kong art.

17) If the CPC were to give up its proletarian stand of independence and initiative, make no distinction between the proletariat and the bourgeoisie, refrain from arousing the masses, and try to appease the bourgeoisie in all matters so as to maintain the united front, it would only weaken the position of the proletariat, put the united front at the mercy of the bourgeoisie, and eventually bring about China's defeat. *Nevertheless*, after he arrived in Yan'an, Wang Ming did everything possible to carry out this "new policy" of the Communist International.

18) The objective reasons were as follows. . . . Many of the troops that had previously been engaged in attempts to encircle and suppress the Workers' and Peasants' Red Army were moved to other battlefields to take part in [the warfare between the new rival warlords], leaving a vacuum in certain areas and an opportunity for the Red Army to grow. *Moreover* (*or*, *better*: What is more), under the rule of the KMT government, the national crisis was aggravated. Every one of the fundamental contradictions in Chinese society became intensified, and the Nanjing government grew increasingly

555

fascist. . . . Discontent was growing even among those who had cherished illusions about the KMT.

19) The principal contradiction in Chinese society in the present stage is the one between the growing material and cultural needs of the people and the backwardness of production. *Accordingly*, to promote the all-round progress of society, we must give priority to the growth of the productive forces and make economic development our central task.

20) The venture, named Huazhong-Warner Transmission Co., Ltd., has a total investment of ¥255 million ($30.72 million), *of which* Borg-Warner is contributing 60 percent.

XIII. Summing it All Up

1) In the Northeast the enemy is still strong and we are still weak.

2) This has aggravated the internal contradictions in the capitalist camp, helped to consolidate and expand the camp of peace and democracy, and strengthened the national and democratic movements in capitalist countries.

3) As we don't have nearly enough technicians, it is very important to train more of them.

4) "Running an operation in China is a great challenge and requires a lot of patience and long-term planning," says Kuang-Ming Lin, president of Dana China. "However, China has a fast-growing economy that offers some good business opportunities."

　　(*Or*: . . . "However, the Chinese economy is growing fast, and it offers some good business opportunities.")

5) There is nothing to fear if the imperialists refuse to do business with us. Their past invasions turned China into a colonial and semi-colonial country. The Chinese people rose up to make revolution because that was the only way they could survive. We certainly cannot rely on the imperialists now.

6) Non-staple foods are daily necessities for people living in the cities and in industrial and mining areas. Indeed, such people consume more non-staple foods than staple ones.

7) A legal aid organization for young people was opened in Guangzhou on Wednesday, China News Service reported. On the same day, the organization launched the Jibuhuan Yunlai Legal Aid Fund.

8) On March 3 the Administration Council of the Central People's Government issued a Decision on Unifying National Financial and Economic Work.

9) A senior financial official reaffirmed yesterday that despite China's having achieved a "soft landing," the ultimate objective of the country's monetary policy is to keep currency values stable.

10) During a meeting with World Bank President James Wolfensohn, Li, who arrived in Hong Kong on Saturday afternoon to attend the annual meeting of the World Bank Group and International Monetary Fund, said China hoped to strengthen cooperation with the Bank.

11) What first appears to visitors entering the town is a spread of green bamboo and lawns dotted here and there with beautifully designed houses, clearly showing the wealth and taste of

the homeowners.

(*Or*: The first thing visitors see on entering the town is a spread of green bamboo . . . .)

12) Compared to a regular automobile, a farm vehicle costs much less (*or*: is much cheaper) to operate.

13) As an outstanding strategist, Bocheng demonstrated his perspicacity not only in directing battles but also in working to build a modern, regular army.

14) To distribute the precious water better among provinces along the river and utilize it more efficiently, we should construct more water conservancy facilities.

15) Encouraged by the strong market demand, Beijing Jeep Corporation has set a sales target of 80,000 units for this year and 100,000 for next year. During the first eight months of 1995, 54,000 units were produced and 52,000 were sold.

16) The required training period for the driver of a car is six months, that for the driver of a farm vehicle only three months.

(*Or*, *better*: For the driver of a car, the required training period is six months; for the driver of a farm vehicle it is only three.)

17) We should know not only how to use the modern equipment but also how it works.

18) When you have built more apartment houses, the people will have a better environment to live in.

19) The loans will be interest-free. Guarantees will be required, however, before they are granted.

20) At that time I was in charge of the work of the Central Committee and the government, and I introduced a series of rectification measures. Before long these measures produced excellent results in every area, but they ran counter to the "cultural revolution" and angered the Gang of Four. So once again I was ousted from office.

Selected Bibliography

In preparing this Guide I have consulted a number of English dictionaries, several printed lectures on translation from Chinese, and many reference works on English grammar, usage, and style. I list below only those sources that are quoted in the text.

Adler, Sol. *A Talk to Comrades of the English Section for the Translation of Volume V of Chairman Mao's Selected Works* (《关于〈毛选〉第五卷翻译问题的报告》). Beijing: Foreign Languages Press (外文出版社), 1978.

Barzun, Jacques. *Simple and Direct: A Rhetoric for Writers*. New York: Harper and Row, 1975.

Barzun, Jacques, and Henry F. Graff. *The Modern Researcher*. New York: Harcourt, Brace & World, 1957.

Cheng Zhenqiu(程镇球). *On Problems of Translation: A Series of Talks Given at the Institute of Journalism*(《论汉译英的几个问题》). Beijing: Foreign Language Teaching and Research Press (外语教学与研究出版社), 1981.

Cobbett, William. *A Grammar of the English Language*. New ed., with introduction by Robert Burchfield, New York: Oxford University Press, 1984. (Previous ed. 1906; first published 1818.)

Cook, Claire Kehrwald. *Line by Line: How to Improve your own Writing*. Boston: Houghton Mifflin, 1985.

Follett, Wilson. *Modern American Usage: A Guide*. Edited and completed by Jacques Barzun. New York: Hill and Wang, 1966.

Fowler, H. Ramsey, and Jane E. Aaron. *The Little*, *Brown Handbook*. 5th ed. New York: HarperCollins, 1992.

Fowler, H. W. *A Dictionary of Modern English Usage*. 2nd ed. Revised and edited by Sir Ernest Gowers. New York: Oxford University Press, 1965. (First published 1926.)

Fowler, H. W., and F. G. Fowler. *The King's English*. 3rd ed. New York: Oxford University Press, 1931. (First published 1906.)

Gowers, Sir Ernest. *The Complete Plain Words*. Revised by Sidney Greenbaum and Janet Whitcut. Boston: David R. Godine, 1988.

Graves, Robert, and Alan Hodge. *The Reader Over Your Shoulder: A Handbook for Writers of English Prose*. 2nd ed. New York: Vintage Books (Random House), 1979.

Johnson, Edward D. *The Handbook of Good English*. New York: Washington Square Press (Pocket Books, Simon & Schuster), 1983.

Kessler, Lauren, and Duncan McDonald. *When Words Collide: A Journalist's Guide to Grammar and Style*. Belmont, California: Wadsworth, 1984.

Strunk, William, Jr., and E. B. White. *The Elements of Style*. 3rd ed. New York: Macmillan, 1979.

Zinsser, William K. *On Writing Well: An Informal Guide to Writing Nonfiction*. 4th ed. New York: HarperCollins, 1990.

561

1986.

1988.

1990.

501